SHADOW
LIGHT

SHADOW LIGHT

LIGHT

ILLUMINATIONS AT THE EDGE OF DARKNESS

KEITH WITT

Copyright 2016 Integral Publishers
SHADOW LIGHT: *Illuminations at the edge of darkness,*
an Integral journey into Shadow

Witt, Keith
Integral Publishers
4845 E. 2nd Street
Tucson, AZ 85711
831-333-9200
ISBN: 978-1-4951-8772-8

Cover and Interior Design by Kathryn Lloyd

TABLE OF CONTENTS

ACKNOWLEDGMENTS

So many people helped this book come into existence! Ken Wilber's work transformed my understanding of the Kosmos, and he has been a friend and guide ever since I first encountered his contribution of Integral Theory to the world. David Riordan lit a fire in me when he asked me to generate a Shadow of Relationships module for a program he was working on for *Integral Life*. Russ Volkmann suggested *Shadow Light* as a title, and Keith Bellamy has been guiding and supporting each step of the way. Lynne Feldman provided editorial wisdom and wonderful feedback. Jeff Salzman has been a friend and muse for many years, as have many others in the Integral community. My wife Becky remains the best teacher and greatest blessing of my life, and my son Ethan and daughter Zoe have always respected the sacred crucible of my work. My clients and students have taught, challenged, and inspired me all throughout my career. Thank you everyone!

PREFACE

I wrote *Shadow Light* because understanding and growing our Shadow transforms us into better people, and we all want to be better people.

Also, it's fun to wake up to new ways of seeing the world—which helps us see *new worlds*! Extending awareness into Shadow—into where we haven't seen before, been before, or felt before—can be scary, but more often it's "This is so cool I need to tell somebody!"

My friend Ron Meyer (who is an author himself) asked me, "Who are you writing this book for?"

Without thinking, I responded, "To the people who listen to *The Shrink and the Pundit*."

My beloved Integral brother-in-arms, Jeff Salzman, has a website, *The Daily Evolver*, which features progressive thinkers from all over the world. He and I have a podcast we do every month or two called *The Shrink and Pundit*, where we talk about luminous topics like Integral Psychology, the Hero's Journey, marriage, sexuality, superior parenting, Integral politics, Shadow, and *The Gift of Shame*. Thousands of people have listened over the years, and I've gotten to know a lot of them—brilliant loving men and women, seekers all.

Seekers are drawn to the alive interfaces between known and unknown—fractal boundaries. Transformative insights, inner struggles, and our personal missions show up when we hang out at those edges of Shadow emerging into conscious awareness.

So to all my *Shrink and Pundit* brothers and sisters, and to seekers everywhere, thank you for inspiring this book!

INTRODUCTION

Knowing your own darkness is the best method for dealing with the darknesses of other people.

—CARL JUNG

In a U.N. study, people rated happiness as more important to them than wealth or getting into heaven.[1] This survey could not be conducted with any other creatures on this planet, because we humans are the only species who can stand apart from how we feel—happy, unhappy, angry, selfish, empathic, fearful, ashamed, bored, interested, or turned on—and observe emotions, thoughts, impulses, and behaviors.

All other living creatures are hard-wired for impulses/instincts/ training/drives to lead directly to action—no pause for self-reflection. That pause for self-reflection is our greatest human super-power, but it's a tricky and capricious super-power, constantly influenced by *impulses/ instincts/drives/unconscious selves*—our Shadow selves.

Often we don't know what to do with self-reflection, and are frustrated and confused by who we seem to be. Why do some people feel good mostly, and some bad mostly? Why do I feel like a worthwhile person some of the time and a worthless person occasionally? Why do some of us have superior judgment in critical situations and others of us horrible judgment in critical situations?

The answer is *Shadow.*

Shadow is the sum total of our learning, drives, habits, values, preferences, and needs flooding constantly up from our non-conscious selves to our conscious selves. Right now your *Shadow-self* is reacting within a tenth of a second to these words (you like them/not like them, find them useful/irritating, want to continue/want to stop reading), but your *consciously-aware-self* experiences and manages these feelings, stories, and impulses a half second to a second and a half later.[2]

Consciously-aware-self has choices how to proceed in thought and action. Choices feed back into your Shadow self and shape it, and here lies the great secret to human happiness, success, and growth. We can grow our Shadow!

Since development is both nurture and nature—our experiences/environments/learning plus our genetic and temperamental tendencies—no one starts out equal in the Shadow sweepstakes. For instance 65 percent of babies are born either easy, difficult, or slow to warm up, and difficult and slow to warm up babies can have more emotional pain than easy babies.[3] More emotional pain means their nervous systems encode more pain regulators like dissociations and defensive states—almost always associated with destructive Shadow programming—than easy babies who feel content most of the time. Some of us have genetic, family, or cultural advantages, and some of us were born distressed or into crazy-making cultures that warp our Shadows to dominate and limit us rather than support and liberate us.

Most approaches to Shadow focus on the dark, dangerous, shameful memories, fantasies, actions, impulses, self-images, and beliefs that rise up unannounced and unwelcome to torment us—what I call destructive Shadow. But this is only half the story. What about intuitions, flashes of insight, generous impulses, compassionate understandings, and caring acts that occur daily for most of us? All of these involve positive non-conscious forces—constructive Shadow.

In general Shadow rises up either *constructively* to help us grow and thrive, or *destructively* to harm us or others in primitive attempts at self-protection and gratification. We can learn to trust constructive Shadow and transform destructive Shadow into constructive Shadow.

Encouraging constructive Shadow and managing destructive Shadow figures prominently in most psychotherapy, change work, moral development, and spiritual practices.

This book dives into constructive and destructive Shadow, melding our conscious intent with our unconscious fountains of emotions, beliefs, memories, values, self-images, impulses, relationships, and stories.

Conscious intent—our conscious thoughts, beliefs, self-sense, and actions—forms feedback loops into our nonconscious Shadow, whether we like it or not.[4] These are both healthy loops radiating wisdom and joy when we think compassionately and act wisely, and unhealthy loops undermining our native hungers to care, share, be fair, and do right by ourselves and others when we surrender to distorted beliefs and destructive impulses. *We all have both kinds of feedback loops into our nonconscious Shadow, healthy and unhealthy, constructive and destructive.*

We can discern constructive Shadow and courageously surrender to it, and catch destructive Shadow and alchemically transmute it into constructive Shadow. These practices open channels to spiritual insight and profound intuitions, to intimate unions with others, and gratitude for life. These understandings can profoundly shift how we hold the stories of our lives—stories about us, others, and everything else.

CONSTRUCTIVE AND DESTRUCTIVE SHADOW

Destructive Shadow often is revealed in selfish or self-destructive stories and impulses.

Constructive Shadow often is revealed in pro-social, empathic, healthy stories and impulses.

Our unconscious—the mysterious depths of our personal histories and drives—processes information, chooses what memories to access, and generates a shifting self-sense of *me* being safe/not safe, virtuous/ transgressive, attractive/unattractive, grateful/ashamed. Our unconscious constantly creates stories of each moment.

When our nervous system feels threatened, primitive fight/flight/freeze reactions tend to instantly arise in a tenth of a second.[5] The memories tend to be of danger, we tend to feel more self-absorbed and distressed, and our impulses tend to be towards violence or flight—this is usually destructive Shadow.[6]

When our nervous system feels safe, our unconscious tends to generate prosocial, more empathic stories and impulses—usually constructive Shadow.

If we're in relationship and I feel threatened, my destructive Shadow cues and communicates with your destructive Shadow—often Shadow to Shadow beneath conscious awareness—and bad things can happen.

Similarly, if we're in relationship and we both feel safe and socially engaged, our constructive Shadows cue and communicate with each other and good things often happen.

Recently I was showing my wife Becky how to record *Say yes to the dress* on our T.V. and she accidentally pushed the wrong button, creating a problem I couldn't solve. I felt a flash of anger and said, "You pushed the wrong button!" She immediately said, "No I didn't," and I felt a flood of rage and impulses to intensely explain *why she was wrong!* She blanked out at my anger, and my son—who was beginning to help—left the room to get away from the sudden bad vibes.

The situation felt wrong. My anger felt too intense. I hate distressing my family. My destructive Shadow had been cued by the episode and was sending violent stories and impulses that my conscious self was struggling with. My constructive Shadow was generating stories of me being caught in a old relational defensive pattern and giving me impulses to breathe deeply, lighten up, and repair with Becky and my son Ethan. My conscious self was half a step behind all this, but knows enough to distrust violent destructive material and surrender to the constructive pro-love material, which is exactly what I did and everything was better in a few minutes. It's taken Becky and me *forty-three years* to learn how to do this efficiently, and still it was hard at the time.

Or course, there are endless combinations of constructive and destructive Shadow in ourselves and in relationships with others. This makes life complex, interesting, anxiety provoking, delightful, tedious, or illuminating as we'll see again and again throughout this book.

Just learning the flavors and textures of constructive and destructive Shadow amps constructive and transforms destructive Shadow—it helps our unconscious Shadow selves integrate and grow.

Helping our Shadows integrate and grow is what *Shadow Light* is all about.

THE POWER OF SHADOW

Managing Shadow is life-and-death serious business. Prince, Janis Joplin, and Amy Winehouse had Shadow-drives to addiction, and Michael Jackson and Bill Cosby Shadow-drives to sexually abuse others. These destructive Shadow forces destroyed all of them, and yet they all produced transcendent art, which always involves constructive Shadow made manifest by the artist.

The best and the worst of humanity arises from our deepest Shadow drives and impulses.

Destructive shadow material—based in our genetic, relational, karmic, cultural, or morphic past—can embarrass, enrage, intimidate, or even drive us mad. Most of us instinctively fear destructive Shadow in ourselves and others, and this has influenced our understanding of Shadow throughout the ages.

For instance, in Shadow literature from psychologists, anthropologists, and spiritual teachers, Shadow is often pathologized. A subtle undercurrent of disapproval and fear of our own frightening or morally reprehensible selves flows through much Shadow writing.

It's true that all authors suggest techniques to detoxify, heal, eliminate, or declaw inner Shadow threats, and all systems offer paths to transforming

Shadow into an ally. But, still, the focus often seems to be on destructive rather than constructive Shadow.

I've found every approach useful and enlightening, especially in the psychotherapy worlds where I've spent most of my life. Psycho/social/ spiritual healing needs to confront destructive Shadow. Who knows what might have happened if Prince and Amy Winehouse chose recovery from addiction, or if Michael Jackson and Bill Cosby sought help for their dark sexual impulses? Destructive Shadow when confronted and dialysized turns into wisdom and strength—and this is the promise of Shadow—to celebrate and enhance our strengths and alchemically transform our vulnerabilities.

Psychotherapy from its first beginnings with Freud and Jung has largely been understood in metaphors—id, superego, ego, animus, anima, pain body, inner critic—but sometimes theorists become lost in their own dark metaphors, neglecting the neurobiological roots of Shadow (explored in Chapters 3 and 4) and the ultimate purpose of Shadow—to protect us and help us survive, thrive, love, and evolve.

Destructive Shadow can't be denied, ignored, or subtly dismissed, it needs to be metabolized into constructive Shadow—*way* stronger and more pervasive than destructive Shadow if supported just a little bit like I did in my argument with Becky.

Most of us are aware of the human drives for dominance, sex, personal survival, and fierce protection of our families, but we have other drives. Most of human evolution over the last two million years has been to help us survive and thrive *in communities*—to be socially successful and effective. As Lynne MacTaggart maintains in *The Bond,* we have genetically based drives to care, share, and be fair with others. These drives organize our non-conscious selves—our Shadow—to do right, to grow, to love, and to contribute. This constructive Shadow is a human gift and superpower. Constructive Shadow delivers beautiful inspirations and impulses to do right, create beauty, and love others.

Some modern thought leaders like Ken Wilber talk about golden shadow of happy, loving, creative material arising from what

psychoanalyst/neuroscientist Allan Schore calls our adaptive unconscious—what I understand as constructive Shadow.[7] They get the
central importance of constructive Shadow in everyone's life. What
these approaches miss is the intricate dynamics of constructive and
destructive Shadow emerging consciously into awareness, requiring
our conscious self to process and manage the constant flood of input.

Whether we call it golden Shadow, adaptive unconscious, or constructive Shadow, we possess inner realms of intuition, wisdom, virtue,
and connections with Spirit. Problems are solved, insights are generated,
and warnings are issued from these realms.

Not only that, destructive thoughts, beliefs, habits, and impulses—
destructive Shadow—can be alchemically transformed *by us* into constructive Shadow. We can grow our adaptive unconscious, our Shadow
selves, with understanding and effort.

Much of this book is about discerning constructive Shadow and
surrendering to its influence, and perceiving destructive Shadow and
transforming it into constructive Shadow. We'll explore this in neurobiological development, life journeys, relationships, sexuality, parenting,
dreams, violence, creativity, and spirituality.

WHO'S DOING THIS?

But first of all, what part of us is doing all this constructive/destruc-
tive information processing, impulse generating, storytelling activity?
Who's figuring our world out anyway? As Walt Whitman said in *Song
of Myself,* "We contain multitudes." As my friend Integral pundit Jeff
Salzman says, "We are larger than we know." In the chapters to come
we'll explore how consciousness came with the price of Shadow, and
how that price is both a curse and a blessing.

I love Shadow and am grateful each day for the flows of constructive
and destructive illumination that cross the fractal barriers between the
unknown and the known in my conscious awareness (more on fractal
boundaries in a little bit).

In *Star Wars*, Luke has huge capacities for channeling constructive Shadow, represented by the Jedi Knight Obi Wan Kenobi, and similar capacities for destructive Shadow, represented by disgraced Jedi Knight and Sith Lord, Darth Vader. They are his two fathers both literally and figuratively, and he reconciles with them in his Hero's Journey—we'll talk much more about the Hero's Journey in Chapter 5.

In the end, by integrating destructive and constructive Shadow in service of principle, Luke generates healing powers, embodies the Warrior, and transcends into Man of Wisdom (whom we'll be discussing in Chapter 6).

We can all be like Luke.

In Chapter 1 we discover Shadow everywhere.

In Chapter 2 we explore how everything is relationships and outline a Unified Field Theory of Shadow.

In Chapter 3 we detail the neurobiology of Shadow, and how we can use this science to grow and thrive.

In Chapter 4 we see how neurobiology helps us understand and enhance Shadow work.

In Chapter 5 we take the Hero's Journey and descend into the Well of the world, exploring how the human drive to create myths has organized Shadow for millennia.

Chapter 6 clarifies the Warrior and Man of Wisdom in each man's developing relationships with Shadow.

In Chapter 7 we honor the Maiden, Sex Goddess, Wife, Queen, and divine Mother—all paths to the Woman of Wisdom.

Chapter 8 dives into sexual Shadow—impossible to be human and not be profoundly influenced by sexual Shadow.

Chapter 9 embraces marital Shadow, and how returning to love through stress and conflict creates great marriages.

Chapter 10 relaxes into family and parental Shadow—how our parents co-shaped us, how we co-shape our kids, and how to invite constructive Shadow to guide us.

Chapter 11 dances with dreams as the royal road to Shadow, existing on multiple levels, all arising from the Universe Dream waking up to itself.

Chapter 12 takes on violence and Shadow, a subtext of every conversation.

Chapter 13 challenges us to surrender to the constant *creation* dance of conscious awareness, action, and Shadow influences.

Chapter 14 expands into spirit Shadow, where we can become injured through spiritual bypasses, or healed and expanded through ascending levels of gross, subtle, causal, and non-dual states.

▶ **Confidentiality sidebar:** *All the client stories and encounters I write about are based on real people and events, but the names are changed and the stories are altered to protect my clients' privacy.*

It's an exciting ride, so let's get started!

1
SHADOW EVERYWHERE

Someday, after mastering the winds, the waves,
the tides and gravity, we shall harness for God the
energies of love, and then, for a second time
in the history of the world, man
will have discovered fire.

—PIERRE TEILHARD DE CHARDIN

In this chapter we will:

- Keep defining Shadow.
- Understand Shadow as emergence.
- Find our Shadow reflected in others.
- Revisit fractals—self-repeating patterns on the cresting wave of evolution—and attune our own fractal interfaces to speed personal evolution.
- See how habits are the bottom line.
- Learn how to metabolize Shadow.
- See our Shadow in everything.
- Return to Shadow as emergence.

WHAT IS SHADOW AGAIN?

Countless experiences, memories, habits, decisions, reactions, relationships, and stories are influencing you at this moment. We are constantly being shaped by new experiences and insights, all the while interrelating with others, the world, and our many selves (in the past, present, and future)—simultaneously driven by habits, emotions, memories, anticipations, principles, and values which are continually shifting as we generate different states throughout the day, encounter different people, and respond to different environments.

Some forces are obvious, like hunger for lunch, desire to call your son, warmth as your husband wishes you good morning, the rituals you go through before your tennis match, or reflexive anger or laughter at some stupid story in the newspaper.

Some forces we can never be fully aware of, like accumulated habits, autonomic balance in our nervous system, or multiple associations on life experiences. Material we aren't fully aware of is often called Shadow, because it is obscured or unknown to us until it moves into the light of conscious awareness.

In this sense, Shadow is the universe pressing through our habits, memories, ego, and desires to be consciously known by us—a never-ending flood that doesn't immobilize us in its immensity only because we've gotten used to constantly riding the rapids of emergence in waking and dreaming life.

We all instinctively know the importance of Shadow, and have our own multiple experiences with Shadow's power.

For instance, at the beginning of this project I felt frozen by the magnitude of Shadow and emergence and wrote to my friend and editor Keith Bellamy:

"I can't find the center of the Shadow book. The deeper I get, the more frustrating it becomes.

Keith wrote back,

"Thank you, thank you, thank you. for your email. It made me burst into laughter (will explain more later). From my minimal experience, shadow is that which hides from yourself and not from the other. When we make break-throughs, the experience is often other-worldly and sometimes downright unreal.

The reason I laugh is because I had what I call a "Shadow Breakthrough" some eight years ago after my mother passed away. I was sad, and shed a tear or two but was holding things together. We were sitting the Jewish Shiva process and on the fourth night my niece's husband offered to make leek and potato soup and bought a freshly baked loaf of bread to have with it. As we sat down to eat, I asked for the butter and was told I couldn't have it because he had used chicken stock (not allowed milk and meat) in the soup.

For me personally everything went quiet and seemed to dim. The rest of the family was at the table talking about something or another. I just exploded at my niece's husband in a way that I cannot ever remember doing. My language was full of expletives and I was full of rage like I cannot remember. My brother-in-law moved me to the living room where I just burst into uncontrollable tears that I still do not fully understand today. What I have assessed in talks with therapists and other integrally informed people was that the sadness and the depth of the sadness was hidden by whatever process I use to create my shadow. Until it was safe to express it, I couldn't acknowledge how sad I really felt.

Keith Bellamy's story relaxed and organized me. Understanding and practically dealing with experiences like Keith sitting Shiva with his family is what I've done for over forty years and fifty-five thousand therapy sessions with men, women, children, families, couples, and groups. We all want to better understand ourselves and each other and keep learning to feel, think, and act more joyfully, lovingly, and successfully. We all keep stumbling and catching ourselves, often buffeted by life's challenges.

Destructive Shadow could have severely injured Keith Bellamy's family. What would have happened if Keith hadn't eventually examined his explosion with compassionate understanding? What if Keith became so locked into his butter and broth rage story he couldn't see there were deeper forces at work? The scene might have lingered for him (and his family) as a signature injury instead of eventually serving Keith's grieving/healing process.

You can see the dangers of avoiding, denying, or thoughtlessly indulging Shadow, and the benefits of exploring and owning Shadow. An obvious choice, don't you think? Become lost in distress and separation (avoiding), or expand power and love (exploring and owning)!

On the other hand, if the choices are so obvious, why do we so often struggle to understand ourselves and others? Why is it so often hard to do right?

Let's start with the basic problem, the constant flood of unknown into known that every human has to somehow reconcile.

Shadow is emergence: Our nervous systems constantly monitor hundreds of thousands of sensory inputs and interior stimulations like memories and fantasies. From this cacophony our brain chooses seven plus or minus two aspects, creates stories with emotions, memories, and impulses, and feeds us those stories in forty to two hundred milliseconds. Our conscious selves catch these stories—*if at all*—at five hundred to fifteen hundred milliseconds as we respond.[8]

This happens constantly. Everything combines into ongoing flow, or emergence, individually by ourselves, in intersubjective relationships with others, and collectively with all the rest of us.

We often instinctively resist awareness of who we are, keeping memories, qualities, and desires in Shadow. We can ignore our virtues as well as our flaws (ignoring either reflects destructive Shadow). We can observe and reflect on the pro-social values of ourselves and our cultures (like family, school, work, or country)—and such healthy curiosity often indicates constructive Shadow.

THE GOOD, THE BAD, AND THE UGLY

My clients are often surprised to find themselves resisting what's strong, beautiful, and creative about themselves and others. Some of our most wonderful attributes seem so ordinary to us that we shrug them off. You might be generally kind—a quality everyone admires—but it feels like no big deal to you. You might construct lovely seasonally nuanced flower beds in your garden, but dismiss your friends' astonished joy at these living works of art that seem so effortless to you.

People often understand Shadow as avoiding or indulging weak, ugly, or shameful material. You might not want to acknowledge or examine your tendency to bully your son when he defies you, or coerce your wife when you disagree, or back away from asking for what you want from your boss or lover.

Discovering and integrating shadow strengths and weaknesses, our inner angels and monsters, is what this book is all about. And, believe me, we all have our angels and monsters!

WE FIND OUR SHADOW REFLECTED IN OTHERS

I find reflections of myself in every person I encounter. This is one of the magnificent, often astonishing aspects of being a psychotherapist, finding yourself again and again—strengths, weaknesses, obsessions, habits, desires, and repulsions—in intimate relationships helping others.

I hope that you'll find yourself again and again as you read the stories in *Shadow Light*. You might find the young mother who cheats on her husband disgusting, or actually secretly identify with (or even support) her decision to reach for passion and excitement. Either way, your reaction reflects *you*—your moral condemnations, secret pleasures, shameful memories, and embodied fantasies and traumas.

You might admire the father who learned to manage his anger so his family didn't have to keep doing it for him, but think to yourself with shame, "I couldn't change as much as he did, or stand up to a bully the way his wife stood up to him." Your admiration probably reflects values of personal growth and taking responsibility. Your shame might reflect habitual self-doubt or self-betrayal—Shadow forces that nonconsciously arise from earliest development to plague us until insight and courageous actions integrate them into our larger Self.

Alchemically transforming self-loathing into self-love is so beautiful! But there are weeds in this garden. We have more power than we know, but not absolute power. Some of us have better opportunities, more favorable genetic legacies, more cultural resources, and just better luck (I always think that meeting my wife Becky in 1973 was the luckiest moment of my life). Some of us end up on the short end of the stick in these areas—not fair, but certainly an absolute of the human condition that we all must reconcile one way or another.

That being said, we all share the human superpowers of focused intent and action, in service of principle, and driven by resolve. Individuals and groups use these superpowers daily to create miracles of technology, intimacy, art, consciousness, and care.

Another human superpower is seeking out and receiving wise influences—being available to shift perspectives and behaviors towards deeper truths and more love. When we're open to both influence and deeper understandings we accelerate our development and can see Shadow messages from our adaptive unconscious more clearly—instead of resisting novelty or change, we become eager for luminous new perspectives.

No one can control or predict outcomes perfectly, but we can identify more or less healthy principles and practices (guided by intuition, experience, and science), and use positive influences from our own and others' wisdom to make adjustments in the face of resistances as we live and love. For instance, mindfulness research has validated again and again how gratitude and compassion are healthier affects/attitudes than anger, anxiety, shame, or cynicism.

Thus Shadow, the unknown, is a huge resource from which we can benefit. We can develop and harness our Shadow to serve us and the world.

You can endlessly keep discovering your strengths and owning them while noticing your mistakes and weaknesses and transforming them. In the process you literally grow your Shadow, developing a non-conscious self which increasingly dialysizes your destructive thoughts and impulses into constructive ones before they even reach your conscious awareness.

WHAT WAS THAT ABOUT FRACTALS?

In nature where there is a boundary that both separates and con-nects—like between sand and sea, air and water, cell membranes, or between known and unknown—fractal boundaries occur. Fractals are self-replicating or self-similar patterns that occur at such boundaries, endlessly repeating at different time and/or size scales, generating endless new configurations—*new configurations biased towards creating more complex, stable, and coherent forms.*[9]

Focus on what you're feeling in your body right now and you're going to the fractal interface between your conscious awareness and sensations/emotions/thoughts ("sensations/emotions/thoughts" because no sensation when it rises to awareness is divorced from an emotional experience and a story supporting the experience).

EXERCISE:
ATTUNEMENT HARMONIZES FRACTAL INTERFACES.

- *I encourage you to buy a journal to record this and future experiences during exercises. Writing about experiences and sharing them amplifies their effects.*
- *Sit or stand comfortably and breathe in deeply (feel your belly expand). Breathe out slowly, paying attention to every nuance of breath. Do this five to ten times until you create a rhythm of slow breathing in and out.*
- *Direct your attention to what you are feeling in your body right now, what you are thinking as you read this, imagining as you consider this, wanting as you become self-aware of desires, or judging as you notice judgments about others and yourself.*

- *Now observe all this—breath, sensations, emotions, thoughts, judgments, and impulses—with acceptance and caring intent.*
- *Think of someone you are critical of, irritated by, or you find threatening. Observe yourself being critical or irritated with acceptance and caring intent.*
- *Think of some aspect of yourself that you're critical of—your weight, temper, shameful secret, or guilty pleasure. Observe yourself being critical or ashamed with acceptance and caring intent.*
- *You probably notice a calming effect of observing these upsetting judgments with acceptance and caring intent. This is your conscious self holding your light and dark simultaneously in accepting awareness—creating a state of attunement.*
- *The instant these sensations, feelings, thoughts, judgments, and desires arise into conscious awareness you are at fractal boundaries between Shadow and light—boundaries you can focus on, ignore, embrace, reject, or guide with acceptance and caring intent towards harmony with your sense of self and all the stories you have about the world. Write in your journal about what you discover doing this attunement.*
- *Notice how such compassionate attention soothes and relaxes you. This is you sending caring attention to fractal interfaces and creating feedback loops into your non-conscious, adding compassion to experience as you reevaluate it.*
- *Compassionate attention shapes your non-conscious—literally accelerating the maturation of your Shadow self. One major reflector of maturation is increasing compassionate understanding of yourself, others and the world.*
- *Do this five minutes a day and you will become wiser, your brain will grow (especially your right frontal lobe[10]), and you will feel more joy and less anxiety. You will be directing yourself to the fractal interfaces of unknown arising into the known, coloring it with acceptance and caring intent, and positively influencing both your current thoughts and behavior and your future Shadow offerings. Write at least a few*

sentences describing your experiences each time you attune, and, after a week of entries share what you've written with someone you trust. Write about your conversation afterward in your journal.

HABITS MATTER

Since consciously attending to all the above all the time would overwhelm us with data and sensations, we have habits of attention, memory, thought, judgment, and relationship that guide awareness. Most of these habits are benign, some are destructive, and all change when we bring our conscious awareness to them—to the boundary between known and unknown, seen and unseen.

When we're in self-destructive states, we resist constructive Shadow because it pushes us towards threatening self-regulatory change—we avoid awareness of those fractal boundaries. Scared, angry, shamed, shut down, and anxious states resist new perspectives, since we are genetically driven to double down on current perspectives when we're stressed.[11] The sixteen-year-old girl screaming, "I hate you! You are a horrible mother!" when her mom tells her she can't go to the unchaperoned Saturday night party is not connected to the part of her who loves her mother and knows the dangers of such parties. That constructive Shadow understanding exists in her, but is being blanked out by rage and a distorted story of her mother unfairly blocking her from having fun with her friends.

When we're in pro-social self-supportive states, we tend to embrace constructive Shadow and observe destructive Shadow with curiosity and acceptance—we can look with interest at those fractal boundaries between known and unknown, and often insight (a more complex, energy efficient understanding) emerges. If in a less stressed moment I point out to this girl that her rage and distorted Mom-just-wants-to-control-me story is blocking her own native good judgment, she might be surprised and say, "Wow! I do stay mad so I don't have to really look at what's going on!"

All throughout nature we find alive fractal boundaries that connect and separate. Chaos theory explains how evolution arises from fractal interfaces self-organizing towards greater coherence—greater complexity in multiple dimensions. This tendency *of all matter* is the *evolutionary impulse,* accelerated in progressive orders of magnitude from:

- Inanimate matter, to
- Living organisms, to
- Complex organisms, to
- The mammalian triune brain, to
- Self-aware consciousness, to
- Intersubjective self-awareness with others, to
- Feeling unity with everything.[12]

Our personal evolutionary edge—the person we are constantly becoming—involves fractal boundaries between ourselves and other people, between our conscience and our drives, and between our different selves and others, nature, and our endless inner experience.

METABOLIZING SHADOW

We naturally metabolize shadow as it emerges—somehow fit it into our understanding of our personal universe—even as it influences thought, action, memories, and judgments. Humans are storytellers and we have multiple stories about ourselves called autobiographical narratives. These narratives—self as good boy, bad boy, good student, passionate lover, hopeless loser, responsible leader, good friend, irresponsible pleasure seeker, etc.—keep changing throughout our lives.[13]

We can broaden and constructively grow all our narratives—all our stories—if we choose! Attending to everything that emerges into consciousness with acceptance and caring intent is a magnificent tool for growing our autobiographical narratives and having clearer, cleaner relationships with others, essentially growing our stories about them.

Being human requires constant self-regulation of feeling, thought and impulse—most of it habitual, but also routinely requiring conscious attention. From birth onward—in relationship with other people, the world, and ourselves—we learn how to walk, think, talk, connect, dress, play, work, and relate, all the while regulating our emotions and behaviors, often in co-regulatory relationships with others. Thus multiple Shadow sources constantly interact both within us and between us and others.

Even as our conscious selves relate, our unconscious Shadow selves relate, sometimes on complementary channels and sometimes in dialectical opposition. You sit across from me and say, "Hi Keith. I want to talk about improving communication with my husband." I might respond, "Sure, what aspects of communication with your husband are you concerned with?"

Below the surface, your Shadow might be saying, "I hate my husband! I fear my husband! I love my husband and miss him! I'm worried we'll never get back to love!" Your face, tone, and bodily movements radiate these messages to me. My Shadow—communicating through my face, tone, and bodily movements—responds with soothing confidence, "I sense your pain and fear, and I believe I can help you can make progress, feel better, and find a way through this mess you're in." In our intersubjectivity, Shadow conversations always underlie the exchanges of words and content.

In psychotherapy, therapists are taught to monitor multiple channels and to continually hold the energetic container of, "You have worth and power and you can make progress." The intersubjective interfaces of these channels between self and other are all fractal interfaces which both connect and separate, and which generate gradually morphing self-repeating patterns.

All these fractal interfaces between what is known and unknown can be disrupted or harmonized by us and by others in relationships with us.

DANA AND AL

Once in a session, a twenty-one year old woman named Dana was describing her new love affair with Al. She concluded by saying, "I don't know what he sees in me."

I said, "I assume Al finds you beautiful, desirable, and interesting."
Dana quickly replied, "I know that's not true! I'll never be beautiful!"
Curious (I found her adorable) I asked, "You believe you are unattractive?" Dana nodded, and I continued, "What does Al say?"

Dana, somewhat reluctantly, replied, "He says I'm beautiful and sexy."

Sensing a potentially productive fractal interface I suggest, "Let's go to that place where he finds you beautiful and sexy, but you are convinced you are unattractive. Let's look with interest at those two together."

Dana responded, "I feel a little relaxed and a little confused." I persist, "Let's just stay there where he finds you beautiful and sexy and you have assumed you are unattractive. What are you feeling and thinking as we do this."

Dana looks thoughtful, "I feel good, and I'm thinking this beautiful thing is more complicated that I've thought before."

This is what arises when we go to fractal interfaces with acceptance and caring intent—more complexity arises. With humans, more complexity is often associated with deeper consciousness and greater compassion.

HOW DO WE MANAGE?

Understanding, observing, and working with Shadow brings illumination to the edge of darkness. We can learn to sense fractal boundaries and harmonize them, identify constructive Shadow and surrender to it, perceive destructive Shadow and transform it.

Sounds good, doesn't it? Embrace all memories, values, relationships, stories, and dreams, cross-validate them across dimensions, and bam! You liberate and empower your creative self, loving self, and soulful self to run the show in your unique universe! Whoo Hoo!

BUT WATCH OUT!

Before we get too intoxicated with golden, constructive Shadow, let's remember the dangers of destructive Shadow! There's violence, prejudice, greed, anxiety, despair, excess, shame, and rage which bubble up and threaten to overwhelm us. We all generate distorted stories, resist change, and sometimes turn away from or indulge shame, rage, fear, terror, numbness, and other painful feelings, memories, and impulses. There is a little bit of crazy in all of us, wanting to surrender to violence and distortion. One of the goals of *Shadow Light* is to show you how to transmute this hard-to-trust destructive Shadow into easy-to-trust constructive Shadow.

Shadow Light explores how shadow arises from cosmic strings (tiny fields), to subatomic particles, to atoms, to molecules, to life, to self-awareness. We'll journey through the major realms of shadow, and detail insights and directions on how to harmonize consciousness to keep refining these continual rivers of experience, emotion, narratives, and impulses into growth, love, and joy.

I encourage you to continue the attunement practice we did earlier in this chapter. It helps you develop new awarenesses of yourself that are actually new sense organs. Every time you notice a new dimension around you—for instance, people shutting down when you become bombastic, or opening up when you are caring—you are developing a new sense organ that can help you better perceive yourself, others, and the universe. In the chapters to come, we will explore dozens of potential new senses you can organize into new perceptions of constructive and destructive Shadow in yourself and others.

Shadow is revealed as the unknown becomes known. We each co-create a personal universe with experience, caregivers, relationships, our personal histories, tragedies, comedies, and dramas. We grow through stages of capacities and understanding in multiple areas—often called multiple intelligences.[14] One such area includes our developing relationships with the unknown as it becomes known— Shadow emerging into the light. This is illumination at the edge of darkness.

As perceptions, thoughts, sensations, feelings, impulses, judgments, desires, memories, and insights arise, they pass from Shadow into conscious awareness, a never ending flood that begins with our first awareness and continues to our last experience.

All these processes occur in relationships with ourselves, others, and the world. In Chapter 2 we examine the relational nature of everything more deeply.

CAVEAT: IT'S NEVER AS EASY AS IT SOUNDS

I look at Henry, my 52-year-old businessman client, and say, "I want to apologize for making this sound so easy."

Henry looks a little puzzled, "I like how clear and simple your explanations are. That's one reason I'm hopeful about this therapy."

Smiling at him I reply, "Thank you! I do try to make things accessible and fun to hear. But I'm actually talking about something a little different."

Intrigued, he asks, "What do you mean?"

I take a deep breath, "It's a paradox really. Inspirational speakers, therapists, spiritual teachers, and all change agents hype how *easy* it is to think and act better. The central theme is endless versions of 'Just decide! You can do almost anything!' I wrote a whole book which integrates a bunch of manifestation systems. Although all of them at some point say change is not an instantaneous or easy process, they *universally imply* huge easy changes are possible by following a few simple steps."

Henry gets it. "I see what you mean. I often think, 'Keith told me to pay attention with caring intent, but I just can't right now! I'm too embarrassed or pissed off!'"

I laugh and agree, "Yes! Exactly!"

I go on to describe in more detail how we like things simple and easy. Audiences enjoy extreme statements and everyone wants quick fixes.

I've concluded that just being a change agent influences you to make extravagant claims. When I write, I kept finding myself suggesting easy progress, while simultaneously emphasizing regular patient practices.

As for quick fixes, the realities of growth are that, sometimes, we dramatically change almost instantaneously with a transformative experience, but that mostly development and progress involve patience and struggle. Even though we can always decide to do better or worse—be more or less healthy—nervous systems resist change and usually incorporate new, healthier, habits of thought and action slowly.

After I told all this to Henry, we sat in companionable silence for a few moments. For several sessions I'd been after him and his wife to just get naked and cuddle together a couple of times a week, something they hadn't done for years. So far they hadn't been able to do the assignment even once.

"Look how hard it's been just to take a shower and fool around for few minutes," I say to Henry. "You guys feel unsafe with each other around your sexuality/sensuality and so you're scared of even tiny changes."

Henry nodded thoughtfully, "It does sound easy—just get naked and cuddle for a little bit, but you're right, we haven't been able to do it."

We spent the rest of the session exploring his resistances to these (apparently) simple instructions, and Henry left more resolved to try the exercise with his wife.

WE GROW THROUGH STAGES

Integral Psychology, developed by Ken Wilber, demonstrates how we grow through developmental stages, which can't be skipped.[15] We need to fully embody our current way of being—be true to our current beliefs and principles—to flow into the next developmental wave. You don't go from beginner to maestro on the violin overnight. You have to do the work.

Spiritual teachers seem to fall into the "it's *so* easy" trap more than most—partially I think because some realizations are easy for *them* to remember and live by (though usually only after years—even decades—of personal work and struggles). For instance, if you're a spiritual teacher with a stable realization of everything connected to everything else across time (you actually *feel* connected most of the time), it's easy to imagine others sharing this experience, and you often can reliably induce a *temporary* peak experience of unity with students and audiences. Many can share such transcendent *state* experiences, but don't stabilize them as new *traits* without extended practice.

Teachers can help people experience expansive states for brief periods—often accelerating the growth process by imagining everyone present stably awakened to new worldviews (always a good idea when you're teaching)—but enduring growth almost always requires efforts over time.

Practice any new *habit* or *state* enough, and it becomes programmed into our Shadow selves as a new *trait*, not requiring much (or any) conscious awareness to naturally arise in our lives.[16] This is one major way we individually evolve.

The pressures of our natural hunger for easy change and marketing's push to amplify hype push teachers to promise easy (or miraculous) transformations, which unfortunately can lead clients, students, and seekers who haven't achieved consistent bliss in the promised time to blame themselves for not trying hard enough.

Most teachers and therapists know that people have powerful internal Shadow forces that regularly make it extremely hard to do the honest and sometimes painful and humbling work of self-reflection and solidifying new habits.

Wise teachers know that their job is to make learning and change sound fascinating, accessible, and doable, without promising easy answers and quick fixes. They guide us to patiently seek the right kinds of information and support for *us*, and practice the right kinds of new behaviors for *us*, so we can gradually make *effective, sustainable* positive changes, with the occasional light bulb going off, "Yes! I've got it!" experience showing up in the process. That's how I've grown throughout my life and I've found the same to be true for my clients and students.

EVOLUTIONARY FORCES PUSH FOR CHANGE AND
RESIST CHANGE

Our nervous systems are so resistant to change—even when we know we need it—because our evolutionary past in the forests and savannahs of ancient Africa shaped our emotional relationships with the world.[17] Ancient hunter-gatherers needed to balance a healthy fear of the unknown with their human craving for discovery and novelty. So a cave-guy might say to himself, "Yeah, I want to see what's on the other side of the hill, but maybe there's a lion over there, so what am I gonna do?"

This kind of push/pull, approach/avoidance type of situation is perfectly reasonable, but has frozen billions of people in their tracks over the last two-hundred thousand years. Our brains and bodies often resist change when feeling unsafe, and are more likely to seek novelty when feeling safe. Angry or hurt couples, depressed or anxious individuals, or anyone unhappy with their current situation usually feels *unsafe*—so instead of reaching out to make changes, they're likely to resist them, not realizing they're surrendering to destructive Shadow.

In other words, those who might most benefit from positive influence—people who feel insecure and disconnected—are often those who are the most steeped in resistance and denial about what could make them feel and act a whole lot better. So change agents like myself try to make progress sound safe, easy, and accessible.

Skilled therapists help clients assess their unique situations and tackle the paradox of wanting change and resisting change simultaneously. My goal is to make new thoughts and behaviors sound so easy that you'll decide to use your superpowers of focused intent and action, in service of principle, and driven by resolve, to reach through resistance and try them. In this I'm just like the spiritual teachers I referenced earlier, with the exception that I'm warning you that it's not as easy as I'm making it sound.

As for Henry, the following week he and his wife took a shower and enjoyed cuddling naked for the first time in years. It was a small step that felt like a major breakthrough, but they knew they needed to do a lot more work to turn their relationship into the warm love affair they both yearned for, and, as far as I know, they continue to progress.

All that being said, sometimes just seeing the world in a new way changes everything. So let's go deeper, starting with recognizing how everything is relationships.

2
WE EXIST IN A
RELATIONAL
UNIVERSE

The essence of everything is relationships.

—Miester Eckhart

THE ILLUSION OF SEPARATENESS

One of the most dangerous aspects of being a conscious human is that we can experience ourselves separate from others, from nature, and from spirit. Such separation experiences can be devastating, even lethal.

In 1965, fifteen-year-old Keith lay in the dark in his filthy room in Covina, California, unable to sleep, wishing for death. Despite having parents who loved me, brothers and other family members who cared about me, teachers who knew and liked me, and friends who wished me well, I was locked in a black depression and felt isolated from everyone and everything.

Rage, despair, and hopeless longing for love roiled within me, and I had no sense of *real* connection to anyone or any hope of happiness or satisfying love. My room reflected my mind—chaotic, unattended, soiled, and dark.

I still vividly recall the sense of isolation and crippling shame at my many weaknesses. Raised in a rational family (my father was a high school biology teacher), I had a scientific empirical bias towards existence. I scoffed at religious hocus-pocus, and was contemptuous of religion or spiritual faith of all forms. Why be alive? What's the point? More suffering? Get a boring job, create a boring family, and then wait for death as my body slowly deteriorates? It all seemed pointless and horrible. I despised myself for my cowardly inability to deal with the world.

My pain turned into indifference towards school and vicious fights with my family, all of whom were dealing with emotional and relational pain of their own. Destructive Shadow was drowning me, silencing the constructive Shadow voices that were struggling to help me choose life.

My parents wisely took us to family therapy and the therapist, Joe Ericson, appalled at the emotional violence, helped my parents commit me to a mental hospital. I remember my father inviting me to drive our 1954 white Ford sedan to look at sports cars, and then stopping in front of the Wells Neuropsychiatric Clinic. "You're going to spend some time here, son." he said, pulling a packed suitcase from the trunk.

Over the next five weeks my treatment involved hanging out, playing ping pong, making ash trays and moccasins in the crafts room, talking to a psychiatric social worker (a nice woman named Mrs. Marisoke), and twenty-three electroconvulsive shock treatments (ECT).

ECT causes amnesia to varying degrees, so I only remember one of them. I'm strapped to a gurney with an IV line inserted in my arm that's sending valium into my bloodstream, a muscle relaxant to prevent me breaking my own bones during the grand mal seizure that accompanies the treatment. The apparatus is strapped over my head, and then blank! All I remember is waking up disoriented.

Sounds horrible, right? But ECT can actually *temporarily* make depression abate in some cases. When it works, it can provide a window or opportunity where the screaming depression subsides and you have a chance to hear deeper voices. With me, the grinding pain had isolated me in a cocoon of suffering, and with it reduced I began to feel *connected*. I wasn't just connected with other people like the staff and other patients, all who seemed pretty nice to me. I felt connected to my own life and body. I felt connected to my future self. I felt connected to a deeper Self who could faintly imagine the possibilities of love and soul. I could envision Keith being someone I wanted to be. It was at that time that I decided to be a psychotherapist and martial artist.

I left that hospital and began improving my relationships with myself and others. The emotional pain and fierce distortions returned, but now there was a resolved Keith-self to help deal with the craziness, a self more connected to my yearnings for love, wisdom, intimacy, and equanimity. More in relationship with myself and the world, I was more able to receive help, more connected to myself and other people. Three years later, I was awarded my black belt in Shotokan Karate. Ten years later, I earned my first license to practice psychotherapy. Both these disciplines led me to spiritual awakenings that continue to this day. Throughout those years and all the subsequent years, I've solidified my conviction that it's all relationships all the time.

IN THIS CHAPTER WE WILL:

- See further how it's all relationships all the time.
- Discover a United Field Theory of Shadow.
- See how Shadow impacted Jane and Jim, an alienated couple seeking love through therapy.
- Discover how therapy speeds things up.
- Explore *your* relationships with Shadow.
- Return to fractals in a relational universe.

IT'S ALL RELATIONSHIPS ALL THE TIME

The vast spaces and intricate networks that decide and process what to bring to consciousness are not just in *me*. From conception to death, none of us exists separate from other people, whether we're aware of it or not.

We are energetically connected to others, and our collective Shadows combine into cultural understandings and standards. I believe we are connected by morphic fields of life and wisdom—energies so subtle that they can't be measured with current instrumentation—which influence us in the most delicate and subtle ways, and sometimes blast us with staggering downloads of knowledge, insight, beauty, and love.

What do I mean by staggering downloads? Mozart used to receive whole concertos as "Round volumes of sound," that he would later laboriously transcribe[18] (more on this in Chapter 13: Creativity—Shadow Demanding Expression). Were these coming from just *him,* or were other forces involved? My genius philosopher friend, Ken Wilber, has written nearly thirty mind-blowing, paradigm-altering books on Integral theory, weaving together multiple threads of science, spirituality, and art. Ken says he studies where his attention takes him, and then wakes one day thinking, "Book!" His first reaction? "Oh Shit! I have to spend the next month writing it out."[19] He's done this *thirty times!* Do these downloads come just from *him?*

I think other forces—relational forces—are also at work.

WE'RE ALL CONNECTED

Right before the Big Bang, the known universe was smaller than an atom. *Everything was connected.*

If we keep looking at tinier and tinier particles, we eventually discover everything is fields arising out of somewhere, self-organizing constantly into the manifest universe.

As the Big Bang exploded, an infinity of tiny fields self-organized into plasma, into hydrogen and helium atoms, into suns, into elements, into us. Nothing was lost—those original fields are what make up you, me and everything. *And fields don't have definable boundaries.* Each field theoretically extends infinitely, so everything is always, and has always been, connected with everything.

Are these fields arising out of nothingness?

Maybe.

Are they comprised of cosmic strings vibrating in eleven dimensions?

Maybe.

Are these fields some other substance/entity/phenomena associated with the Higgs boson field that permeates the cosmos and explains inertia?

Maybe.

Is there some consciousness inherent in all these interconnected fields? Deus ex machina? Spirit? God?

Maybe.

A UNIFIED FIELD THEORY OF SHADOW

The smallest, most fundamental, parts of the universe are almost certainly not *objects.* Objects reduce to atoms, which reduce to subatomic particles, which reduce to oscillating fields in multiple dimensions.

The smallest parts of the universe are almost certainly energetic fields, and fields don't have definite boundaries. Fields theoretically extend with no end, *connecting with all other fields.* So all fields communicate, biased to self-organize towards greater coherence and complexity—they are processes interacting with processes, all moving through time, going someplace—*evolving.*[20]

Not only that, but through quantum entanglement, everything that has shared a field is permanently connected. Every part of us is connected to everything in the universe, *exchanging influence, communicating, relating.*

The universe is hardwired to evolve through infinities of relationships, all involving fractal boundaries (interfaces that both connect and separate), to create more complex novelty out of less complex chaos and rigidity.

The endless flow of creation is always, at its heart, fields co-creating with other fields. Philosopher Alfred North Whitehead called these universal tendencies, "The creative advance into novelty."[21]

You and I are the crest of the wave of the evolution of consciousness—pure Spirit somehow permeating everything and reaching to more coherence and complexity. This is because, as Chaos theory has demonstrated, complex systems of differentiated parts that are linked, arranged hierarchically, energized, and capable of chaotic activity are biased to self-organize towards greater complexity. Complex systems can be purely chemical or living organisms. Human brains, relationships, and social structures are all complex systems, self-organizing over time towards more complexity.

At the self-awareness level—the human level—creation involves unknown arising into known, conscious experience emerging from Shadow. In other words, each new thought, idea, conversation, or creative act involves what was unknown and nonexistent before coming into existence and being known now—the creative advance into novelty.

Shadow emerging into consciousness involves fields interacting with fields—a Unified Field Theory of Shadow which includes constructive/destructive Shadow, Shadow we naturally embrace, Shadow we resist, and individual/collective Shadow. Energetic fields generated by activated neural networks combine to form our sense of self, and organize our experiences, memories, life stories, and emotional states. Practically, each conscious understanding of Shadow suggests action steps to help us grow, heal, love, and thrive.

What I couldn't realize as a depressed teenager was that I was *energetically* connected to all the different parts of myself, the people in my life (and everywhere), and my past/present/future. What no one had ever told me was that *I could influence* all those connections with focused intent and action, in service of principle, and driven by resolve.

For instance, in college I was resolved to become the best psychotherapist I could. That meant feeling connected to the integrity of the profession, discovering and surrendering to gifted therapists and teachers, and dedicating myself to finding and practicing healing relationships. This focus attracted the attention of teachers and practitioners who connected with me in relationships to expand my knowledge and abilities in multiple forms of psychotherapy, a healing approach where *the core of the healing work is first and foremost an intimate psychotherapeutic relationship.*

JIM AND JANE COME INTO THERAPY FEELING DISCONNECTED

A couple in their early forties, Jim and Jane come into a session. They are initially respectful and caring, but disconnected. "We spend time together," Jim says, "but we aren't intimate. We take a walk and have nothing to talk about."

Jane sits silently. I ask, "What's important to you?" and she says, "I'm passionate about caring for our children and my yoga classes."

Jim says despairingly, "There's nothing about me there."

I ask, "How's your sexual/romantic life?"

Jim's voice quivers with anger and frustration, "We haven't had sex in over a year."

"You sound angry about that," I tell him.

"I'm not *angry!*" he responds.

I look over at Jane and, as he complains, she disappears, hurt and spaced out.

Jim, at his wits end, told Jane two weeks ago he might have to separate, breaking up their family and devastating their three young children.

I encourage them to tell their stories, and they each have frustrations with the other, Jim at Jane's inaccessibility and withdrawal, and Jane at Jim's apparent lack of understanding and interest in her and her passions for yoga and spiritual development. Neither hears anything new in the other's recital. Both get progressively more uncomfortable and angry as they talk, trying to be civil but disliking each increasingly as the session progresses.

Imagine you're their therapist. What do you do? There is obvious Shadow material in this example—their unconscious hostility and their deep yearnings for communion and love—but what to do about it?

PSYCHOTHERAPY ACCELERATES TRANSFORMATIVE CHANGE (MOSTLY)

I've often described psychotherapy as traveling through parallel, but intersecting, universes—saturated with past, present, and imagined future relationships with self, others, and the world. A client enters the room, our universes mingle, and we share our intersubjectivity for an hour. With a couple it's their two universes and mine with countless relational intersections.

Most intimate conflicts reflect clashes between two separate, but intimately connected, universes. Jim and Jane come in with Jane yearning for more spiritual authority in her sense of self and deeper understanding from Jim, and Jim, desperate for intimacy, threatened that he might somehow lose Jane. Development has pushed both against transformational barriers and my job is to co-create thresholds to deeper love and understanding and invite each to step through.

I often tell people as they stand at such thresholds, "Each level of awakening creates responsibilities. Are you willing to shoulder new responsibilities along with new gifts?"

WHAT ABOUT JANE AND JIM'S SHADOW?

Constructive Shadow is Jim and Jane's desire to get back to love, driving them into the session. Destructive Shadow is their unconscious assumptions that their hurt/hostile stories are the best reflectors of what is really happening. They both have modern and post-modern worldviews that leave them feeling like shameful failures because of their unhappy marriage and failed love affair, and secret resentment and shame at feeling angry at and superior to their spouse whom they are supposed to feel equal with and loving toward.

I tell them, "Both your stories are distorted towards the negative," and Jim and Jane change states immediately—they become simultaneously confused and relieved.

This is constructive Shadow emerging into consciousness—there is hope! "My story is distorted and can be more true! My spouse can change negative beliefs about me!"

I reassure their sense-of-failure shame, "You can have a successful marriage." I speak to their I-shouldn't-feel-hostile-and-superior shame, "Of course you fear and resent each other in these painful areas, but you can learn to better love and approve of each other as equals in this marriage."

In these new states of consciousness they now look intrigued. Shifting from shame and resistance to interest invites the examination of Shadow.

WHERE'S MY SHADOW AND WHAT DO I DO ABOUT IT?

Let's return briefly to the fractal interfaces we discussed in Chapter 1. In complex systems there are differentiated parts which are linked. The places they are linked are fractal boundaries. Fractal boundaries both separate and connect. At these boundaries are self-repeating patterns that keep appearing with creative variations at different time and size scales. The creative variations are biased towards greater complexity, enduring new patterns which are more energy efficient and stable (less chaotic) while still being fluid and dynamic (less rigid).[22] If we keep examining these fractal interfaces in ourselves we ultimately reach fields interacting with fields—*most of them guided to some extent by consciousness.*

As I mentioned in Chapter 1, a human superpower we all share is our capacity for focused intent and action, in service of principle, and driven by resolve. This superpower applied optimally to personal health and growth is ultimately using consciousness to harmonize the fractal boundaries of fields that determine our interior and interpersonal lives.

What are examples of this? You have moment-to-moment fractal boundaries between:

- Your conscious self and your multitude of inner selves in the past, present, and future.
- You and other people.
- You and nature.
- Your body and your awareness of your body.
- You and your drives and instincts.
- You and your fantasies/values/assumptions and worldviews.

PRACTICE:
PRACTICAL USE OF FRACTAL UNDERSTANDING.

- *Focus on your bodily sensation for a moment. Start from your toes and notice any sensations from your feet to the top of your head. Just sit with bodily sensation for a few seconds. This is a fractal interface between your conscious awareness and your bodily sensation.*
- *Now, think how grateful you are to be alive, to have a body that works in so many millions of ways—blood vessels, heart, digestive system, kidneys, brain, bones, immune system, etc... Concentrate on this until you can feel a sense of gratitude in your chest area for your amazing body—over 500 trillion cells, organized into you. Let the sense of gratitude expand as you breathe slowly in and out from your abdomen. Continue this for at least sixty seconds.*
- *As you do this, what changes about your awareness of your bodily sensation? You probably feel differently than when you started the exercise. What is that difference? I personally feel more of a sense of compassionate acceptance for my precious human body and gratitude that it works as well as it does. Write about your experience in your journal in as much detail as possible.*

- *Repeat the exercise on at least three different days, and then share what you've written with someone you trust, writing about the conversation afterwards.*
- *If you practice this exercise daily whenever you are aware of a bodily sensation, your conscious (and non-conscious) sense of physical coherence will expand. If you continue long enough, your Shadow will grow to the point it will naturally generate bodily awareness and gratitude much of the time.*

You have just used your human superpower of focused intent and action (concentration on sensation and then cultivating gratitude), in service of principle (compassionate acceptance and gratitude are preferable attitudes towards physical experience), and driven by resolve (it required some willpower to do this exercise).

You extended attention to the fractal interface between conscious awareness and bodily sensation and biased it towards compassionate acceptance and gratitude. You just trained your shadow to be a bit wiser and more highly integrated with regards to your body.

We can use focused intent and action in service of principle and driven by resolve to improve relationships. We can use this superpower to be more true to the archetypal forms that most light us up—like Warrior, Man of Wisdom, Woman of Wisdom, Divine Lover, Sex Goddess, or the Youth of a Thousands Summers (much more on these in Chapters 4, 5, and 6). We can expand our powers as lovers, parents, spiritual practitioners, workers, and friends.

HOW DOES THIS APPLY TO JANE AND JIM?

In a subsequent session we explore Jane's tendencies to create hostile stories about Jim, and Jim's tendency to react with coldness. Neither is aware of these destructive Shadow habits in response to stress. Conflict occurs and habitual Shadow reactions organize the ensuing fight, almost like a choreographed dance. I point this out and Jane protests.

"You don't get it! He said I was a bad cook in front of the kids! That's not OK!"

Jim, activated as much by her hostile tone (with all its implicit, "You're so messed up!" destructive Shadow messages) as by her words, fires back, "I didn't say you were a bad cook! I said I didn't like the lasagna!" His words are reasonable but his natural warmth and friendliness are gone as he looks at her contemptuously (broadcasting his demeaning destructive Shadow messages to her).

Stung by Jim's cold contempt, Jane starts to fire back, but I interrupt quickly and turn to Jane (you have to interrupt a lot when you work with couples).

"Wait a minute! How are *you* accelerating this conflict?"

Jane, furious, says, "I put up with his abuse."

I start to laugh, which unsettles both of them. "Come on! You hate his contemptuous tone, and I don't blame you, but it's not abuse. That's an amplification you're making outside of your awareness because you're mad and anger amplifies. That's destructive Shadow. Jim does need to not use that dismissive tone, but right now he's unaware of it."

Jim jumps in indignantly even as Jane nods in agreement, "I'm not being contemptuous!" His moral system says it's wrong to be contemptuous, and Jim believes he doesn't engage in such wrong behavior, so we both must be wrong. Now I start laughing at him.

"Jim, you might not be consciously aware of your contemptuous tone, but it's there, just as Jane isn't aware of how, when she's mad, she amplifies negative stories about you to the point that you're a abusive jerk instead of a great guy having a jerk moment."

Jane feels the truth of this and looks a little embarrassed, a response I want to encourage since embarrassment is her constructive Shadow telling her she's violating a value of being fair. Shame emotions are automatic responses—messages from Shadow—that our non-conscious is experiencing us violating a value. She's an honest person, understands as I point it out how amplifying her story is a form of dishonesty, and her nervous system generates embarrassment (a shame emotion like guilt, regret, humiliation, and mortification) in response.

I look at both of them. "Now I'm going to ask the same question that neither of you answered when I asked the first time, "How are *you* accelerating this conflict?"

Ruefully Jim says, "I guess I'm using a contemptuous tone." Jane visibly relaxes as he says this. I turn to Jane and raise my eyebrows.

She says in a softer tone, "I do exaggerate the negative story when I'm mad."

I smile, "Great! Now look in each other's eyes and tell me how you feel right now." They do this and smile tentatively.

Jim warms up as he looks into Jane's eyes, "I like Jane right now."

Jane lights up a little under this attention. "I feel warmer. I don't want to make things worse when I'm hurt, and I can see right now that I do sometimes."

Look at all the relationships represented here—within them, between them, and with me. Jane and Jim are working at fractal boundaries between non-conscious and conscious, destructive Shadow and constructive Shadow, between each other and with me. In this enactment they're utilizing presence, insight, and compassion from me to dialysize their Shadow material into serving their deeper purpose, which is to love each other better in general and especially when they are caught in defensive patterns. Material that has always been there—the shifts in tones, the distorted perspectives—is now visible to them. It's Shadow emerging into the light of awareness. Just perceiving their part of the negative pattern helps each regulate towards serving love instead of creating painful misattunements.

The relationships revealed in these exchanges are complex, interconnected, and happening at different levels. Jane and Jim have relationships with their destructive and constructive Shadow in themselves and each other. They have relationships with me, and with both their fears and resentments, as well as their love and yearnings.

I have relationships with all these aspects of them, as well as my corresponding reactions and associations with everything that is happening moment to moment. I have meta-relationships with all these relationships as I observe myself during session, looking for guidance and insight from my own constructive and destructive Shadow as it arises.

It's all relationships, all the time.

MORE TO COME

In the chapters to come I'll offer strategies to guide focused intent, suggest principles and ideas to guide understanding, and provide practices to accelerate health and development. Throughout we'll regularly address constructive Shadow, destructive Shadow, the Shadow of simply not knowing, and the Shadow of what we resist. All practices involve conscious attention to managing fractal interfaces between different elements of ourselves and our personal universes.

As I mentioned previously, our brains generate stories, emotions, values, and impulses in 40 to 200 milliseconds, and 500 to 1500 milliseconds later our conscious self *discovers* these feelings, impulses, and stories, and manages them for better or worse. This creates feedback loops back into our unconscious to either enhance or stunt Shadow growth.

Yes, we can literally train our Shadow self—our non-conscious, information processing, impulse/emotion/story generating/right hemisphere-based adaptive unconscious—to become wiser, kinder, more fun, and more reliable.

That's Shadow light. That's illumination at the edge of darkness.

3

THE NEUROBIOLOGY OF SHADOW— CONCEPTION TO DEATH:

"Events that occur during infancy, especially transactions with the social environment, are indelibly imprinted onto the structures that are maturing in the first years of life. The child's first relationship, the one with the mother, acts as a template, as it permanently molds the individual's capacities to enter into all later emotional relationships. These early experiences shape the development of a unique personality, its adaptive capacities, as well as its vulnerabilities to and resistances against particular forms of future pathologies. Indeed, they profoundly influence the emergent organization of an integrated system that is both stable and adaptable, and thereby the formation of the self."

FROM *AFFECT REGULATION AND THE ORIGIN OF THE SELF,*

—ALLAN SCHORE

WHAT?

I know! This is why most people don't get how illuminating and exciting interpersonal neurobiology is. Much of the literature is exactly like the above quote—almost impenetrable, even to people like me who read it all the time and totally love it.

But the neurobiology of Shadow is *so cool!* A lot of it is pretty simple and incredibly useful if you just translate the scientific gibberish into regular language and look for practical understanding.

IN THIS CHAPTER WE WILL:

- See how genes and epigenetics matter in Shadow.
- Go back to our evolutionary imperatives to bond and commune.
- Marvel again at the miracle of self-aware consciousness.
- Discover how judgments and shame are the price of human awareness.
- Use shame as a spiritual guide.
- Understand the relationships between daydreaming, night dreaming, and Shadow.
- See how the neurobiology of memory and consciousness is central to the ongoing floods of Shadow into awareness.
- Explore the evolutionary mandates of defenses, violence, and emotions as ancestral memories guiding us to deal with what's next.
- Go back two-hundred thousand years to the birth of modern human self-aware consciousness.
- Hear the story of the Monk and the Tiger.
- Practice presence.
- Explore why life can be so hard and why brains are social organs.

Let's start with our genetic legacy arising from 13.75 billion years of evolution.

GENES MATTER IN SHADOW

Genes, epigenetic markers, our mother's psychology/biochemistry, and all their interactions with the environment, influence us from conception through birth. Most of this influence is not consciously available. It is Shadow.

Just a few examples are:

- All people are born with varying tendencies toward dependence, cooperativeness, novelty seeking, harm avoidance, persistence, self-directedness and self-transcendence. We make sense of our personal levels of these traits in the stories we generate about our lives as we slowly discover who we are.
- At eight weeks our brains become either masculinized—priming us towards competition and domination, or feminized—priming us towards relationships. *This happens, weirdly, by girls' brains generating an enzyme that neutralizes estrogen. Boys' brains, in the absence of the enzyme, are masculinized by estrogen!*
- A mother's ability to self-soothe when she's upset, especially in the third trimester, influences her baby's neural capacities to self-soothe after birth.[23]

Similarly, how infants and children relate with mother and caregivers creates neurological, relational, and behavioral predispositions that will influence them throughout life. We are all genetically programmed to relate in ways that shape our (and our children's) brain development, for better or worse. Much of this is through epigenesis, described in the sidebar.

▶ **Epigenesis sidebar:** *Humans have 32 chromosomes which hold about 35,000 genes, over half of which are directly or indirectly involved with our nervous systems. Our genes are surrounded by over a million epigenetic markers, proteins that are activated by experience, which in turn activate genes and gene sequences, which profoundly affect every aspect of development. This is one reason why identical twins can be different in so many ways. Their life experiences are different, leading to different epigenetic activations of different genes.*

A few examples of epigenesis—experience activating genes—are:

- By ten months old, if we have a mother who is consistently enough attuned to us so that we consistently feel known, accepted, and protected, we develop *secure attachment* tendencies that optimize pro-social-engagement and pro-security-of-being circuits in our brain, leaving us less likely to lose capacities for self-reflection and empathy when we're stressed. We are all genetically predisposed to be securely attached if given the chance from attuned caregivers loving us well enough to activate the genes to create the brain structures we need for secure relationships.
- 55 percent of American babies have secure attachment styles and 45 percent insecure by ten months old, and most keep these tendencies *throughout their entire lives.* Mom's relationship with baby in the first ten months *helps shape baby's relational brain.* The exceptions are the secure kids who become traumatized or neglected later in childhood (they can *lose* their secure attachment tendencies), and the insecure kids who, through at least one successful intimate relationship, earn secure attachment tendencies later in life (they can *earn* secure attachment tendencies). The brains of secure and insecure kids are wired differently.[24]
- If we're traumatized or neglected our first two years, we have much more probability of developing depression, anxiety, bipolar disorders, and immunological disease in later life. Trauma and neglect activate genes which result in compromised brain circuits.[25]
- If we have a gifted teacher *for just one year* of elementary school—someone who gets us, loves us, and inspires us—we are favored to make tens of thousands more dollars when we enter the work force as adults. That one year of great-teacher-relationship creates stable brain circuits that guide us towards success.
- Genetically, *we're programmed to grow and thrive if given the opportunities and environments that epigenetically activate the right genes.*[26]

This is why mindful self-observation and radical acceptance are crucial for growth. The above examples are just a few of thousands of non-conscious tendencies—Shadow—that we can discover and shape emotionally, behaviorally, and neurologically, as we wake up to ourselves and the world. All of them involve our experience activating different genes that wire our nervous systems and organize our unconscious selves—our sum total of constructive and destructive Shadow.

To integrate material that is scary or threatening (selfishness, destructive impulses, impossible moral demands like, "Don't be sexual!" or "Don't be angry!") we have to first sense them and radically accept what we find. This radical acceptance activates genes to wire new self-reflection circuits in our brains.

We can thus grow and transmute destructive Shadow, but have a lot of trouble doing so if we can't perceive it and accept ourselves as okay people when we do discover it. Knowing the neurobiology of why we do what we do often helps enormously.

HOW IS THIS PRACTICALLY IMPORTANT? SALLY DEALS WITH ROMANTIC SHADOW

Sally, an attractive, vivacious forty-something event organizer, who comes in to a therapy session, smiles radiantly, and says, "Keith I need your help!"

I can feel there's a man involved (her radiance is the giveaway—women in love, like women who are newly pregnant, have an extra glow about them). "Tell me about it. I bet it's a guy."

Sally, "Of course it's a guy! I've been going out with Brent for five weeks and he's critical and demanding. He wants to be adored, and seems bored with what I want unless it's something he likes. He gave me a list of complaints last Saturday. I asked if he'd go to this session, and he said he's smarter than any therapist!"

She smiles and adds. "But we *really* have fun together!"

I immediately see Brent's seductive narcissistic pattern. "I'll bet you two have great sex, he looks good, and he's a blast to be with at parties."

"Yes," she says, "We have lots of fun."

I look into her eyes, "Are you in love?"

"Not yet," she says, and I breathe a sigh of relief, and share some developmental interpersonal neurobiology about Brent, love, and attachment.

"Great! I'm so glad you're not in love yet! Brent's almost certainly a narcissist and will eventually feel super-bad about something you do or don't do. His nervous system will shift into a primitive mode where he has no empathy for you, no self-reflection, and overwhelming impulses to attack you and leave you. Intimacy eventually cues that core pain because it's programmed into his wounded attachment circuits. Brent will feel a black hole of rage and violence in his core. He won't be able to tolerate the pain and will have to blame you and leave you—essentially execute you from his life. While doing this, he'll seem to lose most capacities for understanding and caring and hurt you badly. Narcissists demean and withdraw when they get stressed or challenged."[27]

Sally's nodding her head. She's a smart, sophisticated woman who—like many people—finds narcissists initially attractive, but has been around long enough to feel the truth in what I just said. She asks, "How does this happen, Keith? Why do people become narcissists?"

This turned into an extended discussion about how narcissism typically arises and how Sally was vulnerable to some narcissistic men.

Neurobiological development proceeds in surges, where if you don't get the right attunements from caregivers, you can get arrested development. As a little kid, especially between one and five, Brent probably got praise and accolades, but also neglect and emotional misattunements. Positive attention showed up for looking good or being successful, but he probably wasn't much known—attuned to—emotionally and spiritually by caregivers. This stunted the development of circuits in his cingulate and medial prefrontal cortex. He can understand people, but he's organized around the narcissistic supply he needs from them—praise, attention, admiration, and adoration. Brent's destructive Shadow was programmed to keep seeking narcissistic supply—especially from lovers like Sally who could temporarily deliver the romantic infatuation narcotic.

Unfortunately for all of us, even if a love affair constellates romantic infatuation programming in our brain, mostly the best we can hope for is fun until it fades—our brains are programmed to progress from romantic infatuation into intimate bonding after six months to a couple of years of being crazy in love. Those circuits can be maintained by healthy, self-aware, resolved lovers. With narcissists like Brent, when romantic infatuation fades, watch out!

After we'd discussed all this, Sally looked wistfully out my French doors into the little garden outside my office. "I thought all this was happening, but we have so much fun! Maybe we can just date."

I shook my head, "I know you're having fun, but if you keep being your passionate intimate self with Brent, you're likely to fall in love. If your romantic infatuation circuits get activated with Brent, you'll essentially become obsessed with him and it will break your heart when he does his demean-and-withdraw number."

Sally got it. Passionate and often impulsive in lover relationships, Sally was also an eminently rational woman. The developmental neuroscience helped her see her Shadow attraction to guys like Brent, and her constructive Shadow self trusted me and received my influence. Soon after this session, she broke up with Brent and sent me an email validating everything we'd discussed.

WHY ARE PROGRAMMED THESE WAYS?

Human consciousness is young. Five hundred thousand years ago the human brain expanded to meet the social needs of the tribes that were so wildly successful on the African Veldt that they grew to larger and larger tribes (at least that's what evolutionary anthropologist Robin Dunbar believes). Most primate groups max out at around 30, but human groups naturally max out at around 150 (150 is called the "Dunbar number"), creating much more challenging and complicated social demands which required larger brains. To this day, human groups larger than 150 tend to calve off to form new tribes. This tendency holds true for hunter gatherer groups, villages, and social networks.[28]

Our brains are largely social organs that help us deal with the complexities of such groups—groups that have to manage genetically-driven instincts concerning family, sex, social hierarchies, and often competing needs to be safe, to care, to share, to be fair, to win, and to protect ourselves physically and socially.

Two-hundred thousand years ago a woman was born with mutations on two of 715 sites on her FOXP2 gene. These mutations gave her the abilities to understand I, me, you, and we in the past/present/future, and to generate and understand metaphors and fantasies. The FOXP2 mutations provide incredible abilities to communicate, imagine, remember, and anticipate.[29] All humans now have this mutation and it heavily contributes to our human superpowers—like mental time travel. A chimpanzee (with no equivalent of the FOXP2 mutation) can project about 30 minutes into the future, while a human can project to the beginning of the universe and the end of time.

Brains change over the lifetime and in response to what we think and do—this is called neuroplasticity. We can actually cause our brains to grow, particularly the frontal lobes, by activating them with self-reflection, meditation, problem solving, and attuned relating with ourselves and others.[30] The FOXP2 mutations gave us enhanced capacities for focused attention, language, and conscious awareness, which caused people to grow their frontal lobes more robustly during their lifetimes, creating new capacities in tribes where people with bigger brains had more advantages.

By fifty thousand years ago human frontal lobes had expanded all the way down the front of brains to meet the brainstem. Beginning around this time archeologists and anthropologists have found evidence of civilizations based on agriculture and trade building cities and erecting monuments.[31]

Fifty-eight hundred years ago, a mutation occurred on the ASPM gene that resulted in more folds in our brains. Our heads couldn't get any bigger or babies couldn't be born (it's difficult enough now—ask any mother!), so the only way our brains could expand was to have more folds in our top layer, the cerebral cortex. Those folds form the gyri (peaks) and sulci (valleys) that neuroscientists use to map the cortex. Now almost everybody has the mutated ASPM gene, and you can see for yourself the incredible acceleration of human development over the last six millennia.[32]

SELF-AWARE CONSCIOUSNESS IS NEW, BUT PROBLEMATIC

So, consciousness as we know it is relatively new, and we're not genetically programmed to perfectly manage such power. Human brains grow gradually, punctuated by critical periods of accelerated neurogenesis (the growth of new neural networks) and cell death of unused networks (called apototic cell death). With each developmental surge we acquire new powers and encounter new problems.[33]

HOW DO PROBLEMS GET WIRED INTO BRAINS?

Infants' brains get hardwired to *dissociate*—space out and disconnect—when they're neglected, abused, or have mothers who can't consistently emotionally attune to them. We talked about this earlier in how secure and insecure attachment styles are wired. The more robust an infant's dissociation circuits are, the more intense his or her defenses (like projection, denial, and rationalization) are likely to be later in life.[34]

From ten to eighteen months kids go into shame reactions when disapproved of, creating social learning (necessary and important) but also laying down the neuronetworks of avoiding shame through denial, projection, dissociation, suppression, repression, and all the other psychological defenses that interfere with seeing ourselves and the world clearly. Toddlers' brains are programming these defenses during the first four years, even as they're also learning who they are, how to speak, and how to function in complex human groups likes families, schools, and teams.

From two to three kids develop a theory of mind; they can experience themselves and others as thinking beings. Some of my clients can remember moments of awakening, occasionally as far back as two or three, when they could observe themselves—or imagine themselves—as individual human beings, separate from their parents, who could feel safe or not safe, good or bad, admired or resented.

As our brains mature we become more able to both consciously and non-consciously (from Shadow) observe ourselves. Self-observation activates our judging instincts (yes, we are *instinctually* mandated to constantly judge ourselves and others), and judgment tendencies constantly monitor ourselves and others from a variety of dimensions, including *morally*. From around two onward our adaptive unconscious, our Shadow, makes constant judgments which it sends via feelings/impulses/stories/memories into our conscious awareness to guide us through life.[35]

These judgments are generated through our Shadow programming, based on the cultures we were raised in, but monitored through our current values, often different from our birth cultures since our cultural surrounds (like relationships, communities, families) change as we develop. These dialectics between old values and new values are fractal interfaces which we can observe with acceptance and caring intent, leading to the greater complexity of more nuanced and compassionate value systems both in Shadow and conscious awareness.

CONSTANT JUDGMENTS? WHAT ABOUT BEING NONJUDGMENTAL?

Yes, *constant judgments*! We judge and are judged all the time! Our brains are always reacting to the world, generating feelings, stories, impulses, and moral evaluations in fifty to a hundred milliseconds after some internal cue (from inside myself) or external cue (from outside myself). For instance:

- I see you on the street, smile in greeting, and say, "Hi!"
- Your brain generates a story about me with some emotional valence—Keith is good or bad, likable or irritating, fun to hang out with, or a pain in the ass.
- Your brain also generates a story about *you and me*—Keith likes me or doesn't like me, thinks I'm good or bad, thinks I'm fun to hang out with or a pain in the ass.
- You brain generates an impulse to respond—probably to look back at me and say, "Hi Keith!"
- Your conscious self can catch such stories and impulses at five-hundred to fifteen-hundred milliseconds, and mostly we habitually follow pro-social impulses like, "Hi Keith!"—it is how our constructive Shadow guides us to be a part of the social world.

You notice the judgments in this example about me and also about you in relationship me. This is always happening! Our brains constantly judge everything and everyone and our conscious selves support those judgments or don't support them.

For instance, my neighbor Jason down the street tells me that Sharon on the next block left her husband and kids for her boss, and I have instant critical judgments about Sharon being selfish and irresponsible.

Since I've learned to monitor reactions coming up automatically from Shadow, I notice my critical response and consciously choose a more mature moral perspective than my adaptive unconscious just generated. I remind myself that families are systems, I don't know the whole story, and I feel better when supporting everyone. I suddenly remember that I like Sharon, her husband, and her kids, and they are probably all in distress of some sort.

You'll notice my immediate critical judgment was met and supplanted by my conscious, more compassionate judgment as I considered the situation. We often have moral disconnects between our conscious value systems and Shadow value systems, and these disconnects require self-reflection. Noticing and reconciling such conflicts sends more mature messages back into Shadow and helps our adaptive unconscious grow morally.

It helps me to remember that my adaptive unconscious arose from my genetic roots of surviving in the wild in primitive groups much like chimpanzee tribes today. Extreme defensive reactions and instantaneous flight/fight reflexes are super-adaptive in those environments. Consolidating hostile/frightened stories about, and quick defensive reactions towards, any event or *person* that hurt me *even once* could save my life or a family member's life in such a tribe.

This explains the intensity of defensive reactions and the somewhat counter-intuitive experience of reaching for compassionate understanding and non-violent solutions (both physically and emotionally) in difficult interpersonal situations. In ancient Indiana when it still was populated with Indians, it's estimated that men had a one-in-eight chance of dying from murder by another Indian.[36] Consistent non-violent problem-solving *as a cultural standard* is a relatively new evolutionary achievement in the history of the world.

NOT ONLY ARE JUDGMENTS INEVITABLE, BUT THEY ARE NECESSARY TO GUIDE US AND HELP US GROW OUR SHADOW

Our judgments are necessary for us to care for one another and provide direction in our sometimes bewildering social landscapes. You've heard the term, "A sense of right and wrong," probably hundreds of times in your life, but what does "A sense of right and wrong," actually signify?

Our Shadow monitors us and the world and sends judgments of right and wrong up constantly in response to what we do, think, imagine, or experience. This is often done in intersubjective engagement with others—with the cultures we're embedded in. If *my nervous system* detects a critical judgment from another (I don't have to consciously notice it), it's likely to cue corresponding and complementary critical judgments in me about myself and/or the other. These judgments will rise up from Shadow into my conscious awareness in the forms of thoughts, stories, feelings, and impulses.

Knowing this, we can monitor judgments about ourselves and others like anthropologists and loving parents—we can compassionately self-observe, looking for the patterns and growth opportunities in our dances with culture, Shadow impulses, our emergent values, and our sense of self.

In the above example with Sharon, her lover, and her family, I observed my immediate black-and-white critical judgments (more primitive than relativistic values) and reached for deeper understanding and care. To do this I needed to first consciously notice my reflexive Shadow denunciation (cheating is bad, Sharon is bad for cheating), and reach for a different, more compassionate moral standard to bring to bear on the situation (know the whole story, take a caring stand towards everyone).

GROW YOUR SHADOW

When we meet judgments with curiosity, compassion, and wisdom, we feed superior perspectives back into our adaptive unconscious and it *adapts*. We grow, and Shadow eventually feeds us more refined judgments over time, creating moral development and spiritual expansion. Neurologically, this process involves constellating patterns of more sophisticated and complex neural circuits again and again in our frontal lobes, thus strengthening and expanding them until they become stable brain structures.

When we do this the neural networks get progressively stronger. Activated neural pathways attract cells called oligodendrocytes that wrap the neurons in sheaths of fatty myelin. Myelinated neurons are up to a hundred times faster than unmyelinated neurons, making circuits stronger and more likely to fire. In addition, after a month of activating new networks, stem cells in our brains divide and the daughter cells grow into integrative neurons which hardwire self-regulatory neural networks, particularly in our right frontal lobes.[37]

NONJUDGMENTAL AND ORIGINAL SIN

Nonjudgmental is not neurobiologically possible! It is an impossible standard like, "Never lose," "Be perfect," "Never fear," or "Don't be sexual." I believe that social demands to meet impossible standards is where the idea of original sin comes from. When culture makes neurologically impossible demands, people go crazy.

In my lifetime I've seen this in areas as diverse as sex, violence, racism, child-rearing, and politics. The culture sets ridiculous standards like don't be sexual (or only after you're eighteen), don't have impulses to do violence, never shame your children, or never change your position on an issue—all neurologically impossible, leading people to feel *bad*.

If we don't develop moral frameworks that keep shifting to greater compassion and authenticity with new insights and experiences, we become arrested, dissociated, or cynical. Examples?

- Arrested is stuck in a worldview and fighting any data that might help us change it. For instance, one depressed worldview is, "I am bad and life sucks!" When confronted with data that I might be good and that life might be great, I argue and resist—I am arrested in the depressed worldview.
- Dissociated is not noticing feelings and experiences that might help me grow or change my thoughts, emotions, or beliefs. A common area is with self-esteem. A teenager might have a beautiful body but feel unattractive. The cute guy in history class says, "You look good today!" and you have a brief rush of embarrassment followed by forgetting about the compliment. You have dissociated.
- Cynicism is imputing negative and selfish motives to everyone. Cynicism is particularly nasty, because it's a moral framework

that allows hypocrisy; nobody really tries to be good or anything other than self-interested, so why should I?

For our brains to not get short-circuited, our lives, decisions, and moral frameworks have to increasingly harmonize with our drives and genetic mandates and resist suppressing, repressing, denying, or warping them.

ACCEPT NEUROBIOLOGICAL DEMANDS TO HELP SPIRITUAL PRACTICE

Paradoxically, spiritual practice can injure us if we don't accept neurobiological realities. If someone engages in spiritual practice because they have a belief that they can be free from emotional pain, their representation of being free from suffering is that they can eventually *never feel bad*—impossible neurologically.

The four noble truths of Buddhism got this neurobiologically correct by maintaining that life invariably involves suffering, and that non-attachment from suffering and everything else is liberation. Non-attachment means *we still feel pain*, but are not attached to (identify with) pain. Progressive non-attachment, disidentification rather than dissociation, is neurobiologically possible and preferable (much more on this in Chapter 14: Spiritual Shadow).

If a spiritual seeker believes, "I'm doing beautiful and good spiritual practice only if I'm free from pain, and I'm doing ugly and bad spiritual practice if I feel emotional pain," he limits himself. He can't see his reflexive Shadow moral stance of, "I'm a virtuous practitioner when I don't have emotional pain and I'm a bad, non-virtuous practitioner if I get caught up in anger, lust, fear, greed, and so on." Such interior judgments or disapprovals create shame reactions which make us anxious, and then our destructive Shadow generates defensive impulses and stories to avoid the anxiety and shame.

What a mess!

Instead, if a seeker believes, "The very intent and action of my practice serves me and everyone," the *processes* of life become both less frightening and more luminous. The conscious intent is to meet every experience, even pain and failure, with interest and compassion.

DAY-DREAMING, NIGHT-DREAMING

Brains are wired to constantly create stories (more on this later) and biased to plan for and avoid anxiety, shame, and other threats. When we are not focused on anything in particular, we daydream. The day-dreaming mode is also called the default mode network, where we spend 15 percent to 20 percent of waking life.[38]

At night we are wired to produce night dreams, which use many of the same neural circuits as daydreams. Both daydreams and night dreams regularly send us threats in real and symbolic form, forcing us to deal with them and try to create solutions (we'll dive deeply into these waters in Chapter 11: Dreams, the Royal Road to Shadow).

For example, caught in a traffic jam, you daydream about being late for work, and start an inner dialogue defending yourself to your boss for being late. Your brain focuses you on the imagined problem of your boss's disapproval, your anticipated shame response, and what explanations might work so she won't be mad. That night, you might have a night dream about being stuck on the highway and you're late for work—your Shadow challenging you to somehow solve the problem.

Imagining problems can cue anxiety and shame responses which feel painful and dangerous and your brain wants to avoid them, but also wants to feel more secure. Trying to feel more secure, your unconscious presents problems to you as daydreams and night dreams, craving resolution or a sense of safety in these situations, and so in your daydreams and night dreams you imagine solutions like the fantasy conversation with mad-at-you-for-being-late boss. A significant number of daydreams and night dreams are unsolved problems (mostly in relationships) our brains present us with to ruminate on and try to solve.

IMPLICIT AND EXPLICIT MEMORIES PERMEATE SHADOW

Daydreaming and night dreaming draw from memories that feel like memories—like your first kiss—called *explicit memories*. Explicit memories begin around eighteen months of age and always feel like something is being remembered.

Daydreaming and night dreaming also draw from memories that *don't feel like something's being remembered*—mysterious fears and attractions whose roots we are often unaware of—called *implicit memories*. Brains start encoding implicit memories—anticipations and understandings about ourselves and the world—in the third trimester *and never stop encoding them*. We exist embedded in countless implicit and explicit memories of how we and the world are and will be. We each have a *universe* of memories our adaptive unconscious can choose from, any of which could be used by Shadow to help or hurt us.[39]

We can consciously embrace all memories with the goal of accepting what is and finding what is most beautiful, good, and true. This makes multiple perspectives attractive and acceptable. We benefit by considering everything from as many angles as possible. Generally the more perspectives we have, the more we see and the better we do.

This is especially true for moral conflicts.

THOMAS PAINE OR BENEDICT ARNOLD?

We do better examining moral conflicts and looking for deeper truths than quickly pulling the trigger on reflexive moral condemnations. Take Barack Obama and Eric Snowden.

Eric Snowden was a CIA analyst appalled at the volume of personal information that the government was gathering on everyone. He supported President Obama's presidency partially because Obama publicly agreed that there should be legal limits on such information gathering and constraints on the National Intelligence community.

Obama, when he entered office, was given information from the American Intelligence community that the data harvesting was necessary for national security, and that there were adequate safeguards for personal privacy. His position changed from, "It's wrong to gather so much personal data," to "Respect individual privacy, but gather the data to save lives."

Snowden, alarmed at the potential abuse of power and disenchanted with Obama's shift, felt morally obligated to release millions of pages of secret documents, enlisting news agencies to help him redact material to ensure that individuals would not be harmed by the releases.[40]

Is Snowden a patriot like Thomas Paine, risking all in a courageous "Give me privacy or give me death!" moral stance? Or is he Benedict Arnold betraying his country because he believes he knows better than his country's leaders?

Is Obama a weak leader for changing his position? Or is he a wise leader who allows himself to be influenced by new information and a desire to sacrifice some personal privacies in the interests of the greater good?

I can appreciate all these positions, and suspect that if I had the information that Snowden and Obama have, I'd adjust and readjust my moral stance of what was right and what should be done.

Holding ourselves in such dialectics grows our moral sense and creates and solidifies new neural networks in our frontal lobes, giving us more nuanced moral capacities and upleveling our Shadow judgments as they flow into conscious awareness.

SELF-AWARENESS BRINGS SELF-JUDGMENTS WHICH WE LEARN TO MANAGE

When little kids develop a conscious sense of self, around 18 or 24 months and can observe themselves as thinking beings, they've already had 2 years of neural programming about how to be in the world.

From about 11 to 20 months kids are hyperactive (their adrenaline-driven sympathetic nervous system is dominant during this period) and toddlers hear the word "No" about every nine minutes (as well as countless "Yes's). These "No's" and "Yes's" are parental instructions about what is right and wrong.

A lot of socialization involving approvals and disapprovals from parents and shame reactions and approval reactions in kids occurs during this time. As children start observing themselves at two and three, they start having their own approvals and disapprovals of themselves and their own self-generated shame responses. None of us likes any of the shame emotions (shame, guilt, embarrassment, regret, humiliation), so we tend to avoid them.

Preverbal toddlers' nervous systems don't like shame emotions and instinctively resist them by complying with rules, getting soothing approvals from parents, or by developing defensive patterns. Defenses like denial, projection, projective identification, rumination, repression, and most other defensive systems, are programmed into Shadow starting in the first two years of life.

Toddlers don't have mature enough brains—not enough sense of self or cognitive tools—to self-regulate such defenses. That can't happen until their brains are mature enough as teenagers to self-examine moral reactions in more complex ways. By then, teen brains have had *over a decade* of practicing and intensifying defenses, embedding them into brain structures and constructive and destructive Shadow. Those neural networks have been activated repetitively and are heavily myelinated with cross connections everywhere in the brain.

By the time that all of us reach teenage years, we have an awful lot of reflexive defensive programming—much of which can arise as destructive Shadow. That's why it's a necessary skill if you're a human to be able to self-reflect and develop tools to refine values and defenses as they arise to support or inhibit you.[41]

This is especially important to us when dealing with our tendencies towards violence.

WHY WE HAVE HABITS OF VIOLENCE

You're driving on the freeway, and suddenly a car swerves directly in front of you, causing you to break sharply and feel a flood of adrenaline rush through your body—intense alarm followed by blinding anger. Someone could have been killed! The driver apparently ignores you, and you honk angrily, trying to punish his idiotic and dangerous behavior. He flips you the bird, and you have a murderous impulse to somehow annihilate him from the face of the earth. You roll down your window, offer him your own middle finger salute, and scream, "Fuck you! Asshole!" as he speeds ahead. You glance to your side and see a late model sedan with family of five—two of them young children—in the lane to your right, and they're all looking at you. Your face flushes as you feel a wave of embarrassment.

Throughout evolution, each new capacity gets built on previous capacities. To form the first primitive single-celled creatures billions of years ago in the seas of earth, life needed water, amino acids, and energy. Colony organisms of cells evolved into more sophisticated creatures with different organs and processes, and so on, all the way up to the human nervous system, the current pinnacle of the evolutionary flow.

Along this evolutionary highway one basic fact dominates. You have to be alive and mature to reproduce, so living things act to stay alive, and more evolved life often takes risks to keep young alive. All organisms have some mechanism for self-protection. Amoebas recoil from toxins and extremes of heat and cold. Reptiles run if threatened and fight if cornered.

When mammals hit the scene between two- and three-hundred million years ago, one of their survival advantages was a limbic area in their brain often called the midbrain that is involved in emotions, relationships, motivation, and evaluation. This area learns from experience and is especially adept at lessons of survival. A few encounters with single strand of electrified wire around a yard can keep a horse or dog from trying to escape. Their nervous system encounters the pain of the shock, equates it with physical threat, and eventually *avoids the wire entirely.* The current can be turned off, but the animal still associates the wire—once a source of threatening pain—with danger and stays away.

There is some evidence that our brains *never give up* such defensive programming. Neuroscientist Joseph LeDoux and others say that once our nervous system hardwires a defensive reaction, it is there to stay.[42]

What we *can* do is develop new programming that includes and transcends old programming so effectively that it feels that the old has disappeared entirely. I might learn to feel the rage of being cut off on the freeway, but curb my impulse to honk repetitively and scream profanities. If I engage in this new habit enough times it becomes automatic (reflexively implemented by my affect-regulating right hemisphere), which gives me the sense that I have *worked through* my violent reactions. In reality, my violent impulses have been *included and transcended* in a new habit that feels the anger, has the violent impulses, but then automatically honks once to let the person know they just acted dangerously, and then slows me down and helps me breathe deeply to recover from my distress.

Why do our emotions and reactions require so much attention? Because they are some of our oldest genetic mandates—our ancestral voices.

EMOTIONS ARE ANCESTRAL MEMORIES GUIDING US TO DEAL WITH WHAT'S NEXT

Famous affective neuroscientist Jaak Panksepp said in a 2010 lecture that emotions are ancestral memories, guiding living things to survive and thrive in a dangerous and delicious world.[43]

"Ancestral memories" resonates mythically to me, like a song you can't get out of your head. "Ancestral memories, ancestral memories…" I have visions of hunter-gatherer tribes, ancient mammalian species, and the first life on Earth.

Humans are the advancing edge of evolution in the known universe. You and I embody the current penultimate crest of a 13.75-billion year wave of evolution. Our evolutionary legacy blesses us with capacities for emotional reactions and we mostly *learn* what we like/dislike, fear/desire from our experiences on earth.

My wife Becky smiles and I hug her. A dog snarls and lunges against a fence and I cringe in fear, and then expand in anger. Emotions guide us to the next instant; they tell us to connect, avoid, or defend. Unconscious tendencies—habits of feeling, thinking, and acting—arise from deep learning beginning at conception.

To change habits, we need to become more intimate with the emotions that drive them, more aware and interested. I find it very cool that deeper awareness of bad habits helps change them.

EMOTIONS PREPARE US FOR WHAT'S UP NEXT

Our nervous systems are priming us for *what to do next* when we feel:

- Fear at potential danger
- Sexual attraction at sexy others
- Anger at real or imagined attack
- Grief at loss
- Excitement in happy pursuit
- Joyful play
- Anxiety at what *might* happen
- Nurturance towards children, family, and beloved others

Emotions aren't just about *reacting to* what's happening, but *priming us to deal* with what's happening.

Emotions are ancestral memories guiding us to deal with what's next. These ancestral voices are central in learning and practicing habits of feeling, thinking, and acting with people, objects, and inner experiences. The language of Shadow is first and foremost the language of emotion.

EMOTIONALLY DRIVEN LEARNING KEEPS US ADJUSTING TO THE WORLD

We're born with the *abilities* to feel an infinity of emotional nuances but to a large extent we *learn* exactly what we want, fear, love, hate, and so on, through experience and memory. Brains monitor people, the world, and our inner psychological/physical/social natures, looking for patterns and understanding, leading to emotionally-driven responses encoded into deep memories—Shadow, which arise when cued by similar situations. Smelling chocolate chip cookies in the oven evokes warm feelings of security and pleasant craving (in me anyway). If the tall dark-haired boy next door bullied you, you might feel uncomfortable and insecure around tall dark-haired guys. Most of this learning resides in our adaptive unconscious—our Shadow.

When we're born, we have around eighty-five billion neurons, *but only 18 percent of them are hooked up into neural networks.* Our inherent emotional capacities are *mostly* objectless—not much tied to specific people or experiences.

On the other hand, we do have emotional predispositions such as:

- Infants yearn to see and touch Mother's face and body.
- Masculine people are drawn to competitive dominance and the female form.
- Feminine people yearn towards intimacy and to be seen as light.
- We're born fearing snakes (yes, fear of snakes is a *genetic* predisposition).

Our predispositions plus our constantly-evolving learning generate the emotional soundtracks of our lives—automatic Shadow guides to avoid (like fear of spiders) or approach (like joy at the sight of a beautiful sunset). They alert and guide us the way the scary music lets us know something bad is about to happen in a movie, and the uplifting music tells us something wonderful is occurring.

PRIMARY EMOTIONS

Near the base of our brain, the hypothalamic areas can elicit at least seven primary emotions:

- fear
- panic/separation distress

* anger
* joy/play
* surprise
* seeking/searching
* lust

Run an electric current into one of these spots, and mammals experience that specific emotion. Jaak Panksepp and other neuroscientists have determined these specific sweet spots in or around the hypothalamus generate seven basic emotional control systems—what Panksepp calls "emotional endophenotypes."[44]

I'm certain that additional emotional control systems will be discovered. For example, I suspect special brain circuits exist for spiritual exaltation, shame, disgust, and perplexity.

THOUSANDS OF EMOTIONAL STATES

Just as kaleidoscopes of colors are derived from combinations of primary colors red, green, and blue, emotions are thousands of combinations of basic emotional control systems blended together by the brain/body in response to instinct, learning, and current experience. They evoke memories and associations constantly throughout the day, continually pointing, warning, and guiding from constructive and destructive Shadow.

I look out the window and enjoy the beautiful Santa Barbara Channel Islands, but the mist is a little depressing, and I didn't get enough sleep last night, so I'm kind of cranky. These feelings arise to *prepare me for what's about to happen.* "Depressed" slows me down and makes me cynical, "cranky" readies me for conflict, "sleepy" demands rest. Brains generate emotions, stories, and impulses to protect us from danger, promulgate our genome, and deliver what we crave. The main way brains determine what's safe or unsafe—with corresponding pleasurable or painful emotional guides—is through *learning.*

LEARNING EMOTIONAL REACTIONS

Emotional control systems mostly *learn* to attach emotions to experiences. Brains constantly hook up emotional reactions with all kinds of sensations, behaviors, thoughts, people, impulses, objects, and stories. We have instincts to fear, but we aren't born fearing much. We have instincts to be angry, but we aren't born angry with much. We *are* born with incredible tendencies to learn, and beginning in utero our nervous systems are learning. For example, as I mentioned earlier, in the last trimester an unborn infant hardwires capacities for stress management through how effectively Mom soothes herself when upset.

At birth, watch out! Avalanches of learning create increasing capacities to move, feel, think, react, and relate—everything *emotionally* driven—with many of these capacities organized into our adaptive unconscious.

Usually learning expands and empowers us. Hunger leads us to food, fatigue craves rest, anger demands self-protection, and loneliness seeks warm contact with safe and known others.

Sometime learning takes a sharp turn into crazy, and we can't step on cracks for fear of breaking mothers' backs, or get aroused unless our lover is wearing high heels. When such learning turns into habits of being, it's fiendishly difficult to change, but that's what therapy, recovery, self-help, and social support are for—to help turn bad habits (self-destructive learning) into good habits (self-constructive learning).

THE FOXP2 AND REMEMBERING THE FUTURE

As I mentioned earlier, two-hundred thousand years ago, a woman was born with two sites (of 715) on the human FOXP2 gene, stably mutated to give her the capacities for grammar and symbolic communication. I think of this woman as Eve, because she was the mother of us all. Today every human being has these two mutations.

Grammar and symbolic communication opened the doors to deep understanding, enlightened intimacy, and imagination. "I," "you," "we," and imagination in the past, present, and future, describe the heart of modern human consciousness and all it entails—an accelerating evolutionary tsunami changing the planet and reaching metaphorically and literally to the stars.[45]

The FOXP2 mutations were somewhat unfortunate for us *"emotionally"* because emotions are designed to *anticipate* the future, not particularly anxiety-provoking for most mammals who are only aware of futures for the next five minutes, but can be a real problem for *our* futures which stretch to the end of our lives.

When we anticipate futures, we activate the same neuronetworks involved in remembering the past—yes, we create a future from our imaginations and remember it.

Just as hunger tells us it's time to stock up when we're not really starving to death, fear usually tells us something scary *might* happen. Most animals actually have to see/smell/hear/feel a real threat *about to happen now* to be scared of it, but not you and me! *We* can be scared of stuff *we anticipate, or remember, or just make up!* This is the curse of anxiety, creating and remembering painful futures—destructive Shadow ruining our lives. Healthy anxiety warns us of real danger and keeps us alert and safe, then fades into pleasurable presence when we are secure (as we are almost all the time).

SOME CURSES CAN BE MANAGED AND INTEGRATED INTO BLESSINGS

When humans achieved the capacities to live simultaneously in the past, present, and future, they also received the capacities to *worry about* the past, present, and future, and to empathically resonate with others' worrying. This wrecked our natural mammalian nature of not stressing if there's no current problem. The relaxed satisfaction of a grizzly bear satiated in a blueberry field, the mindless contentment of a field mouse snug in her burrow, or the timeless oneness with nature the deer feels standing motionless in the deep forest, were all compromised by human memory of painful past episodes or anticipation of what bad events *might* happen.

Everyone has become lost in superheated recollections of past threats and offenses. Everyone occasionally focuses on and amplifies current threats and offenses. Worst of all, everyone has lost sleep and been utterly distracted anticipating future threats and offenses. Such obsessions block instinctual unity with nature unless we become deep enough to remain present and open in the current moment, *while maintaining contact with the past and future.*[46]

Integrated states where the present moment is enhanced by past/future memory and fantasy are also human birthrights (making it completely worthwhile to give up naive mammalian innocence), but usually require life-long self-development. Key to this process is living so fully in the present moment that we harmonize with the worried ancestral voices calling urgently about past, present, and future threats—especially future threats since emotions are always *priming us to deal with what's next.*

Worrying about something in the future is called, "anticipatory anxiety." Anticipatory anxiety diminishes consciousness—it is the great enemy of development, the fly in the evolutionary ointment, the Everest to climb on the journey to enlightenment. The remedy for anticipatory anxiety is *presence.*

THE MONK AND THE TIGER

One of my favorite Buddhist stories involves a Zen Monk walking through a verdant forest and suddenly encountering a tiger, bent down low to the ground, ready to spring. Frightened for his life, the Monk takes off with the tiger in pursuit. Seeing a precipice ahead, the Monk—preferring a fall to being mauled—leaps out into the chasm. In the nick of time, he grabs a vine, leaving him clinging to the side of the mountain. As he hangs against the jungle cliff, two mice come out of a hole and begin nibbling at the vine he's hanging from. Raising his eyes, he sees the tiger on the cliff's edge growling horrifically. Catching a delicate fragrance from a tiny fissure in the rock face, he sees a lone strawberry plant with a beautiful strawberry on it growing in a little pocket of soil. He reaches out and plucks the strawberry, puts it in his mouth, and slowly eats it, delighted and absorbed in sweet taste, texture, and unity with nature.

PRESENCE

I love this monk. I want to embrace each moment just like he does hanging on that cliff. Contemplative practice, receiving influence from those who love us, reaching for the highest good—they all guide us to *presence*. I encourage daily practices that foster all forms of presence. Absorption in the present moment, surrender to radiant love, and unity with pure consciousness are three of my favorites.

EXERCISE:
TRY PRESENCE RIGHT NOW

- *Take a deep breath and relax your body.*
- *Feel your feet, legs, pelvis, torso, belly, chest, throat, neck, arms, hands, face, and head with acceptance.*
- *Be aware of all your senses—sounds, clothes on your skin, wind in your hair, sun on your back, tightness or looseness in your body...all experience—with acceptance and compassion.*
- *Relax into this state of global awareness of right now with calm acceptance, and maintain it for two minutes. As you finish, move into your day with the intent to continually adjust towards global awareness with calm acceptance. Write about your experiences in your journal and, after a few entries share them with someone you trust.*

Presence, compassion, and depth of consciousness lead us to observe what's right and beautiful. They guide us in *feeling* emotions and then *acting on* them to make good things happen. When we lose our way in defensive states or bad habits, depth of consciousness can bring us back to full presence, where all feelings are priceless guides.

This integrates our brains and grows our Shadow!

We all can get lost in the past and future. Maybe you start to obsess angrily about your son not cleaning his room, or blush with embarrassment remembering spilling dinner on your lap in the restaurant last night. Whatever the painful pull, try telling yourself, "Oops! I'm obsessing about the past/future/memory/fear/resentment/whatever. Snap out of it! Embrace presence."

PRESENCE IS CONNECTION

Even better, presence resonates with others in a tantric dance of accelerating technological, artistic, and spiritual creation. We know that almost all manifestation is collaborative (everything is relationships)—people joining together to harmonize their gifts. Writers need editors, directors need actors and producers, quarterbacks need receivers, builders need architects, children need parents, and lovers need each other.

This is not just individual evolution! We are the *only* species consciously accelerating the evolution *of all* life—almost always in tantric engagement with conscious others. We actualize our unique selves and our collective selves in relationship with other people, creating intersubjective fields of love, art, innovation, and poetry.[47] All these processes involve creating complexity in our brains, which grows our Shadow.

4

NEUROBIOLOGY INFORMS SHADOW WORK

Two things awe me most, the starry sky above me and the moral law within me.

—IMMANUEL KANT

One and the same thing can at the same time be good, bad, and indifferent, e.g., music is good to the melancholy, bad to those who mourn, and neither good nor bad to the deaf.

—BARUCH SPINOZA

IN THIS CHAPTER WE:

- Revisit defenses.
- Dive into drives.
- Learn the flavors of Shadow, and our resistances to Shadow.
- Return to brains as social organs.
- Set the stage for the Hero's Journey.

Psychological defenses are necessary to help us thrive. We need instincts to warn and guide us when our nervous systems read danger and our nervous systems are incredibly sensitive. If I show you an angry face for 40 milliseconds, you'll have no conscious awareness that anything has happened, while your nervous system registers fear— your Shadow warning and guiding you. Your adaptive unconscious has determined threat and is priming you with fear to fight or flee if the threat intensifies—all out of conscious awareness in Shadow.

Of course, to a large extent, our psychological defenses established as reflexes from conception onward, often cause suffering due to their primitive origins and habitual natures, rising reflexively as they do from destructive Shadow at the least hint of threat.

Defensive states inevitably involve amplified or numbed emotions, distorted perspectives, destructive impulses, and diminished capacities for empathy and self-reflection—practically never optimal reactions to most situations.[48]

Working with defenses is always at the edge of awareness, always Shadow work. Much Shadow work directs awareness to defensive barriers—fractal boundaries—where we resist perception of critical judgments, forbidden passions, and self-destructive defensive states. With the help of guides like our own interior principles and wise others, we can penetrate those barriers, find the material, and refine our values to become increasingly relativistic and mature. As we do that we become more coherent neurobiologically. That's what Sally was first doing earlier in the last chapter talking about her narcissist boyfriend. When I initially threatened her relationship by saying he was probably a narcissist, she felt a surge of emotional resistance, a distorted perspective of, "But we have fun together," (implying fun was worth the risk of an emotionally dangerous lover), diminished capacities to really look at herself and him, and the destructive impulse to keep seeing him.

As we become more coherent neurobiologically we tend to develop deeper consciousness and more compassion. We can observe defensive states and *disidentify* from the pain and distortions without becoming lost in distress. Sally, an emotionally healthy woman, quickly shifted to a state of healthy response to the present moment when I challenged her defensive desire to not lose her dangerous playmate—she more clearly saw her risk.

Disidentification is not *dissociation*, where we have no conscious awareness of Shadow feelings, stories or impulses. Pathological dissociation—reflexively cutting ourselves off from awareness and truth—is at the heart of all destructive Shadow and causes worlds of problems.[49] It's hard to be mean to your friend without dissociating from the fact that you care for her and she cares for you. It's hard to feel worthless without dissociating from your essential goodness and desires to grow and love.

▶ **Trauma sidebar:** *Trauma can instantaneously reprogram our nervous system, burden us with overwhelming emotions, disorganize our lives, and amplify destructive Shadow. Big "T" traumas like assaults, molestations, or horrendous accidents, and small "t" traumas like school bullying or petty humiliations can alter our sense of self and condition us to blank out and dissociate, try to run from, or push down traumatic material.[50] If you discover any kind of trauma as you expand your understanding of your Shadow, take it to someone you trust and give it whatever attention it needs to resolve into a deeper wiser sense of self.*

Trauma work is always Shadow work and modern psychotherapy has developed powerful techniques such as memory reconsolidation, dual focus therapies, sensorimotor psychotherapy, neurofeedback, and Eye Movement Desensitization Reprogramming (EMDR). If you are burdened or frightened by any trauma, there is no need to keep suffering if you have the courage to seek help.

BEING A HUMAN BEING IS ENORMOUSLY
CHALLENGING AND SHADOW WORK IS TRICKY

Unfortunately, throughout history people who've developed Shadow work have by necessity done it extensively with metaphors, never cross-validated with neurobiology. This is true for both the Western and Eastern religions as well as modern psychoanalysis, all of whom have Shadow conceptions and interventions. There were no fMRI, PET, or EEG imaging machines in Tibet to help the growth of Vajrayana Buddhism or in the early twentieth century when Freud and Jung were doing their seminal work. All Freud and Jung's constructs such as ego, superego, id, anima, animus, Puer, Synex, etc., are metaphors; they had no tools for seeing what the brain correlates and limitations were for these constructs.

The problem with metaphors is that you can do anything with a metaphor. This can leave metaphoric systems over-promising (since metaphors are poetic in nature, they are especially vulnerable to fevered hyperbole). Some examples:

- Your pain is the devil corrupting your soul. Embrace old-time religion and the devil will be cast out. You will no longer be plagued with doubt, lust, fear, greed, pride, or envy. If you do feel doubt, lust, fear, greed, pride, or envy, it means you haven't done a good enough job embracing old-time religion or casting out the devil.
- Suffering is caused by attachment to what we like and don't like. Let go of attachment and suffering ceases. Be distracted *at all* by what you like and don't like and you are still too attached.
- Anxiety, shame, obsessions, pride, rage, and distortions, are caused by internalized conflicts. Resolve the internalized conflicts and these problems dissipate.

Metaphoric over-promises generate Shadow over-expectations. Because we all have an instinct for self-transcendence (personality researcher

Robert Cloniger found humans to be temperamentally predisposed to self-transcend[51]), any system that leaves us dissatisfied with *what is actually possible* recapitulates the original sin models that permeate most major religions—cultural pressures to pathologize ourselves for genetic mandates and normal human experience—like feeling doubt, lust, fear, greed, anger, envy, pride, and attachments.

If our instinct for self-transcendence gets turned into chronic dissatisfaction or chronic shame, one of humankind's best temperamental gifts—self-transcendence—becomes corrupted into continual self attacks and screws up our lives. This blocks growth or, even worse, can set us up to define dissociation as growth. If I block awareness of doubt, lust, fear, greed, envy, anger, pride, and attachment, I've essentially walled myself off from constructive Shadow impulses to address them.

DRIVES, NEEDS, AND SOCIAL CAPACITIES

When we dissociate *from drives, needs,* and *social capacities,* we get sick. Examples are:

- *Drives* like sex and aggression—I insist, "I don't covet my neighbor's wife," or "I don't want to smack you when you diss my daughter," and deny my angry defense when you point out my lust or aggression.
- *Needs* like, "I need to feel secure," "I need to care for others," "I need to be cared for by others," "I need to feel personal meaning," etc. I dissociate from these needs and feel lonely, unhappy, angry, or phobic, and don't know why.
- *Social capacities* like empathy and self-reflection—"My culture demands I make others—like foreigners or the poor—disappear as emotional beings when pursuing my egocentric or ideological goals." I follow these cultural demands, and lose touch with my compassion for other people.

When we dissociate from drives, needs, and social capacities—besides such suppression and repression tending to strengthen destructive Shadow—we are fragmenting our selves, not integrating ourselves. If we define such fragmentation as "maturity," or "growth," we are actually embracing distorted pseudo-growth, and we can see the fruits of this in nationalism, racism, elitism, and all forms of psychopathology and general cluelessness.

Understanding those principles we can embrace developmental strategies where Shadow work takes into account *how brains actually work in relationship with other brains*. Integrating what's neurologically possible and necessary with what feels morally preferable accelerates coherence and it eliminates some of those conflicts between our instinctive Shadow moral judgments and our more mature conscious moral judgments. We can hold both sets in an alive dialectic tension where we search for unifying principles and truths—thus refining our values and growing our constructive Shadow.

Classic examples of such dialectics occur in almost every dystopian future movie from *The Hunger Games* to the *Divergent* movies. The dystopian moral system pressures our heroine to do violence to herself or others, while her Shadow morality—constructive Shadow which knows fascism is toxic—protests that something is gravely wrong. She holds these two opposing forces in dialectical tension until care and justice win out and she assumes a new moral stance—violence to fascism is moral if it is the only recourse to fascism. Real world examples are the allied response to the Axis Powers in WWII, and President Bill Clinton's intervention in Bosnia to stop genocide.

WE RESIST FLAVORS OF SHADOW

Shadow is the unknown emerging into the known—many flavors. Let's check some out, and look at how we might be resisting them:

WE CAN RESIST KNOWLEDGE WE DON'T HAVE THAT'S JUST FUN, YUMMY KNOWLEDGE:

Some new awareness of the world can be easy to absorb and adjust to.

- The earth is 93 million miles from the sun.
- There's a super-massive black hole at the center of our galaxy.
- Many studies show that men tend to be attracted to clear skin, blond shiny hair, and nice smelling women because all those are indicators of youth and fertility.

This new knowledge might not do much for me in terms of how I live my life, or it might, but either way I don't resist it. It's easy new insight and understanding. I have no habitual threat or resistance to it. If it has enough emotional charge (positive or negative) I'll likely remember it.

WE CAN RESIST AWARENESS OF DESTRUCTIVE SHADOW

When I point out his Warrior nature to a man (more on the Warrior in Chapters 5 and 6), it can evoke deep yearnings to experience himself as courageously true to his principles. If he has internalized destructive Shadow neuroprogramming of identifying himself as weak, or internalized cultural prohibitions against embracing his inner Warrior, his momentary sense of strength disappears like a cloud of smoke.

When I point out a woman's secret sadism in looking for reasons to attack her husband, she might deny my observations or attack me for making them. My confrontation was perceived by her nervous system (Steven Porges calls such nervous-system-perception "neuroception" [52]) as threatening, and it instantly instantiates a defensive state of amplified emotion, distorted perspectives, diminished empathy and self-reflection, and destructive impulses. We don't learn much when surrendering to defensive states.

Shadow we resist perceiving is especially problematic. The material we resist perceiving is often the most significant and relevant Shadow for health, intimacy, psychotherapy, and spiritual development because that resistance creates dissociations which block our growth and compromise health. Brains routinely resist encoding such challenging knowledge—generating defensive instincts to look away, forget, and suppress.

Brains, biased as they are towards avoiding threat, avoid knowledge that seems threatening unless consciousness takes over and insists on considering and being influenced by new perspectives. This is why our capacities to receive caring influence mark our development on so many developmental lines like the self line, moral line, psychosexual line, values line, and cognitive line. Receiving caring influence literally opens up our nervous systems to be changed and molded by trusted others.

> **Developmental lines sidebar:** *Ken Wilber in his book* Integral Psychology[53] *details how almost all our multiple intelligences (like psychosexual, psychosocial, moral, values, kinesthetic, artistic, mathematical, etc.) constitute developmental lines that grow through progressive stages, with each stage having a broader view and wider embrace, more open to new perspectives. For instance, cognitively we grow from the sensorimotor awareness of infants, to the magical thinking of toddlers, to the concrete either/or thinking of grade schoolers, to the rational/relativistic formal operational thinking of adolescents, to further levels beyond. Everyone starts at level one and progresses through the stages, and we don't skip levels—this is what characterizes a developmental line.*

WE CAN RESIST CONSTRUCTIVE SHADOW

We don't just resist destructive Shadow material about ourselves, but also constructive Shadow. For instance, you might resist identifying yourself as a virtuous person—a value-added person who's committed to doing right. You might resist identifying yourself as a healthy person even though you exercise regularly, sleep well, and eat healthy food.

Not seeing yourself as someone committed to goodness, health, and growth can actually be more of a problem than not seeing the parts of yourself that you're angry at, ashamed of, afraid of, and so on. Some small children are trained to have instinctive moral condemnations of themselves when they celebrate victories or strengths. Some parents consider such celebrations indicators of the sin of pride. We can see the residue of this in the NFL banning end zone celebrations after touchdowns. This was especially true of the Greatest Generation, who endured the Great Depression and fought in WWII. Their children, my generation of Baby Boomers, were often attacked by our parents when appearing to think too much of ourselves. Our rebellion against such suppression ironically supported the eventual narcissism that plagued the youth cultures of the sixties and seventies, continuing into the expanding narcissism of Gen X and Gen Y (as hilariously chronicled by Jean Twinge and Keith Campbell in *The Narcissism Epidemic*[54]).

Speaking of narcissism—yes, there is a marked increase in narcissism over the last thirty years, partly a function of the child-centric family orientations of many modern parents (more on this in Chapter 10: Parental Shadow). But the positives of focusing on child development outweigh the negatives. Most of us try hard to be good and successful, and it's important to acknowledge this. I've found modern teens and twenty-somethings to be more mature, caring, and insightful than previous generations.

WE'RE MOSTLY GOOD, MOST OF THE TIME

Modern developmental research overwhelmingly supports the reality that most of us spend a lifetime trying to be good. "Good," of course, is tricky, depending upon the cultures we're raised in. In fundamentalist Christian or Muslim cultures, it's morally correct to assign non-believers diminished rights and consign them to Hell if they don't see the light. That being said, humans groups always generate moral codes of good and bad behavior, and we are programmed to generally prefer to be good.

If we additionally commit to ongoing growth, we increasingly develop on our moral lines towards less violent and more inclusive. If we keep growing we ultimately discover that we are instruments of spirit on earth, and there is no room for false modesty in such depth and authenticity.[55] Shadow inhibitions can actually resist acknowledging and integrating our own power and beauty, and the positive parts of what we don't see are as important as the negative parts. A big part of Shadow work is embracing beautiful truths about ourselves. When we do embrace such beautiful truths about ourselves, we support development in our frontal lobes, coherence in our EEG, and robust heart rate variability.

▶ **Sidebar on heart rate variability:** *Heart rate variability is the difference between our heart rate increasing with inhalation and decreasing with exhalation. The more variable this is, the more our tenth cranial nerve, the Vagus, which extends to our heart and then back to our brain, keeps us optimally dialed into the present moment. Heart rate variability increases with secure attachment, loving contact, meditation, massage, and exercise. It is the single most accurate reflector of general health we have.*[56]

BUT WHAT MAKES LIFE SO HARD?

At the center of everything is our human experience, which is complicated by our conscious selves managing drives, instincts, and impulses. We constantly manage multiple flows of processes. Life is so intense, and most of us regularly feel emotionally fragile. For instance, one characteristic that slows everyone down is procrastination.

Destructive Shadow wants to help us avoid what we fear, and so sends impulses to procrastinate when we resist some responsibility or action. When we temporarily turn away—procrastinate—our nervous systems generate a tiny surge of relief, which reinforces turning away and teaches our Shadow that procrastination is what we want to do. This trains our brain to be more clueless!

Such destructive Shadow directs us away from purpose; we feel a little relief and our nervous systems and adaptive unconscious have become a little more certain that procrastination is what we need to do. This creates huge problems (one estimate of internet use was that 30 percent of the time it was in service of procrastination).[57]

Knowing we don't want to reinforce turning away from responsibility, that it's best to face resistance and take assertive action, that doing so strengthens non-conscious neurological constructive Shadow programming, we can use our human superpowers of focused intent and action in service of principle, and driven by resolve to use each impulse to procrastinate as a cue for powerful, responsible action. This turns the liability of procrastination into the strength of mature resolve.

EXERCISE: PROCRASTINATION INTO STRENGTH

Pay attention to when you procrastinate throughout the day and write what you discover in a journal.

- *After two days of this, pick one activity you commonly procrastinate on—like doing the dishes, answering email, taking out the recycling, or kissing your husband—and do it every time you are aware you're procrastinating. Use your impulse to procrastinate as a signal to actually engage in the activity you're resisting.*
- *After a week of using the impulse to procrastinate to actually get things accomplished, write how you feel differently about yourself, the tasks, and procrastination in general.*
- *Share what you've written with someone you trust.*

BRAINS ARE SOCIAL ORGANS

Our nervous system runs our lives to a large extent. We have drives, emotions, instinctual needs, and predispositions that influence us on a moment to moment basis. They don't just influence us alone; they influence us in relationship with other people who are influenced by us—a relational Heisenberg principle (the principle that observing something affects it). Intersubjective fields of relating naturally constellate when people are in proximity. If you are sitting with several others in a waiting room, apparently not interacting at all, everyone will notice if one person leaves the room—the intersubjectivity has shifted.

As we each walk through our universe, we're infusing everything in our universe with ourselves. That means we don't just see a separate universe; we see ourselves reflected back from the universe to us, particularly reflected back through other people's reactions to us, and ours to them.

You and I talk, and I'm seeing Keith reflected through you as you see yourself reflected through Keith reflected through you, reflected through Keith, etc. Every assembly point of reflection has its own Shadow material, and it all has neurobiological correlates. We all have mirror neurons in our brains—motor neurons that mimic others' voices, expressions, moods, and intent when we relate with them. This is one of the foundations of empathy and why feelings can be so intensified when shared with others.

> **Mirror neuron sidebar:** *Mirror neurons are motor neurons in our brains that subtly recapitulate movements, sounds, and states of people we're in contact with. When you talk with me, mirror neurons are actually causing me to subvocalize your speech below my conscious awareness. If you smile at me, mirror neurons cause me to unconsciously recapitulate your state and intentionality.[58] This is one reason escalating conflicts speed up so fast—the hurt/anger/attack is bouncing back and forth in a positive feedback system which, if not interrupted, leads to some kind of relational breakdown.*

As we learn about ourselves, as we grow, as we develop relationships, we have practices and principles that are either consistent with our neurobiology or inconsistent with our neurobiology. When it's inconsistent, we get scrambled neurologically and socially.

ON TO OUR PERSONAL JOURNEYS

Human brains individually and collectively are programmed to constantly create stories of the present moment, the world, relationships, and the past/present/future.[59] With the evolutionary impulse driving our nervous system's limitations and staggering powers, what are the stories we *instinctively* choose to live? What tends to become sacred in our lives?

In *Chapter 5: Archetypal Shadow: The Hero's Descent Into the Well of the World*, we look at the stories/myths/archetypes that guide and inspire humans, rising as they do from every culture—Shadow forces and forms in that we often are not conscious of (and never *fully* conscious of) all the elements that influence the stories of our lives we create and discover. Cultural archetypes like the hero, the heroine, the divinely inspired leader, or the selfish power-God villain, are mandated by genetic imperatives like our desires to fit in, stand out, serve ourselves, dominate others, find love, protect our family, self-transcend, and create beauty.

With self-awareness came the human tendencies to take all the drives and turn them into art. The art of our lives is reflected in the stories of our lives, and those stories center around the Hero and Heroine's journey.

5

ARCHETYPAL SHADOW: THE HERO'S DESCENT INTO THE WELL OF THE WORLD

No one answered. The noon-bell rang. Still no one spoke. Frodo glanced at all the faces, but they were not turned to him. All the Council sat with downcast eyes, as if in deep thought. A great dread fell on him, as if he was awaiting the pronouncement of some doom that he had long foreseen and vainly hoped might after all never be spoken. An overwhelming longing to rest and remain at peace by Bilbo's side in Rivendell filled all his heart. At last with an effort he spoke, and wondered to hear his own words, as if some other will was using his small voice.

"I will take the Ring," he said, "though I do not know the way."

—From *The Fellowship of the Ring*, by J. R. R. Tolkien

THE CALL

Why did Frodo sign on for such a suicide mission?
Why do men and women volunteer for Navy Seal training (or Army Ranger training, or firefighting, or police work), knowing that

it is dangerous, painful, and—if they are successful—will only lead to more danger and pain?

Why did Steve Jobs and Steve Wozniak commit their lives and money to creating a personal computer?

Why did Charles Darwin eagerly agree to a long and dangerous journey to the other side of the world on the Beagle?

The hero is called by a person, spirit, need, disaster, sign, or epiphany, sometimes many times, and finally accepts the mission. The first step of the Hero's journey is hearing the call.

IN THIS CHAPTER WE WILL:

- Understand the importance of primary metaphors.
- Dive into the Hero's Journey.
- Identity *your* current Hero's Journey.
- Understand we are all Batman and Wonder Woman, and ask, "Now what?"
- Explore the stages of the Hero's Journey, and find constructive and destructive Shadow revealed in every stage.

SHADOW INFLUENCES OF PRIMARY METAPHORS

In 1980, George and Mark Johnsen published *Metaphors We Live By*. In it, they describe primary metaphors which are metaphors—frequently cross-cultural—that most humans understand intuitively. "I'm feeling up," "I'm feeling down," "It's a new day," "He had a dark thought," or "The story of his life," are all primary metaphors which evoke similar associations in most humans.

Primary metaphors are Shadow programming that universally arises from human culture, formally taught by none, instinctively known by all.

Primary metaphors are the basis of all wisdom traditions because the way ancient genius humans understood the living realities of evolutionary psychology and interpersonal neurobiology was through metaphors that *felt* right and true. They had to understand and express complex forces and states with evocative symbols. The Egyptian Chariot of the Sun riding across the skies each day, Zeus hurling lightning bolts out of the thunderstorm, or Scheherazade's feminine wisdom healing the Caliph's insanity, are all metaphors for complex human and natural forces.

WHERE DO PRIMARY METAPHORS COME FROM? HUMANS ARE THE STORYTELLING SPECIES

Out of conscious awareness, our brains constantly create stories, or autobiographical narratives, of ourselves and our lives. Self-conscious awareness in the past/present/future, plus our genetically-driven fascination with social dynamics, plus our neurological bias to create stories where problems arise and we solve them, plus the hunger of conscious awareness to understand and explain the universe, plus our instincts to compete, cooperate, seek safety or excitement, procreate, bond, advance, care, share, be fair, and to self-transcend, translate into humans as the storytelling species.[60]

We don't just *generate* stories, we *resonate* with stories. We encounter stories everywhere in conversations and media and have reactions governed by Shadow forces in us that attract or repel us to different stories. Once engaged in a story—seeing, hearing, reading, anticipating, or remembering—mirror neurons in our brains resonate with the characters, putting our feelings, thoughts, behaviors, and bodies into the conflicts, triumphs, and adventures.

We all know how completely absorbed we can become with books, movies, articles, and narratives of all kinds. Hunger for stories starts early. Toddlers who can't understand more than ten or twenty words will sit quietly as Daddy reads *Green Eggs and Ham*.

Even pre-verbal, pre-conceptual infants love stories, and relax when mothers provide ongoing commentary about their feeling/behaving states. These simple stories like, "You look so happy right now! You're having fun with your rattle," "Is something wrong, you have a something's-wrong frown," "Isn't it nice here by the water? You love the ocean," somehow contribute to ongoing narratives *in the baby* about how baby is feeling and behaving. Mothers who talk like this to their infants improve the children's abilities to later identify and regulate emotional states as preschoolers and beyond.

When kids learn how to talk, we can help their brain development and narrative capacities from around three onward by telling them the story of their day at bedtime. Kids usually find this fascinating. "You woke up and had oatmeal with sunflower seeds for breakfast. You went to preschool and played with Emily, and you and she took turns on the slide. You cried when she wanted to stop. This afternoon we went to the Zoo and saw the lion...." Do this regularly with your child and new brain circuits are created and myelinated (insulated with fatty sheaths of myelin, making them *way* faster and more powerful), setting his or her brain up for more coherent autobiographical narratives later in life.

At around five, kid's brains mature enough (especially the memory center hippocampus right behind our orbital frontal cortex behind our eyes) so they can consciously have an autobiographical narrative. They can conceive of their life as a story with them as the central figure. It's often at this age that kids encounter the reality of their own death. "Mommy, am I going to grow old and die?"

We proceed through life with countless autobiographical narratives—us as son, daughter, father, lover, teenager, friend, worker, boss, etc.,—which morph and shift as we mature and continue to reevaluate our life stories from (hopefully) progressively more mature perspectives.

These stories are centered in our intuitive, non-verbal, emotional, poetic, metaphorical, non-linear, body centered, intuitive right hemisphere. Our life stories—autobiographical narratives—influence us constantly by informing us what our current role is in a particular narrative. Primary metaphors and autobiographical narratives are largely *non-conscious*—in other words, mostly *Shadow*.[61]

LIFE IS A JOURNEY: THE HERO IS CALLED, ACCEPTS THE CALL, NEGOTIATES THE HERO'S JOURNEY, AND COMES HOME TRANSFORMED WITH GIFTS FOR ALL

One of the most widely understood primary metaphors that organizes all our autobiographical narratives is, "Life is a journey."

Life as a journey arises in all cultures, and we know that journeys can have better or worse outcomes. The outcomes that light us up are the happy endings where the hero transcends and the world has been made a better place—Frodo destroys the ring of power, the Navy Seals kill Osama Bin Laden, Jobs and Wosniak bring the personal computer to ordinary people, and Charles Darwin revolutionizes human understanding of how life came to be.

You'll notice that all these examples involve protagonists being called to some enterprise that they commit to at some cost to themselves. This is not coincidence. Being called for important creation/action/service/need is built into human consciousness. Almost certainly, hunger for achievement and sacred service was such a powerful supporter of kin selection—the evolutionary drive to protect and care for the tribe—that it is now installed in each person's DNA. It is our craving for the Hero's Journey.[62]

HOW HAVE YOU BEEN CALLED?

Have you ever discovered an injustice you had to remedy, a new form that had to be birthed, a new capacity you yearned to embody, some service you had to perform? Have you ever encountered a suggestion, pronouncement, blessing, or curse from someone else that activated you and motivated you to do *something important*?

THE HERO'S JOURNEY

Joseph Campbell studied the mythologies—enduring stories—of over a hundred-and-forty-four cultures, and found a common thread in all the myths and legends—the Hero's Journey. His book, *Hero with a Thousand Faces*[63], hit me like a lightning bolt when I was seventeen and seeking meaning.

In the Hero's Journey, an ordinary person with some extraordinary capacities (which describes all of us!) is called to some mission that will disrupt and change his or her life, and he or she—eventually—says "Yes!"

When I was a kid, before videos and audio books, kids and teens were fascinated by comic books about superheroes and supervillains and science fiction books (mostly written by scientists who had to take their fantasies, creative predictions, and future possibilities somewhere other than dry, disbelieving lecture halls). Comic books were all about missions. Batman fought for justice and Wonder Woman showed how a woman could stand up for herself and others. Science fiction was all about adventures with infinite possibilities—protagonists engaged in interstellar travel, psychic powers, extraterrestrial intelligence, immortality, and alternate universes.

Who's your favorite superhero? Frodo? Superman? Albert Einstein? Carl Jung? Plato? Jesus? Buddha? Mother Teresa? Yoda? Bill Gates? Barack Obama? The hero from your favorite book?

Who's your worst villain? Hitler? The Joker? Dracula? Your most-hated politician? The mean girls from junior high? Charley Sigurson who bullied you in high school?

All these attractive and repulsive archetypal figures evoke strong reactions in you, and thus reveal Shadow material about your type of person. Who we are is often best revealed by what attracts and repulses us.

EXERCISE:
SUPERHEROES AS MIRRORS

- *Write down five superheroes—real or fictional characters—you particularly are drawn to.*

- *Now write two or three qualities that you admire in each of them. Take all these qualities and put them in a column on the left side of a piece of paper.*
- *Opposite them, on the right side, write where you have embodied, or wished you had embodied, each quality at some time. Courage, compassion, self-sacrifice, intuitive genius, physical strength, deep understanding, etc.*
- *Now, write down five villains—real or fictional characters—you personally can't stand.*
- *Next to each write two or three qualities that most characterize each of them.*
- *Take all these qualities and put them in a column on the left side of another piece of paper, and on the right side write where you have embodied each quality at some time. Cowardice, selfishness, violence, bullying, victiming, self-indulgence, cluelessness, bigotry, idiotic bad judgment, etc.*
- *Put these two sheets side by side and you have representation of many of your constructive and destructive Shadow forces. You have a scaffolding of qualities that comprise your unique type of person.*
- *Share this with someone you trust, and record what you learned and experienced in the conversation.*

EXERCISE:
WHAT IS YOUR CURRENT MISSION?

- *How do you want to further embody your positives and transform your negatives? What would you like to accomplish doing this besides becoming a more integrated, powerful, and whole person? In other words, do you have a mission? Some service you want to provide to your family, community, country, or the world? Some artifact or art you want to create? Some goal you urgently wish to accomplish? Write this down on a sheet of paper.*

- *After you do all this, look at this sheet and the two others from the previous exercise as a whole, a framework of your strengths, weaknesses, yearnings, shames, and passions. Is there a theme? Is there a mission? Is there purpose? If you find any of these, you have a beginning roadmap for your Hero's journey—perhaps even a call!*

WE ARE ALL BATMAN AND WONDER WOMAN. NOW WHAT?

Myths arise endlessly from each of us and all of us. Archetypal forms emerge from human collectives—informing all of us whether we know it or not.

Archetypes influence us in multiple ways. Primary influences are simply which archetypes compel us. This is completely personal. When my wife Becky was asked at ten-years-old what she wanted to be, she said, "A Mommy." The Mother archetype lit her up—in Greek mythology this is Hestla, the Goddess of the Hearth. When I asked her in her twenties what she wanted, she responded from her Seeker self, "I want to expand my consciousness"—the path of Woman of Wisdom lit her up (Hera in the Greek, Shakti in the Hindu, Changing Woman in the Navajo).

Secondary effects arise from negotiating archetypal demands and influences with culture. Culture is quite friendly to some archetypes and incredibly hostile to others.

A woman who resonates powerfully with the Sex Goddess will have inner conflicts and bewildering shame if raised in a fundamentalist, anti-sexuality family or community. Her yummy Sex Goddess self feels sinful, Shame surges.

Similarly, Women of Wisdom have had to mask or turn away from their power in families and cultures that suppress women. The last eight thousand years of agrarian societies have been hard on acknowledging and supporting women in general and Women of Wisdom in particular (who've had to handle a lot of clueless and dangerous men just to survive).

My maternal grandfather was a Warrior raised in a Quaker culture. When he volunteered to fight in WWI he was the first in three generations to go to war, probably not popular with some of his family and congregation.

If a central archetype is celebrated by our cultural surround, it's great!

The Athena athlete warrior princess archetype is often encouraged and admired by parents who delight in her striving and courage. Serena Williams, for instance, was supported this way, first by her family and then by the world.

The Maiden and Divine Lover tend to be supported by families who value beauty and sensuality. They're encouraged to blossom and thrive towards warm community and happy families.

Honorable Husband and Wise Father archetypes are supported by most families and communities.

The star quarterback who resolves to help his teammates be better and to keep improving himself is celebrated by his school and community.

Our personal and cultural archetypes constantly influence us, both consciously and non-consciously. Our Shadow selves *inform us* from the values and passions of our personal constellations of archetypal figures and stories.

What archetypes turn you on or repel you? Both reveal your basic nature and your current address on the epic journey of your life. We discover ourselves by what attracts or repels us in:

- Books, plays, or movies
- Games, sports, competitions
- Activities we enjoy or are repelled by, including recreational and professional ones
- Friends—who we choose, who chooses us, and how we relate
- Family members, lovers, in-laws, and other tribal members
- Fetishes, obsessions, night dreams (especially repetitive dreams), and daydreams
- Attributions, blessings, condemnations, and inspirations towards and from others
- Characters/themes/relationships/missions that move us in some fashion

All these and more reflect our archetypal Shadow influences.

EXERCISE:
FIND YOUR PERSONAL MYTHOS THROUGH FEELINGS, DREAMS, AND DIALOGUE

- *Write a daily journal about what draws you in (attracts and enlivens you) and pushes you away (what repulses or disgusts you).*
- *In addition, write your dreams each morning—complete with characters, themes, and emotions.*
- *Every month review what you've written and share your thoughts and insights with someone you trust.*
- *Over time your mythic constellation—your person mythos—will become clearer and clearer. As it does write about it and share it.*

As we discover ourselves, our archetypes emerge from shadow into the light, where we can consciously shape them as we wish. Authentic growth is always in keeping with our deeper purpose, life missions, and loving relationships—constantly revealed to us in constructive Shadow. Disease is disconnection, self-betrayal, turning away from healthy intimacy and self-knowledge—revealed to us in destructive Shadow.

The hero's and heroine's journey reflects these processes for men and women, for masculine and feminine.

THE HERO'S JOURNEY AS META-ARCHETYPE

The Hero's Journey—with deep genetic roots—mandates us to be the hero and serve the hero. On it we deepen personal archetypes like the Warrior, Healer, or Leader, and encounter numerous archetypal relationships, like discovering and receiving magical aid from a personal angel, or reconciliation with the Mother or the Father.

All cultures have a version of the Hero's Journey—epic stories arising from the life cycles of human families and tribes as universal stations on the human journey through life.

YOU ARE THE HERO

All of us are on a Hero's Journey, whether we know it or not. We're on little journeys that can last a couple of hours or a day, and we're on epic adventures that can last till death. Knowing the myths and archetypes that turn us on and knowing what our station is in our particular Hero's Journey helps us live good lives. It helps us serve the world.

JOSEPH CAMPBELL AND *THE HERO WITH A THOUSAND FACES*

Joseph Campbell loved myth and feared it. He saw vast benefits from myth as metaphor and horrendous atrocities from myth as literal truth, justifying violence in imagined service to literal interpretations of sacred texts.

The Hero with a Thousand Faces was published in 1949, becoming an instant classic. In it, Campbell draws from the myths and legends of 144 cultures to reveal the timeless patterns of the Hero's Journey—from the first call, to the struggle with the threshold guardian to crossing the boundary into the other world, onto the road of trials, into conflict and reconciliation with conflicted power figures like Father, Mother, and God, and finally, personally transformed, back through the threshold bringing wisdom and healing to the tribe.

In the first part of the twentieth century it was the psychoanalytic movement that popularized the idea of personal myths and inner Shadow forces affecting us constantly. Carl Jung and Freud were two individuals that brought into popular understanding the possibility that every single one of us has mythological forms arising from dreams, fantasies, insights, and, of course, relationships. Campbell was heavily influenced by both men.

Myths are collective understandings of how everything works and how we should be together. They arise and change as cultures arise and change.

Tribal cultures (like hunter-gatherers) have tribal myths, where the kin relatives of the tribe are exalted above all other people. The Navajo creation myth had Begochiddy, the Child of the Son, leading the Navaho through four worlds, each one being progressively wrecked until they finally arrived in this world, centered around the Navajo.

Ethnocentric cultures have myths that exalt those who share the beliefs and values of sacred texts such as the Bible or the Koran. The call to the ethnocentric hero is to bring the salvation enshrined in the sacred texts to the unsaved. Thus Christians were called to the Crusades and to save souls in the New World. Today many radical Muslims are called to form Islamic states and attack secular modernity.

Rational cultures have myths of victory on merit-based hierarchies and the transcendence of the strongest, smartest, and most advanced. Sports heroes like Michael Jordan and Peyton Manning are called to lead their teams to championships. Roger Federer is called to be the best tennis player ever. Corporate titans like Warren Buffet, Steve Jobs, and Bill Gates are called to change the world, creating stupendous international corporations with unimaginable wealth and power. Thought leaders like Ken Wilber, Arnold J. Toynbee, Teilhard de Chardin, and Albert Einstein are called to generate ideas and discover natural laws that change our understanding of the cosmos.

Within the context of all cultures—tribal, ethnocentric, and rational—remains the question of how does the individual live his or her life?

THE PARADOX OF THE COLLECTIVE AND INDIVIDUAL

A seminal understanding in the depths of the collective (our shared human identity) is that none of us exists alone, independent from the collective, and yet all of us have the responsibility to direct our *individual* consciousness through the universe that came into being the moment we were conceived. That's the paradox; I feel my essential uniqueness as a consciousness, and yet I'm aware of how I'm intimately interconnected with a wide variety of social networks, other human beings, all life, and the universe itself. So how do I make sense of this?

Well, The Hero's Journey is the form that naturally arises out of human consciousness to help each individual understand his or her own life journey.

THE HERO IS CALLED

The Hero's Journey begins with a call to action. The hero is never (or at least rarely) called by God saying, "Keith, come on. There's something important I want you to do!" The hero is called by obvious or subtle events communicating that somehow the Hero is not fully in harmony with the world and something needs to be done about it. The call always involves something that was not known before (in Shadow) emerging into consciousness to disrupt our world and demand our participation.

The call might appear to be a random event. You miss your plane, which is blown up by terrorists, and you feel you've been spared to contribute something to the world (this actually happened to a friend of mine). Often the call is a big mistake. A woman marries an abusive man, fights her way free of codependent domestic violence, and is moved to create safe houses for battered women. Sometimes the call is a trauma or a catastrophe; 9/11 inspired many Americans to enlist in the armed forces. Sometimes the call is a feverish excitement about a particular area. As a teen I found myself completely absorbed by psychological growth, psychological wounds, healing, and transcendence. I felt compelled to study and master psychotherapy.

Whatever the call is, it pulls us out of our ordinary existence, and our immediate reaction is often to say "No way!" "No, no! It's too much trouble! It's too soon! It's too late! I'm too busy!"

In *The Hobbit*, the first time that Gandalf asks Bilbo if he wants to go to the Lonely Mountain and help the dwarf king Thorin regain his throne, Bilbo says (and I'm paraphrasing here), "Are you f#@*ing kidding me, Gandalf? There's no way that I'm leaving my comfortable

Hobbit Hole in Bag End and going to the Lonely Mountain! Get out of here!" And so he had to be called again (Gandalf sent thirteen dwarfs to his house one or two at a time to eat dinner and win him over). Eventually Bilbo says, "Yes." As we're called again and again, eventually some part of us wakes up, some chord rings in our ears, and we say, "Yes!" That "Yes!" is us responding to a moral demand to surrender to a passionate vision or process. In this sense, constructive Shadow is the voice of our deepest moral instincts, generating impulses to surrender to the Hero's journey.

Worldview caveat: *Our deepest moral instincts are functions of our current and past worldviews, and so there is certainly a progressive hierarchy of moral relativism we grow through from birth onward. Our moral line of development starts at egocentric and progresses through ethnocentric, worldcentric, and cosmocentric. Historically, whole cultures espouse and normalize moral standards leaning towards the pre eminent worldview of that culture. For instance:*

- In the power-God court of Genghis Kahn, anything that appeared to disrespect Genghis was wrong. In fascist states informers feel moral imperatives to turn in acquaintances—and even friends or relatives—who might be disloyal to the regime.
- In the conformist (fundamentalist) middle ages, tens of thousands of fervent European Christians felt a moral imperative to invade the middle East.
- CEOs and boards of directors have felt moral imperatives to lie to the public or harm the environment to protect profits, the tobacco and oil industry being classic examples.
- Self-righteous egalitarian pluralists have felt moral imperatives to blanketly denounce those who don't sign on to their progressive values.

In general, we grow through the above stages towards moral positions that find it wrong to harm anyone or anything unnecessarily, and right to seek compassionate understanding in all arenas. These characteristics are universal in the highest stages of moral development.

After we accept the call, companions and aid start showing up. Your therapist gives you a copy of *The Hero with a Thousand Faces*. Your professor suggests you apply for a certain grant. You answer an ad on Craigslist for that position as sound engineer. One of my clients took a black studies class in college. The cultural perspectives in that class blew this young woman's mind, lit her up, and called her to a life of social service. We receive the call and then guides show up. As guides show up, we start moving towards our goal and, at a particular point, there's a threshold, protected by the Threshold Guardian.

THE THRESHOLD AND THE THRESHOLD GUARDIAN

A threshold is a passageway into an identity that we haven't had before. In all the myths there are always Guardians of that threshold— forces that discourage us from stepping into the unknown—like the three-headed dog Cerberus who guarded the gates of Hades in Greek mythology. In each of our lives, whenever we encounter a scary threshold to something new, there is some barrier or figure—the Threshold Guardian—who blocks our progress.

The guardian might be some boss who doesn't value our creative contributions, or the mortgage where, "I can't answer the Call because I might not be able to pay the mortgage." The Threshold Guardian might be some physical fear or limitation. "I'm afraid that if I learn how to scuba dive that I would die, but I'm really called to learn how to scuba dive!"

Somehow we have to trick or defeat the Threshold Guardian and step through into the unknown. When we step through, we discover enhanced power. Some part of us expands and suddenly we're on the road of adventures, the road of trials. This is where storytellers just go crazy and have a fantastical good time.

WE ALMOST ALWAYS HAVE MAGICAL AID TO HELP US THROUGH THE THRESHOLD

Luke had Obi-Wan Kenobi, Frodo and Bilbo had Gandalf. One of my sources of magical aid was Ernie Woods.

I was a senior in college and had no plans of moving forward. I knew I wanted to be a therapist, but was clueless about next steps. One of my friends was Ernie Woods, a therapist at the UCSB Counseling Center, who stopped me one day on campus and said, "Keith, you want to be a psychotherapist?" I said, "Yes, of course!" He said, "Well, you know, you need a degree and a license."

I said, "I really haven't planned anything yet. I'm just focusing on graduating."

He said, "Look. Apply to the Counseling Psychology graduate program here at UCSB. I think they'll take you." I said, "Why would they take me? I'm a hippie with long, stringy hair and an anti-establishment attitude. Graduate programs don't like to take people from their own University, and only a small percentage of applicants get accepted to public counseling psychology programs anyway, including this one!"

Ernie laughed (he had a great laugh) and said, "All true, Keith! But, I don't know, There's something about you. I think they'd take you." So I applied (my only application) and, by God, they took me. The rest was history as far as I was concerned. I got my MA, my Marriage Family Therapist license, and then later my PhD from the Fielding Institute and my Clinical Psychologist license. Ernie was my magical aid that arrived right when I needed him. He was my angel, and I had the good sense to listen to him and follow his advice and it helped me defeat the Threshold Guardian of my passive confusion and step through onto the road of adventures that has led me to writing these words to you.

THE THRESHOLD GUARDIAN CAN TAKE MANY FORMS

The guardians aren't just monsters. They can be fears, biases, habits, and limitations. For instance:

Fear of change can be the Guardian. If I marry this person or divorce this person, I'm going to change. If I have that child, I'm going to be a different person.

The Guardian might be somebody. It might be a parent, teacher, or high school counselor who says, "No, you can't!"

The Guardian might be doubt and weakness. "I'm called to teach, but I'm terrified of public speaking."

Bill O'Hanlon, one of my favorite teachers, is an introvert and was a horrible, horrible public speaker when I first saw him. I signed up for a workshop on trauma given by him at the beginning of his career in the eighties and he was a miserable presenter. I remember thinking, "I paid one-hundred-fifty bucks to come and listen to this guy talk all day?" He would drone on about hypnosis—then mumble, mumble, mumble—then more boring talk. I almost went to sleep and not because he was hypnotizing me.

Fifteen years later, I bought six hours of his Positive Psychology lectures and he was brilliant![64] He was charismatic! He told incredible stories. His messages, techniques, and stories organized and then reorganized and then super-organized my understanding of the material. He blew my mind. I thought, "This guy is one of the best presenters I've ever heard!"

Bill O'Hanlon was not going to let being a boring introvert stop him from his mission of bringing hypnotherapy and brief psychotherapy into the psychotherapy community. As he later described it, he was blissed by Milton Ericson and his unique forms of hypnosis and therapy, blessed by Ericson's and others' encouragement, dissed by traditional therapists who were dismissive of his brief therapy and positive orientation, and pissed about twentieth-century psychology pathologizing everybody instead of focusing on health, happiness, and fulfilling relationships. His mission required him to become a powerful, pleasurable, and entertaining guy, and so he crossed the threshold and did it!

The Hero has to best the monster—defeat the Threshold Guardian. Often you have to wrestle with some inner demon of doubt, rage, fear, or anxiety to move forward on your journey. Defeating the Guardian and crossing the threshold always requires enduring beyond comfort zones for a greater cause:

- You have to study relentlessly to score well enough on the MCAT to get into med school.
- You have to leave the security of your current job to try another job.
- You have to risk rejection to write that manuscript and send it to a publisher.
- You have to face fear of being a bad parent to have your first child.
- You have tolerate your fear of constraint to commit to someone you love.
- You must soothe your fear of commitment and responsibility to risk marriage and family.

As you can see, Threshold Guardians are all over the place, but if we have courage and resolve we'll make it through the Threshold. Once through the Threshold, we discover enhanced powers. When you surrender to a call and cross the threshold you become a larger person. You have new abilities, and you'll need them for the ordeals coming on the Road of Trials.

THE ROAD OF TRIALS

After you've defeated the gateway guardian, you're launched onto the road of trials that will lead you circuitously towards your goals. The road of trials involves the adventures, monsters, problems, and ordeals that threaten and distract us from the Way. Storytellers love battles with dragons, solving riddles, outwitting evil witches, and discerning secret paths through the dark woods, but—make no mistake—there are real dangers on the road of trials!

You work for years to get into medical school and now you need to take the courses and endure the trials of the next five to eight years. You've left your job, gotten the small business loan, and now need to do all the hard work and problem-solving involved in making your entrepreneurial dream come true. You've been accepted into the ballet company and now need to grow as a dancer to find your place in the culture.

The deeper truths below the adventures and trials are that profound dangers arise when we take up challenges. Sometimes we die. Sometimes we are caught in the teeth of the monster and literally die. Jay Moriarty, a famous surfer and free diver, was obsessed with how deeply he could free dive into the ocean without breathing equipment. He just kept pushing the edge until he finally went too deep and died. This can happen when challenges become more important than the mission. We can just keep pushing the edge until, suddenly, we've gone too far.

This is why we need wise guides and companions to help keep us focused and to call us back when we stray.

THE BELLY OF THE WHALE, THE WELL OF THE WORLD

On the other hand, mostly when we push too far we don't die. We survive the accident, we rebuild our company, we seek out another relationship, we rehabilitate our injury, we repent our selfish mistake, we work our way through the depression, and the process becomes another call into some form of service.

Both triumphs and disasters can lead us to what Campbell called the Belly of the Whale, or the Well of the World, where the hero goes into a profound depression or into a darkness so hopeless that he or she despairs. Often in modern society we'll experience this literally as depression, anxiety, or a failed relationship, and it seems like we're going nowhere and there's nothing that we can do. It can feel like death—a dead life, a dead job, or a dead relationship. In the Belly of the Whale our impulse is to collapse and surrender to darkness, and sometimes we do. Suicide, homicide, addiction, despair, exploitation, victimization, are all forms of collapse that can crush us in the Well of the World.

In that depression, there in the Well of the World, a magical insight, an ethereal guide, or some enchanted help will come if we allow it. As we receive this help, a reconciliation with the Beloved, the Father, the Mother, and other Shadow archetypes occurs.

Magical aid somehow helps love and wisdom enter the dark corridors of despair to enliven us, to give us a Way through. In Tolkien's *The Two Towers*, the Elf Queen Galadriel gives Frodo a gift, a little vial of sacred water. He asks, "What's this?" She responds, "It's a light that will guide you through dark places," and it does. If we look for it and have faith in it, there is always a light that will guide us through dark places. If we lose faith in a way through we can surrender to the darkness. Suicide, homicide, addiction, and deep depression are all forms of becoming lost in dark places.

Reconciliations occur when we come face-to-face with wounded relationships or developmental arrests, often wounds in our relationships with Mother, Father, Spirit, and Self. In these confrontations are opportunities to resolve wounds into love, wisdom, and growth. I've supported this in thousands of therapy sessions over the last four decades, helping people find the old conflicts in their current pain and resolve them into deeper wisdom and love—often redefining their relationships with fathers, mothers, siblings, and other significant life figures. These transformations are not just *conceptual,* but actual uplevelings of our Shadow selves—our instinctual adaptive unconscious—to more maturity and complexity.

Often the Belly of the Whale opens us up. As we collapse into the destructive Shadow that engulfs us, we can paradoxically open ourselves to change. Divine help comes as light, insight, a message, or a messenger. Bill Wilson, one of the two founders of Alcoholics Anonymous, felt a "Wind of Spirit" come over him in a drunk tank, and he found the courage to get sober and dedicate himself to helping alcoholics everywhere by founding AA.

I've heard it from hundreds of clients over the years, describing turning points in their lives. Magical aid—a dream, teacher, friend, book, image, minister, or therapist—directs us into resolving a conflict with Shadow, where we find ourselves as Hero and Heroine.

APOTHEOSIS

Campbell, influenced as he was by psychoanalysis, believed that the Well of the World conflicts were often sourced in basic unresolved issues with archetypal Father and/or Mother blocking our power, doubting our abilities, or otherwise distracting us from our Way. In courageously addressing these conflicts the Hero claims adult power and better integrates masculine and the feminine, resulting in profound transformation. This is the apotheosis where a gift comes to the Hero—a gift so precious that he must take it back to the tribe.

At the end of the Tolkien epic, in *The Return of the King*, the four Hobbits return to the Shire to find it enslaved by evil men. But these are not the four bumbling and frightened hobbits that fled the Shire a year earlier. They have all been transformed by their experiences—the road of adventures, the Belly of the Whale, the apotheosis and transformation—and have embodied the Warrior and Man of Wisdom archetypes. They easily defeat the oppressors and free the Hobbit people.

Jung in his system called adult development individuation. Ultimately he said for someone to be an individuated human being he or she needed to integrate the archetypal masculine, feminine, and Shadow. If you think of this process in terms of a family, a child grows from looking up at father and mother as authorities, to looking straight across at them as other adults engaged as partners in supporting growth and life. He grows from unconsciously being directed by Shadow impulses and stories, to consciously examining them, refining them, and choosing what fits his higher purpose. Spiritual teacher and world-class practical theoretician about masculine and feminine essences and aspects, David Deida, says discipline is listening to the deeper voices,[65] the constructive Shadow that grows as we grow. When we integrate weak and strong, masculine and feminine, light and shadow, we transform. This transformation creates gifts that we are moved to share.

We want to bring our new consciousness and gifts back to the tribe and so we're called to return through the threshold. Some people don't return. There are lots of myths where people were asked to come back and they say, "Forget about it! I don't I want to go back!" Towards the end of "The Odyssey," after enduring twenty years of risk and hardship, Odysseus's remaining men refused to leave the land of the Lotus-Eaters. They wanted to hang out and get high all day in a life of ease. They had no interest in returning to Greece. Odysseus, on a mission to return to his wife Penelope and regain his kingdom, had to go forward alone.

Or worse, we make the journey, bring back the gift, but become corrupted by our new power. Some people are tempted to take their power and control everybody. Often, the hero of one myth becomes the evil emperor of the next myth because, like in regular society, he fears loss of power and tries to control the flow of history for selfish purposes. A lot of boomers, idealistic in the sixties, are not particularly idealistic right now, and we know who some of them are. They're in the news. They were given power and they got very interested in keeping and expanding their power rather than continuing the transformative process that myth is supposed to support. In the nineteenth century, Lord Acton, a noted philosopher at the time, said, "Power tends to corrupt, and absolute power corrupts absolutely." A paradox of human consciousness is that, even though we resist change, we need to keep growing or else we deteriorate and suffer.

Resistance to change in dialectical engagement with the need to keep growing is reflected in most myths. That's why each generation needs to hear the Call, say "Yes," and make the Hero's Journey.

When the Hero accepts the call of return and crosses the threshold back into the regular world he comes back transformed, a master of two worlds. Rejoining the community he becomes a conduit, a bridge between worlds. Often a central experience and message of the returned Hero is that the illumination from the other world is all around us all the time.

DUNE AND THE OTHER WORLD ALL AROUND US

One of my favorite mythological texts of the twentieth Century is the science fiction book, *Dune,* by Frank Herbert, about an alternative universe where the genetic capacities for psychic powers are cultivated over many generations and activated by training, drugs, and moral authority. In *Dune,* the hero, Paul, at fifteen and just awakening to his call, is talking to his teacher Dr. Yueh, who eventually betrays him, surrendering to his own destructive Shadow. Friend and guide transformed into betrayer is a common archetype since most of us betray and are betrayed at some time. Yueh gives Paul a bible from his murdered wife Winni and says, "Open it to the marked passage," intending Paul to read an inspirational passage on leadership. Instead, Paul instinctively opens to Winni's favorite verse:

"Think you that a deaf person cannot hear.

What deafness then might we not all possess?

What senses do we lack that we cannot see and hear another world all around us?"

The passage hits Paul like a thunderbolt, burning away his childhood, filling him with "terrible purpose," and leaving him changed forever, a conduit between two worlds.

The Hero sees and hears the other world and brings his vision back to the collective. Joseph Campbell believed that each generation needs cleansing and renewal. Cultures rise and fall, become decadent, and then revive, altered every time by new knowledge and evolutionary forces. The collective is renewed again and again by the Hero's journey. It's in our genome to fall into corruption, into the temptations of the flesh, the temptations of power, the temptations of fear. So Heroes have to endlessly answer the Call, encounter the purifying fires of the Hero's

Journey, and create bridges into Spirit to renew the people—to help them *"...see and hear another world all around us."*

The Hero comes back and offers his gifts, often inspiring others to embody the better parts of themselves.

I believe all humans are called. Many times we say, "No!" and then something bad happens. Eventually, many of us join Frodo and proclaim our version of, "I will go, though I do not know the way."

In the West, in modernity and post-modernity, we need to recognize that the mythic form—the larger-than-life qualities and sacred missions—are necessary, mandated as they are by our very genes.

In this sense we remythologize the culture with the emergent myths and Heros of our time. We currently do it with movie stars, rock stars, political figures, and so on. Ronald Reagan, Bill Clinton, Gandhi, Desmond Tutu, Mother Teresa, Lincoln, Martin Luther King, Taylor Swift, Bono, the Beatles, and Marilyn Monroe, are all examples—regular people who somehow are elevated to become symbols as well as individuals.

Sometimes certain people discover that they have been given the job of occupying a mythological form—they've been called and said, "Yes!" Pope Francis is one of my current favorites. He has surrendered to his sacred Mission and someday will be sainted by the very institution—the Catholic Church—which is currently reeling from his revolutionary changes.

I once gave a science fiction book called, *Lord of Light* [66], to Ken Wilber (author of *Sex, Ecology, and Spirituality*), because I thought he would see himself in it.

In *Lord of Light,* people colonized a planet and found a way to grow new bodies so that they could have multiple lifetimes—essentially recapitulating the Hindu and Buddhist ideas of reincarnation. As the centuries passed, a few kept developing some aspect of personality until they became a pure expression of that aspect, essentially a larger-than-life bridge between two worlds. They became Kubera, the Divine Artificer who could imbue feelings into structures, or

Kali, the Goddess of destruction spreading chaos, or Maitreya the Lord of Light.

An archetypal person, a mythological embodiment, is someone who has become the purest expression of who he or she uniquely is—an integration of Shadow and light into a coherent force. At that particular point they have entered the area of enhanced power, have become a larger human being, achieved an apotheosis, and are ready for the next stage of the Journey. Such individuals are often better connected to the fields that surround all of us, can inform all of us, and can empower us if we take the Call and survive the journey.

SPIRITUALITY PERMEATES THE HERO'S JOURNEY

Spirit is the heart of the our archetypal matrixes, our mythic natures. We all intuitively feel something, someone, some organizing power beyond our understanding. God, Spirit, the Void, the Goddess, morphic fields, the Higgs boson field, the Absolute, or pure emptiness—we have many names for transcendent forces unimaginably immense, but can yet feel real and personal to us. Spirit in material form is the central theme of all myth, all human archetypes. The Hero creating a bridge from the material world to the Spirit world is a central element in every Hero's Journey.

We can see how the evolution of consciousness is always accompanied by some felt sense of spiritual connectedness in the evolution of the stories that men have told and recorded over the centuries. As we look back through history, we can see that as consciousness evolved the stories evolved—stories evolving through hunter-gatherer nature mysticism and magic, through agrarian pantheons and sacred texts, through industrial and informational egalitarian value systems and modern physics. The myths are still evolving.

Spiritually, myths provide a series of steps from God down to us and from us up to God. You see this in all the Creation myths. One of my favorite is a Tibetan Buddhist creation myth—Yab was eternity who gave birth to Yum who was time. Yab and Yum, eternity and time, gave birth to the present world.

What I particularly like about the Yab/Yum myth is that, like several others, it anticipates modern physics because that's exactly what happened. Out of eternity came the big bang, and time came into existence along with everything else, biased to evolve. Together time, matter, and the evolutionary impulse, created the present world.

SHADOW REVEALED IN YOUR HERO'S JOURNEY

As you read through this chapter you had different reactions to the stories, ideas, and principles revealed in myths, archetypes, and the Hero's Journey. I suggest you skim back over this chapter and write in your journal about what was interesting/boring, yummy/yucky, and personally relevant/personally irrelevant.

Wait a day and then review your notes, looking for what you know now that you didn't know before, feel now that you didn't feel before, or believe now that you didn't believe before.

This is you discovering and integrating your Shadow via the Hero's Journey. It is Shadow Light, illumination at the edge of darkness.

6

WARRIOR AND
MAN OF WISDOM

...the Way of the Warrior is the resolute acceptance of death.

—Myamoto Musashi

I n the early eighties I was walking to my car with my last client of the day, a young therapist named James who was working on identity and relationship issues. He was complimenting my work in the session and said something along the lines of, "I really enjoy you encouraging me to be like a warrior."

I was briefly confused and a bit irritated, and wasn't clear why until after I thanked him politely and was driving home. In the car I figured out what bugged me and finished the conversation in my mind, "James, I'm not encouraging you to be *like* a Warrior. I'm encouraging you to *be* a Warrior!"

DESTRUCTIVE AND CONSTRUCTIVE WARRIOR
SHADOW IN A TERRORIST INCIDENT

On August 21, 2015, there was a terrorist incident on a high-speed train traveling from Amsterdam to Paris.[67] A 26-year-old Moroccan man named Ayoub el Khazani entered the train with a pistol, a Kalashnikov automatic rifle, and a box cutter. He opened fire with his handgun, hitting several people with an apparent agenda of killing as many as possible. In the car were three American friends, servicemen Spencer Stone of Sacramento and Alek Skarlotos of Roseburg, Oregon, and Anthony Sadler, a senior at Sacramento State University. They were on holiday together, and quickly realizing something needed to be done, they charged and subdued the gunman.

As Mr. Sadler related it, "We heard a gunshot, and we heard glass breaking behind us, and saw a train employee sprint past us down the aisle." He said they saw a gunman entering the train car with an automatic rifle.

"As he was cocking it to shoot it, Alek just yells, 'Spencer, go!' And Spencer runs down the aisle. Spencer makes first contact; he tackles the guy. Alek wrestles the gun away from him and the gunman pulls out a box cutter and slices Spencer a few times. And the three of us beat him until he was unconscious."

"The gunman never said a word except, 'Give me my gun! Give me my gun!'" he added.

Mr. Stone then helped another passenger who had been wounded in the throat, even though his thumb had been nearly severed by the box cutter.

Ayoub el Khazani clearly was driven by deadly interior forces. Whatever his conscious beliefs, his Warrior nature had been corrupted and amplified by a non-conscious self utterly convinced that mass killing was right action. Somehow his non-conscious Shadow self had been warped into pursuing the murder of innocents. It is impossible to imagine him engaging in this act while living a happy, healthy, self-reflective life, intimately connected in loving relationships—violence almost always arises from misery and emotional pain.

Meanwhile, Sadler and Stone, their Warrior natures conditioned as they were to protect others—a foundation principle of American military philosophy and training—instinctively organized themselves to put aside their own welfare to save others. Trained to harness their own violent instincts to do right, their attack on the terrorist was as inspiring as Mr. El Khazani's attack on the passengers was horrific. It is easy to imagine them engaged in normal lives with satisfying relationships—loving self-sacrifice often arises from pro-social values and impulses.

Their quick actions involved instantaneous instinctive reactions, impulses, and beliefs from constructive Shadow—their non-conscious selves instantly organizing them to do right at enormous personal risk. Doing right at personal cost or risk is one definition of the Warrior. In this case, doing right involved harnessing their dangerous instinctual violence for just this kind of action. Instinctive violence is often destructive Shadow, but Warrior training and deepening awareness can turn it into power and dark beauty.

Healthy Warrior training reinforces loops of commitment to protect others at personal risk, producing capacities for the kind of heroic impulses and actions demonstrated by the three young Americans. In contrast, we can see the results of unhealthy Warrior training in the warped Moroccan gunman—obviously the victim of the kind of mind control and destructive Shadow amplification that supports sick loops of indulging violent thoughts, actions, and perspectives.

The Warrior and Man of Wisdom archetypes are not metaphors; rather they are central figures in most men's lives—sources of strength and comfort when cleanly embodied, and sources of collapse and suffering when ignored or compromised.

Masculine Shadow holds and transmits Warrior and Man of Wisdom. We can ignore, suppress, and distort Warrior and Man of Wisdom resulting in destructive Shadow screwing us up, or we can listen, surrender, and embody their inherent constructive Shadow power to serve our deepest purpose.

It's our choice.

IN THIS CHAPTER WE WILL:

- Define the Warrior and Man of Wisdom as a developmental progression.
- Learn how being true to our Warrior leads us to our Man of Wisdom.
- Explore how to meet the monsters we encounter and consume them.
- Connect the Warrior and Man of Wisdom to living, parenting, working, loving, and all relationships.
- See how human evolution created the Warrior and Man of Wisdom.
- Visit the destructive Shadow inherent in every Warrior.
- Delve into two of my favorite sacred texts: *Bhagavad-Gita,* and *The Book of Five Rings,* and explore how ancient Wisdom traditions can guide us to our Warrior and Man of Wisdom.
- Understand how the sages of old anticipated our upcoming Integral Age.
- See the development of Warrior and Man of Wisdom from birth to death.
- Discover Two Rules for Guys.

THE WARRIOR AND MAN OF WISDOM ARE AT THE HEART OF THE HERO'S JOURNEY

The Hero's Journey is omnipresent in the genetically-driven archetypal forms that arise from all cultures. For men, embracing his Warrior nature and transforming through his quest into the Man of Wisdom is at the heart of the masculine Journey.

The Hero, when he finally heeds the call, embraces his Warrior self, develops, strengthens, and clarifies through ordeal and struggle, and struggles courageously to resolve his apotheosis into the Man of Wisdom. This is an include and transcend developmental trajectory—we develop our Warrior and expand into Man of Wisdom.

To do this we must face our demons in service of our mission—Theseus and the Minotaur, Hercules and his twelve labors, David and Goliath, Harry Potter and Voldemort—the Hero, the monster, and the transformative mission. Luke Skywalker into Jedi Knight, Muhammad Ali into World Champion, and Douglas MacArthur from WWI foot soldier into de facto Japanese emperor overseeing post WWII Japan's political reconstruction—Warrior into Man of Wisdom.

The three young Americans who charged the armed terrorist on the Brussels to Paris bullet train were embodying the Warrior archetype, being true to their principles at some risk to themselves. When a man consistently embraces and lives his Warrior, he eventually transforms into the Man of Wisdom—channeling Spirit into the tribe.

WARRIOR AND MAN OF WISDOM ARISE SIMULTANEOUSLY

There is always some Man of Wisdom in Warrior and some Warrior in Man of Wisdom. Radical priest Mathew Fox said in a *Sun* interview with Leslee Goodman, "The mystic in us is the lover—the mystic says, 'Yes,' but the prophet in us is the Warrior, and the Warrior says, 'No, this is unjust. No, this is suffering that we can work to relieve.' That's the rhythm of the Mystic and the Prophet, the Lover and the Warrior."[68]

The shift over a lifetime from Warrior to Man of Wisdom is one of emphasis, but the two are always intimately intertwined.

HOW DO WE DEVELOP OUR WARRIOR?

Thirty-five year old Weston sits in front of me, furious at his critical and litigious ex-wife, but fiercely dedicated to his seven-year-old daughter, and his calling as a healer and leader.

Earlier in our work we began by organizing his rage at his wife and his commitment to his daughter into a coherent balance to address his destructive Shadow influences to attack her, cheat on her, give up on his mission, or allow her to take his son away. As he wrestled successfully with these issues, he deepened, became more impeccable, divorced his wife, stood up for 50 percent time with his daughter, and was just elected leader in an important community organization.

Weston is a largely rational man, somewhat contemptuous of New Age woo woo, but to become the therapist and leader he aspires to be he needs a stable connection with the Other World, and it's my job to help him. He resists contemplative practice, but sees the validity of movement yogas like karate, Tai Chi, and Chi Gong, and I've taught him a few basic exercises.

Today I ask him, "Weston, do you have a sense of something connecting all of us, larger than us, and energetic in nature?"

Weston looks thoughtful, exploring his thoughts and feelings, "Yes, I think we all are connected by energy fields, I guess by Spirit in some fashion."

I breathe deeply, looking into his eyes and attuning to myself and Weston, connecting with Spirit in all my chakras. I know that this amplifies our intersubjective experience, making more Shadow material visible and feelable to him, "Do you feel connected at this moment?"

Weston gets very still, and speaks with quiet authority, "Yes. I feel connected at this moment."

I challenge him, Man of Wisdom to Warrior, "You need to practice this so it is a stable capacity—so that it's there whenever you call on it. This connection will protect you from pride and grandiosity. It will be a place to go when you need clarity and compassion."

Weston instantly gets it and responds with Warrior resolve, "I see that. I will practice this and the yogas you showed me. Thanks!"

I feel the warm pleasure of having helped a young Warrior to an important threshold and seeing him step through.

UNIVERSAL ARCHETYPES

The Warrior and Man of Wisdom are universal archetypes that inform almost every man's (and many women's) development, but how do we find our Warrior nature? How can we tell constructive Shadow leading us into a healthy Warrior, or destructive Shadow influencing us towards a corrupted Warrior, using power for harm and egocentric gratification?

We become the Warrior when we are willing to endure discomfort and put ourselves at risk for our principles. Seventeenth century "Sword Saint" Miamoto Musashi (much more about him later in this chapter) maintained that the resolute acceptance of death in serving your purpose—your current mission—is the signature hallmark of the Warrior. Principle over comfort and safety seems to be a central organizing principle in most teachings about the Warrior and Man of Wisdom and is consistent with the evolutionary roots of the archetypes. I've also found it to be true for my clients and me over the last forty-three years and fifty-five thousand therapy sessions.

When a man becomes stable in his Warrior consciousness, discerning what's true or false, and is more moved to serve others' development and less absorbed with testing himself, he's often transitioning into Man of Wisdom.

The Warrior mostly involves men, but appeals to the masculine in all of us. Women can animate their masculine to rock the warrior archetype. My favorite? It has to be Ripley in *Aliens*. She risked everything to serve her principles and save people she loved.

A woman can be a Warrior leading into a Woman of Wisdom, but has more archetypal developmental paths to Woman of Wisdom—for instance, the Divine Mother, Lover, Artist, and Wife can all transform into Woman of Wisdom. We'll be exploring Feminine archetypes more in Chapter 7: Many Paths to Woman of Wisdom.

Why is the Warrior archetype so necessary for men? Male competition and dominance is built into the human genome just as it is in chimpanzees, walruses, wolves, and countless other species. This instinct is met putting principle ahead of personal comfort or safety in critical situations.

The Hero's journey—the universal human attraction to being on a mission—often involves an initial transition into the Warrior who, through traveling the road of trials, transforms into the Man of Wisdom.

The hero in the hero's journey, by definition, expands his Warrior nature. He hears the call, says, "Yes!" faces and defeats the threshold guardian, and crosses the threshold onto the road of trials and ordeals. The Warrior, receiving transformational spiritual guidance, feels in his heart when he's on or off his mission and adjusts back to his mission, even under extreme duress.

Ordeals lead to the Well of the World—the Belly of the Whale—where he must reconcile Masculine and Feminine, Father and Mother, Light and Shadow. As he does, his identity is progressing towards Man of Wisdom who returns through the threshold, a living bridge to the Other World. Great examples?

- Luke embodying the Jedi Knight into defeating and then reconciling with the wounded father—Darth Vader.
- Harry Potter finding deep compassion, even as he destroys Voldemort.
- Bill Clinton facing the humiliations of his impeachment and wounded sexuality and continuing on to serve the world in multiple ways.
- Einstein first surrendering to his calling to more deeply understand the cosmos, in the face of much adversity, and going on to be a powerful philosophical voice for unity.

The core of the Hero's Journey is Shadow challenging us to grow or collapse. We are called, we resist the call, we finally accept the call, and embark on our personal Odyssey—choosing the adventure and coming home transformed. The monsters arise from within and without, seeking to consume us, craving violence. Attack! Flee! Attack you! Run from you! Attack me! Run from me! A man discovers his Warrior nature facing the monster with principle and resolve.

EACH TIME WE MEET AND CONSUME THE MONSTER, WE DEEPEN

This dynamic is the core of the Warrior's journey.

I was a high school athlete who wrestled, practiced Shotokan Karate, played tennis, and ran cross country. My fears of pain, opponents, injury, and failure were the monsters who said, "Don't risk that try-out, don't get on the mat with that opponent, don't take that ten-mile run, you will never do well in that race." I had to meet those monsters and consume them, absorb their energy and step through the resistance thresholds into the training and contests, the victories and the defeats. Each time I faced them and stepped through them, I found my Warrior self just a little bit—I absorbed a little of the resistance power and alchemically transformed it into a little more courage to step forward the next time in service of my principles.

This is the beauty of merit-based hierarchies likes sports, dance, theater, and heartfelt projects, especially for adolescents who are discovering their adult identities through success and failures, temptations and ordeals.

This is also consistent with modern research on willpower. As Roy Baumeister details in his *Willpower: Rediscovering the Greatest Human Strength,*[69] willpower is resisting a lesser impulse (like procrastination) in service of a deeper, more meaningful impulse, and is associated with increased happiness, success, health, and love. Of three dozen personality characteristics, willpower was the only one that, at four years old, could predict future college GPA.

Also, whether we naturally have more or less willpower as children, *we can develop willpower with practice.* Remember the human superpowers of focused intent and action, in service of principle, and driven by resolve? Consciously choosing goals/principles and utilizing our superpowers to pursue them increases willpower and develops our Warrior selves.

Most guys are lit up by the Warrior archetype. The Warrior is someone willing to sacrifice comfort or safety for his principles. Every single time a guy endures risk or discomfort or sacrifices in service of principle, he nourishes his Warrior nature. The desire to do this rises up in men. If you're not true to your principles, you suffer. If you are true to your principles, you find your Warrior self each time you hold your ground, face your fear, or embody your purpose.

We want to find ourselves as Warriors. Many men I've discussed this with craved this from earliest memories. I wanted to find myself as warrior when I was three, five, eleven, fifteen, and thirty—the hunger was always there. I didn't know exactly what I was reaching for, but I yearned for power and purpose, like my favorite characters in books and movies. Looking back I can see them clearly—Mighty Mouse, Mowgli (from Kipling's *The Jungle Book*), Super Man, and The Man from UNCLE. All were Warriors serving the higher good.

The Warrior and the Man of Wisdom are an include-and-transcend developmental progression—if you don't somehow embody the Warrior, you can never fully embody the Man of Wisdom.

As a boy grows from child, to teen, to man, he expands into the Warrior. He finds meaning at the edge of death—either actually or symbolically by risking injury, failure, or defeat. He takes the Hero's Journey—sometimes again and again. When we're tested and rise to the task, we find our Warrior selves—a blissful experience to the masculine. And life tests us again and again, leading to successes and failures, both potentially supporting our Warrior selves.

At a particular point in adult development, something changes—we no longer need to *find* our best selves as much as to consistently *embody* our best selves. This marks the transition in Man of Wisdom. As we shift into Man of Wisdom we're less drawn to ordeal and more to service—a vertical developmental leap. I suspect this archetype arose in our misty genetic past when age diminished men's physical capacities, but experience expanded their judgment and discernment. Tribes who accessed this wisdom had distinct evolutionary advantages.

The Man of Wisdom naturally embodies his principles. He transmits compassion and wisdom into the world, and is moved to care. Man of Wisdom is often less drawn to competition and trials for himself, but loves to help others, especially the young Warriors. Man of Wisdom discerns between truth and bullshit and naturally prefers truth.

WARRIOR TO MAN OF WISDOM IS A DEVELOPMENTAL PROGRESSION IMPORTANT TO:

Parenting: Child, into teen, into Warrior, into Man of Wisdom is a developmental process that we need to understand so we can help our children with it, and help each other with it.

Relationships: The above transitions are tantric processes—meaning they happen in relationships with other people, with our own bodies, with our past/present/future, and with the world. This is especially true with our chosen partner. She suffers when we collapse and finds us more trustable when we are true to our Warrior core.

Life rhythms: Development of the Warrior proceeds through stages and there's a rhythm to the stages. We feel a desire or a yearning that turns into a resolve, which turns into responsibilities, which lead us into ordeals, where in meeting them we find ourselves in some fashion—gradually transforming and growing in the process. Our new selves eventually feel new desires or yearnings that turn into expanded resolves, and so on and on. This under-pins the life of the Warrior and Man of Wisdom. Or, as David Deida puts it, a man's life is success, failure, success, failure, success, failure . . . death.[70]

If you're a guy and you fully commit to your yearnings and resolve, you're going to progress into the Warrior archetype. Guys who are at peace with themselves as a Warrior are different kinds of guys. We all know that, right? Your favorite heroes—both fictional or non-fictional—will have that committed-to-purpose feel about them. When I discuss this in classes, almost everyone—men and women—intuitively know what I'm talking about.

WARRIOR AND RELATIONSHIPS

If you've determined your principles in your relationships (as you should!) and you're true to those principles, those relationships will mostly grow well or end well.

What I mean my "end well," is that, if you're true to your principles and open to wise influence and your relationship still ends, it's likely to end relatively cleanly and your next relationship will probably be a better one. A reflection of this is that second marriages are statistically more happy but also shorter than first marriages. How does that work statistically with large groups of second marriages? Well, it works because many people are smarter and more discerning going into a second marriage and so *choose* better partners and *are* better partners (often making a happier second marriage). They also are wiser in knowing when to cut their losses and get out earlier if a relationship can't be improved (often making for a shorter marriage).[71]

The Warrior and Man of Wisdom find themselves in relationships with others, and their Warrior/Man of Wisdom values are enacted in relationship with others.

You can see how the Warrior and the Man of Wisdom are universal archetypes in human cultures. Further, as we'll soon see, every culture has Warrior and man of Wisdom archetypes because they are *genetically mandated.*

EXERCISE:
HOW TO HELP YOUR WARRIOR
AND MAN OF WISDOM GROW

I suggest you take your journal to a private place that feels beautiful and comfortable to you.

- *Remember a time you were extremely angry and acted badly by your standards, and write it down in detail.*
- *Remember a time you were extremely angry and acted well by your standards, and write it down in detail.*
- *Remember a time you were extremely fearful or anxious and acted badly by your standards, and write it down in detail.*

- *Remember a time you were extremely fearful or anxious and acted well by your standards, and write it down in detail.*
- *Imagine yourself facing the younger you that acted well and say something to him (like "I admire your wisdom and courage in the clutch"). Observe his imagined expression or how you imagine him responding in words or actions, and write it down.*
- *Imagine yourself facing the younger you that acted badly through fear or anger. What are you most deeply moved to say to him right now? It might be something like, "I'm ashamed of what you did." or "I'm frightened of you." Say it to him in your imagination, and observe how his imagined expression changes, or how he responds in words or actions. Write down what you experience.*
- *Continue these dialogues daily for a week, writing down what happens and what you learn.*
- *Share everything with someone you trust and write what comes of the conversation.*

EXERCISE: CULTIVATE THE WISE WITNESS:

- *The "you" who just talked to your younger self is probably deeper, wiser, and more courageous than your younger self. Resolve to be this deeper self more minutes every day—do not think about being this wiser self, but be your wiser self. Look through his eyes and speak with his voice.*
- *As you move through your life, keep noticing when you act well or badly by your standards and give yourself the same attention you gave yourself in the previous exercise. Write about this and share it with someone you trust.*
- *These practices will amplify your Warrior nature and accelerate your development into Man of Wisdom.*

HOW ARE THE WARRIOR AND MAN OF WISDOM EVOLUTIONARILY MANDATED?

Five to eight million years ago, cataclysmic geological events—earthquakes and volcanoes generated by huge plates shifting under the earth—created the Great Rift Valleys of Africa. This transformed the continent's heavily wooded ecosystems into grasslands and savannahs with much more variable weather, forcing many species, including our ancestors, out of the trees and onto the veldt. The human foot evolved to better adapt to walking rather than climbing, and our social structures underwent a remarkable reprogramming.

When we came out of the trees, human beings developed tendencies to pair-bond and form nuclear families. Why? Well, first of all, homo sapiens' feet couldn't easily climb up into the trees anymore, and in the savannahs of ancient Africa there were fewer trees anyway. Even more of a problem, a woman carrying around a 30-pound kid in one arm cannot effectively fight or flee, and she certainly can't scamper into a tree like a chimp mother with a toddler on her back. It's not really possible for her to consistently and effectively protect herself and her child out on the veldt. She needs others—and especially *one fully committed other*—focused on protecting her and that child, so the nuclear family was born.[72]

Men and women who formed teams—pair-bonds—had huge survival advantages. A pair-bond means two sexual partners fixate on each other and their children. Very unusual. Only 3 percent of mammals pair-bond, and most of them do so just for just one breeding cycle.[73] Our distant ancestors were already wired to want to have position in merit-based hierarchies—status in the tribe—like chimpanzees and other primates, but the pair-bond was a new evolutionary wrinkle that intensely connected man, woman, and children in a pair-bonded nuclear family with special luminance and demanding impulses to belong and *protect*.

So human beings evolved beyond other primates. We became a unique pair-bonding species. Human women are the only mammals that are sexually available (theoretically anyway) any day of the month. Human men and women are programmed to be attracted to each other to create romantic infatuations where they are intoxicated *specifically with each other* for six months to two years. As romantic infatuation fades, intimate bonding remains where couples feel deep connections with nuclear family.[74]

This pair-bonding dynamic created the Warrior—a guy willing to sacrifice himself for his mate and children. I find this so beautiful! These distant relatives were barely three feet tall and had tiny brains by modern standards. They had rudimentary speech, primitive tools, and didn't even have fire until a million years ago. But these barely self-aware men were willing to sacrifice themselves for the women they loved, for their children, and for their tribes. The Warrior archetype was born.

Kin selection is common in mammals, a bias towards blood relatives in a group or pack. Pair-bonding and nuclear families created an additional evolutionary force—kin selection bias towards men and women *genetically compelled* to help their mate and children survive and thrive. What better protector for a mate and children than a Warrior—someone willing to die in service of his family as well as his tribe?

These groups were *extremely* successful. As I mentioned in Chapter 3, modern primate groups max out about 30 (with some exceptions—some baboon groups are as large as 250). Most apes and monkeys can't handle the social complexities of more than 30 other individuals (if that). About five hundred thousand years ago the human brain expanded, and many believe that corresponded to a time when tribes got bigger. Evolutionary anthropologist, Robin Dunbar, believes an expanded brain was needed to handle the complex social demands of larger groups. His research strongly suggests that modern humans are wired to max out at groups of around 150—much more numerous than other primates. When communities grow larger than 150, new groups tend to calve off into additional communities. The social demands of larger tribes demanded a lot more brainpower.[75]

Most of our brain is designed to be social. There's a very narrow strip running like a mohawk through top of our brain that has to do just with *me* separate from *you*. All the rest of the brain has to do with relationships—with others, the world, and the various aspects of self.

Why did evolution favor these changes? Let's look at the three kinds of selection that power evolution and see:

- **Natural selection**—the survival of the fittest. If I can continue to live and thrive, I'm more likely to pass on my genes. If my tribe or family is disrupted or taken away, my chances of personal survival go down, so fierce protection of family and tribe is favored.
- **Sexual selection**—the survival of the sexiest. If I can successfully mate, I'm more likely to pass on my genes. Pair-bonding guarantees men at least one mate and the social surround to protect offspring. In addition, larger groups provided more opportunities for sexual partners (we're all wired for both monogamy and to cheat if we have the chance). If a guy cheats he has more of a chance of passing on his genes. If a woman cheats, she has more chance of enlisting another man in protecting her and her children. If everybody cheats, there's more genetic diversity which favors stronger offspring.
- **Kin selection**—the survival of the tribe. If I can increase my blood-kinship group's chances of thriving, my genes will be more likely passed on. Extending my sense of family beyond my nuclear family to my kin-related group evokes Warrior energies in service of the tribe. Larger communities can compete more successfully with other groups, and have more resources to bring to bear in hunting, gathering, and mutual support.[76]

What powerful forces! The drive to bond with one partner, have children whom you favor over all others, and the Shadow mandate to protect them to your utmost abilities gave huge evolutionary advantages to families and tribes with pair-bonded Warrior parents. This drive was such a potent mutation that it became universal in the human genome. Every guy has some urge and ability to create his own kind of tribe where he effectively is responsible for everybody's welfare—putting his personal safety and welfare second to theirs. Every guy has the capacity to make his mate, family, and kin group more important than his immediate personal comfort or welfare.

As consciousness evolved, these biological demands, based in pair bonding and kin selection in tribes, generalized and expanded into men standing up for personally sacred principles. One powerful definition of the Warrior is somebody who is willing to die for his principles or his passions.

MODERN BRAINS ARRIVED ONLY FIFTY THOUSAND YEARS AGO, AND ARE STILL EVOLVING

As we discussed earlier, fifty thousand years ago the human frontal cortex expanded to the point where the frontal lobes extended all the way down the front of the brain to the brainstem, and the modern human brain came into existence. Evolution took off like a rocket.[77]

Physical evolution accelerated enormously. When people started forming cities, *physical evolution* increased *a hundred times*—that's *ten thousand percent* faster! One example is a mutation on the ASPM gene that appeared just fifty-eight hundred years ago which increased the amount of folds in the cerebral cortex, effectively expanding the cerebral cortex.[78]

Human skulls couldn't evolve any bigger because human babies can barely get their heads through the birth canal, but more brain territory means more brain power, which creates significant evolutionary advantages. The cerebral cortex is the area covering the brain and is composed of five credit-card-thick layers of brain cells. If stretched flat, it's huge, but in the brain it's crinkled up into folds creating peaks (gyri) and valleys (sulci). For the brain to expand it could only do so by generating more folds in the existing space, thus giving us more capacities—which is exactly what the ASPM gene mutation did. Almost every human today has this ASPM variant.

Humans continue to evolve, and we're evolving progressively faster to the point that geneticists are now *consciously altering the human genome.* I know! The potentials for catastrophes and abuses are astronomic! But such research is another reflection of the evolutionary impulse extending through self-aware consciousness and accelerating human evolution. We now are evolution's self-aware emissaries turbocharging the evolutionary process for better or worse.

WHAT ABOUT THE EVOLUTION OF THE MAN OF WISDOM?

With larger groups came distributions of labor and more complex social hierarchies. Humans, with phenomenal memory capacities, unprecedented information processing, language, and extreme sensitivity to nature and the rhythms of the seasons and wildlife, now could accumulate knowledge and use it in coherent ways via complex social structures. They could also *pass this knowledge down* from parents, friends, teachers, and *wise elders.*

Larger and more successful groups, with some men and women living longer, generated individuals with more knowledge and skills which could be transmitted through social learning. Expert tool artificers, better hunters, effective social balancers, and deeper thinkers all contributed mightily to tribes surviving and thriving.

Some leaders had natural authority and superior discernment. Some Shamans had stable connections to the other world and vast insight and intuition. Tribes guided by such individuals had significant advantages, and so the Man of Wisdom arose as the archetype for wise leader, shaman, and sage (we'll discuss the Woman of Wisdom in the next chapter). This archetype kept developing through the Philosopher Kings extolled by Plato in *The Republic,* and continues to develop today in the Wise Father, Enlightened Leader, Spiritual Teacher, Selfless Coach or Therapist, and Sage.

In 1985, a movie called, *The Emerald Forest*, was released. The premise involved an American man whose son had been abducted by a Brazilian hunter gatherer tribe. The father, a Warrior on a mission, led expedition after expedition relentlessly into the forest to rescue his son, until, finally years later, he found him. Unfortunately for the father, this tribe was one of these idealized retro-romantic groups that everybody imagines lives blissfully in the rainforest (apparently some actually do, as Jean Liedloff chronicled in *The Continuum Concept*[79]), and when he finally finds his son, the young man is married and second in command of the tribe. The kid has no wish to return to civilization. The father desperately entreats the chief, "You're the Chief! Tell my son to come back with me!" The chief, a Man of Wisdom teaching the father (who himself is the epitome of the Warrior risking all for his son) responds, "If I told people to do what felt wrong in their hearts, I wouldn't be chief very long."

The Wise Leader, Healer/Shaman who guides, protects, and reconciles conflicting forces is intuitively valued by all. As Lynne MacTaggart details in *The Bond*, humans naturally have drives to share, care, and be fair, and they hunger for leaders, Men and Women of Wisdom, to sustain social frameworks that support these drives.[80]

THE DARK SIDE—DESTRUCTIVE SHADOW AS WARRIOR

Warrior resolve is a double-edged sword. You can be willing to die for your principles or passions for power-based needs, like dictators and tyrants have from time immemorial—somebody who is all about, "I will dominate!" "I want to be CEO and screw you!" "I will do anything to win this tournament/contest and values be damned!" "I want, I want, I want!" That's one form of Warrior, where the mission comes ahead of personal welfare and larger principles, and the mission is all about *me*. Such Warrior power can generate results—there can only be one heavyweight champion of the world for instance—but can also cause harm when not moderated by communitarian principles. Such personal ambition can generate vast power for good or not so good.

Similarly, Warrior resolve can be for purely egocentric purposes and meaning. A man can find his Warrior nature surrendering to a passion.

Rabid sports fans, motorcycle enthusiasts, competitive chess players, dedicated surfers, or tennis maniacs are all examples. These passions, moderated with responsibilities to others and personal welfare (not taking inappropriate risks in service of your passion), strengthen the healthy Warrior. These passions obscuring responsibilities to self and others can be dangerous and block development.

Unhealthy Warrior resolve can arise in destructive Shadow form. Domestic violence, bullying, rape, crime, violent political positions, jingoistic philosophies, colonialism, radical Islam, aggressive Christian fundamentalism, narcissistic entitlement, and rapacious exploitation all can involve corruptions of the Warrior energy manifested through destructive Shadow.

As I mentioned earlier talking about moral development, destructive Shadow can arise from social standards where, "I am more human or more worthy than another person or group," so another person or group deserves less rights and less care than me or mine." Racism and all bigotry are examples of this.

Often destructive Shadow says it's moral for me to vilify, exploit, injure, or aggressively dismiss some others or classes of others. When we can *perceive* such impulses, in a moral context of *it violates our principles* to surrender to such impulses, we can protect ourselves and the world from our destructive Warrior Shadow. When Pope Francis addressed the U.S. Congress on September 24, 2015, he entreated them to view each immigrant in the European migration crisis as a separate human being with family, dreams, aspirations, and struggles. Man of Wisdom Pope Francis knew that it's harder to turn away from a real, living, suffering human being than from a threatening faceless mass of desperate humanity.

PROTECTING OTHERS FROM HARM IS GENERALLY CONSTRUCTIVE SHADOW

When the masculine developmental arc involves surrendering to a sense of confidence and solidity in his healthy Warrior core, based in caring principles of being fair and just with all people, men tend to do well—they often have a peacefulness about them that is attractive and admirable to other men and women. Men who do this, at any developmental level, also tend to more frequently and consistently *feel* more strong, masculine, and coherent. They are more likely to want to protect the innocent and take stands for social justice.

Men who refuse the call, turn away from the trials the world presents, or surrender to dark impulses to harm themselves or others, tend to remain clueless of their native hunger to stand firm by their principles in the face of anything. Such men are likely to suffer shame, self-doubt, anxiety, depression, and confusion. They are more likely turn away from challenges to care for others.

HUMANS TURN DRIVES INTO ART

We human beings take the drives and turn them into art. We take hunger and food cultivation/preparation and turn it into culinary art. We take lust and we turn it in the art of romance and passion. We take our desires to care for children and turn it into the art of parenting—maximizing our children's developmental progress in multiple dimensions. We take our drives toward the Warrior and Man of Wisdom and turn them into the Wisdom traditions and Spiritual journeys that permeate all cultures.

The enlightenment beginning three hundred years ago ushered in the radical concept of universal rights. As individual rights have become more prevalent in the world, so to have individual responsibilities to live according to our principles. With the technological and interpersonal advances of the last hundred years, all this has been accelerating, accelerating, accelerating...

Of course, we still have fascist states like North Korea where the responsibilities are to the leader at the cost of individuals, or fundamentalist worldview like radical Islam, where the others deserve exclusion and death. Not surprisingly, people generally do not thrive in such cultures.

The East European countries in the Soviet Empire routinely came out least happy on U.N. happiness surveys. Interestingly, when jihadists are captured and *effectively* interrogated, the overwhelmingly most effective methods involve creating human relationships with them where the interrogators engage in dialectics challenging murder as the will of God.

SACRED TEXTS

With the advent of writing, human social evolution was turbocharged by this new ability to pass wisdom and knowledge forward, and most of the wisdom traditions created sacred texts to organize and quantify their teaching. Famous examples are the Talmud, Koran, Tao Te Ching, and the Bible. Other works, designed to be empirically accurate, like Plato's *The Republic,* Plotinus' *The Enneads,* and Newton's *Principia Mathematica,* took on spiritual luminance as the years passed and the teachings reverberated.

There were two manuscripts that became personally sacred texts to me, the *Bhagavad-Gita,* and *A Book of Five Rings.*

The *Bhagavad-Gita* (or Gita), is a part of the Hindu epic text, the Mahabharata.[81] The Gita is almost entirely a conversation between the Warrior/King Arjuna and the God Krishna serving as his Charioteer in a great battle.

Arjuna is appalled at the slaughter to come, and protests the damage of war. Krishna reminds him of his times and responsibilities as king.

They discuss multiple yogas, or ways of being, and Arjuna asks about Karma Yoga (nonattached service to Spirit). Krishna tells him to decide upon right action, engage in it as fully as possible, and to give up attachment to whatever outcome ensues. In short, he suggests Arjuna do his best to make everything he does an expression of God.

Krishna, the archetypal Man of Wisdom has no doubts. Krishna discerns between true and false and asserts from the Other World. Arjuna has lots of doubts. His personality and attachments—fear, anger, pride, shame, destructive Shadow, and defensive states—all get in the way as they do with every human, but he sets his Warrior resolve to listen to Krishna, do right, and be true to his mission.

Krishna doesn't have personality get in his way. Krishna doesn't have much of a personality really. He's a God. But we trust him because he radiates Man of Wisdom.

These figures and principles have always rung completely true to my Warrior self. I encountered the Gita at twenty-two in a UCSB religious studies class when I had been practicing and teaching Shotokan Karate for seven years. It was the first traditional sacred text that touched me deeply.

But the Gita is a myth and that was a problem for me. I didn't trust some of the principles from a conformist agrarian cultural story (with much ritual and symbolic action), to guide me in my day-to-day martial arts or spiritual seeking. As a Warrior I yearned for a guide I could absolutely trust to practically organize my training and purpose *now* in the 1980s.

Strangely, the source I found was from over three hundred years ago—Miyamoto Musashi's *A Book of Five Rings*.[82]

A BOOK OF FIVE RINGS

I discovered the warrior archetype in the sense I understand it today when I was about 30 years old.

At the time I was studying Taoist healing and Chinese martial arts with healer/martial artist, John Davidson. He was a crazy Narcissist, but a brilliant healer and deadly fighter.[83] He combined psychotherapy with bodywork in an incredibly dynamic and dangerous system called Symbol Linking Therapy. He was a kung fu master and I couldn't defeat him in combat (and I was six years younger than John, and was trained in many systems of combat). He told me Miyamoto Musashi's *A Book of Five Rings* was the definitive text on the Way of the Warrior, and he was right.

A Book of Five Rings blew my mind. To me it rang true as a practical and potent physical/tactical/strategic/moral/spiritual scaffolding. *A Book of Five Rings* instantly became a sacred text, and I've practiced Musashi's strategies and been guided by his wisdom ever since.

MIYAMOTO MUSASHI WAS THE PREEMINENT SAMURAI WARRIOR OF 17TH CENTURY JAPAN

Let's just pause for a moment and think about what *preeminent samurai warrior of seventeenth-century Japan* means.

Seventeenth-century Japan had the best sword fencers in the world. Miyamoto Musashi, by the time he was 31, had fought and won 60 duels with the best fighters in the land, killing many of them. Samurai didn't screw around in those duels. A katana sword is diamond-hard, razor-sharp, and wielded with extraordinary power. Duels *often* ended in death or catastrophic injury. These were violent feudal times. At thirteen Musashi killed his first opponent, a samurai named Arima Kihei, who had come to Musashi's village and issued a general challenge for single combat. Apparently, Miyamoto got in trouble for it with his uncle and teacher, the Buddhist Monk Dorin.

Musashi continued to train and duel, and never lost in over sixty deadly encounters. After twenty-eight he fought only with a wooden sword and after thirty-one never killed another man in a duel, though he fought many of them. In his early fifties there are several documented cases of Mushashi defeating men merely by approaching them with his two wooden swords at crossed guard, his Warrior gaze burning into their eyes, and simply backing them into a corner where they were unable to strike a blow.

Miyamoto Musashi embodied attributes deeper and more powerful than his contemporaries (*who were the most deadly sword fighters in the world*). He possessed a dominating power and brilliant strategic mind, but it was his completely practical orientation and Spiritual intensity that resonated with me. How did he develop such powers?

Musashi said that whenever you take a sword in your hand you should, "Think always of the cutting." He encouraged practitioners to learn all the martial arts, the Five Sword Attitudes, the basic stances, expressions, and techniques of his school, but when you face an opponent, think always of the cutting.

Weirdly, as with much of his teaching, I found clarifying direction for my psychotherapy. "Think always of the healing," is at the heart of all the work I do, and some of my students have commented that this one injunction rings the loudest for them from everything that I've taught them.

Musashi lived in violent times and he didn't start out perfectly formed. Truth be told, as a teenager Miyamoto Musashi was somewhat of a dick, often dismissive of other schools, even arrogant in his mastery.

To beat people in battle you must objectify them, and obviously Musashi learned to have no compassion for his opponents. But the killing obviously weighed upon him eventually. As he developed his technique and philosophy, he deepened spiritually. At twenty-eight, after a famous duel where Musashi killed a sword master named Sasaki Kojiro using a wooden sword he'd carved from an oar, he always fought with a wooden sword and after the age of thirty-one never killed in a duel again.

His writings became more spiritually oriented, and he painted beautiful renditions of nature, birds, and people. He expanded into more enlightened perspectives.

In 1643, at the age of fifty-nine, he retired to a cave named Reigendo on Mount Ito and wrote *A Book of Five Rings*. In it, he transmits his accumulated wisdom of the Way of the Warrior.

He had Nine Rules of Conduct:

1. Do not think dishonestly.
2. The Way is in training.
3. Become acquainted with every art.
4. Know the Ways of all professions.
5. Distinguish between gain and loss in worldly matters.
6. Develop intuitive judgment and understanding for everything.
7. Perceive those things which cannot be seen.
8. Pay attention even to trifles.
9. Do nothing which is of no use.

A student of many schools, Musashi discerned substance from bullshit, and The Book of Five Rings is the most substance, and least bullshit, Warrior text I know.

MUSASHI ANTICIPATED THE INTEGRAL AGE

His principles, "The first thing in the Way of the Warrior is the resolute acceptance of death," "Know the Ways of all professions," and "Have intuitive judgment about everything," detailed what consciousness research has been revealing for the last forty years.

In Integral studies we've observed that when someone *feels* appreciation for everything and diminished fear of death, they've entered a different world—a complex human community with Spirit, a familiar presence everywhere. Desire to serve the world arises in this level of ego development, and it was to everyone that Miyamoto wrote *The book of Five Rings.*

Similarly, "The Way is in training" reflects the growth mindset studies by Carol Dweck in the 1980s and 1990s that showed focus on effort and progress yields superior results in health, love, business, and parenting—far better than focus on outcome or personal image. Life is less about getting it *right,* winning *every time,* or *never making mistakes,* and more about managing processes *better,* rather than managing them *worse.* There is no perfect right way, no end to any growth process. We never get there. We're always growing. "The Way is in training."

You'll notice that number one of his nine rules is, "Do not think dishonestly." In Integral we say that everybody gets to be right, but nobody is right all the time, and that all knowledge is partial. Our task as avatars of pure consciousness is to discern truth from falsehood as best we can.

The last part of *The Book of Five Rings* is *The Book of the Void,* where Musashi attempts to transmit his understanding of emptiness, form, and Spiritual authority. At the end he says, "In the void is virtue and no evil. Wisdom has existence. Principle has existence. The Way has existence. Spirit is nothingness."

Musashi's teachings have guided me as a Warrior and Man of Wisdom over the last thirty-five years. "Principle has existence" and "The Way has existence" point to quintessential organizing principles to guide a man into his Warrior nature. Know your principles, follow your principles, and you will find your Way.

I once worked with a tremendously successful business man named Allen who came to me in despair because his beloved wife Karen was threatening to leave him over a secret affair that she had just discovered he'd been conducting for over eighteen months. Not used to failure, he was tortured by his inability to control the flow of events that had ensued from her discovery. He easily separated from his lover (devastating for her, but not for him) but Karen couldn't trust him after such major deception and betrayal. Allen teetered at the edge of losing her, his children, and their shared life that he so valued (70 percent of people having affairs describe their marriage—even their marital sex life—as good, so cheating is often not primarily driven by unhappiness at home[84]).

In our work it became clear that he had violated his own principles of integrity by his cheating, lying, and rationalizing. Interestingly, he intensely valued his *professional* integrity and prided himself on being known as an honorable man in his business.

I told him, "You collapsed. You didn't live your principles. Do you feel how your Warrior nature is appalled at what you did?"

Allen: "Absolutely. Sherri [his lover] was so hot though! I couldn't help myself."

Keith: "Really? You had no choice eh?"

Allen, laughing, "I get it—I always have a choice and I chose to screw up."

Keith: "Yeah, both literally and figuratively! If you believe you have no choice, you're setting yourself up to collapse in similar situations in the future."

Allen, looking more resolved, "I will *never* do that again!"

Keith: "Notice how you feel differently saying this?"

Allen: "Yes. I can't do this to Karen ever again, and I won't."

Keith: "This is your Warrior self, willing to do what it takes to live your principles."

WHAT ARE YOUR SACRED TEXTS?

What books speak deep truths to you. What are your principles that resonate with their teaching and are guided by their wisdom?

EXERCISE:
EXPLORE YOUR SACRED TEXT FOR YOUR PRINCIPLES

- *Write principles from your sacred text (or texts) in a list and put down next to each how committed you are to it, using a rating scale of 1 (barely committed) to 10 (fully committed).*
- *Daily read what you've written.*
- *In two weeks rate how you feel about each again. Are you more or less committed? Share this with someone you trust.*

THE WARRIOR DEVELOPMENTALLY

Since everything is relationships, our Warrior and Man of Wisdom natures have their roots in our relational history, going back to the very beginning of life itself.

Development is include and transcend. The tendencies to survive and reproduce in single-celled organisms were included and transcended in multi-celled organisms and so on up the evolutionary ladder. We are the repositories of billions of years of evolutionary programming, with each level of added complexity including and transcending previous levels. At the human level, all these ascending levels of complexity are played out in the stories of our lives and the archetypal forms of our cultures.

Thus all archetypes begin in utero with the electromagnetic field that comes into existence the moment an egg is fertilized. At that moment, the cumulative influences of our entire evolutionary past are set in motion. The broad scaffolding of our genetic legacy harnessed to whatever exists in and through that electromagnetic field, in complete relationship with the womb, has begun the developmental dance for this new person.

Through myriad forces the fetus matures, the baby is born, and the developmental journey continues, with some archetypes more demanding and some less. There are broad categories—types—that apply to each of us (like extrovert/introvert, thrill-seeking/risk-adverse, heterosexual/homosexual), but each human becomes his or her own unique type of person.[85] Since development of every sort affects who we are and how we deal with the world, Shadow is there from the very beginning, developing as we develop, informing us with constructive and destructive stories and impulses.

Fast forward—little boys tend to struggle more, strive more, and compete more than little girls. Little girls tend to relate more, cooperate more, and empathize more than little boys. Little boys are more into rules and rights, while little girls are more into caring. Countless studies—many cross-cultural—have shown such consistent differences between boys and girls developmentally.[86]

Let's just talk about little boys for now. Starting around one, kids have a sense of personal dignity. If you violate that sense of personal dignity, a child reacts. Sometimes he collapses and feels bad about himself, particularly if he is in a hostile environment (abusive or neglectful home or culture) which insists that children comply, even that they violate their native desires for justice and care. This causes a lot of wounds, and has been driving people to therapists' offices ever since psychotherapy started at the end of the nineteenth century. For a little child to stand up to a huge adult is a big deal, but if he stands firm for his dignity, he's just discovered and strengthened his Warrior self.

I remember when I was five years old. I was in an early kindergarten class. The teacher got pissed at us for something. She started talking baby talk, and I told her to stop doing that. That was one of the first times I got kicked out of a class. My dignity was offended, I spoke up, and I discovered a little bit of my Warrior self.

Now, there have been other times in my life where I didn't speak up, where I collapsed, where I surrendered, where I felt like a coward. I felt horrible about those times, and that suffering drove me to seek power, integrity, and my Warrior nature.

Ordeals and problems arise naturally in each human's life. The nine-year-old joins AYSO and isn't very good, so he works hard to get better. Training naturally moves from progress, to plateau, to progress, always punctuated by successes and failures, both of which can create problems/ordeals. As this boy hits these ordeals—making mistakes, struggling to improve, criticism from peers, criticism from coaches—he either collapses or transcends. If he collapses, becomes a poor loser or a poor winner, or gives up on a personally important goal, it's up to the wise adults in the family (usually Mom or Dad) to help him dialysize his collapse into further strength. The goal is always to resolve the ordeal into deeper understanding and more strength. Guided by wise others, he can face his destructive Shadow and discover a little bit more of his Warrior self.

As children hit adolescence, they become more acutely aware of authenticity in themselves and others. Hypocrisy drives teenagers crazy. So a teenager who stands up for authenticity and against hypocrisy finds a little bit of his Warrior self.

As adolescents become young adults, perhaps go to college or get a job, social justice can become a big deal—issues such as equal opportunity, fairness in the workplace, and respect at all levels. You stand up for social justice and find your Warrior self, or you surrender to the entropic forces of corruption that exist in all institutions and cultures and become diminished. Why do college students overwhelmingly flock to Barack Obama and Bernie Sanders? They both are fierce advocates for integrity, authenticity, and social justice.

Growth usually involves self-discovery, and as we mature we discover missions that guide us. A college degree, our own business, becoming a Marine, or creating a loving family are all examples of calls that invite us onto the Hero's journey. We thrive when we commit to the journey, and wither when we turn away.

But a Warrior doesn't just have his mission, he has relationships. We're conceived and born in relationships. We're raised in relationships. We are literally addicted to other people, and managing that addiction for better or worse is part of the Warrior's path. You take someone away from other people and isolate them, they go crazy. They go into withdrawal, activating the same brain circuits involved in withdrawal from drug addiction. So the Warrior is always living, breathing, and acting in intricate tapestries of relationships.

MY MISSION AND MY RELATIONSHIPS

So two interconnected demanding forces of a Warrior are *mission* and *relationships*, which can often be in conflict. For the Warrior, committed to his Way, mission usually comes first with relationships a close second. This is dictated not just from our masculine hearts, but also from our feminine partners. Clear examples are in save-the-world stories.

We've seen it again and again in books, movies, and TV shows. The guy comes home and says to his wife or sweetheart, "I've got to save the world," "The nuclear triggers are missing," "The virus has been released," "The villain has escaped from maximum security," "I'm the right man for the job, so they've given me the call."

At first his wife says, "Don't do that! It's very risky trying to save the world! You might get killed! Horrible things could happen!"

The guy *never* seriously replies, "Yeah, you're right. I don't want you to lose your man. I don't want our kids to lose their father. I'm not going to go save the world. I'm going to stay home."

If he did refuse the call, she would be instantly relieved (as would he), but ultimately he would be diminished in both their eyes. A woman is usually uncomfortable with a man who is willing to compromise his mission for anything, including her. Whenever I've presented this to audiences, most women in the groups heartily agree with this—it has resonated with their sense of themselves and their men.

Negotiating mission and relationship is an ongoing challenge in the Way of the Warrior, and they're both centrally important. Why? Because with each station on your Hero's journey, and with every new level of intimacy, comes new responsibilities. And with new responsibilities come new challenges and ordeals in following through on those responsibilities. Principle has existence. Wisdom has existence. The wise choice for the Warrior and Man of Wisdom is to stand for your principles, both in your mission and in your relationships.

When you fall in love, you have new responsibilities to be true to your partner and support her development. When you have a child, you have new responsibilities to nurture the baby and your partner. With each new level of intimacy come new responsibilities.

TWO RULES FOR GUYS—DON'T BE A DICK, DON'T BE A PUSSY

I've done three TEDx talks, and the last one was *Two Rules for Guys*, essentially a shorthand approach to being the Warrior (check it out at https://www.youtube.com/watch?v=T5YZ9CttznE). Rule number one is, "Don't be a dick!" So if you're bullying other people you might be using your power, but probably not in service of your principles (unless you have a principle that it's a great thing to bully other people). Bullies actually have a lot of self-esteem, but they don't have a lot of self-awareness, their relationships suck, and they tend to be unhappy. That's the first rule for guys—*Don't be a dick!*

Rule number two is *"Don't be a pussy!"* You're a pussy if you allow somebody to dominate you inappropriately, or if you say "Yes" when you need to say "No." If you don't stand up for your principles—don't take your stand with, "This is what's right" in the face of something you believe is wrong—you surrender to external coercion and become a pussy. Often in such cases, the rational is, "My boss made me do it," "My wife insisted," "I couldn't help it," etc.

We've seen such collapses a lot in the last twenty or thirty years in the political arena. People who come out of an administration often write a book and say, "Well, the decisions I made (going to war, lying, hurting poor people, surrendering to special interests) went against my principles, but I did it because I was ordered to."

"I was just following orders" is what the world was contemptuous of in the Nuremberg trials of Nazi war criminals. But it's interesting how often that gets pulled out when somebody working for some boss or institution violates personal principles. So if you have a principle, don't violate it. If you do violate it, you suffer—*don't be a pussy!*

EXERCISE:
LET YOUR WARRIOR AND MAN OF WISDOM HELP WITH YOUR DICK AND PUSSY SELVES.

- *Remember a time you felt deeply ashamed in relationship with another. Be your Warrior self observing your ashamed self, and give yourself feedback on that episode.*
- *Now be your Man of Wisdom self observing your shamed self, and give yourself feedback.*
- *Check in daily with your Warrior self and Man of Wisdom self. Each day have a dialogue between you and your Warrior and Man of Wisdom and write about your experiences. As you become familiar with being your Warrior and Man of Wisdom, try inhabiting those selves at work, at home, and with friends.*
- *After two weeks, share everything with someone you trust.*

SUMMARY

Let's end this chapter with a quick summary. The Warrior and Man of Wisdom are deep archetypal forms that speak to us from Shadow, growing as we grow, honored by us or ignored by us.

Healthy Warrior and Man of Wisdom are quintessential masculine channels for constructive Shadow to flow into our lives and every life we touch.

THE WARRIOR:

- **The Warrior is true to his principles at some cost to himself.** He discovers his Warrior nature in accepting and transcending the ordeals the world brings him.
- **Boys and men instinctively seek paths to the Warrior.** Warrior training and consciousness permeates sports, games, competition, bullying, fiction, art, and film—a universal archetype of humankind.
- **The Warrior cultivates radical acceptance of what is.** We all can see farther than we can be. Humility is looking with similar interest at both success and failure—present and on purpose *right now.*
- **The Warrior resolves dialectics into unity.** Part of development as a Warrior is to accept/acknowledge current power and capacities while knowing everything can be improved and that the journey is always the destination.
- **Shadow wisdom. Our spirits discern.** Brain/mind/spirit systems are crazy smart. If we listen for the best messages and embody them, our systems get crazy smarter. If we surrender to bullshit and violence, our systems become corrupted, our discernment is suspect, and our resolve diluted.
- **Warrior in relationship** takes the responsibilities to keep choosing health and love with each new relationship challenge, responsibility, and capacity—no excuses.
- **The Warrior** is moved to find himself again and again, to discover and rediscover his Warrior nature. He yearns for a sacred mission, and to feel courage on the edge of death. The Hero's journey captures him in some form and he accepts the call, returning home transformed through training, ordeal, and initiation, usually with gifts for the collective as he embodies a bridge between two worlds.

RELATIONSHIPS REFLECT PARADOXES IN THE WARRIOR PATH

- **We crave the autonomy** of standing firm in the face of adversity, completely self-responsible.
- **We grow in interdependent relationships** with others and the many different aspects of ourselves.
- **The Warrior wants freedom, but craves commitments to ideals,** individuals, and groups that transcend his personal desires and fears.
- **The Warrior craves strength, but must embrace his weaknesses.** The Warrior wants to feel masculine strong and good, while needing to love and unify with his feminine self, weak self, cowardly self, violent self, egocentric self, and all Shadow.

THE MAN OF WISDOM:

- **Is grateful for what is.**
- **Discerns love and truth from bs,** "Perceives those things which cannot be seen."
- **Harmonizes relationships** within himself (including his Shadow and inner feminine) and his relationships with his feminine partner, others, his mission, and the world.
- **Is confident in his principles and the Way.**
- **Is in tune with the deeper rhythms** of when to surrender and when to take a stand. As Musashi said, "There is timing in everything.... There is timing in the whole life of the Warrior, in his thriving and declining, in his harmony and discord."
- **Man of Wisdom perspectives broaden as he develops**, making him progressively more relativistic where intuitive knowledge of the highest good can instantaneously transform even his principles.
- **The Man of Wisdom has compassionate understanding,** with intuitive knowledge of everything. He's moved to channel

spiritually correct truths and directions into the world. After years of embodying the warrior, he feels less hunger to compete and strive, and more desire to share hard-earned perspectives.

A **Warrior** commits to love. A **Man of Wisdom** lives in love.

As the Warrior matures towards Man of Wisdom, actions and beliefs that don't consider the highest good for everyone feel partial and unsatisfying. Actions and beliefs that do seek the highest good feel yummier and yummier.

"The Way has existence." The Way leads the masculine into Warrior and then beyond into Man of Wisdom.

7

MANY PATHS TO WOMAN OF WISDOM

Woman is by nature a shaman.

—CHUKCHEE PROVERB

THE GODDESS WITH A THOUSAND FACES

Over the years I've seen women grow to Woman of Wisdom from a wild array of archetypes, often interconnected and changing over the life span—Handless Maiden, Ingénue, Sex Goddess, Wife, Divine Mother, Healer, Huntress/athlete, Seeker, and Artist, all progressing towards Woman of Wisdom. Any or all of these can light up a woman's life and guide her forward at different times, always in intricate inter-twined relationships with countless aspects of herself, her partner, her family/community, and nature.

A common thread? As a woman discovers herself drawn to a form, surrenders to its healthy aspects, and opens to constructive Shadow guidance, she inevitably progresses towards Woman of Wisdom.

IN THIS CHAPTER WE WILL:

- Discover how many archetypes lead towards Woman of Wisdom.
- Explore universal central forms.
- Ride the three waves of feminism.
- Dive into the agony and ecstasy of dealing with men throughout the ages.
- Detail how to create sexual interest in a guy, and how to motivate him to care for you.
- Talk about inclusive and exclusive boundaries—both necessary for happy healthy living and relating.
- Delineate similarities and differences between the Hero's Journey and the Heroine's Journey, and help you discover where you are right now.

Every woman's Shadow contains *all* the archetypes, whether she ever consciously experiences them or not. We have a collective Shadow—what Carl Jung called the "collective unconscious"—where all the forms arise in human cultures to speak to us through dreams, daydreams, relationships, yearnings, repulsions, attractions, and countless conversations and interactions in our social universe.[87] As a woman learns to listen to these voices, they become clearer and clearer. As a woman learns to discern constructive from destructive Shadow, and cultivate the courage to act on her discernments, she inevitably progresses towards Woman of Wisdom.

Woman of Wisdom is much like Man of Wisdom and this is not surprising. Healthy development with all people converges towards common principles and capacities. For instance, little girls' moral frameworks lean towards *care* for others, while little boys' moral frameworks lead towards *rights* for others. As they mature morally, the "others" group for both males and females expands beyond themselves to include family, tribe, nation, humanity as a whole, and life itself;

this is a predictable moral progression. The upper levels of both men's and women's moral development involves felt concern *for both rights and care for all.*[88]

So, like the Man of Wisdom, the Woman of Wisdom:

- **Is grateful for what is.**
- **Discerns love and truth from bs,** "Perceives those things which cannot be seen," As Miyamoto Musashi said about the Warrior.
- **Harmonizes relationships** within herself (including her Shadow and inner masculine), and her relationships with her masculine partner, others, her purpose, and the world.
- **Is confident in her principles and the Way.**
- **Is in tune with the deeper rhythms** of when to surrender and when to take a stand. She respects the masculine but doesn't fear the masculine, and so can access it in herself and enjoy it in men.
- **Woman of Wisdom perspectives broaden as she develops,** making her progressively more relativistic where intuitive knowledge of the highest good can instantaneously transform her opinions and actions.
- **The Woman of Wisdom has compassionate understanding,** with intuitive knowledge of everything. She's moved to channel spiritually correct truths and directions into the world.
- A **Woman of Wisdom** lives in love—the universe is saturated with love which informs everything.
- **As she matures towards Woman of Wisdom,** actions and beliefs that don't consider the highest good for everyone feel partial and unsatisfying. Actions and beliefs that do seek the highest good become more obvious and essential.

Even though the seeds of Woman of Wisdom exist in all women, we grow through stages and archetypes towards this integrated self. No one starts out at Woman of Wisdom the same way infants don't start out as fully grown adults. As we wake up to ourselves as children, adolescents, and grownups, certain paths shine with more luminance. Following these paths to best serve love leads to Woman of Wisdom.

Let's explore some of the most common archetypal forms that light up and inform women.

The Handless Maiden discovers herself not anchored in her power and autonomous authority, seemingly helpless in the face of the world's demands, judgments, and coercions. In spite of her felt helplessness, she can courageously embrace the Heroine's Journey when called by yearning, disaster, circumstance, or relationship. By looking inward, receiving guidance and help, and surrendering to her deepest soul and wise guides, she can eventually discover herself as the Woman of Wisdom, but the forces of powerlessness and helplessness will always periodically arise as destructive Shadow which demands attention and integration.

The Ingénue ("Puella" is the Jungian name) is the darling of the ball, the eternal radiant young goddess of purity and love. She can offer her innocence to the world—opening to love and closing to violence—allowing herself to gradually be transformed into Woman of Wisdom. Her development is learning to discern innocence from naiveté, spontaneity from narcissistic self-absorption, and devotional love from unhealthy dependence. Awakening to these forces arising out of Shadow guides her towards Woman of Wisdom.

The Sex Goddess can mobilize her power, channel sensual/erotic pleasure into the world—often becoming the Divine Lover to her chosen partner—progressing from serving her own hungers and cultural demands to leading the tribe in passionate embodiment—the Woman of Wisdom.

The Divine Mother dedicates herself to children thriving—seeing Spirit in each moment of every child's life. She supports, guides, and adjusts to her children's shifting needs, even as she supports, guides, and adjusts to her partner, her family, and her own growth. Her children thrive, individuate, and co-construct unique lives with her and others. As she adjusts and responds with love to the ever shifting demands, she transforms into Woman of Wisdom.

The Divine Wife surrenders to love with a trustable man. She shows him her suffering at his collapses and her delight at his integrity and presence. She empowers herself and is committed to empowering him. She commits to supporting her own and her man's fulfillment emotionally, sexually, and spiritually. She is often the gatekeeper to their social networks, organizing and discerning what serves everyone best. In partnership with her beloved she moves into Woman of Wisdom.

The Healer harnesses her native desires to care with nature's hunger for balance and harmony. She finds her healing modes and allows them to grow in her as she serves the world. As she practices her healing gifts her confidence expands, her connections with the other world stabilize, and she becomes the Woman of Wisdom.

Huntress/Athlete (Athena in Greek Mythology) harnesses physical strength and courage with penetrating insight. She is drawn to striving and conflict in service of competition (think Olympic athletes or Mixed Martial Arts world champion Rhonda Rousey), or protection (think Zena, Warrior Princess). The Goddess Athena was generally portrayed as a virgin—I assume partly because the complexity of combining Athena Warrior Feminine with Aphrodite (Goddess of love—devotional erotic surrender to the beloved) was too much of a reach for ancient Greeks. Current post-modern cultures include dialectics like Warrior domination and feminine devotional surrender. The kick-ass woman CEO can come home and be ravished by her strong and trustable masculine partner.

The Seeker knows intuitively that everything is Spirit, and dedicates herself to surrendering to Spirit, developing insight and power to share her spiritual light, and affiliating with like-minded others to form spiritual communities. As she progresses on her Way, she discovers herself as Woman of Wisdom.

The Artist sees beauty everywhere and is moved to generate beauty as a central calling. As she transforms inspirations into artifacts of words, objects (like food, clothes, paintings, or gardens), images, movements, relationships, experiences, or sounds, she moves towards Woman of Wisdom.

These are a sampling of core feminine archetypes. Women can channel any or all of them, with each woman a unique configuration of drives, yearnings, and experiences.

More than any other time in human history, our current era privileges individual desires and paths over conformity to external standards, even though external standards are always guiding and informing us. Western progressive cultures have normalized the idea that we grow through different identifications and passions and we are increasingly accepting of individual variations. Thinking developmentally helps us understand how expanding any level of expertise/discernment leads through progressive interpenetrating archetypes towards Woman of Wisdom.

EXERCISE
WHAT ARE MY CURRENT ARCHETYPES?

- *In your journal, write down the archetypes I've described in a column.*
- *After each one, give it a score from -5 (minus 5) where you just can't stand her, to +5 (plus 5) where you totally love her. Zero is you being completely indifferent, though we are rarely completely indifferent about anything.*
- *After you're done, look at your ratings, especially the highs and lows. The archetypes you especially like and especially hate reveal Shadow attractions and repulsions that will lead you to important parts of yourself.*
- *Make an effort to radically accept all your reactions and be curious about what they may tell you about your current self, life, and relationships. Write down any insights and observations.*
- *What you most liked, your highest scores, probably represent yearnings and personal strengths and should be loved and cultivated.*
- *What you most disliked probably reflect personal Shadow you have trouble accepting and loving. If you are repulsed or put off by the Divine Mother, Sex Goddess, Warrior/Athlete, or any other feminine*

form, you probably have Shadow resistance to them. What might your resistance be? Write about it in your journal.
- *Share everything you've written with someone you trust.*

THREE WAVES OF AMERICAN FEMINISM

American feminism has progressed through at least three waves in the last century.[89]

First-wave feminism fought for basic rights—to vote, to own property, to have the same constitutional rights as men.

Second-wave feminism fought for cultural equality and the deconstruction of male dominance which permeated the Shadow of America. I remember my women friends and lovers not shaving their legs and armpits, throwing away their bras, and being contemptuous of makeup. They resented any suggestion that their paths involved compromising comfort or health to attract men or comply with societal demands.

Third-wave feminism is less about male repression and much more about female development and empowerment in a complex world with incredible stresses and demands, and shifting needs through the life span. Third wave feminism tends to see men as welcome and necessary allies, and is accepting of whatever lifestyle choices women make about appearance, relationship, and employment.

A problem that has arisen with both second- and third-wave feminism is the idea that, since women *can* inhabit multiple archetypes, they *should* embody multiple archetypes. They *should* have it all—fulfilling job, hot love affair in a fulfilling relationship, children, friends, athletics, spiritual practices, etc. As you may have discovered for yourself, nobody can have it all, especially *have it all at the same time.* Talk about a recipe for self-doubt and self-criticism!

Most of us live many lives as we age from child, to adolescent, to adult, to family member, and so on. Each stage of our life has different passions, drives, and focus. The women I've known and worked with are happiest in rhythm with what is currently most important and meaningful in their current life, and so they constellate different combinations of central archetypes as they mature towards Woman of Wisdom. Trying to *have it all at the same time* often stresses women into cascades of self-doubt and burn out.

The modern world requires women to attend to their own ongoing equation of rest/activity, connection/solitude, affiliation/self-absorption, service-to-others/service-to-self. Wired as women are to relate and care, approached as they are to attend to children, friends, lovers, partners, and family—the responsibilities of love—it can be enormously difficult to keep their body/mind/spirits in self/culture/nature harmonized. This is where women's relational capacities are priceless, if they can mobilize them for self-nurturance, by finding women and men to help them serve themselves as well as others.

Humans are intensely relational and women are by nature more relational than men. One fMRI study evaluated how many areas of men's and women's brains lit up (had more blood flow) while actively relating with another person. Two areas lit up in men's brains and six areas lit up in women's brains. Under stress, women are genetically driven to seek affiliation with other people (sometimes called the "tend and befriend response"), while stress (particularly anger and rage) more often drives men to solitude.[90]

This means that a woman's archetypes need to harmonize with her relational networks (lover, family, friends, and community) or she risks living a conflicted life. Finding Men and Women of Wisdom as guides is priceless in this journey of becoming.

THE HANDLESS MAIDEN INTO THE WOMAN OF POWER

For example Kim, an athletic forty-four-year-old Chief Operations Officer at a successful law firm came to me in a major depression—daily thinking longingly about death. As we talked, it gradually emerged that her marriage was loveless, her husband Sam exploited her professional success, her critical and demanding grandmother intruded regularly into her life, and at work she never pushed for pay commensurate with her value to the firm.

I asked her, "Kim, have you ever heard of the handless maiden?" She shakes her head, "No. It sounds like some native American thing."

I agreed, "It is. I learned it from a psychologist named Anne Davin who lived with Pueblo Indians for years. The handless Maiden becomes the victim of the world's demands, not feeling her power, authority, or responsibilities."

Kim looks puzzled and a little irritated, "What do you mean responsibilities? I am the most conscientious person I know!"

I look into her left eye and channel my Man of Wisdom, "I respectfully disagree. You desert yourself daily. You put up with incredible neglect and exploitation from your husband and family. You feel no sense of responsibility for your own joy and fulfillment. You're a beautiful woman who calls herself unattractive. You're a passionate woman who tolerates your husband's neglect and disinterest. You have abandoned Kim and live a double standard of one set of rights and care for everyone else, and a diminished set of rights and care for yourself."

Kim suddenly looks thoughtful, "You're right, but I get so confused when I think of disappointing any of them."

I ask her, "Can you imagine leaving Sam, telling your grandmother 'No!' when she makes outrageous demands, or wearing a pretty dress to a conference and having a hot affair with some cool guy you meet there?"

She laughs at this, her beautiful smile radiant. I press on, "See how imagining this makes you happy? She nods and I continue, "So what do you think your deepest Self, your constructive Shadow is telling you right now?"

Kim gets it, "That I want all that!" which makes me laugh and respond, "Yes! Finally you understand your work. It's not to kill yourself. It's to create what I just described—to transform from the Handless Maiden into the Woman of Power, Woman of Wisdom."

CULTURE MATTERS

Cultures of family, communities, and schools either support or inhibit a woman's chosen archetypes. For instance:

Kim's family culture had conditioned her into becoming the Handless Maiden—feeling responsible to say, "Yes," to any other family member's demands. Her husband had capitalized on this to use her shamelessly. It was a joy for me to see Kim in subsequent months kick Sam out of her house, say, "No," consistently to her family's unreasonable demands (especially to her tyrannical grandmother), and to start a hot love affair with an appreciative lover. The last time we talked she was happy and grateful to be alive.

Through most of history, Women have had to mask or turn away from their emotional, intellectual, sexual, and relational powers in patriarchal families or communities that suppress women. If they wanted to exert influence or provide leadership, their offerings often had to placate or manipulate dominant males rather than directly influence the group—otherwise they risked vicious reprisals and rejections. For instance, my maternal grandmother was fired from her college teaching job for including sex education in her curriculum.

MEN HAVE DOMINATED WOMEN AND CULTURE FOR MOST OF THE LAST TEN THOUSAND YEARS

Anthropologists believe that the hunter-gatherer groups which constituted most of human history generally had more or less equal power and authority between men and women. We find this in a few hunter-gatherers who exist today—equal numbers of female and male deities, women having the same relational choices as men, and women intertwined in the power dynamics of the tribe.

As the success of tribes led to horticulture and then agriculture, this all changed. Starting around ten thousand years ago, agriculture created power hierarchies, concentrated wealth, and the widespread practice of slavery for the backbreaking work of farming and building.

In agricultural societies, men dominate, and women—to varying degrees—become property. We see it today in the stark contrasts between modern and traditional groups in countries like India and China. In the cities, where modernity prevails, women (especially educated women) have rights and power. In the rural countrysides, women are often forced into marriages, denied education, and physically and sexually abused—all with cultural acceptance.

Let's not get too self-satisfied in the West. The first U.S. conviction for marital rape was in *1983*! Until then, the holdover of women-as-property gave American men the legal right to rape their wives.

MEN ARE NECESSARY

Attracting men, relating with men, and understanding men are central struggles in most women's lives. All women have their own form of beauty, of feminine light. Feminine radiance is the light that shines from a feminine person and nourishes the masculine like sunlight nourishes the forest. Understanding her feminine light and consciously using it in service of love is central to most feminine archetypes.

The feminine hunger for trustable masculine attention and partnership is matched by the masculine hunger for feminine light and relationship. These are based in ancient drives that we share with all mammals.

Most guys are programmed to protect women and be drawn to feminine light. Women want masculine attention, but also can fear it and be injured by it. Author and teacher Alison Armstrong suggests that much feminine suffering with men arises from confusion about what kinds of attention women want, when they want it, and *from whom* they want it.[91]

I especially like her ideas about what draws sexual attention and what moves men to be "charmed and enchanted."

SEXUAL ATTENTION

If you crave sexual attention—to incite a man to *want sex right now*—she maintains that the four instigators are:

- Generating sexual energy (by thinking about and feeling your sexuality).

- Indulging any or all of your senses in the pleasures of touch, taste, sound, color, art, smell, and all things sensual.
- Enjoying and displaying your shapely body (*every* feminine curve and shape has enthusiastic male admirers).
- Have shiny hair—a sign of fertility, since less than 12 percent body fat compromises fertility and dulls hair.

▶ **Multi-gender sidebar:** *The LGBTIQ community has educated the modern and post-modern world to the reality of humans having multiple gender choices. I have been a fierce supporter of gender rights all my life, and am delighted that the twenty-first century seems to be normalizing multiple genders. I've also found variations in masculine and feminine dynamics between and within every gender choice. It would require an entire book to do justice to even the most frequent ones, and so I'm limiting myself generally to heterosexual relationships in this book.*

That being said, there are consistent principles of masculine/feminine aspects/essence in development and erotic polarity that generally apply to most gender choices, so I find it useful to have general understanding while always being sensitive to variations in individuals and relationships.

CHARMED AND ENCHANTED

If you want a guy to be charmed and enchanted—to crave relationship with you and want to take care of you—she suggests:

- Be self-confident.
- Be authentic.
- Share your passion, whatever you're passionate about.
- Be receptive to his care and appreciative of his noble qualities.

What I like about Alison's teaching is how she encourages every woman to have confidence in her worth and radiance—increasingly conscious of what energies she's radiating at any given moment. These are keys to living the life you want and co-creating the kind of love you want with your chosen man.

This fits nicely into the masculine/feminine dynamics of:

- Masculine integrity eliciting feminine light.
- Masculine collapse creating feminine suffering.
- Feminine radiance nourishing masculine purpose.
- Feminine care moderating masculine drive for dominance.

As David Deida maintains in numerous books and teachings, we all have both masculine and feminine aspects, but our deepest sexual essence is usually more masculine or more feminine, and the archetypes that draw us will resonate with our unique blend of masculine/feminine aspects/essence.

STAGE DEVELOPMENT

We develop through stages. Child, to adolescent, to young woman, to partnered woman, to professional woman, to mother, etc. Women don't have to embody any one of these—a woman can decide to never be a mother for instance—but every woman will grow through stages, and these stages generally each involve developing relationships with men.

Women find that at each stage of their development they need to reevaluate:

- Both wanting and fearing masculine attention.
- Wanting and being offended by male sexual desire.
- Their reactions and principles regarding anger, shame, and fear in themselves and men.
- Competition with other women and with men.

INCLUSIVE AND EXCLUSIVE BOUNDARIES

Each stage requires boundaries, both inclusive and exclusive, for me and others. Inclusive boundaries are qualities and actions you insist on having—like respect, understanding, and a growth orientation. Exclusive boundaries are qualities and actions you refuse to tolerate—like betrayal, abuse, and moral blindness.[92]

The inclusive boundaries Kim and I worked toward were:

- Include your "No!" Never automatically say, "Yes," to a yucky feeling. Always say, "I'll get back to you" when you feel the least bit of resistance to "Yes."
- Only stay with a partner your heart says is the right one.
- When your heart doubts, engage your partner in dialogue about your doubts. If the dialogue doesn't turn into more love, go to a therapist.
- If your work with a partner in therapy doesn't create more love, separate.
- Create better, more mature love in your life.
- Regard your needs and desires as equally important to others' needs and desires.

Exclusive boundaries—what you insist on not allowing—are equally important. Kim eventually learned to set exclusive boundaries for Sam (eventually making him an ex-husband), and her family.

To her Grandmother and other family members, "No, you cannot come over without calling!"

To Sam, "If you don't sign the papers my lawyer will file a motion with the judge."

As Kim set mature and powerful inclusive and exclusive boundaries, she felt more solid and worthwhile, and this is generally true for a woman caught up in the Handless Maiden archetype who faces her condition and courageously reaches for growth.

WHAT IS MY CURRENT HEROINE'S JOURNEY?

Answer these questions in your journal.

- *What stages of life am I most expressing at this time? Am I in adolescence, young womanhood, the Woman Warrior, the Sex Goddess, the lover, the Bride, the Young Mother, the Brilliant Woman Creator, the Feminine Leader, the Divine Mother, the Healer, the Woman of Wisdom? What most draws my attention, excites my interest, or demands my obligation? I am probably some combination of these and other archetypal forms.*
- *How do I move through this stage of my life being true to myself and my responsibilities?*
- *How do I tell what inclusive and exclusive boundaries to set for me, partner, children, friends, or anyone?*
- *What are the three most important principles that guide me?*
- *Who are my best guides? What input from them do I welcome and embody, and what input do I resist and refuse?*

Share all that you've written with someone you trust. Write about your conversation in your journal.

Answering these questions guides you to your current station on your Heroine's Journey.

THE HEROINE'S JOURNEY

I once had a series of sessions with Mandy, a 50-year-old mother, and her 27-year-old-daughter, Judy. They loved one another deeply, but regularly fell into bitter conflicts, with each feeling misunderstood and unsupported. I asked them what they wanted from the other.

Mandy replied, "I want Judy to not get so critical and unaccepting."

Judy said, "I want my Mom to understand me and stop interrupting and controlling me."

I step in, "So Judy, you want your mother to understand and listen to you better, and Mandy, you want your daughter to not be so critical and correcting." They both agreed.

Later in the session, discussing Judy feeling offended that Mandy wouldn't drop everything and take her to an appointment in LA, both got hurt and shut down. I challenge them a little, "This is not a fun conversation, right?" Both agree. "I'd like you to make this conversation more enjoyable."

At first, dead silence, followed by the same tired argument.

Interrupting, I point out, "Right now you are each in your separated wounded feminine, wanting the other to help you out. Judy, you feel interrupted and misunderstood, and Mandy, you feel criticized and corrected. You want the understanding and acceptance we were talking about earlier."

Mandy protests, "I just want what's fair!"

I focus on her distress and desire for deeper love with her daughter. I respond, "The way you each are asking for it is by amplifying your emotional pain and regressing to children who believe that if you feel bad enough, Mom will step in and take care of it."

I go on, "You see how you're relaxing as I speak." They nod. "I'm providing masculine direction right now, because both of you are too hurt to take the initiative—you're both in your wounded feminine." I turned to Mandy, "In these cases it's the mom's job, *if she can,* to activate her Woman of Wisdom and lead back to love. You can do this by focusing on understanding and validating what Judy's trying to say."

Mandy, a veteran of both psychotherapy and yoga, had good self-reflection skills. She turned to her daughter and, in a loving tone, said, "I get it you felt hurt I wouldn't take the day off to drive you to LA. I can see how you'd feel unimportant at that."

Judy sighed and smiled a tiny smile, "This feels better."

I complimented both of them for the shift (the feminine often grows best in the presence of loving praise). "Mandy, you just activated your

Woman of Wisdom and let *her* guide you with Judy. And Judy, you felt your mom's warmth and integrity and surrendered to trusting her. That's a feminine superpower—devotional love."

Here are two women, each on her own Heroine's Journey, each at a nexus point of having to reconcile mother and daughter, agency and communion, and receiving aid from me in deepening their powers to understand, accept, and love.

Since Joseph Campbell published *The Hero with a Thousand Faces*, women have been asserting that the Heroine's Journey is different. Yes, the Heroine's Journey tracks many of the same stages as the Hero's Journey—there is a call, a threshold, a threshold guardian, magical aid, a road of trials, an apotheosis, and the transformation into becoming a bridge between two worlds—but women often encounter different trials and discover different powers than men.

In 1990, Maureen Murdock published *The Heroine's Journey*. A student of Campbell, Murdock expressed second-wave feminist frustration with his apparent relegation of the feminine to the enduring archetypes of nurturance, receptivity, and unity with nature. As a therapist, she knew firsthand about women's struggles against their own demons and cultural restrictions to grow and flourish. It seemed to her that, to have agency in the world, women were being forced to turn their backs on their feminine hearts and activate their inner masculine.

Her *Heroine's Journey* postulated the need for a woman to alienate herself from the mother to access patriarchal power. Identifying with the masculine, the road of trials leads to both agency—success and recognition—but also the awakening to the spiritual aridity of disconnection from the Goddess. In then pursuing the Goddess, women heal the original mother/daughter split, integrate masculine and feminine in climatic apotheosis, and finally individuate, essentially becoming Woman of Wisdom.[93]

In the last twenty years, third-wave feminism has built on the foundations of equality, feminine empowerment, and equal opportunity to understand the Heroine's Journey as less driven by reaction to patriarchy, and more driven by the native feminine voices that speak out through all women. This post-modern approach is broadly inclusive of the healthy manifestations of all feminine roles, all feminine yearnings, and draws from science, the wisdom traditions, nature mysticism, the fashion industry, the arts, the alternative health industry, and Shamanism. There is less about masculine oppression and more about communal development.

I especially like the approach of therapist, teacher, and mystic, Ann Davin, in her program, *The Heroine's Journey*. She conceptualizes the Heroine's Journey as progressing through five phases:

- **Phase 1—Everyday Woman**: Beginning as the Handless Maiden, out of touch with her agency and hungering for self-care, self-awareness, and self-possession, a woman takes responsibility for what she experiences and does and recognizes herself as a reflection of the divine.
- **Phase 2—Rupture:** Her Journey takes her into chaos through activating events where she is challenged to surrender to her becoming. She enters the Belly of The Whale, the Well of the World, and grieves her losses and everyone's losses. Fear and doubt, when faced, transform into spiritual courage and confidence. Through these trials she dies and is reborn into her native beauty and lively energy.
- **Phase 3—Transparency:** Rigorous self-observation expands her inner Witness, and she faces the Shadow aspects of her strengths and weaknesses, triumphs and heartbreaks, cultivating radical acceptance of all her inner selves, including the Handless Maiden. Chaos intrudes, feelings of victimization and powerlessness overwhelm and need to be faced by her with the help of guides/friends/community, which leads her to...
- **Phase 4—Receiving:** She says "Yes!" to love, sensuality, contact, community, and the subtle realms of dreams, visions, and Spirit in all her forms. Alison Armstrong says receptivity is the sine qua

non, the deal breaker or deal maker, in a woman's relationship with a man—and I think with nature and the world also. Receive love, receive guidance, receive the pleasures of life, receive your man's finest qualities, and you advance on the Heroine's Journey. John Gottman, the world's preeminent couples' researcher, found that receiving positive influence to be one of the main characteristics of the "masters" of relationships, and a major deficit of the "disasters" of relationships.[94]

- **Phase 5—Action:** Finding deep purpose, she expresses herself through service that restores, energizes, and transforms her. She revisits old wounds, finding power in the polarities between connection and loss, love and pain, acceptance and rejection. Co-dependency becomes interdependency, and her Woman of Wisdom self becomes mostly available when needed.[95]

EXERCISE
WHERE ARE *YOU* ON YOUR CURRENT HEROINE'S JOURNEY?

In your journal, answer the following questions:

- *What current life activity feels the most important and meaningful to me? Is it my spiritual seeking, parenting, service, self-maintenance, lover relationship, friends, community, art? Is it some combination of these?*
- *What am I currently doing to support my most important and meaningful life activities?*
- *What are my dreams and yearnings? Make a list that includes even your wildest fantasies.*
- *What am I currently doing to embody my dreams and yearnings?*
- *What am I currently doing to sabotage my dreams and yearnings? This could be over-commitment, fatigue, fear, self-doubt, or reluctance to ask for support and help.*

- *How does all of the above fit into my Heroine's Journey? What is my call, my magical aids (or potential magical aids), the threshold and threshold guardians? What obstacles and opponents in myself and the world am I currently struggling with? What different aspects of me need more acceptance, empowerment, and support? Who are the teachers and guides that most light me up right now? What is the emerging Woman of Wisdom in me like—how does she feel and how do I access her?*
- *Share everything you've written with someone you love,*

As we discover ourselves, as our archetypes emerge from Shadow into the light, we can consciously shape them as we wish. Growth is always in keeping with our deeper purpose, life missions, and loving relationships. Disease is disconnection, self-betrayal, turning away from healthy intimacy and self-knowledge.

What archetypes turn you on or repel you? Both attraction and repulsion reveal your basic nature and your current address on the epic journey of your life. Books, movies, games, sports, activities, friends, family members, lovers, fetishes, obsessions, dreams (especially repetitive dreams), attributions, blessings, condemnations, inspirations, and characters/themes/relationships/missions can all inform your mythic constellation, your current position on the Heroine's Journey.

As you can both observe and intuit, all paths with a heart lead you into your Heroine's journey towards Woman of Wisdom.

8

SEXUAL SHADOW

*To grow through the three stages of intimacy we must come
to terms with our deepest desires and give and receive our
sexual, emotional, and spiritual gifts. We may find that we
are hiding some of our real desires, thinking they are unfair
or taboo. Before we can learn to give and receive our deepest
gifts, whether gently or wildly, we must understand why
we often confine our loving, and how we can liberate the
mysterious force of love that lies yearning in our hearts.*

—DAVID DEIDA, FROM *INTIMATE COMMUNION*

SEX SHAME

Are you 100 percent accepting of everything you've ever thought
or experienced sexually?

Are you 100 percent sexually fulfilled?

Have you *never* been offended at (or embarrassingly absorbed by) a
sexual image or act?

Have you *never* felt guilty or ashamed of something sexual?

I didn't think so.

SEX BLISS

On the other hand, what's the best time you ever had in your life? What's the most intense pleasure you've ever felt in intimate physical interconnection with another person?

I thought so!

IN THIS CHAPTER WE WILL:

- Learn the difference between constructive and destructive sex Shadow.
- Make peace with sexual drives.
- Debunk the myth of long-term happy promiscuity.
- Explore masculine and feminine aspects and essence.
- See how male and female sex drives are equally powerful, but *different.*
- Learn what it takes to have enduring sexual fulfillment—see the *necessity* of conscious tantric intimacy.
- Identify blocks to mutual erotic fulfillment and start deconstructing them.
- Further appreciate shame dynamics.
- Identify destructive sexual Shadow—then learn how to alchemically transmute it to constructive sexual Shadow.
- Generate your lust map and your partner's lust map, and then bring them together.
- Identify sexual pathology and wounding and see where healing needs to take place.
- Have fun with sexual fantasies, because what better way to end a sexual Shadow chapter?

Here we go....

CONSTRUCTIVE/DESTRUCTIVE SEX SHADOW

Like all of us, you have sex Shadow, constructive and destructive. As usual, the destructive sex Shadow gets more press, but constructive sex Shadow is pure gold.

Let's go a little deeper.

SEX AND VIOLENCE

Sex Shadow and violence Shadow fascinate everyone one way or another—usually attraction, disgust, excitement, or shame, but *never* complete indifference. Interestingly, sex and violence are often connected in people's minds, as if the level of forbiddenness somehow relates them. "Sex and violence," "Sex and violence," Sex and violence"...how many times have you heard them paired?

But why do sex and violence become connected, really? Think about it, sex and violence together don't make sense. Sex is usually our most cooperative, creative, and loving playground. Sex is at the core of our most intimate, vulnerable, and passionate moments in relationship. Violence—destructive/non-cooperative/exploitative—causes most of the world's worst problems (much more on this in Chapter 12). And yet somehow they end up paired together.

Freud was quite taken with sex and violence, seeing destruction/death as Thanatos, our cumulative destructive drives, and sex/eroticism as Eros, our cumulative erotic/creative/forbidden/libidinous drives. He organized his central ideas of superego, libido, and repression around our fascination and horror with sex and violence.[96]

▶ **Jung sidebar:** *Jung was much more sanguine about sexuality, but then again, Jung had sex with patients—a practice that will get you thrown in jail in twenty-first century America.*

It makes sense that Freud connected sex and violence, I guess, given the psychoanalytic contexts from which he generated his theories. His Victorian patients were ashamed and horrified by various sex and violence imagery, fantasies, and experiences. The sex drives and the violence drives are some of the most socially volatile human instincts. Arguably, unregulated sex and violence can destroy any social fabric—which explains the omnipresence of sex and violence taboos.

Rules and taboos are necessary foundations of human culture. To successfully survive, tribes needed to regulate aggressive and sexual impulses somehow. Our genes mandate moral standards where Shadow inhibitions *internally constrain destructive thoughts and impulses.* But *moral standards can keep growing.* In our current post-modern society, we grow towards more individualistic, inclusive, and relativistic moral standards, which is especially important with sexuality since we are each a unique sexual being.[97]

Understanding and accepting our *own unique sexual mosaic* is a necessary step in *growing and developing* our sexuality and sexual standards. Much of our sexuality is shrouded in Shadow, and bringing compassionate light to bear can be revealing and exciting!

We'll deal with violence Shadow much more in Chapter 12. In this chapter we focus on sex.

LET'S MAKE PEACE WITH OUR DRIVES

To be happy, we have to make peace with our drives. Suppression (*consciously* pushing an idea/impulse/image away) and repression (*automatically* denying and resisting ideas/impulses/images) amplify shame and distort beliefs. Suppression and repression usually make things worse in the long run.

What is suppression? Try not to think of your first passionate kiss for the next ten seconds..............How did you do? Most people think *more* about a charged emotional image/event when they try to not think about it.

Suppression tends to amplify the object of attention and makes us less comfortable and less self-accepting. Awareness, acceptance, and compassionate understanding—opposites of suppression—make everything better.

What is repression? If we turn away enough from feelings, thoughts, memories, or desires, we eventually start automatically avoiding them—they become repressed, which is essentially a form of dissociation where we have conditioned ourselves to not be aware of our own Shadow images, feelings, and stories arising.

Generally, the Western Christian traditions have been more anti-sexual than pro-sexual, which is often true for fundamentalism. Based in agrarian cultures with patriarchal gods and oppression of women, fundamentalism of all sorts historically pathologizes the feminine and suppresses sexuality. Fundamentalism demands blind conformity to social standards, and conformity is anchored in rules that demand we subjugate our individual desires and drives to culture's demands.

Throughout my lifetime America has been gradually becoming more pro-sexual, and I have been an enthusiastic advocate of healthy sexual expression since my teen years (though God knows I've had an ocean of my own sexual material to work through!).

Unfortunately, America is not particularly *pro-sexual-development*. Parents rarely have a coherent strategy to support their children's sexual development, and the whole concept of age appropriate sexual play at almost any age is generally a forbidden topic.

For instance, as Judith Levine reports in *Harmful to Minors*, in Fundamentalist Christian doctrine (protected by law in many states) families should be in charge of sex education for their children, and institutions like schools should never mention sex, much less educate and *encourage* healthy sexuality. Yet studies show that in 70 percent of fundamentalist homes, there *is never* any meaningful conversation about sex, leaving the children in ignorance or at the mercy of whatever their friends, culture, or pornography (omnipresent and easily available on the internet) reveals to them.[98]

So, sexual Shadow has deep roots and multiple minefields to trap the unwary. Let's explore some scientific truths, and I'll suggest ideas and exercises to help us grow our sexual Shadow.

THE MYTH OF HAPPY PROMISCUITY

In the sixties and seventies it was accepted wisdom in the groups I hung out with that you could not be sexually fulfilled over time with just one partner. That led me on a fruitless (often hilarious) quest to try to find the best polyamory solution to create sexual fulfillment.

Sexual fulfillment was my primary goal, though I wasn't fully conscious of it at the time—my fruitless yearning for plenty of partners was constructive Shadow straining to inform me that I wanted sexual fulfillment with *one special partner*. Over years of experimentation and struggles (which generated some great stories but not a whole lot of satisfaction), I finally discovered that for me and most others, sexual fulfillment *requires* monogamy.

What?!

I can especially hear some of my polyamory millennial friends (not to mention the 25 percent to 45 percent of married people who have had or will have secret affairs[99]) gasping in disbelief.

Yes, even though we are genetically wired to lust after attractive others, fall in romantic infatuation with certain people, and intimately bond with longer term partners *all at once*,[100] it doesn't work in our current society to do this with multiple partners.

In barely verbal hunter-gatherer groups a million years ago, where the average life expectancy was around thirty, passing on genes and maximizing your children's resources with combining pair-bonding with secret liaisons and opportunistic sex made genetic sense.

In agrarian societies over the last ten-thousand years where men dominated and women were property, men stockpiling women and having opportunistic sex, and women latching onto the most successful man they could attract made genetic sense.

Increasingly over the last thirty years, neurobiologists, evolutionary psychologists, and biologists keep finding that genetic mandates have more impact than we know.

Examples?

A brilliant but controversial evolutionary biologist named Robert Trivers speculated that parents would unconsciously favor having boy or girl children depending on their social prospects—especially wealth or poverty. Trivers is an academic iconoclast—bi-polar, an open sexual enthusiast, and contemptuous of his critics, whom he keeps disproving.[101]

Trivers' work has borne up under scrutiny. Studies show that poor families tend to produce more daughters and rich families more sons, probably because it favors poor families to have their daughters potentially chosen by wealthier men, and favors rich families to maintain status with male offspring. Even further, parents from more male dominated professions like engineers and scientists tend to have more sons, while more female dominated professions like teachers and nurses tend to have more daughters.[102]

What is the mechanism of action in these situations? Harsh conditions during pregnancy favor more girls, since girl fetuses are somewhat hardier than boy fetuses. Beyond that our current explanations are just speculation. Selective miscarriage in response to different environments is the leading candidate, but we really don't yet know.

WHERE DOES MONOGAMY FIT INTO ALL THIS?

In modern society with equal financial/professional/sexual/parental power for men and women, life expectancies of 70 or more, and the potential for deepening consciousness and intimacy over a long lifetime, joyful monogamy produces the most health, growth, and success for individuals and the most happy/healthy children.

Lust is the drive that sends our attention and desire to sexy others—impersonal and powerful.

Romantic infatuation makes monogamy relatively easy. We are obsessed and intoxicated with a special other, want sex frequently with them, and are hungry to know and be known, to claim and be claimed. Sexy neuromodulators testosterone, dopamine, and estrogen are up, encouraging sex. Bonding neurotransmitters oxytocin and vasopressin are up, encouraging trust. Serotonin is down, encouraging us to be obsessed with our lover. Unfortunately, we are programmed to pass into intimate bonding after a genetically limited six-month to two-year romantic infatuation joyride, and monogamy becomes more problematic.

When we are in the **intimate bonding** stage of a relationship, sex and romance become less urgent and easy. The excitement/sexy neurotransmitters dopamine and testosterone are down, serotonin is up helping us be less obsessed with our partner, but the bonding/attachment neurotransmitters oxytocin and vasopressin continue to influence lovers to feel more securely connected while less obsessively "In love."[103]

Even though we feel less sexually urgent, intimate bonding is *important*—as in life-partner important. Our Shadow identifies with—*claims*—our partner. Even in marriages with high conflict or very little sex, if one partner discovers the other has cheated, his or her nervous system freaks out into jealousy, depression, obsession, and outrage.

DRIVES NEVER STOP DRIVING

The lust and romantic infatuation drives crave the heat of desire and infatuation, so even in satisfying intimate bonding we can find ourselves longing for the sweet rushes of lust and romance. These are the forces that cause us to seek loopholes in our monogamy commitments—what I call, "The Theory of Loopholes."

We can amplify lust and romance in intimate bonding, but it usually requires two people putting in some effort. For example, since novelty, risk, and excitement tend to raise dopamine (and correspondingly testosterone) levels, people often get sexual boosts from novel experiences they share with their intimate partner. These can range from roller coasters, to hotel rooms, to vacations, to having your wife's old college roommate join you in bed.

The problem with bringing other sexual partners into an intimate relationship is that it messes with our evolutionary programming in potentially disastrous ways. Once you start having sex with someone, you and he or she risk moving into romantic infatuation where one or both of you *specifically* takes on romantic luminance to the other. Remember, we can lust for one person, be "in love" with another, and be intimately bonded with a third—they are three distinct (though interrelated) *drives,* just as mate protection when someone seems to be claiming your partner is a *drive.* It might be OK and fun with you and your wife to have a three-way with her friend (I've actually found it rare when all three people have a great time in a three-way), but your wife will go crazy if you and her friend fall in love. Similarly, if your wife has brief fling at a conference, it might be a trivial sexual adventure to her, but it's likely to drive you crazy that she cheated on you.

Sex experts from Dan Savage to Esther Perel often reprise the familiar refrain of, "If couples can just talk about extra-marital sex like rational adults, almost anything is possible." This reminds me of a horrible night I spent in the summer of 1975 when Becky and I were trying to have a non-exclusive relationship (after heroic efforts to the contrary, we eventually decided we were monogamous). My friend Noel had approached me to see if I would mind if he asked Becky out, and twenty-four-year-old-stupid-Keith foolishly answered, "Why not? We're all sexually liberated adults. We're not bound by the conventions of the past. It's up to her." I remember feeling particularly free saying this to Noel, not knowing what was to come.

Like a slow-motion train wreck, events gradually unfolded over the next week. Noel asked Becky out. Becky talked with me about it and I gave her the same new-age-non-exclusive rap. The night arrived and they went out. And here I was, driving my Rambler Ambassador alone through the summer night, smelling orange blossoms on the night air, and trying unsuccessfully to not think of them up at Noel's house at the top of San Marcos Pass, making love on the bed he had suspended beneath a skylight that opened the room to the moon and stars.

As I kept trying to manage the shocking waves of grief, rage, and sexual frustration that washed over me, I told myself, "Keith, remember this. Some things you can't negotiate." It wasn't until decades later that anthropology and neurobiology revealed the genetic roots of my suffering that night.

> **Behaviorism sidebar:** *At that time I was finishing my MA in Counseling Psychology at University of California at Santa Barbara. My program was an amalgam of Humanistic Psychology and Behavior Therapy. That night I tried to ease my jealous suffering with flooding or prolonged exposure—a behavioral technique where you pile on the distressing images until they lose their power. Not surprisingly (and validated by subsequent trauma research) flooding myself with images of them having sex just made everything nightmarishly worse.*

Suffice to say, Becky and I had a long talk and she stopped dating Noel. Noel, in just that one night, fell for Becky—full-on romantic infatuation (I can't blame him, she's great)—and essentially stalked her the next several months. He eventually had enough presence to stay away and get over it.

I—stubborn and arrogant young man that I was—needed to get my emotional ass kicked a few more times before I realized that, once the romantic infatuation/intimate bonding circuits are activated, multiple partners aren't going to work. Becky and I finally got it and have been happily monogamous ever since.

Sex, romance, and mate protection are drives that can awaken irresistible evolutionary forces. The statistics tell the story. A million women and four-hundred-thousand men report being stalked every year in

America, mostly involving erotic attachments (and that's just the tip of the iceberg since people often don't report stalking). Untold depression and suicide comes from romantic betrayal and relationship breakups. Over 25 percent of murders in this country involve lovers, spouses, and love triangles, the darkest reflection of the power of sexual bonding.[104] We can play pretend games and gamble with our biochemistry—sometimes successfully as in the three-way that actually doesn't leave anybody feeling distressed, ripped off, or deserted—but for the most part when you play with sexual fire, people get burned.

You can't reason your nervous system out of millions of years of evolutionary conditioning. Save such miracles for masturbation fantasies—usually harmless sources of sexual/romantic variety. In the real world, partners can harmonize, adjust, and support each other to keep sex growing and romance alive, but you can't reverse or ignore biological drives just because it sounds like it might be fun. Someone will inevitably get hurt.

On the other hand, intimate bonding where partners take care of the marital love affair can create the deepest, most dynamic intimacy that's every existed—emotional, spiritual, sexual, and familial attunements that enhance intimacy and accelerate development. This is the promise of modern monogamy.[105]

Even though men and women are driven by lust, romantic infatuation, and intimate bonding drives, and even though we have equal power in modern relationships, it doesn't mean that men and women are wired exactly the same sexually or relationally. One of my favorite examples of this involves two famous studies by Clark and Hatfield.

THE CLARK AND HATFIELD EXPERIMENTS

In 1989, Russell Clark and Elaine Hatfield published a paper with the results of two studies that had been conducted in 1978 and 1982.[106] In these studies, nine moderately attractive twenty-two-year-old men and women circulated around a college and approached forty-eight men and forty-eight women (of opposite sex) with some version of, "I've noticed you around campus, you seem like a nice and attractive person, and I want to introduce myself." After the introduction, they asked the other the following questions:

- "Would you go out with me tonight?"
- "Will you come over to my apartment?"
- "Will you have sex with me?"

Of the men approached by women, 50 percent agreed to the date, 69 percent agreed to come over to the apartment, and a staggering 72 percent agreed to sex.

Of the women approached by men, 50 percent agreed to the date, 3 percent agreed to come over to the apartment, and zero percent agreed to sex.

In 2011, Terri Conley replicated this study *in fantasy*. She asked men and women if they'd have casual sex if the person was especially good looking, was famous, or was good in bed. In this study the men answered about the same as with Clark and Hatfield, but the women's answers were dramatically different. Of the women, 24 percent *imagined* they'd say "yes" to sex if the man was good looking and 40 percent *imagined* they'd say "yes" if the guy was good in bed.[107]

Fantasy allows us to consider a situation without personal projection or fear. These 24 percent yes-to-good-looking and 40 percent yes-to-good-in-bed women could move into what I call "Romance Novel" mode, romantic fantasy where women don't feel threatened by a concrete in-your-face man's desire. *In real life,* women are instinctively much more cautious about casual sex with strangers, and there's evolutionary neuro-biological reasons for this.

Neuroimaging studies by Helen Fisher have verified that women activate more social evaluation circuits with lovers and potential lovers than men do—almost certainly because genetically there is more on the line for a woman when it comes to sex. Pregnancy and childbirth are dangerous. Raising a child is energy-consuming and exhausting.

Our ancient women ancestors who did more social evaluation of sex partners had an evolutionary advantage. On the other hand, men who impregnated the most women (leaving as many progeny as possible) had an evolutionary advantage, and so opportunistically indulging desire served men much better than expanded social evaluation.[108]

We instantaneously evaluate people we meet in multiple ways and then project a personality onto that person, usually fairly accurate, but never perfectly so. Personal projection is what we immediately attribute to a real person in front of us. In the Clark/Hatfield study for instance, the women perceived the men asking-for-a-date/come-over-tonight/have-sex-now as *less* intelligent, socially/sexually adept, and *less* attractive than the men who were asked by women evaluated the women askers (on 1–10 scales).

The men asked by women perceived the women as being *more* intelligent, socially/sexually adept, and more attractive (on the same 1–10 scales). In Conley's *fantasy* experiment, the women created fantasy men who were much more intelligent, socially/sexually adept, and more attractive, which expanded the women's imagined willingness for casual sex from zero to up to 40 percent. In related experiments, women have found intelligent men to be more attractive for sexual liaisons than men they don't find particularly intelligent.

Since Clark and Hatfield controlled for intelligence, social skills, and attractiveness, the lower scores for men were at least partially results of *projections* by the women they were approaching. In the cultural contexts of 1978 and 1982 campus life (which I participated in and remember vividly), these kinds of overtures were considered more sexy from women to men, and more icky from men to women.

Also, in fantasy the women were not as afraid of an overture as the women approached by real men. Men are more dangerous to women than women are to men in many ways. Women are actually genetically more predisposed to fear men's anger than men to fear women's—all this doubtless due to men's testosterone-driven greater height, size, strength, and aggressiveness. The implication of Conley's fantasy experiment is that when you reduce fear of harm, young women get much more interested in casual sex, and this is supported by the studies showing most (especially young) women accepting of casual sex, and up to 40 percent of single women engaging in casual sex.

You'll probably notice that you have opinions and judgments about everyone in the above experiments. How would *you* feel if an attractive other asked you on a date, to come over tonight, or to have sex right now? Titillated? More likely if you're a guy. Put off? More likely if you're a woman. Surprised by your answer? You've just unveiled a little bit of your sexual Shadow.

MALE AND FEMALE SEXUALITY: EQUALLY STRONG BUT DIFFERENT

Even though guys think about sex much more than women, anthropologist Helen Fisher believes the male and female sex drives are equally strong, just *different.*

Guys are more visual sexually, have more steady sexual interest, and tend to be more single-mindedly focused than women, due primarily to having 16 to 30 times more testosterone—the hormone of sexual desire and focused attention.

Women's sexuality is more episodic and contextual (arising from romantic or arousing situations) and often more intense (with many women having more orgasms per encounter than men).[109] David Deida is fond of saying that any one woman can sexually reduce any man to a quivering wreck.[110]

I've written extensively about the masculine and feminine in other books (*Waking Up, Sessions, The Gift of Shame, The Attuned Family,* and *Integral Mindfulness*).

Suffice to say, we all have masculine and feminine *aspects*. Specifically:

- The masculine in us is drawn to emptiness, courage at the edge of death, direction, presence, and feminine light. The masculine finds holding true principles in the face of threat beautiful and relaxes when he is on his mission.

- The feminine in us is drawn to fullness, being a wellspring of love, the senses, community, dance, and free-flowing emotion. The feminine finds being true to her deepest heart beautiful and relaxes in the presence of trustable masculine presence and direction.

In the sexual occasion, most of us are more purely masculine or feminine, and this is our *sexual essence.*

Erotic engagement, like dance, requires a masculine leader and a feminine follower, and almost all of us are more drawn to being one or the other in the sexual occasion.

Sometimes men have critical judgments or conditioned disapproval about their feminine aspects, or women about their masculine aspects, which drives this material into Shadow where we respond by dissociating (becoming unaware), denying (refusing to accept a part of ourselves), or projecting/attacking (seeing this in others and hating and despising *them* to protect ourselves from acknowledging forbidden parts of ourselves). Examples are how it can be confusing and distressing to a guy who values toughness to collapse into vulnerability, or for a woman who values social harmony to ragefully kick ass.

EXERCISE:

- *Who are the consenting adults you especially despise or condemn sexually? Porn stars? Prudes? Cheaters? Masturbators? Openly gay or lesbian public displays of affection? Cross-dressers? Sadomasochism enthusiasts? Even keeping to consenting adults, the list can stretch out pretty far for many of us.*
- *Write about these person or groups of people in your journal, and describe their sexuality in as much detail as possible, including how you imagine their sexual practices play out and how each person feels while he or she is having sex.*
- *Now read what you've written and pay attention to your body and imagination as you do. Is there a thrill anywhere? Is there a little tingle*

of arousal? Is there disgust or shame? Write this down, and consider how it might reflect your sexual Shadow.

- *If there is some practice or image you find particularly disgusting or offensive, focus on it for a bit, and imagine yourself doing this practice with enthusiasm. What do you experience? Distress, guilt, arousal, anger at me for suggesting you do this? Write what you discover.*
- *Try telling yourself the following phrase about this person (or these people), "They have the right to be who they are," and see how you feel. Write about that and look for insight about you.*
- *Read everything you've written and look for new understanding of your own sexual Shadow. Write what you find.*
- *Share everything you've written with someone you trust.*

COUPLES NEED TO CONSCIOUSLY COOPERATE FOR ENDURING SEXUAL BLISS

Both women and men are wired to be attracted to certain others, fall in love with demanding sexual urgency when resonating with the right person, and then become habituated to sex over months and years of intimate bonding—requiring *conscious efforts* to stay hot through a committed relationship.[111]

What kind of conscious efforts? Chrisanna Northrop, in a massive online study of 70,000 people (from many countries), found that people whose marriages stayed erotic and romantic past romantic infatuation engaged in the following activities:[112]

- Connected touching
- Public displays of affection
- Frequent "I love you's"
- Cuddling
- Romantic gifts
- Compliments
- Passionate kisses

- Dates
- Getaways
- Caressing
- Talking during sex
- Passionate sex, oral sex, and intercourse

I assume *some* couples *naturally* do all these for decades, through childbirth and childrearing and extending into old age. I *am certain* from my forty-three years of clinical experience that most couples who embrace even some of these activities over many years have had to regularly put *conscious collaborative effort* in to keep their eroticism alive and well.

WHAT'S STOPPING US?

It seems pretty obvious when you look at the data. We want to keep passion alive past romantic infatuation. Couples who do manage to keep a mutually fulfilling sex life have fewer problems and more stability.[113] We know what it takes to make this happen. Why aren't all couples making these practices daily/weekly priorities?

The answer, of course, is sexual Shadow.

Sex/romance/intimate bonding are *drives*, like hunger and thirst. Drives can't be denied, successfully suppressed, or reasoned away, they must be integrated into a satisfying life, and *they are always there, ready to generate constructive or destructive Shadow impulses and ideas given the right cues.*

Drives channeled through constructive Shadow support our health and fulfillment as well as the health or our cultural surrounds. Drives channeled through destructive Shadow compromise our health and fulfillment and are generally harmful to our social surround. The sex drive can influence us to be exploitative, ashamed, or obsessive sexually—destructive Shadow—or happy, engaged, and fulfilled sexually—constructive Shadow.

The sex drive is especially complicated because, due to the shame dynamics and socialization influences we discussed in Chapters 3 and 4, we all have aspects of our sexuality (and our partner's sexuality) that we are ashamed of, resist knowledge of, or even fear.[114]

Further, how men and women initiate sex changes from romantic infatuation into intimate bonding, because the desire-leads-to-arousal mechanisms present in both men and women in lust and romantic infatuation often shift *in women* to arousal-lead-to-desire during intimate bonding.

During intimate bonding when sexual urgency diminishes and familiarity/routines/responsibilities accelerate, men keep their desire-leads-to-arousal tendencies because they are *visually erotic*—the sight of their partner's curves and smile evokes desire-leading-to-arousal interest in sex right now.

Women in intimate bonding have the same diminished sexual urgency and burdens of familiarity/routines/responsibilities, but often shift into *arousal-leads-to-desire* in their committed relationship.[115] In other words, women in longer-term relationships *often don't know they want to have sex until they're having sex*. Since modern women have been taught by well meaning others to say "No" if they don't feel like it, this can lead to gradually diminished and increasingly conflicted sex in intimately bonded relationships.

Don Symons, evolutionary psychologist, demonstrated with a series of studies that in modern relationships, women are probably the determiners of sexual frequency. Lesbian and straight couples tended to have about the same number of sexual encounters per week. Gay male couples had way more partners and sexual frequency.[116] Whatever the frequency or sexual orientation, couples who want to remain erotically mutually fulfilled usually need to collaboratively negotiate the intimate bonding sexual challenge.

If couples can't *consciously* adapt to this new configuration, they risk losing each other as lovers.

This is probably one of the explanations for John Gottman's finding that when one partner initiates sex, the other says "No," and the initiator remains loving and positive, that the couple tends to have plenty of sex. Couples where the "No" was met with neutral or negative responses reported less and less satisfying sex.[117]

I believe that loving response to "No" is the tip of the iceberg, revealing much more about a couple than just that one dynamic. With many couples I've worked with, a positive response to a "No" to sexual initiation indicates a comfort with initiation, with "Yes," with "No," and with a bias towards saying, "Yes" to sex in general—in other words a conscious, cooperative shared sexuality.

EXERCISE:

- *Write in your journal the ideal formula for you and your partner to both feel sexually fulfilled. Tender words, date nights, scheduled love making, once-a-week, twice-a-week, three-times-a-week frequency, sex games—put everything on the table, and write what in your opinion would keep both of you connected and happy.*
- *Write which stage of relating you are in. Have you just met and are lusting for your lover? Are you passionately attached and obsessed with your lover, still in romantic infatuation territory? Have you passed into intimate bonding where you feel like intimate family but are not as consistently hot for each other? Do you have children under five? Five to ten? Ten to twenty? Have you progressed to middle age?*
- *If you are currently making a both-sexually-fulfilled formula happen, write how you and your lover are managing it.*
- *If you are not making this ideal formula happen, what's stopping you? Cluelessness? Mindlessness? Fatigue? Disinterest? Lack of trust? Hopelessness? Your partner's refusal to grow sexually? Your refusal to grow? Rationalizations about sex, marriage, or your partner that seem like legitimate reasons to neglect mutual fulfillment? Write what's stopping you two from creating the ideal mutually-fulfilled formula, and especially include your part in not making the ideal happen.*

- *Share everything you've written with your partner, and use the conversation to create more love and sexual fulfillment in your relationships. If that doesn't happen, go see a therapist for help.*
- *Don't wait to see a therapist. The average couple sees a therapist six years after problems start, and that's a lot of negative momentum and regrettable incidents. Believe me, as a therapist it's a lot easier to deal with, "We've been disconnected the last two months and we want to fix it," than, "We haven't had sex in five years".*

DESTRUCTIVE SEX SHADOW

Destructive sex Shadow impulses can be devastating when we indulge them. Common examples of destructive sex Shadow impulses are going for the "Bad Boy," refusing to admit yearning to be ravished by your husband, disconnecting/dissociating from your native sexuality—being cut off from your healthy native sexuality—through trauma or cheating on your wife when the hot woman at the conference asks you to her room for a drink.

Destructive sex Shadow impulses can be illuminating and liberating when we observe them with acceptance and caring intent and look for how to integrate them into healthy sexual expressions (like playing "Bad Boy" games with your lover, ravishing games with your husband or wife, entering therapy with the goal of waking up your dissociated sexual self, or imagining your wife to be the bikini babe you just saw on the beach while you and she are in a hot embrace).

How to liberate constructive sexual Shadow and integrate destructive sexual Shadow?

FIRST: RADICAL ACCEPTANCE

An attitude of absolute acceptance for who you are and what gets you off and who your partner is and what gets him or her off supports integration. Radical acceptance begins with attuning to ourselves and attending to all sexual attractions, repulsions, and reactions with interest and compassion—then we do the same with our partner.

Accepting a sexual thought/impulse/memory is not the same as *indulging* a sexual thought/impulse/memory. Accepting allows us to *perceive* our sexual Shadow, which then gives us opportunities to grow our intimacy and sexual satisfaction. Accepting makes it easier to share who we are sexually with our partner and help them share with us— necessary conversation to improve romance and sex.

The *form* of sexual expression is less important than the *process* of sexual expression. We can see this clearly in kinky sex. Bondage, submission, fetishes, sexual humiliation, role playing, etc., can be healthy if incorporated into a respectful caring relationship, or unhealthy if used to injure or emotionally avoid a partner.

How to learn to be aware, accept, and share? A great way to invite sex material out of Shadow into our conscious awareness is by creating *lust maps* to help us explore our sexuality and talk about it with our lover.

WHAT IS A LUST MAP?

Every activity, sight, sound, behavior, look, smell, taste, fantasy, or touch that increases your sexual arousal is part of your personal *lust map*. It is unique; no two people have exactly the same lust map.

Lust maps are a subcategory of love maps, which I first heard about from couples' researcher John Gottman.

By early adolescence we develop a *"love map"* of who we go for in intimate relationships—looks, education, voice, vibe, smell, taste, height, interpersonal patterns, etc.,—which includes sexuality, but also lots of other factors like smile, emotional stability, cultural history, education level, parenting style, interests, and friends.

Love maps guide who we seek for relationships.

Loosely included in our love map is a lust map on who and what gets us off sexually, *and your partner has a lust map too!*

LUST MAPS DON'T PERFECTLY TRACK LOVE MAPS

Many studies have shown men and women going sexually for people they don't necessarily want to be in a relationship with.[118]

For instance, women might go for edgy guys—bikers, narcissists, 10-day beards on hard-drinking charmers, or sensitive poets who don't mind you're cheating on your husband—knowing they might be horrible relationship choices, but, ummm, "I just want to be taken by that guy!"

Men might lust after the "whore" end of the "Madonna/whore" continuum—really going for the super-sexual, porn-star-slutty-babe-sex object, but often completely dismissing her as a candidate for a committed relationship.

Every person has a different "lust-map," so don't feel weird that yours is unique! All lust maps are unique!

Supportive partners cultivate curiosity and acceptance of their partner's lust map.

Projecting and announcing acceptance of your partner's lust map is a big deal because, like *you,* he or she probably feels weird about something sexual!

Revealing your lust map and being curious *and accepting* about your partner's lust map is a wonderful way to talk about sex. Talking in a positive constructive way about sex potentially increases all the activities that Chrisanna Northrup's study said were associated with long-term hotness. You'll find it incredibly useful to you, and potentially reassuring and delightful for your partner to be curious and non-threatened about what is most yummy and yucky to each of you about sex and eroticism.

This is not as easy as it sounds! We all have sexual judgments about people getting off on what we don't like, or others being critical about what gets us off. As you probably discovered in the exercise we did earlier, we all have Shadow resistances to aspects of our own and other's sexuality.

> **Cultural sidebar:** *I've often thought that the sexual constraint laws so popular in nineteenth and twentieth century countries (no sodomy, no oral sex, no homosexual or lesbian sex, no sexual images, lots of "No!") arose from male legislators wanting to make illegal what they found disgusting on their lust maps or what they found secretly erotic and were ashamed of. I suspect this is at the root of many of the anti-gay-legislator-caught-with-hot-guy/girl scandals we've seen over the last few decades.*

You might like your partner to stroke your breasts lightly, or grab them *really hard*. If he's critical of either desire, you're likely to feel shame/humiliation/rage in response.

Say your partner likes you to lick his testicles and you think that's gross and put him down for liking testicle licking—big mistake! Now *he* might go into shame/humiliation/rage.

You might like your partner to dress in slutty lingerie. If she finds this offensive or degrading you're likely to feel shame/humiliation/rage.

Remember, you can accept your lover's desire and still say "No" to it if it repels you or even if it doesn't get you off just a little bit. On the other hand, often you don't know what you like until you've tried it a few times.

WE DISCOVER DISAPPROVALS, BUT CHOOSE HOW WE PROCESS THEM

Disapprovals are reflexes that we *discover* and then either strengthen— you know, build a case for why we should disapprove and why our partner is bad—or process compassionately, like saying to ourselves, "I'm not into that, but he or she certainly has a right to want to have sex in the backyard where we might be seen."

When disapproval or disgust starts—remember, these reactions are non-conscious and occur within a tenth of a second—they're reflexes which you only become *consciously aware of* a half-second to several seconds later.

But, when you become conscious of your disapproval, disgust, or threat, you can adjust to *acceptance and compassion*—that's best! That's taking responsibility for your reactions and processing them to create more love. Even more, this acceptance and compassion stance feeds back into your adaptive unconscious—your Shadow self—and helps it grow and become wiser, strengthening constructive Shadow and transmuting destructive Shadow.

You can be turned off by her liking her toes sucked on, but still accept that *it's fine that she likes her toes sucked*. That kind of acceptance supports healthy talk about sex, and healthy sex talk leads to expanding eroticism!

It's disappointing and potentially frustrating for you or your partner to be repelled by something that turns the other on, so we help each other with compassionate acceptance and occasional experimentation.

I might not want to do anal sex with you, but I need to accept that anal turns you on, or you'll feel shamed by me. You might not want to lick whipped cream off my naked body, but if you accept it turns me on, I can still feel sexually validated by you. If we really don't know whether we like those activities or not, we can try them and see.

INITIATION IS A BIG DEAL

Sex usually begins when both of us somehow decide, "We're being sexual right now." It usually needs an overture, and often one person— more often the guy—is the designated signaler of "Let's get sexual."

Remember how John Gottman found that couples where a "No" to a sex overture met with positive emotion—love, warmth, approval from the person receiving the "No"—had plenty of sex, and that couples where "No" was met with neutral or negative affect had progressively less sex? *This one characteristic* reliably predicted plenty-of-sex from diminishing-sex couples. The take-home message? Make sexual overtures and always respond to "No" with positive affect.

There are other ways sex happens.

Desire might start you being frisky, but also you might have scheduled some premeditated sex and the schedule starts you! Either way, sex gets started with the mutual intent of going further.

WHAT YOU LIKE CAN CHANGE WITH LEVELS OF AROUSAL

Often, you gradually get turned on, then really turned on, and then somebody has an orgasm. On average, 30 percent of women and 75 percent of men have orgasms during intercourse.[119]

Sex progresses through stages and can happen fast or slow, hard or soft, or any number of other ways. In Integral we call these "state stages" because they are a progression of related states of consciousness.

You might not like deep wet kissing in the beginning of love making, but melt into it when you're moderately or majorly turned on.

You might like soft stroking rhythms at the beginning and hard pounding rhythms at the end.

Acceptance of you and your partner is accepting what gets either of you off at different stages of sex—*while only saying "Yes" to actually doing stuff that you enjoy at least somewhat* at every stage.

"Enjoy at least somewhat" means you have no problem doing the activity, it's mildly pleasant, even if it doesn't particularly get *you* off. For instance, you don't have to really like biting his nipples if you *kind of like* biting them because he gets super turned on when you do.

EXERCISE
CREATE A LUST MAP.

Get a big sheet of paper and put "My lust map" in a three-inch circle in the center.

- *Then make wavy lines out from the center circle, and at the end of each one write something that turns you on or off—yes, what turns you off is also part of your lust map. You can use different colors, draw pictures, paste images, whatever you like.*
- *Keep elaborating on what turns you on and off until you have created a personal masterpiece of a lust map.*

EXERCISE:
SHARE YOUR LUST MAP WITH YOUR PARTNER
OR SOMEONE YOU TRUST.

That's right! Share it, describe it, and encourage him or her to make his or her own lust map to share with you.

- *If this exercise turns into major problems, find a therapist and take your maps into the sessions.*
- ***Stay present!*** *We are taught to dissociate from sex in ourselves and others when we're the least bit stressed. Present is attuned to yourself, attuned to your partner, and focused on radical acceptance.*
- *Look for constructive and destructive Shadow in your lust maps and in your conversations. What is hard to accept in you or your partner? What is disappointing? What is a pleasant or sexy surprise? Write all this in your journal and share it with your partner.*

An awful lot of input around sex—like all guys like blow jobs and all women like guys to go down on them—is not necessarily true in some people's individual lust maps—often leading us to feel weird about what we like.

We like what we like, and no couple does or likes *everything* that either one of them likes—sex is always an ongoing work in progress.

EXERCISE:

What's something you like or don't like sexually that feels weird or not normal to you? For instance, say you like to say sexual words during intercourse, but that feels abnormal, or you don't particularly like the missionary position and that feel abnormal. (One woman I worked with was concerned because her Catholic lover always exclaimed, "Jesus Fucking Christ!" when he had a orgasm. I encouraged her to both normalize it and talk to him about her discomfort, which she did, with the result of it fading into a non-issue.) Write about it this in detail in your journal.

- *Discuss this with your partner or someone you trust and write about the conversation.*
- *Do you feel more or less weird or normal after the conversation, and why? Write your reactions.*

SEXUAL COMPULSIVITY IS COMPLICATED

We've been mostly talking about sex Shadow arising from ancient drives and inhibitions, and gone on to explore and normalize what we like and don't like. This is pro-sexual kumbaya and much of the work for most of us in dealing with sexual Shadow. But sexual material and reactions *can* be dangerous and destructive. There can be devastating problems when destructive Shadow is harnessed to sexual compulsivity or aggression towards self or others.[120]

Sexual compulsives can have wildly different kinds and degrees of obsessions. I've helped men and women who were absolutely "Sexually addicted." They urgently craved self-destructive sex like compulsive philandering, prostitutes, and exhibitionism, and recklessly indulged to the point their lives were falling apart. These people really benefited from addiction models of abstinence and recovery, often helped by Sex Addicts Anonymous as well as psychotherapy.

But there are different forms and levels of sexual compulsivity, and—to a certain extent—all drives, including sex and bonding, are compulsive. But there are relativistic levels of sex crazy.

For instance, there are probably significant differences in craziness between a guy who accesses porn for regular masturbation sessions and a guy who secretly goes to prostitutes every week. How about a woman who has a secret affair for years and a woman who has a brief fling on a business trip? Sex and bonding problems are too intricate and complicated to put into one framework like "sexual addiction." I'm sure Patric Carnes—the father of the sex addiction recovery movement—would agree that sex/intimacy problems additionally require broader, more developmentally oriented, sexual understandings.

ABSTINENCE FROM SEX CAN'T BE THE FINAL ANSWER

Cocaine, alcohol, and gambling addictions can be resolved by abstinence—stop using the substance and get lots of support to stay away from it. Problems with drives such as hunger and lust can't be dealt with using pure abstinence models. Stay away from an addictive substance long enough, and your body adjusts to not having it (unless it's a nutrient like vitamin C, or chocolate—just kidding about the chocolate, but we do crave and get sick when we don't get enough vitamin C).

We can see this in how the craving for substances like drugs and alcohol diminishes markedly over time when you're not pumping them into your body. In studies on relapse rate for alcoholics, incidence of relapse was as high as 80 percent the first two years of recovery, and dropped precipitously after two years of abstinence from alcohol.[121] Apparently people's body/mind/brain systems can let go of urgently craving non-necessary-for-healthy-existence substances like alcohol. We aren't genetically programmed to need cocaine, alcohol, gambling, or drugs—they are not inherent human *drives*, even though they hijack drive circuitry in our brains.

BASIC DRIVES ARE DIFFERENT

Psychotherapy helps people organize and make sense of *drives* like dominance, hunger, thirst, lust, romantic infatuation, and attachment to other people—physiological imperatives. To consciously grow we need to know and accept our drives into our larger Self in healthy ways. We can't stop eating, drinking, or lusting, but we can learn to keep them in harmony with a healthy fulfilling life.

Many average twenty-something guys think about sex every five minutes—so are *all* these twenty-something guys sexually obsessive? Many twenty-something women think about sex daily and can easily have a love affair dominate their world—so are *all* these women sex and love addicts? I don't think so.

I think drives are powerful, urgent forces that need attention and acceptance to be integrated into healthy lives.

Ask any sex therapist—they'll tell you people want permission to be sexual, information about their masculine and feminine natures, and direction towards satisfying love.

A good example of this is how many people relax when autoeroticism is normalized. Most of us are conditioned to be ashamed of masturbating. A friend of mine used to do an exercise with groups where she had them first imagine being walked in on while making love with a person, and then being walked in on while masturbating. Everybody felt more embarrassed and humiliated at the image of being caught in mid-masturbation than in enthusiastic sex with a partner.

Some guys just need their natural reactions normalized. I've seen countless men visibly relax in relief when I say some version of, "It is perfectly normal to see a hot woman and want her *right now.*" Similarly many women are relieved that their, "I want Mr. Hot to ravish me!" fantasies are shared by millions of other women around the world, and are based in evolutionary drives.

Lust, romantic infatuation, and intimate bonding are evolutionary forces that contribute heavily to the myths of our lives—the stories we tell ourselves about who we are and what we're about. "I am lovable," "I am not lovable," "I am desirable," "I am not desirable," "I am erotically fulfilled," or "I am erotically starved," figure heavily into our personal myths. Such beliefs about ourselves contribute to individual archetypal narratives that can amp up craziness (like those 25 percent of murders which involve sexual jealousy or betrayal) or provide opportunities for deeper awakening (like those couples we love who seem to embody the dream of long-term fulfillment). Seeking out new truths and deeper compassionate understanding of our personal sexual narratives grows our constructive sexual Shadow.

DESTRUCTIVE CULTURAL SEX SHADOW MAKES IT HARDER TO HELP CHILDREN WITH ALL THIS COMPLEXITY

Sexual development, like social, moral, and cognitive development, happens from birth onward and benefits from education. As I mentioned earlier, most Americans frown on explicit sexual talk or explicit permission for sexual feelings and age-appropriate sexual play in children of all ages.[122] If a five-year-old likes to play looking/touching games with her best friends, what can Mom and Dad do to help her develop well? If your ten-year-old is sexually interested, don't you want to help him be deeper and wiser about what's happening rather than teach him he shouldn't share his feelings or experiments with anyone? If your fourteen-year-old is wondering whether she should have oral sex with her boyfriend, shouldn't she have mature guidance from someone she trusts?

Let's face it, most people don't want to have these conversations with their kids. Most parents avoid these conversations, and get *outraged* if other people have them with their kids. An occasional exception is that we sometimes allow our children to talk with their friends about sex, which relegates sex education to the least sexually educated among us.

OK, we don't have to be good at everything. If you don't want to discuss this stuff with your kids, find quality sex educators who'll help your family start conversations and keep them going, even potentially disturbing conversations that involve your children's emergent sexuality.

This last point reflects another colossal blind spot in American child-rearing—the fact that sex education is best delivered to *families*—not just kids. Healthy sexual development is best served as part of ongoing family dialogues that include conversations about physical development, academic development, and social development.

In the 1960s, Holland shifted sex education to be pro-pleasure, pro-communication, and broadly inclusive of gay, straight, transgender, birth control, and women's right to choose abortion. Parents were routinely included in the programs. After a few years of this, they found in surveys that boys and girls still thought sex revolved around the boy's needs, so they instituted an education component emphasizing girls' sexual pleasure and boys' responsibilities to make sure their partners had positive sexual experiences. In 2016, Holland's young people have one seventh the abortions of their American peers, one seventeenth the number of teen pregnancies, and 88 percent of girls and 91 percent of boys report their first sexual experience as being positive with someone they cared deeply about. Parents and children routinely discuss all things sexual, and it is the norm for fifteen- to seventeen-year-old lovers to have sleepovers in each other's homes. In America, it's rare for teens to talk comfortably about sex with parents, and 70 percent of teens express regrets about their first sexual experience, saying they did it because of opportunity or peer pressure.[123]

Some American schools are meeting the challenge of upleveling (dramatically improving) family sex education in America. A few years ago a woman told me that in her ten-year-old's class, the parents all gave permission for a sex educator to teach a class about sex and relationships. The boys and girls were talked to as a group by a friendly, knowledgeable grown-up in terms that were understandable to them. The children were then asked to each write an important question anonymously and hand it in. All the questions were transcribed, answered, and send home with the kids for further discussion with parents. I find this to be a beautiful and inspiring story, and I confidently predict that such superior education will become a standard in the years to come.

I also predict that these children are less likely to develop sexual compulsive disorders than their less educated peers, and more likely to have fulfilling, healthy sexual relationships. They will have less destructive sexual Shadow to have to deal with, and more constructive sexual Shadow to support healthy relationships.

SEXUAL TRAUMA

Up to 5 percent of boys and 20 percent of girls experience some sexual intrusion—a molestation, an assault, harassment, or rape,[124] and 20 percent of college women are sexually harassed or raped. When our first sexual experiences are exploitations by older and/or crazy others, it can scramble our sexual circuits in any number of ways. We can feel inhibitions, compulsions, and dissociations that contaminate our sexual pleasures, blank us out sexually, or compromise joyful sexuality with ourselves and healthy lovers.

Like most therapists, I've worked with countless men, women, and kids who have been sexually traumatized, and the good news is that all of us can heal sexual wounds and reclaim our birthrights of vibrant, pro-social, loving sexuality. To do so we often must be willing to face the destructive Shadow generated from our abuse and all that arose from it concerning sex, our bodies, intimacy, and sense of self.

If any such traumas have come up for you reading this chapter or doing any of the exercises, that's your constructive Shadow inviting you to look at your wounds and take responsibility to heal them. If so, find a therapist experienced in this work and dedicate yourself to love, personal integrity, and clean vibrant sexuality.

As a psychotherapist, I find it a privilege every time a courageous person comes to me with such issues and begins the Hero's or Heroine's journey into wholeness.

Even if you've had sexual pain and trauma, it's important to remember that passionate sexual joy and union is our natural state! Our bodies guide us in this, harmonizing with ancestral voices.

We are sexual beings who crave fulfilling sexual expression!

Mostly, sex is great!

ALL FANTASIES ARE FINE, AND FANTASIES AND REALITY ARE OFTEN NOT THE SAME!

I want to end this sexual Shadow chapter talking about sex fantasies. Fantasies that draw our attention are direct links to Shadow. Pleasant or distressing, they reveal our wiring and demand recognition and acceptance.

Let's start with the most basic sex Shadow fantasy facts—all of us have sex fantasies and all fantasies are fine because *fantasy is not reality!*

Just because you fantasize sex with others doesn't make you unfaithful to your partner!

Just because you fantasize extreme sexual activities doesn't mean you'd even enjoy them in real life, or need to embody them in the actual world.

I've known faithful spouses to have promiscuous fantasies, shy people to have dominator fantasies, and dominant men and women to have sexual submission fantasies. It's all fine!

Guy fantasies are often having sex with attractive others. There is wide variety, but, generally, guys have themes, bodies, and scenes that get them off.

One guy liked two brunettes getting it on.

Another guy fantasized great times with his wife.

One guy only had real sex with women, but fantasy sex with other men.

Humans are capable of infinite sexual fantasy variation, and it's *mostly* all good.

One caution with sex fantasies—try not to fantasize actual people you relate with. Fantasizing your best friend's wife or husband actually might create distracting attractions with them.

Fantasizing the man or woman at work might tempt you to cross boundaries.

Fantasizing sex with your boss might actually lead to a secret affair.

Porn is fine if not used addictively. Know the difference between casual use and compulsive use.

Casual use is fitting porn/masturbation into a good life and a good sexual relationship with your partner.

Compulsive use can be daily, extending for hours, interfering with relationships, or creating obsessive rumination (though, in fairness, many normal young men think about sex almost every minute).

Women's fantasies have lots of variation, but usually fall into two categories: scripted and unscripted.[125]

Scripted fantasies have themes and stories, and there are a lot of fun books written about women's scripted sexual fantasies—*My Secret Garden* being one of the most famous. After tens of thousands of therapy sessions and a fair amount of easy-to-read research, it seems to me that women's scripted fantasies involve variations on six major themes:

#1: The pretty maiden is the object of another's desire. I am the adorable sexy embodiment of feminine sexuality who magnetizes my ideal lover. This is an actual genetically-based brain system. Feeling beautiful and desirable elicits physical arousal in many women.

#2: I am the sexual victim, the object of humiliation and violence—the ravishment fantasy. Remember, *fantasy is not reality!* If this fantasy gets you off, you don't want to *really* be raped and humiliated, it is a scene that you control in your fantasy.

If you do play ravish/humiliation games with a lover, you'll notice that great trust and affection is involved, and you know you can stop the scene at a moment's notice.

(Interestingly, some studies have shown men to have more fantasies of being restrained, dominated, or spanked, so this is actually more likely a guy's sexual fantasy.)

That being said, women have a brain system dedicated to surrendering into arousal, even orgasm, when being sexually forced—based obviously on our hunter-gatherer roots when physically stronger males forced weaker females in the free-for-all of primitive tribes, and the biological anomaly of human women being the only mammal who is sexually available (at least biologically) at all times, not just monthly or seasonally.[126]

Sexual availability sidebar: *This sexually-available-at-any-time system helped bond men monogamously to women, given that we have dedicated mate protection circuits that are activated when someone else expresses interest in our partner, and sex releases the bonding hormones oxytocin in women and vasopressin in men with each sexual experience.*

Also, automatic arousal when being forced helped women survive the potential hazards of male desire and superior strength. What hazards? Sexual arousal prepares the vagina for penetration, expanding it, and lubricating it. Penetration without arousal increases the likelihood of injuries to the vagina during sex. The collapse-into-arousal-when-forced system protected women being raped from potentially catastrophic infections from having sex when their genitals were not biologically receptive. The collapse-into-arousal-when-forced is a physiological response which enlarges and lubricates the vagina independently of social contexts.

It's left modern women with a "ravish me" arousal system where it's a turn-on for the right guy, at the right time, to sweep me up erotically right now!

#3: "I am the wild sexual woman! I passionately initiate sex which ignites my lover to huge desire for me. Lost in abandoned lust, I consume and overwhelm him with my sexual fire.

#4: "I am the dominatrix exerting power, bending my partner to my sexual desires." Here you dominate and humiliate, creating an atmosphere of your sexual power controlling, arousing, even humiliating the other.

#5: "I am the voyeur, observing others having passionate sex." You watch them either secretly or openly, becoming more aroused as they progress through their passion.

#6: "I am the beloved." Here you are intimately engaged in lovemaking with a lover of equal power in mutual adoration and passion.

Unscripted fantasies are images or sensations—often fleeting—which can be cued by objects or the environment. In unscripted fantasies there is often a symbolic image focusing on sensual/erotic charge building, building, building...and releasing! The image could be a train reaching a summit, a wave breaking, or a flower blossoming.

Fantasies often reflect our coming-of-age sexuality. Many of us have basically the same sexual fantasies from teenage onward; our lust map often is set by our teens and then elaborated through life, but often not majorly changed.

I've noticed that as I age, I keep adding older women to the women I'm attracted to—one welcome consequence of aging, finding a wider range of women sexually attractive.

EXERCISE:

- *Write down your favorite go-to sexual fantasies, and explore how they fit into the frameworks I've just described. Write down on a scale of 1 to 10 just how embarrassing each one is to reveal to a lover (10 is maximum shame/embarrassment/humiliation, 1 is no-big-deal).*

EXERCISE:

- *Share these with your lover and ask him or her to do the same with you. If you begin to get turned on, have hot sex! If it begins to turn into a fight, and you can't de-escalate in three minutes, talk about it later. If you can't discuss it comfortably at all, take up the conversation with a therapist to help.*

SEX SHADOW EVERYWHERE

I suggest you skim through this chapter and look back over the notes in your journal and your lust map. Has anything changed in the way you understand your sexuality and your sex Shadow? I find something new every time I explore this material, and I've been teaching and doing therapy—including lots of sex therapy—for over four decades. Sex Shadow is always bubbling up to inform and transform us.

Our job is to listen, accept, and welcome our sexual Shadow and help our lovers with theirs. This doesn't just benefit us sexually, it loosens up and liberates all our constructive Shadow as it constantly flows from not aware into aware, from not acceptable into acceptable.

9

MARITAL SHADOW

*Like everything which is not the involuntary result of fleeting
emotion but the creation of time and will, any marriage,
happy or unhappy, is infinitely more interesting
than any romance, however passionate.*

—W. H. AUDEN

*Marriage may be the closest thing to Heaven or Hell
any of us know on this earth.*

—EDWIN LOUIS COLE

*Marriage is a wonderful institution
but who wants to live in an institution?*

—GROUCHO MARX

Talk about your easy targets! Marriage has been the subject of commentary and humor from time immemorial. Homer said, "There

is nothing nobler or more admirable than when two people who see eye to eye keep house as man and wife, confounding their enemies and delighting their friends." That was in 1,000 B.C.

Why is it that you're on average 35 percent happier if you live next door to a good friend, but only 8 percent happier when you live with a spouse?[127]

Why does everyone start out hopeful and starry-eyed, and yet 50 percent divorce, and many others continue to cohabitate in misery?

One good answer to these questions is that we have yet to institutionalize effectively managing marital Shadow.

WHAT IS MARITAL SHADOW?

Mark and Judith came to me struggling with horrible fights that swept through their relationship like hurricanes, leaving them exhausted and emotionally bruised. CEO Mark and corporate lawyer Judith had survived messy divorces with previous spouses to eventually find each other and create a blended family with their four adolescent children. Both were active, attractive, and sexually hot when they weren't going for the jugular.

Powerful, opinionated, and ruthless in conflict, neither backed down in an argument, making them ruinously vulnerable to escalating conflict—one of the most robust predictors of divorce. In our third sessions Judith began with an indictment—like a good lawyer she presented a well-reasoned case.

"Mark is completely selfish! It's his plan or no plan. When I want to visit my daughter Janey in San Francisco, he complains about how long I'm gone, but when he wants to help his son Michael move into his apartment in New York, I'm supposed to drop everything!"

Mark, snapping up the bait, violently disagrees. "You are so wrong! How about when Janey got meningitis, you..."

Judith interrupts contemptuously, "Oh? You helped? Visiting her once in the hospital and demanding that I go to your office party that night is helping?"

I interrupt, "Stop! Neither of you is aware of what you're doing at this moment. You are so driven by hostile Shadow habits to attack and diminish each other that you're both completely missing what you really want!"

Mark and Judith are not so far gone that this doesn't pique their interest. Judith responds first. "What do you mean about 'Shadow habits' and 'Missing what we really want?'" Mark nods. They're accustomed to going in and out of extreme anger—a good sign they can shift states. Abilities to give and receive positive influence, even when you're upset, create happy couples—Judith and Mark can't do it with each other yet when pissed off, but they just did it with me.

I take a deep breath and exhale slowly, watching how they unconsciously mirror me and relax a bit. I relax my face and modulate my voice to soothe.

"You want to get back to love. When you're arguing you believe *convincing* works—that *convincing* gets you back to love. No it doesn't. Love gets you back to love." My goal here was to encourage them to *observe* themselves trying to angrily convince, and *believe* that angry convincing is wrong—ineffective and essentially immoral. I'm working to directly influence the growth of their constructive Shadow around conflict.

▶ **Attacking sidebar: Attacking sucks!** *It's a horrible habit to automatically and habitually attack when you feel distressed, misunderstood, or criticized. It's Shadow because you don't see that you're making things worse—you just do it again and again, and it never works!*

Anger is important in relationships. Anger happens and must be acknowledged and processed into resolution and more love to be productive. Anger does not have to turn into attack, and will be consistently destructive if angry attacks are normalized.

Judith, still angry, disagrees and returns to her case. "If Mark wasn't so selfish, we wouldn't have these problems." Mark counters, "It's never your fault, is it? You can never..." I interrupt, "Wait! I need to tell Judith something. "Judith, you just did it again. Your trying to convince him he's selfish."

She looks startled, and this time stays thoughtfully quiet—a good sign. I continue. "It's hard to catch, isn't it?"

She smiles, "You're right. It is a habit. It happens so fast!"

I look at Mark, "How are you feeling at this moment?"

Mark, tempted by his hostile story, visibly catches himself and shows up as more mature man. "Actually, I'm kind of impressed with what Judith just did." She blushes in unexpected pleasure.

This is just a glimpse of the Shadow material flowing and swirling around their unique intersubjectivity. Our Shadow selves communicate as our conscious selves communicate.[128] When the two conversations are congruent, everything is working in the same direction, but what if consciously I'm trying to connect positively and unconsciously trying to attack, while you're doing the same? Such situations produce characteristic destructive patterns of relating, which is what Mark and Judith were engaged in. If they can perceive these patterns *when upset* and self-soothe, and then reach for marital bliss, everything changes—their Shadow agendas become congruent with their conscious agendas of loving better, which is the reason they entered therapy in the first place, to love better.

If Mark and Judith get back to love from conflict quickly and frequently, getting back to love eventually becomes a *positive attractor state*—a pro-social place they go to easily *and naturally*. Positive attractor states are shared attuned states we *habitually* go to—priceless in conflict. I point this out. "Look into each other's eyes and tell me how you feel—closer or farther away."

They look at each other and tentatively smile. Mark speaks first, "Definitely closer." Judith nods agreement as I continue.

"This is what I mean by getting back to love, what you *really* want when you start fighting."

IN THIS CHAPTER WE WILL:

- Explore how Mark and Judith's experience reflects marital Shadow.
- Talk about the relational stages of marital Shadow.
- Learn how to watch out for marital defensive patterns, and examine a few ways to transform them into constructive Shadow programming.
- Define "relational entropy" and discover how all of us need to address it or risk deteriorating marriages.
- See how effective repair of small to major injuries is a cornerstone of joyful marriages, and I'll teach you some dynamite techniques for quick repair.
- Understand why we shouldn't trust what we think when we're in defensive states.
- Identify how the two commitments of relationships, "I'll stay as long as..." and "I'll do what it takes..." are both important and necessary in marriage.
- Revisit normal crazy and extra crazy, and how understanding them is central to marital health.
- Spend a little time in the secret affair minefield.
- See how creating an open friendship and a vibrant marital love affair is protective of secret affairs and other attachment injuries.
- Conclude with some beautiful tantric processes of helping each other grow constructive Shadow and alchemically dialysize/transform destructive Shadow into constructive Shadow.
- I'll explain the Five Star method for understanding and improving every aspect of your marriage.

PRETENDING DESTRUCTIVE SHADOW IS VALID CREATES CATASTROPHES

Mark and Judith began the above session pretending their hostile feelings were proportionate, and their critical beliefs 100 percent accurate. They were making the huge mistake of trusting what they felt, thought, or wanted when distressed. When you pretend destructive Shadow is as valid as constructive Shadow, you're in big trouble. In marriages this mistake leads to misery and divorce.

"Trust your feelings" has been a mantra of humanism for over fifty years (not to mention a staple of Obi-Wan Kenobe flavored, "Trust your feelings Luke!" Star Wars geekdom). *In reality,* when you're angry, ashamed, frightened, devastated, or highly anxious, your emotions are amplified or numbed, your thoughts are distorted, and your impulses are more likely to be coming from destructive Shadow than constructive Shadow.[129]

When you're in a defensive state, *don't trust your feelings, thoughts, or impulses!* Soothe yourself back into a state of social engagement, help your spouse do the same, and then reach for compassionate understanding and loving action. Compassionate understanding *will change your beliefs about distressing situations* towards less painful/destructive and more accurate/constructive.

You can usually tell destructive Shadow in marital conflict from the emotional signatures of anxiety, depression, sadness, shame, contempt, numbness, and/or rage.

Similarly, constructive Shadow usually has the emotional signatures of joy, compassion, love, lively interest, care, and/or patience.

To grow your marital Shadow, *take responsibility when you're distressed* to soothe yourself, cultivate compassionate understanding, and always do your best to get back to love with your spouse.

RELATIONAL STAGES OF SHADOW

Every stage of human development brings new Shadow challenges. For instance, the kind of Shadow you have to deal with when lusting for the woman across the dance floor is different from the kind you encounter falling in love, which is different from the kind of shadow that you have to manage passing into intimate bonding after your love affair has simmered down.

Shadow in lust arises from our genetically coded desire to *have sex now* when cued by the presence or interest of an attractive other. Lust is often impersonal, in that we see the beautiful woman or talk briefly with the charming, handsome man and start feeling little tingles or major surges of sexual energy running through our bodies. When two people are harmonizing such tingles they are amplifying *erotic polarity* between one's masculine energies and the other's feminine energies. At this point our brains begin to talk us into flirting and connecting—they want us to have sex right now! Without consciously adding awareness of what we're experiencing and doing, we can talk ourselves into distracting attractions where we obsess about another, or even love affairs that don't take into account whether this person is a healthy partner for us or not.

Shadow in romantic infatuation is not paying attention to potential problems. Romantic infatuation—falling in hot love with another person—activates circuits in our brain where we can notice another person's faults but not much care about those faults.[130] This is why it's a great idea when you begin dating someone to introduce them to your friends before you fall in love. Especially introduce them to your women friends who generally have more social evaluation circuits in their brains than men. If your friends think this is a bad match for you, they're probably right!

Shadow in intimate bonding often arises from ignorance about how we are programmed to love in stages. Before birth control, falling in love drove couples to pair-bond, have sex frequently, and often conceive and deliver a child. By the time romantic infatuation faded and intimate bonding predominated, the child was born, the family had a felt coherence (a central feature of intimate bonding), and the partners had attached with each other and the baby so that they were moved to protect and care for their family.

In our ancient past, this is how humans found each other, fell in love, had a child, and raised it until the kid was old enough to begin to be more autonomous.

Modernity has thrown a wrench into the evolutionary works. Couples meet later in life, consciously take charge of reproduction so they often have children in their late twenties and thirties, and often pass into intimate bonding before pregnancy.

We still want to be with our partner during intimate bonding. Friendship, attraction, and commitment endure past the obsessive sexy joyride of romantic infatuation, and often couples become more stably committed the more children they have and the more life experiences they've shared. Older more informed adults tend to create more stable and enduring relationships. Especially, couples who are college educated and marry later tend to have more stable marriages than less educated couples who tend to bond and have children in their late teens and early twenties.[131]

When you fall in love with somebody it's a good idea to have conversations with them about what's on the horizon. These conversations are mostly some version of, "At some point, it's not going to be as easy or as fun or as effortless as it is now and what are we going to do about that when it happens?" This conversation invites both of you to open up to relational Shadow and discuss it cooperatively while you're still romantic-infatuation-intoxicated.

INTIMATE BONDING SHADOW IS CONNECTED WITH OUR PARTNER FEELING LIKE FAMILY

Intimate bonding involves diminished sexual urgency and obsession, but it also drives us to relate to our partner as a life partner. We want to be domestic together, and often start seriously planning a shared life. He or she begins to feel like *family*.

When we recapitulate family-of-origin feelings of connection with someone, defensive states we originally developed in our families are much more likely to emerge, just as we become less in-love-intoxicated with our partner and more likely to notice his or her faults or grating habits. Maybe her flightiness was adorable during romantic infatuation, but irritates the hell out of you in intimate bonding when you're trying to nail down the itinerary for your Europe trip. His wacky humor might have made you helplessly laugh during romantic infatuation, but embarrasses you in front of your parents after you're married.

DON'T PRACTICE RELATIONAL DEFENSIVE PATTERNS!

Distress tends to make us feel unsafe and thus elicit defensive states, which in turn tend to threaten our partner and elicit complementary defensive states in him or her. The more often we do this, the more we and our partners co-create enduring relational defensive patterns. As relational defensive patterns continue, we keep activating and practicing them when either of us feels threatened, with each iteration more deeply embedding them into our two nervous systems.

The Holy Grail of happy marriages is the *positive habit* of quickly repairing distress back to love. Once both partner's constructive Shadow impulses are simultaneously harnessed to reliably and reflexively seek compassionate understanding and quick repair when in pain, the couple has transformed much of their destructive marital Shadow into constructive marital Shadow.

Judith and Mark in our earlier example had established their escalating criticism defenses as children, constellated an escalating-criticism pattern early on with each other, and had been practicing it for years when they finally made it into my office.

DESTRUCTIVE INTIMATE BONDING SHADOW OFTEN RESULTS IN LESS SEX AND FUN

As we explored in the last chapter, sex and fun often require more effort for a couple during intimate bonding. Since sexual urgency fades and defenses amplify during intimate bonding, couples can find themselves having less romance/sex/play (which they miss and *usually* blame the other for) and more conflict (which they *always* blame the other for).

EXERCISE:
CONSTRUCTIVE AND DESTRUCTIVE
SHADOW IN YOUR MARRIAGE

* *Over the last week, what was the moment you felt the most love for your spouse? Write about this in detail in your journal.*
* *Over the last week, what moment did you feel the most distress with your spouse? Write about this in detail in your journal.*
* *Tell your spouse the first story (most love moment) and ask for his or her reactions—then talk about it. Write about this in detail in your journal.*
* *Tell your spouse the second story (most distress) and ask for his or her reactions—then talk about it. Write about this in detail in your journal.*
* *Read everything you've written and look for constructive and destructive Shadow material in you—especially your typical defensive states. Write about this in detail in your journal.*
* *Read everything you've written and look for conflict patterns and love patterns of relating that cause more love or more suffering with you and your spouse. Write about these patterns in detail in your journal.*
* *Share your insights with your spouse and have a discussion. Write about the conversation in your journal.*

RELATIONSHIP ENTROPY

Romantic infatuation is a self-sustaining, testosterone/dopamine-driven joyride not requiring much effortful conscious action. Relationship entropy involves the liveliness, the juice, of a relationship slowly dissipating over time after you pass out of romantic infatuation into intimate bonding.

Humans create routines and normalize repetitive patterns of living and relating. During intimate bonding we become habituated to our spouse, and are vulnerable to taking our marriage for granted. If we don't consciously counteract these forces, our love, interest, attraction, passion, and commitment can slowly dissipate over the years until our marriage feels empty, even loveless.

I think about this every time I hear couples exchange wedding vows. "I promise to cherish, to love, to be there for you..." You've heard such vows and probably have exchanged them yourself. *Promises are useless unless you back them up with sustained daily action!*

When Becky and I got married, we didn't promise anything—we made statements of intent. I told her, "I intend to wake each day and take care of my love for you, and I intend to help you do the same for me." In the subsequent decades I've missed a few days, but not many. I've seen too many couples succumb to relationship entropy and lose each other (even more, I'd feel like a hypocrite preaching active intentional love all day and then coming home and not doing it myself).

Relationship entropy happens largely out of awareness. Work is demanding, raising kids is overwhelming, taking care of our physical health becomes more challenging as we age. There's never enough time for everything, and well meaning responsible people tend to sacrifice self-care, sleep, and their marriage in the interests of work, children, and other life demands.

This can be devastating to marriages. We gradually find it a little bit more difficult to be into each other, a little less likely to take joy in each other, a little bit easier to be irritated with each other. Our energy for shared joy, fun, and love gradually dissipates without us really noticing what's happening.

These gradual changes, if they stay in Shadow (if we don't pay attention and adjust towards love from indifference or conflict), can gather momentum over the years. It's very much like how a steady wind over hundreds of miles of ocean eventually produces big waves. Little subtle influences to be less positive with each other, gradual habituation resulting in less appreciation and loving attention, increasing external demands leaving us gradually less invested in being excellent with one another—all these gradually diminish love and increase indifference and irritation.

MAKE RELATIONSHIP ENTROPY CONSCIOUS AND COUNTERACT IT

We can become aware of relationship entropy and develop constructive Shadow habits to always be reversing it. How?

- We can accept the inevitability of relational entropy and your responsibility to keep putting energy into your marriage. It's like taking a canoe into the Missouri river and learning that you have to keep padding up stream or you'll eventually drift to the sea. We need to always be paddling upstream to keep our marriages not just good but growing.
- We can consciously invest energy each day in connecting positively to our spouse both physically and emotionally. Compliments, caresses, interest in his or her life, sharing personal feelings and dreams, and ceremonies of connection like date night, breakfast or dinner together, scheduled sex, spontaneous sex, play, family time, and support for his or her issues and needs all add positive energy to a marriage—they all grow constructive relational Shadow.
- When in conflict, we can stay loving and repair *fast*. The research on repair is overwhelming. We know that people who start conflict nastily, or who can't resolve back to love, are usually doomed to divorce and unhappiness. Couples who start conflicts gently and insist on repairing back to love have *lots* more bliss and stability.

EFFECTIVE REPAIR IS THE CORNERSTONE OF HAPPY MARRIAGES

Conflict comes with the territory of marriage. Effective repair has six major components:

- First, stay positive with your spouse as much as possible so you both generally feel fondness and admiration for one another.
- Second, start a conflict talk gently (especially with tone)—"Honey, I know you've been working hard to remember to do the yard work, but the last couple of weeks I've noticed a lot more football watching and a lot less grass mowing." You'll notice how gentle humor helps a lot. This is not cutting humor where we contemptuously humiliate or use disgusted tones, but engaging humor that makes our spouse smile.
- Third, if your spouse initiates a conflict talk (80 percent of the time wives initiate such conversations), respond gently—"I don't like how you remind me so much about house jobs on the weekend, but I know I space out and you have to say something."
- Fourth, both of you need to feel heard and validated for your feelings and desires. Heard and validated sounds something like, "I know the lawn looks terrible and I've slacked off on mowing." "I know I ask you to do a lot of repairs and maintenance around the house during the weekend when you want to relax and have fun."
- Fifth, after you talk, you both feel you've made a little progress on your issue—"I will mow the lawn today." "I will try to not ask you to use all your spare time fixing up the house." Most couples' issues are never fully resolved, but happy couples get better at managing them and making progress.
- Sixth, you both feel affectionate connection at the end. This last is *crucial!* Feeling affectionate connection is not *pretending to feel* affectionate connection, it is actually feeling it and sharing it with your partner with a hug, caress, or heartfelt "I love you!" or "You're wonderful!"

> ▶ **Affectionate connection sidebar:** *When Becky gets mad at me and we talk about it, I'll ask her a couple of minutes later, "Are you still mad?" If she is, she'll say, "Yes! I'll be over it soon, but I'm not quite there yet!" I usually find this incredibly endearing, because I know the shift to tasty Becky warmth is just a couple of minutes away. This looks easy when we do it, but it is the result of decades of work.*

Here's a repair I facilitated with Mark and Judith about Judith wanting her daughter Janey to stay the summer and Mark resisting.

Judith: "Why don't you like Janey? She's a good kid!"

Mark: "I love Janey! I just can't stand her sleeping late, sitting around all day, and then partying with her friends every night. What are we, her personal B&B?"

Judith: "Your such a hypocrite! That's exactly what you do when we go to Hawaii!"

Mark: "I have a job! And you gave me such grief when Michael wanted to spend August with us before college. You're the hypocrite!"

I interrupt: "Listen to your tones and content. We've discussed this. You're pissed off and believing your critical negative stories about the other guy. Your trying to solve the issue by attacking each other. Is that a good idea? Really, is attacking going to make things better? Be honest! What are your tones and words actually communicating right now?"

Judith has practiced this with me before and is a particularly self-aware woman when she's not white-hot-infuriated. She visibly relaxes and even laughs a little ruefully. "I guess I'm contemptuously dismissing Mark as a man, parent, stepparent, and husband!" We all laugh, and I tease her, "Good luck with that!"

Mark, who's worked hard to see destructive Shadow and cultivate constructive Shadow is attuning to the repair process. "I'm using a bullying tone and not giving her an inch."

Keith: "So, what's valid about the other's point and what are you willing to do about it?"

Judith: "Mark's right about Janey laying around, and I'm going to tell her she needs to get a summer job."

Mark: "I really appreciate the job thing. That makes it much easier for me. Of course she's welcome to stay the summer, and I'll keep reminding myself she'd 19 not 29."

They're still tense from the previous heat so I push for affectionate connection. "Look each other in the eye and think about the effort that you both just made to love each other better." They start a little strained, but quickly smile and warm up. I press on, "That's affectionate connection you're feeling right now. The rule is *always* end with affectionate connection. If you can't do it right away, go read a book or take a walk, think about your part of the problem and what's valid about the other guy's part, and then come back and make affectionate connection.

They both nod, and we've taken another little step towards them learning how to make effective repairs, practicing until quick repair is a new habit, and reversing marital entropy.

REPAIR GIMMICK #1: BREAK GRIDLOCK WITH OPEN-ENDED QUESTIONS ABOUT THE YEARNING OR DREAM BENEATH THE RESENTMENT

Sometimes couples get locked into points of view and can't change—they become stuck. For instance, if Mark refused to let Janey stay the summer and Judith insisted Janey stay for the summer, the discussion would quickly devolve into personal attack, since neither would be willing to validate the other's position or shift their own opinions. One technique which works (if you both can do it during a fight!) is to ask the other three consecutive open-ended questions about the yearning/dream/desire at the base of his or her stuck position, and just listen to the answers, not refute or argue. Every strongly held opinion has a principle, dream, or desire at its core. Open ended questions require an explanation ("What was it like sailing to the islands?" or "What do you believe is the right approach to planning our vacation?"). In contrast, closed ended questions can be answered easily with one word ("How tall are you?" or, "Do you like brussel sprouts?").

Judith could ask Mark open-ended questions like,

- "What most concerns you for us and Janey?"
- "How do you want Janey to grow during the summer?"
- "What could I do to make Janey staying good for you?"

Mark could ask questions like,

- "What's important to you about having Janey here over the summer?"
- "How do you think Janey staying could be good for our family and our marriage?"
- "What have you observed are the ways I relate with Janey which help her grow?"

DON'T TRUST WHAT YOU'RE THINKING IN DEFENSIVE STATES

One of the first things I had to teach Mark and Judith was when they got pissed off and shifted from loving and enjoying each other to being angry, to not trust what they were thinking.

In our beginning sessions, I'd often point out, "Anger and fear distort thought. You're angry and worried right now, and so your thinking is totally skewed towards the negative. Your opinion about the other is dark, and you've forgotten your genuine love and appreciation for who she/he is and how important he/she is to you."

As we've explored previously, defensive states involve amplified or numbed emotions, distorted perspectives, destructive impulses, and diminished capacities for empathy and self-reflection. This is not a problem if we can *observe ourselves* entering defensive states (notice our destructive Shadow), and *take the responsibility* to adjust to a state of healthy response to the present moment (turn destructive Shadow into constructive Shadow).

REPAIR GIMMICK #2: PUBLICLY ADMIT YOU DON'T TRUST WHAT YOU'RE THINKING RIGHT NOW

When I enter a defensive state with Becky, and just tell her, "I don't trust what I'm thinking right now. I'm defensive." This often breaks the spell of the defensive state, but can be difficult because the charged resistance in defensive states tends to be sticky and pernicious since it's associated neurologically with self-protection. Once the spell is broken, I can reach for proportionate and loving emotions, caring perspectives, healthy alternatives, empathetic attunement with Becky, and compassionate self-observation of my own feelings/thoughts/impulses.

THE TWO COMMITMENTS, "I'LL STAY AS LONG AS..." AND "I'LL DO WHAT IT TAKES..."

"I'll stay as long as..." commitments involve consciously having conditions that need to be met for us to stay in relationship. "I'll stay as long as I'm sexually happy." "I'll stay unless I find someone better."

"I'll do what it takes..." commitments *assume* that when we have a problem we will work together to get through it and back to love. "We've been having sex problems, let's start improving sex and get help if we need to." "You can trust me to be faithful and to work on us if we have issues." This is one reason secret affairs and other betrayals are so devastating, one partner has assumed a shared, "I'll do what it takes..." commitment and discovers their spouse wasn't able or willing to walk the walk of such a commitment.

Our adaptive unconscious, our Shadow, drives us to form intimate relationships, have sex, and be embedded in families and tribes. In a free society where we have relationship choices, we naturally *start* relationships with "I'll stay as long as…" commitments. "I'll stay as long as I'm getting my needs met." "I'll stay as long as I feel love happening with us." "I'll stay until I'm reassigned to another posting." "I'll stay as long as I think we're healthy together." "I'll stay as long as I don't feel trapped by our relationship."

"I'll stay as long as…" is a healthy way to begin a relationship because it takes time to know another person, and no matter how interesting or hot someone is in the beginning, his or her destructive Shadow eventually emerges (as does our own) and we discover how effectively we can get back to love through conflict and trials. We *should* begin relationships with "I'll stay as long as…" commitments, and should *always have bottom lines* (inclusive and exclusive boundaries) about what we need from our partner to remain intimate. Some problems like physical or sexual abuse, criminal behavior, or addiction *require us* to put the relationship on the line.

That being said, as we get closer and progress through romantic infatuation into intimate bonding, we have taken our partner's measure and found out how present and able we ourselves can be in service of love. If we've developed confidence in our own and our partner's character, and have faith that we'll both do the work of countering relationship entropy, we shift into "I'll do what it takes," commitments. As I mentioned earlier, wedding ceremonies are filled with "I'll do what it takes," commitments, but they need to be embodied daily over years to be more than empty promises.

"I'll do what it takes," commitments are associated with longer marriages and more efforts to repair conflicts and improve connections when problems arise.

Destructive relational Shadow often emerges in conflicts by shifting someone from an "I'll do what it takes…" commitment to "I'll stay as long as…" commitment, without their conscious knowledge. This emerges in therapy sessions when one partner starts putting the relationship on the line. I'll hear sentences like:

- "I don't want to be in a marriage where..."
- "If you can't learn how to listen, we'll never..."
- "I see other couples be happy and friendly. Why is it we can't..."
- "How can I stay with someone who..."

There are often a lot of absolute words spoken in these conflicts—words like "never," "always," "constantly," "Every time..." etc. Whenever you hear yourself or your partner using absolute terms like this, or putting the relationship on the line, most likely destructive Shadow is distorting the moment and needs to be addressed.

REPAIR GIMMICK #3: CATCH YOURSELF PUTTING THE RELATIONSHIP ON THE LINE, OR USING ABSOLUTES, AND IMMEDIATELY APOLOGIZE

Apologies are priceless in marriages. Trying to have an intimate relationship without ever apologizing is like trying to play tennis and never hitting a forehand—it drastically limits you. Catch yourself using an absolute word—always, never, etc—or putting the relationship on the line, and immediately apologize.

In general, look for your part of a problem, acknowledge it, and apologize to your partner. "I'm sorry! I just got snarky." "I didn't intend to put you down. I'm sorry I hurt you." "You thought I was injured when I lost my cell phone. I'm sorry! That must have been scary for you." "Gary told you I was flirting with the plumber, but we were just laughing about the leak. I'm sorry you had to go through that!"

You'll notice you can apologize just because your partner felt injured or distressed. You don't have to have made a mistake or be in the wrong, you just need to apologize (with sincerity and kindness) every chance you get.

I've heard, "He/she never apologizes," hundreds of times over the last 43 years, and almost every time it reflects a destructive Shadow pattern that needs to be addressed before the couple can consistently return to love.

NORMAL CRAZY AND EXTRA CRAZY

As we've discussed, no human makes it out of childhood without some defensive states hardwired to show up under perceived threat. This is *normal crazy* which everyone has to deal with one way or another. When you're normal crazy in a defensive state, you're distorted and destructive, but have some capacity to notice and adjust back to attunement with yourself and then others. Sometimes you need help, like taking a break, soothing yourself, or recruiting a caring someone to help you feel safe by asking him or her for advice and comfort. When we're normal crazy we can with help usually adjust from normal crazy back to attunement. This is what Mark and Judith did in our earlier example.

Extra crazy is rarer and more dangerous. Extra crazy gets crazier when challenged, and sometimes no soothing or input can make a dent in distorted perspectives or slow down destructive impulses. All of us have been extra crazy at some point or another, usually in extreme circumstances—high anxiety where we can't be comforted, rage states where nothing can stop us from attacking because we are *so mad,* or so bummed and blanked out that no one can reach us. When extra crazy is a habit of consciousness, we *regularly* get distorted and inaccessible. In extra crazy, when someone tries to calm us or help us get undistorted, we double down and get crazier. Consider the two following dialogues between Judith and Mark:

NORMAL CRAZY;

Judith: "Where were you last night?"

Mark: "I had a drink with Bill and then came home."

Judith: "I don't believe you. I think you and Bill were out chasing women. You know what a dog he is."

Mark: Laughing, "Come on! We had a drink and I came home. Is there something bothering you?"

Judith: "When I went to your office today, I saw you smiling and chatting with that young associate, Georgia. You two looked pretty cozy."

Mark: "I'm sorry you felt jealous. I was being friendly but you know I'll never cheat."

Judith: "I'm sorry I got jealous. I don't know what came over me."

EXTRA CRAZY:

Judith: "Where were you last night?"

Mark: "I had a drink with Bill and then came home."

Judith: "I don't believe you. I think you and Bill were out chasing women. You know what a dog he is."

Mark: Laughing, "Come on! We had a drink and I came home. Is there something bothering you?"

Judith: "You're lying! You're such a liar!"

Mark: "That's crazy, Judith! We had a drink at Joe's and I came right home!"

Judith: "Oh? Now I'm crazy? I'm not cheating and lying."

Mark: "Well, screw you then! I'm not putting up with this—I'll see you later!"

You notice how extra crazy in one partner activates extra crazy in the other. In escalating conflict this can cycle into chronic emotional or even physical abuse—extra crazy.

If extra crazy happens regularly with you or your spouse—daily, weekly, or involving even occasional emotional or physical abuse—your marriage is in trouble and you should find a therapist *now*.

PROJECTIVE IDENTIFICATION, DESTRUCTIVE SHADOW ON STEROIDS

One particularly pernicious form of extra crazy is projective iden-tification, a distinguishing characteristic of borderline and narcissistic personality disorders, but something most people have experienced at one time or another. Projective identification is unconsciously projecting your nastiest, ugliest side, onto another person and then either chronically tormenting them (borderline reaction) or contemptuously dismissing them from your life (narcissistic reaction).[132]

Projective identification in marriages leads to instability and emotional and physical violence—clinging and torturing with borderlines and demeaning and withdrawing with narcissists.

If you challenge your partner clinging and torturing or demeaning and withdrawing and they consistently get more violent, or if you are challenged by your spouse and *you* consistently get more violent, see a therapist *now!*

Self-help is wonderful, and you can learn incredible knowledge and skills from books like this, or classes from experts like myself who are dedicated to love and healing.

But extra crazy needs more than books or classes, it needs ongoing psychotherapy focused on *extra crazy*. Without major work, extra crazy can plague individuals, couples, and families for lifetimes. With as little as three years' work borderline and narcissistic personality disorders can be healed and integrated into healthy, normal crazy people, but you have to do the work.

SECRET AFFAIRS—ALMOST ALWAYS A WRONG TURN

How do you handle anger with your partner? Romantic or sexual yearning? Play? Shame? Concern? Potentially threatening information like attractions to others, or secrets you might keep from him or her?

Not sure? Well, if hiding such material frequently seems like a good idea, your marriage is probably in trouble. We need to trust our partner with almost everything. What we hide often gives destructive Shadow power to hurt us.

Even worse, when we don't talk with our spouse about emotionally charged material, the feelings of loneliness and separation makes us vulnerable to an attractive other who is interested in us and easy to talk to. This is one way cluelessness and/or self-indulgence can lead to secret affairs—devastating to marriages. Secret affairs create huge outflows of destructive Shadow.

A woman named Sylvia came in to see me one time, bored with her husband Luke and her life with their two small children. She had developed a special friendship with Mario at work with whom she had fascinating conversations. They met to share hikes in the mountains, poetry, and happy talk about the world. Sylvia said they were, "Just friends."

I tried to warn her, "Sylvia! You are romantically infatuated with Mario and at the edge of a secret affair. It will be yummy beyond belief at first, and then a total shitstorm in your marriage and family. Tell Mario no more hikes, tell Luke what happened, and then get into couples' therapy."

Sylvia would have none of it, "My life is boring! All Luke does is drink beer and watch TV. Mario loves art, writes poetry, has political insights. We can keep it to being friends."

I look at her skeptically, "Really?"

Sylvia doubled down, "Luke can't handle the truth, but I'll think about what you've told me." She left the session and I didn't see her again until six months later after Luke discovered her secret affair with Mario—cell phones and modern technology are making secret affairs progressively harder, which is a good thing in my opinion.

Overwhelmed with fear of losing her family, and wanting Luke's affection and trust back, Sylvia insisted on everybody doing therapy to clean up the mess.

All this left Sylvia miserable, losing weight, simultaneously grieving for Mario and trying to salvage Luke, whom she suddenly was in danger of losing.

Destructive Shadow was flooding everybody, and it was only through hard work and courageous actions that Sylvia and Luke eventually came back to trust, friendship, and love.

Our lust and romantic infatuation drives are cued by random erotic polarities—a guy catches the eye of an attractive woman, a woman blushes with pleasure when an attractive man compliments her dress. When we keep these reactions in Shadow—out of conscious awareness—they can accelerate into flirting, distracting attractions, and secret affairs. The earlier we catch these Shadow impulses and regulate them according to our principles, the better.

How do we inoculate ourselves from secret affairs as well as a host of other attachment injuries?

Here's how. We cultivate an open friendship with our spouse and insist on nourishing our marital love affair.

CULTIVATING AN OPEN FRIENDSHIP WITH MY SPOUSE

As I mentioned at the beginning of this chapter, one happiness study found that people were on average 35 percent happier when they lived next door to a good friend, and 8 percent happier living with a spouse.[133]

Excuse me, *what?*

Obviously there are a lot of married couples who are not currently good friends. Why is this?

First of all, let's define good friend and distinguish a good friend from a constantly-to-occasionally difficult friend.

A *good* friend is someone you seek out for contact and play. A *good* friend takes your side and supports you reliably. A *good* friend is there for you when you need him or her, and doesn't let you down.

Good friend is a fairly demanding relationship—characterized by a lot of commitment and understanding. When we're around good friends our blood pressure goes down, our heart rate goes down, stress hormones (like cortisol and CRF) diminish, and our heart rate variability goes up (remember, heart rate variability is perhaps the single most robust predictor of general health and well-being).

Other kinds of friends might be constantly difficult or occasionally difficult for us to be with. Being around constantly-or-occasionally difficult friends causes stress hormone levels, blood pressure, and heart rate to elevate. Weirdly, in one study occasionally-difficult-friends caused more stress elevations than constantly-difficult friends, and now we're beginning to see the genesis of the 35 percent vs. 8 percent statistic.

If we're *good* friends with our spouse, we both benefit, but if we're constantly-to-occasionally difficult friends with our spouse, our life stress increases. I suspect that this is why women in long-term unhappy marriages don't live as long on average as single women. Happily married women and any kind of married guys (happily or unhappily married) tend to live the longest (I guess even having a woman around who doesn't like you still makes a man healthier).

So we want to be *good* friends with our spouse, which involves doing a lot of positive behaviors and not doing a lot of negative ones. This always includes *consistently surrendering to* constructive Shadow influences and *consistently regulating* destructive Shadow.

Here are some examples of what good friends consistently do:

- Almost always respond positively to bids for attention or affection.
- Be interested in each other's lives and be supportive of both plea-surable and painful experiences.
- Always hold the other as a good person.
- If there is an injury, assume it was a mistake or miscommunication of some sort that can be healed by supportive dialogue, and be fully available to engage in supportive dialogue, acknowledging your part of the problem and apologizing your any pain you might have caused.
- Give and receive positive influence easily.

Here are some examples of what good friends consistently regulate in themselves to not hurt each other:

- Get progressively better at noticing injuries like discounts, hostile or contemptuous tones, or failure to support, and immediately apologize and work to repair.
- In conflict ask open-ended questions with the goals of compas-sionate understanding and resolution back to affection, until

there is shared acceptance and understanding, even if there are still disagreements.

• Avoid betrayals and injuries like affairs, financial shenanigans, lies, put-downs, and public humiliations.

WHAT DO YOU MEAN BY "OPEN" IN "CULTIVATING AN OPEN FRIENDSHIP WITH MY SPOUSE?"

Openness does not mean complete transparency. Couples don't need to reveal everything they think, do, and imagine to each other. No one has the time, patience, or interest to know *everything* about another person, even a beloved spouse.

There is also personal material that we don't share unless our spouse asks us about it—and then we answer honestly. Becky doesn't need to hear about every time I desire an attractive woman, and I don't need to hear about every time she gets irritated at me because I don't like doing yard work. If she asks, I'll tell her, and if I ask, she'll tell me—we are not *hiding*, we are adjusting and protecting.

Sometimes our spouse makes a non-repetitive mistake—leaves his socks on the floor when he usually picks them up, or she leaves the dishes when she's usually pretty good about cleaning the kitchen—and we give the other a pass. If it's me, I tell myself some version of, "This is no big deal, it's not a pattern, and Becky's great," and I feel better and forget about the episode. Patterns often need discussion—occasional mistakes can often be simply let go.

The standard for material we don't disclose but aren't hiding is that, if our spouse finds out about it, we would feel morally justified about not telling him or her at the time.

Openness *does* mean *not hiding anything important to our spouse.* We know the material our spouse would feel injured not hearing. If I get a bad medical diagnosis and don't tell my wife, she'll be justifiably pissed off. If George at work makes passes at you and you don't tell me, I'll be offended.

The standard for material we hide in unhealthy ways is that, if our spouse found out about it, they'd feel betrayed and we'd feel ashamed.

YOU ONLY KNOW WHAT YOU KNOW

Since Shadow is unknown until it emerges, happy couples only hold each other responsible for what they are conscious of. Say I forget to pick up your dry cleaning (I didn't want to do it in the first place), and you tell me it bugs you and you think I "Forgot on purpose." I try that on, consider it, remember being irritated about you asking, and the destructive Shadow of forgetting the errand makes it into the light of my conscious awareness. I say, " I'm sorry! I think you're right! I probably was indirectly expressing irritation. I didn't want to do it, but said 'yes' anyway. What can I do to help you feel better?" You soften as I validate and offer repair.

You recognize I adjusted as soon as I became conscious of my mistake, and you forgive me for my hostile act because I'm taking responsibility for it *as soon as I am aware of it*. I'm also concerned for your feelings, and willing to make amends. Happy couples don't demand perfect knowledge of destructive Shadow, only that each takes responsibility for it when it arises.

On the other hand, I might say, "I think I just forgot, and I'm sorry. I'll keep paying attention to see if it's a pattern." I can't really validate your theory of me being passive aggressive as I look at myself. At that point it's a good idea for you to go, "I might be wrong, but thanks for paying attention." We assume we're both doing our best to tell the truth.

So that's the "Open friendship" part of inoculating marriages from attachment traumas, but what about the "Cultivating the marital love affair" part?

THE MARITAL LOVE AFFAIR, CULTURAL SHADOW, AND BEATING THE ODDS

The marital love affair is one of the main differences between a friendship and a marriage. We don't have sex with our friends (a least not when we're married—if we do we're literally screwing up our lives). An alarming number of couples either take the marital love affair for granted, or, even worse, give up on the marital love affair because it requires too much effort to keep sex and romance consistently alive and growing through life challenges of work, children, aging, defensive states, and other sources of destructive sexual Shadow.

In Chapter 8 on Sexual Shadow and in this chapter we've discussed how sexual urgency often fades after romantic infatuation progresses into intimate bonding. Western culture certainly loves couples who maintain eroticism and romance during all the life stages, but doesn't provide a whole lot of direction about how to do it.

A key to supporting the marital love affair is revealed by the John Gottman distinguishing characteristic of couples who had "plenty of sex" from couples who were sexually dissatisfied and alienated.

When a plenty-of-sex partner initiated sex and his or her spouse said, "No," he or she responded with love. Not negative criticism or whining, or even neutral nonchalance or disengagement—he or she responded to "No" with affection and warmth.

As I said in the last chapter, I believe that this characteristic of meeting a potential rejection with warmth is the tip of an iceberg comprised of many more positive connections and capacities in plenty-of-sex couples. To me it suggests willingness to normalize talking about sex, safety with "Yes" and "No" in many contexts, a general attitude of support in the relationship, and, maybe most of all, a genuine friendship between the partners. This has been true for plenty-of-sex couples that I've worked with over the years.

But responding with warmth to a "No," is not *pretending* to respond with warmth, and we can't just dial up confidence and warmth in the face of a potential sexual rejections. People are incredibly vulnerable and sensitive about sex, perceived rejection, and even about initiating sex. Some partners simply stop initiating if they experience *even one* sexual rejection. Some partners *cannot* initiate—they have been programmed by life and trauma to literally be unable to suggest lovemaking.

Half of marriages end in divorce. Of the couples who stay together, I suspect at least half feel dissatisfied and unfulfilled sexually—and I think this is a conservative estimate. That gives newlyweds at best a 50 percent chance of staying together and a 25 percent chance of having a plenty-of-sex long term marriage. These are miserable statistics that we need to change as a culture. How do we do it? Let's start with you!

If you're in a plenty-of-sex marriage, I suggest you go out this week and celebrate being in the top 25 percent of married couples in the U.S. when it comes to sexual fulfillment. Have a good time and toast each other with the beverages of your choice.

If you're not a plenty-of-sex marriage, check out my six core concept mini-courses on *Talking Sex,* or my audio course *Loving Completely* (both on my drkeithwitt.com website). If sex doesn't get better and keep getting better, find a therapist who likes you, likes sex, and knows how to help couples work through problems, and work with that therapist until you feel fulfilled sexually most of the time.

I know that this *sounds* simple, and this is where marital Shadow is heavily involved. Most couples don't enter therapy until years after problems start (on average, six years[134]). Many people would rather not talk explicitly about sex, and that goes triple for sexual blocks, conflicts, and traumas. Destructive Shadow leads people away from addressing sexual issues with forgetting, denial, secret affairs, embarrassment, misinterpreted religious messages, and "I'm too tired tonight," types of excuses that stretch into *years* of sexual deprivation.

EXERCISE:
COMMIT TO BEING A PLENTY-OF-SEX COUPLE.

Read this chapter with your spouse and resolve to be a plenty of sex marriage. Discuss your strengths and vulnerabilities as lovers, and come up with at least one improvement for each vulnerability. Make efforts to follow through on those improvements. Make a list of the top five forms of contact and pleasure that help you feel sexually fulfilled and share it with your partner. Try to offer at least two of your partner's top five in the next three days. If all this doesn't result in progress, find a good couples' therapist and receive his or her influence to grow and love better.

What are some common problems in creating a plenty-of-sex marriage?

- One person wants more frequency and the other feels pressured, put upon, or inadequate.
- One person has a kink-like bondage, S&M, or some fetish like heels, lingerie, or semi-public sex, and the other is turned off.
- Someone feels bad about his or her body because of body image issues like weight, scarring, or age.
- One person is inhibited to have sex with other people in the house and they have children so there are *always* other people in the house.
- One person is frightened of the other's anger, anxiety, depression, or habitual contempt or criticism.
- The more masculine partner is unresolved or ambivalent about learning and practicing masculine presence, or has trouble being a trustable, confident lover.
- The more feminine partner is conflicted about being a fountain of love, offering free-flowing emotion and devotional surrender to trustable masculine direction.
- A couple unconsciously avoids explicit talk about sex.
- One or both partners have secret sexual Shadow shame (like molestations, signature injuries with their spouse, or crippling sexual inhibitions) that they've never shared, or have trouble sharing.

All these problems can be overwhelming, and any one of them deserves to be taken seriously.

Most sex helper types lean more towards either sexual enrichment (give people permission, information, and suggestions and they blossom), or sex therapy (find the wounds and heal them). I've found that couples usually begin with sexual enrichment and then dive into sex therapy when blocks emerge.

The most important principle for supporting the marital love affair is to talk regularly about sexual fulfillment and get help if you're not making satisfactory progress.

▶ **Sex therapy sidebar:** *Back in the 1970s when I did my initial sex therapy training in California, there were dozens of sex therapy clinics and hundreds of "Sex Therapists" of many persuasions scattered across the state. By 1980 most of them were out of business. Why did that happen?*

In those ten years, the culture changed to somewhat normalize explicitly talking about the marital love affair, and all the couples who just needed permission, information, and a few suggestions had gotten their input and were doing okay by the standards of the day. What was left were couples who had problems with their friendship, substance abuse, sexual compulsivity, infidelity, unresolved early trauma, or other complex destructive Shadow patterns. These couples needed more experienced therapists who could focus on these underlying issues, and many of the we-just-work-on-sex therapists went out of business.

HELPING EACH OTHER SURRENDER TO CONSTRUCTIVE SHADOW AND DIALYSIZE DESTRUCTIVE SHADOW IS A TANTRIC PROCESS

We marry to support and love each other and to help one another grow into better people. This is a tantric process of using the fabric of everyday existence and relationship to deepen emotionally and spiritually. Incorporating attuned awareness of your Shadow and your partner's Shadow, both constructive and destructive, leads to numerous powerful tantric practices—tantric meaning finding spiritual significance in body, relationships, and sensation. Most of the exercises in this chapter and Chapter 8 are tantric practices.

SIGNS OF GROWTH AND DEEPENING LOVE

As you become attuned to the fractal interfaces between your conscious self and Shadow, between you and your spouse, and between you and the world, the fabric of your marriage is revealed. As you monitor whether you seem to be progressing to more or less intimacy, more or less fulfillment, more or less conflict, and more or less distortion and clarity, you can share with your spouse, repair injuries, and create positive rituals of friendship, family, and eroticism. All these awarenesses and activities strengthen constructive Shadow and highlight destructive Shadow when it arises, giving us opportunities to consciously dialysize it into constructive Shadow.

USE THE FIVE STARS AS RELATIONSHIP MAINTENANCE TOOLS

In my audio class, *Loving Completely,* I recommend people evaluate potential lovers, themselves, and their spouse by asking five central questions, which I call the Five Stars.[135]

The Five Stars are the five questions:

1. **Is there erotic polarity, a spark of attraction, between me and my spouse?** We have energetic polarities with everyone we encounter, but some polarities have an erotic tingle. If you're a guy, you probably look at your wife sometimes and feel a subtle to huge sexual desire. If you're a woman, you might occasionally

think about your husband, "He's sweet," or feel a pleasant (or maybe uncomfortable) awareness of your body as he compliments how hot your new dress is.

2. **Does my spouse maintain his or her physical and psychological health?** They don't have to be buff, they just need to seem interested in staying reasonably healthy and happy, and willing to put regular effort into health. For instance, does he or she eat healthy food, exercise at least moderately, avoid cigarettes and addictions, and ask for and receive help from you and others when having physical or emotional problems?

3. **When we're in conflict, is my spouse able and willing to do what it takes to get back to love?** "Able" asks if he or she has the depth, knowledge, skills, and maturity to deal productively with conflict. "Willing" asks if they can manage their own fears, resentments, and impulses to attack and flee enough to hang in with you in conflict and work back to understanding and affection.

4. **How does my spouse show up as a parent or family member?** We all grew up in some family experience. Does my spouse put him or herself second when needed by a child? Does he or she relate well and set appropriate boundaries with different family members?

5. **Does my spouse have deep soul's purpose, something larger than themselves, in their life, and does he or she feel appreciation and admiration for what's deeply meaningful—even sacred—to me?** We all have some sense of the sacred, and, after the initial romantic infatuation stage of a relationship burns out, we usually don't want a partner whose *sole reason for being is to be with us.* His or her life must also matter to them separate from us. Also, we need partners who respect and at least somewhat understand what's important or sacred to us. If I take my relationship with God, spirit, or the infinite seriously, I need you to understand and respect how special that is. If you find a deeper connectedness and sense of unity doing yoga, parenting your child, volunteering

for youth soccer, or having integrity in your job, you need me to recognize and honor this special area for you.

Using the five stars as five dimensions to continually evaluate yourself and your marriage is one way of making sure you don't let important issues slip through the cracks. Remember, marital entropy requires constant attention.

EXERCISE:

Using the Five Stars as a tantric practice with yourself and your spouse.

- *Ask yourself the Five Stars about your spouse and write about it in your journal.*
- *Ask yourself the Five Stars about yourself and write about it in your journal.*
- *Share all this with your spouse and invite him or her to do the same.*
- *If problems arise that you can't repair after several conversations, get help from a good therapist.*
- *Every month or so have a Five Star conversation with your spouse to see how you two are doing, and what adjustments you can make now towards fun, love, repair, passion, and growth.*

10
PARENTAL SHADOW

Our friends are getting older, I guess that we are too
Without their loving kindness, I don't know what I'd do
The wine bottle is half empty, the money is all spent
We're a cross between our parents and hippies in a tent.
Love calls like a wild thing, it's another day
A spring wind blew my list of things to do away.

—GREG BROWN, LOVE CALLS

Are you a parent?

If you are, you know what happens when your first baby is born—everything changes! If you're not a parent, consider how your birth completely transformed *your* parents' lives. Many of our most intimate and influential social/emotional/spiritual bonds spring from family relationships.

Do we want to be better parents? How could we not? We love our children so much and want what's best for them.

Good parenting in the fifties and sixties cultures I grew up in meant providing safety, love, support, good nutrition, physical activities, social stimulation, and educational opportunities—incredibly caring and sophisticated parenting by historical standards. That being said, those cultures were blind to parental Shadow in countless ways. For example:

- Spanking was routinely practiced, and corporal punishment with paddles was accepted practice in many private and some public schools.
- Humiliating children—including publicly—was considered effective parenting, and appropriate on occasion.
- The idea that non-conscious forces drive parents and children was incomprehensible to many of the Greatest Generation. They came out of the depression *into* WWII! Providing love, safety, and financial security in a traditional family felt pretty good to them, and the idea that incredibly complex psychological dynamics permeated families and development seemed esoteric—even self-indulgent.
- Family as an emotional system with deep ties and intergenerational transfer of habits and biases was just beginning to be researched and popularized in psychology, and was viewed dismissively by many psychotherapists who believed in working with individuals, not families.
- In the fifties we had practically no knowledge of how brains developed in connection with other brains, and neuroscientists/developmentalists were often clueless or deluded about memory, emotion, motivation, intimacy, basic drives, and thought.

Through neuroresearch and social research we've learned an incredible amount about families, development, and parenting in the last sixty years.

We now know:

- That secure attachment styles (briefly mentioned in Chapter 3) in parents and children support happiness and optimal development *significantly* better than insecure attachment styles. Infants and children who get the attunement, space, and attention they need tend to feel solid in the world and confident that parents will be

Neuroscience sidebar: *Even today there are fierce debates. For instance, some neuroscientists believe specific parts of the brain act somewhat autonomously—like the right hemisphere "containing" intuition, the adaptive unconscious, habits, and our autobiographical memory.[136] These conclusions arise largely from fMRI studies of brains. The fMRI uses electromagnetic imaging to measure increased blood flow to specific areas associated with an experience. Put a person in the fMRI scanner, present an evocative image, sound, or story, and then measure where blood flow increases. It makes sense that if the blood flow goes up, that part of the brain is associated somehow with the experience, but is the activity separate from the rest of the nervous system?*

Some neuroscientists believe that increased-blood-flow-areas reflect switching/organizing centers that activate whole-brain responses—that we're always harnessing the whole brain in any moment.[137]

I lean towards both approaches myself: 85 billion neurons, hooked up with more connections than there are stars in the universe, generating a coherent electromagnetic field that keeps self-organizing just to the edge of chaos, right on evolution's crest.[138] I vote for more-complexity-and-wholeness both/and explanations when offered differing perspectives.

around, safe, and effective. Kids who are neglected, abused, or poorly attuned to tend to struggle—they're more likely to shut down, act out, suffer extreme anxiety, or sink into depression.[139]

- Goodness of fit between parent and child can be improved with conscious parenting. Our kids are born with hard-wired personality characteristics like activity level, rhythmicity, and shyness. Parents who can understand their child's type and adjust accordingly have happier more successful children.[140]

- Authoritative parenting is better than authoritarian, permissive, or disengaged parenting. Parents in charge, but flexible, fair, and attuned, have healthier children and better marriages than parents who are hostile/controlling, disengaged, or permissive.[141]

- Parents who have a good relationship with each other have healthier kids. A couple taking care of their love helps kids at every age.

- Emotionally coaching attitudes are mostly better for kids than emotionally dismissing attitudes. Viewing emotions as teaching opportunities that need dialogue, labeling of feelings, and problem solving/boundary setting predicts academic and social success, resilience, and a solid sense of self in kids.[142]

- Liberation hierarchies are much better than dominator or chaotic hierarchies. Creating a family structure with compassionate parents firmly in charge, but open to feedback and concerned with care and fairness supports healthy development hugely more than parents who bully, neglect, or can't attune with love.[143]

- Open systems are better than closed systems. Healthy families welcome outside input and enrichment opportunities—they are open to new ideas and new people.

- Growth mindsets are better than fixed mindsets. Effort and progress orientations generate more joy and success than get-the-A/win-the-game-at-all-costs/failure-is-shameful orientations.

- Parents who receive influence to grow are better for kids than parents who think they know it all. Being a superior parent means dedicating yourself to a lifetime of learning how to love your children more effectively.[144]

You see a framework emerging. We want to create secure attachment styles in our kids, and be securely attached to our spouse. We want to support each child's unique temperament. We want to practice authoritative parenting. We want to embody emotional coaching attitudes and behaviors. We want to create liberation hierarchies in our family where things are fair, we share, and we care for each other. We want our families to be open systems rather than closed systems. We want to encourage growth mindsets and not encourage fixed mindsets in both our children and ourselves. We want to keep improving and growing as parents.

What stops us from doing all this all the time?

Shadow.

PARENTAL SHADOW EXERCISE #1:

- *What was your best moment with you and your mother? Your father? Write about these moments in detail in your journal. What parental characteristics were each of them embodying in these wonderful moments?*
- *How do you embody these positive parental characteristics? Write how you do.*
- *What was your worst moment with you and your mother? Your father? Write about these moments in detail. What less-than-optimal parental characteristics were each of them embodying in these painful moments?*
- *How do you embody these less-than-optimal parental characteristics? Write how in as much detail as possible.*
- *Write how these moments reflect your constructive and destructive parental Shadow—be alert for the interfaces (similarities, differences, and influences) between who you are now and how your parents were when you were growing up.*
- *Share all this with your partner. Write about your conversation.*
- *Share all this with your kids—at any age! There is age-appropriate language for discussing Shadow at every developmental fulcrum— just adjust to your kid's language and thinking abilities and reach to understand his or her interior sense of the world. Interiors are you kid's feelings, beliefs, and subjective experiences. Write about your conversations.*

- *Read everything you've written and make a list of parental virtues you need to accept and honor in yourself, and then another list of destructive habits you need to improve.*
- *Share this with someone you love, with an emphasis on how this exercise opens up windows to some of your core constructive and destructive parental Shadow. Write about your conversation.*

IN THIS CHAPTER WE WILL:

- Explore parental Shadow—mine, yours, everyone's.
- Define "Superior parent."
- Draw a family genogram, and find Shadow reflected in it.
- Look more deeply at secure and insecure attachment in children and parents.
- Listen to some ancestral voices of genetic Shadow.
- Hear how Stella Chess and Alexander Thomas pioneered understanding children as unique expressions of consciousness.
- Create a goodness-of-fit chart for you and your family.
- Further explore how epigenetics influences gene expression, and revisit the weird world of the Willard/Trivers hypothesis.
- Explain further how authoritative parenting works better than authoritarian, permissive, or uninvolved parenting.
- Detail practices to help grow and integrate parental Shadow.

MOST IMPORTANT JOB

Parenting has got to be the most important job we'll ever have, and we usually spend more time learning how to drive our cars than learning how to parent our children.

Since I think good parenting is being attuned, caring, and serving the moment—arguably core values for relating to everyone—I believe we are responsible for parenting the world.

We are especially responsible to help *our* kids thrive—ancient ancestral voices, speaking through genetic mandates, motivate us to protect, help, and support our children. Constructive parental Shadow optimally serves these drives by optimizing our children's developmental environments and being informed by the kinds of frameworks and practices mentioned above. Destructive parental Shadow injures our children and families as we indulge destructive impulses to attack, avoid, or resist caring influences from others.

Constructive parental Shadow generates compassionate perspectives and impulses to attune to and nurture others—especially our children. Destructive parental Shadow generates distorted perspectives and impulses to disconnect from and hurt others—especially our children.

Parents' drives to nourish and protect children and family are enormously challenging in modern and post-modern society where we don't have much tribal support to guide us and provide constant help. In one hunter-gatherer tribe, babies were held by ten adults every hour and almost the whole tribe every day.[145] Modern mothers are not surrounded by such support.

In fundamentalist cultures—where tradition and spiritual mandates from sacred texts dominate day-to-day life, parent and child roles and responsibilities are mapped out and unquestioned. This provides guidance, but also allows spare-the-rod-and-spoil-the-child-type destructive Shadow forces to contaminate parenting and hurt children's development.

Modern and post-modern parents don't subscribe to blind obedience to rigid rules. For instance, "Do it because I say!" is no longer OK with many modern parents—we know bullying children hurts them. We want to parent well, but are often unclear about what that means.

This is where social research is invaluable, beginning with a relatively simple formula for being a superior parent.

WHAT IS A SUPERIOR PARENT?

A superior parent is simply a parent who does his or her best to protect and care for children and is open to a lifetime of receiving influence to be a better parent.

That's it. It doesn't matter as much where you start as whether you're willing to keep improving. You can start as a miserable parent, but if you do your best to protect and support your child and are willing to receive caring influence from wise others, in the twenty-first century you will grow into a superior parent.

Parenting changes us in ways that can't be fully described to non-parents. As we change, we can consciously utilize feedback of all sorts from our children, our spouse, experts, and from the outside world about what works better and what works worse for each of our children. This process naturally takes us again and again into constructive and destructive parental Shadow—amplifying constructive and dialysizing destructive Shadow in ways that grow our adaptive unconscious parental selves. That's being superior parents, and the process never stops.

My kids, Ethan and Zoe, are currently 30 and 27 respectively. I expect to be a better parent next year to them than I am this year. Why? I'm open to new perspectives, I study human thriving and striving, and I know what I believe right now is just my *current best understanding*. Looking back, I'm shocked with how little I knew about infants when Ethan was born and how much more I know about toddlers and children today than when my kids were growing up. I'm appalled at how immature I was in so many ways as Ethan and Zoe progressed through complicated developmental fulcrums. That being said, I did the best I could during those years, and knew far more than my parents' generation (and most of my contemporaries) about almost everything to do with families and childrearing.

On my deathbed I'll hopefully still be working on being a better parent to my children.

> **Deathbed sidebar:** *Speaking of deathbeds, Australian Bronnie Ware worked as a caregiver for dying people, and asked all of them what they would have changed in their lives—what regrets they had. She found five themes:*[146]

- *I wish I had the courage to live a life true to myself.*
- *I wished I hadn't worked so hard.*
- *I wish I had the courage to express my feelings.*
- *I wish I'd stayed in touch with my friends.*
- *I wish I'd let myself be happier.*

All of these in one way or another involve children and family. Even more, how someone embodies each of these has profound effects on his or her children. All five regrets reflect qualities these people not only yearned to embody more fully themselves, but often wished to help their children embody more fully.

Consider deciding to embody all five starting right now! Live a life true to yourself. Work in a way that supports a balanced life. Express your feelings—with acceptance and caring intent for your experience and others' experience. Stay in touch with the friends and family that bring you joy and love. Consciously recognize each hour of each day that happiness is a choice and you can decide to be happier right now.

If you resist improving in these areas you are at a fractal interface between your conscious self and your destructive Shadow—a growth opportunity! Be curious about your resistance and engage in self-reflective dialogue with someone you trust about what might be stopping you and how to make progress in these areas.

PARENTAL SHADOW EVERYWHERE

The twenty-first century parental standard is increasingly that each human is unique, and as parents it's our responsibility to provide the parenting that's best for our unique child.

Every day in my practice parents struggle with how to respond to infants, toddlers, kids, teens, and grown children with a staggering range of issues and personalities. Always beneath the surface in these relationships are Shadow selves harmonizing, conflicting, and informing, with parents holding the ultimate responsibility in managing the parent/child relationships.

Massive constructive and destructive Shadow forces are stirred up and unleashed as we become parents. Our biological priming, our family of origin programming, our defensive tendencies, our relationship with our spouse (challenged by the transition into parenthood and the demands of family), and whatever cultures we are embedded in all contribute to our Shadow selves delivering regular waves of impulses, reactions, stories, and relational patterns. These all interact in complex ways with our children, our spouse, and our communities, which generates more individual and interpersonal patterns, more Shadow programming, and more challenges.

> ▶ **Psychotherapy sidebar:** *This is why all therapists are taught to not do therapy with their own family members. There is way too much Shadow material that bubbles up in the emotional crucible of the therapy session for a therapist to keep his bearings and be effective with people he shares so much personal history, longings, dreams, and desires with.*

Our children grow in these cauldrons of Shadow, developing their own sense of self and their own Shadow programming. We want to optimize their development but often don't have maps for dealing with ourselves, our children, and our spouses in different situations.

This chapter will provide some maps, beginning with exploring how our extended family shapes constructive and destructive Shadow.

OUR FAMILY OF ORIGIN—WHAT A GENOGRAM CAN TELL US ABOUT FAMILY AND PARENTING

Jeremy is forty-six, Helen is forty-two, and they have three children, Jim and Jake, eight and six respectively, and three-year-old Sara. Jeremy prides himself on being an involved father and coaches Jim's basketball team. Here they are at an important game with cross-town rivals, and Jim is not playing particularly well.

"Pass the ball, Jim! Pass the ball!" Jeremy yells from the sideline. "No! Don't dribble into the corner!" He turns to Helen furiously, "Talk to him during the break! He's not concentrating! Tell him he has to pass the damn ball better!" Sara huddles next to Helen, trying to stay invisible. Jake is at a play date.

Helen tries to calm Sara and Jeremy simultaneously, "Okay. I'll talk to him. Everything's fine!"

Not easily soothed, Jeremy continues to berate and scream directions until Jim runs crying from the gym, with Helen giving chase to try to bring him down from his outraged distress, and Jeremy attempting to comfort the now distraught Sara. Later Helen tells me how frustrated and infuriated she was at Jeremy's behavior.

Jeremy and Jim's team won the game. Great. The real issue, everyone's destructive Shadow, is mostly invisible except to Helen. She can feel the need for emotional soothing and process-oriented parenting—*how* events are unfolding being much more important than winning, losing, or what happens—but when she and Jeremy are upset they have no shared platform to talk productively. When she tries to discuss the incident later at home, it quickly accelerates into mutual accusations and despair.

A week after the incident, we talk about it in session.

"I don't know why I yell like that." Jeremy says. "I'm so sorry Helen."

Helen is still angry and protective. "You always apologize afterwards, Jeremy, but that doesn't help the kids!"

I ask them, "Have either of you ever done a genogram?" Both shake their heads no. "A genogram is getting a big sheet of paper and putting your name in the center, and everyone in your extended family ordered around you in a generational hierarchy with oldest on top. Then you put different lines to brothers, sisters, mothers, fathers, spouses, children—everybody—with a solid line meaning a nurturing relationship, dotted line meaning a tenuous or even nonexistent relationship, and a line with horizontal slashes in it a conflicted relationship. Then underneath each name you put a few descriptors that characterize that person—gentle, harsh, alcoholic, unfaithful, faithful, happy, loving, erratic, steady, abusive, nurturing—and especially how they were with you. Monica McGoldrick and Randy Gerson developed the genogram techniques from the ideas of a psychiatrist/researcher named Murray Bowen who studied families around eighty years ago."[147]

One of Helen's destructive Shadow impulses is hostile analysis, and she is super-sharp and super-quick. "Jeremy's father was totally demanding and over-involved!"

Jeremy rolls his eyes, "Well *your* mother is a pain-in-the-ass perfectionist you can't stand!"

Helen jumps to her Mother's defense (though her mother regularly drives her crazy). "She loves me and supports who I am!"

I interject, "Wait a second! Jeremy said, 'I don't know why I yell like that,' and I think we should explore why he yells like that." I turn to him, "So, what characterized your relationship with your dad?"

Jeremy looks thoughtful, "We were close. He coached my teams and went to every game. He was totally dedicated to my two sisters and me."

Looking into his left eye (wanting to engage his emotionally dominant right hemisphere), I ask, "How was he when you lost?"

Jeremy instantly tears up. "He was disappointed, but always supportive. *I* couldn't stand it when I lost."

I hold his gaze just a moment until he makes the connection to him and his kids. He gets some of it, "I really hate it when the boys' teams lose—I take it personally. But I tell them it's fine."

I go on. "They can feel your dread of losing and your pain when they make mistakes, just as you felt your father's. This conditions their adaptive unconscious—their Shadow—to urgently try to avoid the distress. Some kids unconsciously strive super-hard, or don't try, or freeze up, or break down into tears or rage. That's Jim when he loses it. Some kids work hard constantly and are never satisfied except momentarily—that was you as a child and today as a grown up. You feel compelled to *constantly* excel and win to protect you from the humiliation of not being the best." Both Jeremy and Helen are nodding now, interested. I go on.

"Kids grow best with a focus on effort and progress being the standard and outcomes being secondary. Ideally, poor performance guides your efforts to improve, and great performance feels good and validates your efforts. You win, you lose, the painting is great, it's a mess, but are you progressing? Are you improving at something that is important to you? What's the current technique or skill that you're working on, and let's play with that. This is called a growth mindset which generally results in more progress, happiness, and success.[148]

To encourage this while teaching, education researchers have found that kids learn best when you show them something, let them fool around while you ignore mistakes until they do something successful, and then you comment on how they got it right and give them another tip."

Jeremy laughs, "Boy! I was never coached that way!"

I laugh with him, "Me neither, and I hated losing. In retrospect, that dramatically slowed my progress in the sports I loved. Even worse, it dramatically lessened my *enjoyment* of the sports I loved."

PARENTING TIP: CULTIVATE GROWTH MINDSETS

- *Notice when you are more focused on outcomes with your child—like winning, getting the right answer, getting an A, painting the perfect picture—and when you are more focused on how they are engaged. Are they interested, making efforts, progressing?*
- *Try to politely acknowledge successes, but visibly enjoy effort, interest, and progress with your kid in everything from chores to schoolwork. Let them know your admiration when they are making efforts and expanding.*

• *After doing this for a week, ask your spouse how you've been doing as a parent. Others often see us better than we see ourselves, and your spouse will probably report pleasure at your efforts and progress.*

EXERCISE:
DRAW YOUR GENOGRAM

• *Get a big sheet of paper and put your name in the center, and everyone in your extended family ordered around you in a generational hierarchy with oldest on top, youngest children on the bottom. Go at least as far in the past as your grandparents, and at least as far into your extended family as your uncles, aunts, and cousins. You can paste pictures of people—or images, drawings, or symbols—next to their names if you'd like.*
• *Connect everyone with lines—with a solid line meaning a nurturing relationship, dotted line meaning a tenuous or even mostly nonexistent relationship, and a line with horizontal slashes for a conflicted relationship.*
• *Underneath each name put a few descriptors that characterize that person—gentle, harsh, alcoholic, faithful, unfaithful, happy, loving, erratic, abusive, nurturing—and especially how they were with you if you had any contact with them.*
• *Look at everyone and consider that you probably have some capacity to be like many of them, have tendencies similar to some of them, and have destructive and constructive Shadow programming to some extent related with all of them. Write any observations, insights, ideas, and possibilities you discover in your journal.*
• *Many of these people are parents. Look at their styles of parenting—strengths and weaknesses—and consider that you probably share many of those qualities or have developed reactions to things they did. For instance, your father might have been a stoic suck-it-up-and-carry-on type of guy, so you might either be that way yourself, or have resolved to be especially attentive to your child's emotions because your father wasn't particularly attentive to yours. Write about what you discover in your journal.*

- *Share all this with your spouse, and write about your conversation in your journal.*
- *If your kids are at all interested—and they can be at any age—share this material with each of them and write down your conversations, looking for insights on your strengths and weaknesses as a parent, and what areas you'd like to focus on growing.*
- *Share what you've written and discovered so far with your spouse, and pay attention to whether it's a fun conversation or not. If not, try to make it more fun. If you can't make it more fun, ask a therapist to help you two be able to discuss parenting more enjoyably. If parents radically disagree on parenting styles—especially if one is a suck-it-up, avoid-negative-emotions, emotionally dismissing parent, and the other is an emotions-matter, let's-explore-and-learn-from-everything emotionally coaching parent—it predicts divorce with 80 percent accuracy without therapy, so harmonizing parenting styles is vital for marriages.*

▶ **Ready to be a parent sidebar:** *One of my favorite teachers, Denton Roberts, owned a horse-packing franchise in the High Sierras, and would take groups of therapists into the mountains to teach, fish, and hang out. We were on one of those trips, sitting around a campfire in a beautiful river valley high up in the mountains and he asked me about Becky and me having children. I told him, "Denton, we're waiting until we're ready."*

Denton, who had two wonderful teen-aged boys, laughed, "You're never ready to have kids, Keith! Being a parent makes you ready to be a parent!" His words have echoed through my mind countless times in the last 35 years.

EACH CHILD IS DIFFERENT, PERSONALITY MATTERS

Parenting is such a massive set of tasks that none of us, no matter how much we prepare, are completely ready for the transition into parenthood, or for the idiosyncratic needs of each child who arrives in our family.

To complicate parenting even further, our personalities both shape and are shaped by our children's personalities—often largely out of awareness in Shadow. We have difficulty changing what we can't see, and often reflexively avoid seeing our destructive parenting Shadow because it's scary, embarrassing, or frustrating. When my two kids were born, my lack of patience with small kid demands was embarrassing to me. I realized I needed to become more relaxed and patient when Ethan and Zoe were difficult, and struggled to get better at it. It was hard, but I progressed slowly through the years, following Denton's principle and my own belief that my job was to keep working to be a better parent, no matter how hard it was.

Parenting *always* comes up in therapy with parents, no matter what they originally came in for. One father I worked with always used reasonable *language* with his kids, but when frustrated his *tone* became more and more urgent—even contemptuous. Until I pointed this out, his tone was completely invisible to him—a destructive Shadow habit that caused his wife and children to cringe and withdraw, even when the *content* of what he was saying made sense. Their reactions left him more frustrated, and he thought the problem was that they weren't *listening*—while the main problem was really him not listening to his own tone.

I fell into this trap myself more than once as my children were growing up, and eventually Becky and the kids helped me see that if my tone wasn't compassionate, nothing I said was of any use.

A big step in understanding parental Shadow is looking at underlying personality and attachment systems in parents and children, and what to do to help everybody encourage constructive Shadow and transform destructive Shadow. How secure we are with intimates is especially important to how we parent.

SECURE AND INSECURE ATTACHMENT[149]

By now most new parents have heard the term, "Attachment parenting," meaning doing your best to help a child feel secure in self, family, and the world. English psychologist John Bowlby, his student Mary Ainsworth, and Berkeley professors Mary Main and Eric Hesse, among many others have shown reliable connections between parents' attachment style and their children's levels of security of attachment. Briefly:

Secure parents tend to create securely attached babies. Parents who have a positive feeling of how their own life makes sense, and who are able to be consistently present and attuned to their baby's needs, tend to have babies who are securely attached. These babies feel comfortable in the world, are easily soothed when upset, explore when given the chance, and confidently approach parents for contact. Securely attached children tend to grow into adults who have a positive feeling of how their own life makes sense. About 55 percent of American babies are securely attached.

PREOCCUPIED PARENTS TEND TO CREATE ANXIOUS AMBIVALENT BABIES

- Parents who are easily lost in distress or who become preoccupied with unpleasant feelings, thoughts, memories, or fantasies tend to have babies who are anxious, clingy, and not easily soothed. These kids are likely to grow into preoccupied/anxious/irritable adults. About 20 percent of American babies have anxious ambivalent attachment styles.
- We all get preoccupied with emotionally charged incidents and memories occasionally. When was the last time you were so hurt,

scared, or angry that all you could think about was what the biopsy was going to show, whether you were going to get the job or not, or how mean your husband was when he yelled at you? Now imagine spending most of your time feeling this preoccupied—when you hang out with your husband, drive your kids to school, make love with your wife, or try to concentrate at work. You can see how such preoccupation would make it impossible to consistently attune to yourself or your kids, and how your kids would grow up having your attention some of the time and having to deal with your preoccupations the rest of the time.

DISMISSIVE PARENTS TEND TO CREATE AVOIDANT BABIES

* Parents who are dismissive of emotion, don't recognize emotional states easily, and who tend to be unaware of their child's inner experience tend to produce avoidant babies, kids who play by themselves, don't display much emotion, and who are often vaguely hostile. About 15 percent of American babies have avoidant attachment styles.

* Remember the last time you blanked out—just couldn't think or be connected to what you were feeling in your body. This often happens immediately after a shock, accident, or catastrophe. This blankness is called dissociation, and kids don't like it in parents. All of us blank out—dissociate—sometimes, but then we pull ourselves back to our body and feelings. What if you could hardly ever pull yourself back? What if your answer when asked, "How do you feel?" was almost always, "I don't know," accompanied by a vague irritation that you weren't even aware of? What if you were suspicious of emotions and felt you should just ignore what you're feeling and carry on? Your kids would probably learn to contract inward themselves, developing their own emotional numbness—leading to an avoidant attachment style.

DISORGANIZED/DISORIENTED PARENTS TEND TO CREATE DISORGANIZED/DISORIENTED BABIES

- Parents who struggle to stay connected to reality have difficulty having any coherent strategy for dealing with distress, and who are frightened or frightening to babies tend to produce disorganized/ disoriented babies who are prone to a wide array of psychological disorders. About 10 percent of American babies have disorganized/ disoriented attachment styles.
- If parents are frightening, frightened, or just not there, babies can literally go into dissociation on steroids. Their brains learn to check out and either collapse and/or explode in response to an impossible world. This sets up their nervous systems to be extra crazy, and things just keep getting worse unless major healing interventions occur—the sooner the better!
- This is one of the countless reasons I am such a fierce advocate for supporting pregnant mothers and children, and especially disadvantaged parents and children. The earlier we address problems, the more impact we can have quicker and the less time, money, and suffering is spent later on dealing with distressed teens and adults.

It's fascinating to me that all humans are predisposed to secure attachment. Minus autism and other pervasive developmental disorders, research strongly suggests that any baby with caregivers who are present, attuned, and responsive is likely to develop a secure attachment style.

Even more, kids with insecure attachment styles *can develop security!* This is called "earned secure" attachment because the person has to grow through his or her insecure style to create a life that makes positive sense. A common denominator in earned secure attachment seems to be successful attuned intimate relationships with caregivers, therapists, teachers, or other important figures.

I love this! Love heals. Intimacy heals. We are none of us condemned to separation or unhappiness. Taking responsibility for our constructive and destructive Shadow, participating in a healthy intimate relationship, and receiving positive influence from others, we can grow through our wounds and deficits towards joy and intimacy.

GENETIC INFLUENCES

As I've mentioned in previous chapters, our genes are ancestral voices, speaking to us through emotions, attractions, repulsions, and tendencies. Children are born with many personality characteristics already in place. Some of these are simply genetic predispositions. Most parents will tell you that their kids' personalities were noticeable within weeks or months of birth and in many ways stayed the same throughout childhood. Robert Cloniger, rigorous personality researcher, found that everyone seems to have varying amounts of harm avoidance, novelty seeking, dependence, persistence, cooperativeness, self directedness, and self transcendence. He found each individual to be a mix of varying levels of these core characteristics.[150]

Our genes influence who we are attracted to, how we make sense of the world at different ages, what interests and skills we have, and how we will be in family relationships.

How a mother is during pregnancy also affects her baby. For instance, babies whose mothers are happy and good at self-soothing in the last trimester tend to be better at self-soothing and have healthier kidneys and later onset of puberty than babies whose mothers are chronically stressed out during the last trimester.

In terms of child development, how parents' and children's temperaments match up seems to have profound effects on a child's personality. Folk wisdom has known this forever, but some seminal research was done in the middle of the last century that brought the scientific community on board.

GOODNESS OF FIT

Back in 1956, married couple Stella Chess and Alexander Thomas along with Herbert Birch started an extensive study of parents and children evaluating nine temperamental qualities in 161 children:[151]

1. Activity level—How much the kid moved around and sought physical motion.
2. Intensity—How emotionally intense the child was about interests and issues.
3. Regularity—How naturally the child created and followed physiological routines like eating, sleeping, and elimination, and psychological routines like family dinners and errands.
4. Sensory threshold—How much sight, sound, touch, taste, and other sensory inputs a child could tolerate comfortably without distress.
5. Approach/withdrawal—The extent to which a child approached or withdrew from different forms of social engagement.
6. Adaptability—How easily or painfully a child adjusted to changes in activity, environment, or relationship.
7. Distractibility—How easily a child drifted from one focus of attention to another.
8. Persistence—How engaged a child stayed with a focus or activity in the face of frustrations or distractions.
9. Mood—The typical affective tone of the child's life—happy, sad, anxious, joyful, social, withdrawn, or angry.

They found 40 percent of children to be easy—meaning adaptable and easily attuned to social environments, 10 percent difficult—reactive, rebellious or regularly hard to manage, and 15 percent slow to warm up—instinctively withdrawn, shy, or cautious. The other 35 percent demonstrated more complex combinations.

Their work—along with many others—reveals that how well children do depends a lot on how parental personalities and parenting styles fit with each child's temperament. This has been called *goodness of fit*.

You can see in Jeremy and Helen's family, from our previous example, how Jeremy and his son Jim are both high on intensity and activity level, with low sensory thresholds. Jeremy needs to learn how to calm himself, slow down, and raise his ability to tolerate frustrating situations, to improve his chances of helping Jim learn how to do the same.

When Jeremy got this, he could tell Jim, "Son, you and I get excited and frustrated easily. Neither of us likes to lose or make mistakes. I'm working on relaxing, doing my best, learning from whatever happens, and appreciating the moment, and I want to help you do the same."

It was a lot easier for Jim to hear this as work that he *shares* with his father, rather than hearing his explosions are a problem everyone has to deal with.

▶ **Everyone-has-their-work-to-do sidebar:** *This is why I like to tell couples and families that a healthy family helps everyone develop— Mom, Dad, kids, and even extended family. We all have our current work to do in self-care, emotional regulation, relating better with each other, attuning to ourselves and others, and following our Way. I've found that families with this orientation tend do well.*

EXERCISE:
GOODNESS OF FIT

- *Get a big sheet of paper and create vertical columns for each member of your family—you, your spouse, each child, and other major caregivers of your children. List everyone's name across the top of the sheet.*
- *On the left side of the paper, make a vertical list of the above nine temperamental qualities.*

- *In the boxes that naturally form across the page, rate everyone from 1–10 on each quality. For instance, if you are completely laid back about everything, put down a 1 on intensity. If you are passionate about almost everything, put down a 10 on intensity.*
- *For each of your children write what special attention they need for every quality. For instance, if they are very adaptable, they might need acknowledgement for being able to shift modes easily, and perhaps extra interest in what they want as contrasted with what others want from them (a problem with being too adaptable is that you can lose your own agenda adapting to other's desires or demands).*
- *For you and your spouse, write what special skills you need to practice to help each child. For instance, if you're high intensity and your child has an anxious mood, you might want to practice self soothing and mindful awareness to be a calmer presence.*
- *Study your chart and write in your journal about how to create more goodness of fit in your family.*
- *Share everything with your spouse or someone you love, and talk about how to get support to create more goodness of fit in your parenting.*

You now have a goodness of fit roadmap for your family. *You can share this with your kids.* Yes! Let them know how you understand them and yourself, and what you're doing to help everyone thrive and grow. This normalizes a growth mindset for the family—"We're all different. We all have strengths and vulnerabilities. We work to acknowledge and expand our strengths and acknowledge and improve our vulnerabilities. Dad has his, Mom has hers, and each of you kids has yours."

If your child disagrees, change his or her designation to feel more accurate *to him or her.* The purpose is to consider what type of person we are with interest, not to perfectly get every quality right. If you personally find it either super-easy or next-to-impossible to shift your opinions, go back to your 1–10 score on adaptability and see if it predicts your reaction.

Making this chart naturally reveals constructive and destructive parental Shadow in you and your family; it brings the unseen to light. Each day, remind yourself to acknowledge your constructive Shadow strengths and those of your spouse and kids. These are a family reservoir of skills and resources, and we all should know and appreciate our virtues. Each day, remind yourself to acknowledge destructive Shadow tendencies in you and everyone and have regular conversations about how to improve in those areas, normalizing the reality that none of us are perfect, but we can always be growing and learning.

THE WILLARD-TRIVERS HYPOTHESIS, OR WHY RICH PEOPLE HAVE MORE SONS, AND POOR PEOPLE MORE DAUGHTERS

We are affected completely out of awareness by genetically programmed drives which are generally invisible to us. For instance, men with constitutionally high testosterone tend to marry less, divorce more, and be more violent in marriage.[152] Men with more copies of the vasopressin expression gene tend to be less monogamous.[153]

Our environments also affect our genetic expressions. As I've mentioned in previous chapters, we have around thirty thousand genes, but up to a million genetic markers, called *epigenetic* markers, surrounding those genes. Environmental conditions tend to activate certain epigenetic markers, which in turn, selectively activate certain genes. For example, children raised together before 41 months old tend to be disinterested in each other sexually as they mature. This is called the Westermarck effect after Finnish anthropologist Edward Westermarck who described the tendency in his 1891 book, *The History of Marriage*.[154]

One of the most amazing examples of environment affecting gene expression is known as the Willard/Trivers hypothesis.

In 1973, Robert Willard and Dan Trivers proposed the remarkable hypothesis that maternal conditions influenced the ratios of girls to

> **Historical sidebar:** *Freud dismissed Westermarck's findings because they contradicted some of his developmental theories—a tragic mistake for Freud who spent 20 years in his early career studying the nervous systems of animals like lampreys and crayfish, hoping to make a major breakthrough neurobiology. If he would have embraced the Westermarck effect, brilliant theorist that Freud was, he might have intuited the epigenetic process of environment effecting the expression of genes, and won a Nobel Prize.*

boys in large groups, with mothers having more girls in conditions that favor girls, and more boys in conditions that favor boys. They had no idea *how* this happened. One suggestion was unconscious selective miscarriage, and subsequent data continues to support this in human and animal research.[155]

Conditions that seem to favor girls include:

- Poverty, since poor boys have added challenges competing with rich boys, and it's historically easier for girls to "marry up."
- Parents in more historically female professions like nursing and teaching.
- Beautiful parents tend to have more girls, since beauty favors a girl's genetic chances.

Conditions that seem to favor boys include:

- Wealth, since wealthy boys have more resources and mate choices.
- Parents in more historically male professions like engineering or science.
- Tall parents have more boys, since height gives boys an edge.

Sure enough, when all these areas were researched, there were more boys or girls being born in the expected directions, sometimes with huge effect sizes like 140 boys to 100 girls for engineers and scientists, and 135 girls to 100 boys for nurses and school teachers.

The Willard/Trivers effect is culture affecting gene expression out of awareness—in Shadow.

CONSCIOUSNESS CAN CREATE AN ANTI-WILLARD/ TRIVERS EFFECT

On the other hand, the Chinese one-child policy over the last twenty-plus years was consciousness *in opposition to culturally influenced genetic predisposition*, a kind of anti-Willard/Trivers effect. The Chinese one-child policy (abruptly ended in 2015 when Chinese officials began to see the catastrophic consequences of not enough women for men in a rapidly aging workforce) resulted in discrepancies of as much as 130 boys to 100 girls in many parts of China. Around 1995, the combination of easy identification of gender, state sponsored abortion, and the rural bias towards *consciously* wanting a son rather than a daughter in a one-child country led to many more girl fetuses being aborted than boy fetuses. Some speculate that such a demographic will result in a more hostile and militaristic culture, since crime is generally committed by young men in association with other young men, but it will be ten to twenty years before we'll see if this happens in China (and in other countries like India where parents use selective abortion to favor boys).

The poor rural families in China and India would typically have more girls from a Willard/Trivers perspective—both poverty and environmental stressors favor more girls—but they've had access to easy gender identification and selective abortion since the mid-nineties. Rural cultures *consciously* favor boys over girls, so consciousness plus rural culture favoring sons over daughters won out over more the subtle epigenetic influences involved in the Willard/Trivers effect.

It's good to be aware that we and our kids are shaped by genetic and epigenetic forces, but what matters to most parents is, "How can I be a better parent to my child now?"

As it turns out, certain parental styles work better than others, and parents being happy with each other has huge positive effects on kids.

FOUR PARENTING STYLES, AUTHORITATIVE IS BEST

Diana Baumrind is a Berkeley psychologist who identified four major styles of parenting—authoritarian, permissive, uninvolved, and authoritative. Of these four, authoritative consistently had the best child outcomes. Briefly:

- Authoritarian is "My way or the highway. Just shut up and do what I say!" Authoritarian parenting doesn't work very well. It creates problems in children, because it normalizes bullying in the family. Authoritarian parenting creates dominator hierarchies of parents enforcing rules with fear and violence. Not surprisingly, children from such families are more likely to be physically violent or violently victimized themselves.
- Permissive is, "Sure, do anything you want to do. You want candy, have some candy. You want to break the piano, break the piano." Permissive parenting can turn kids into crazy narcissists.
- Uninvolved is parents communicating on many levels to kids that, "I'm not connected with you because I'm gone, I'm distracted, I don't want to, I'm not interested, or I'm clueless." Uninvolved sucks, but it's not just parents who are responsible—this is a cultural pathology in America where we work more hours than any other industrialized country. When Mom has to work three jobs and comes home exhausted, she doesn't have much time to connect with the kids—especially if she is among the single moms who are raising over a fifth of the children in this country. When Dad has to put in 55 hours a

week to keep up and be successful, there's not much juice left for children. So what happens to kids with uninvolved parents? Usually they're raised by other kids like brothers, sisters, and friends—not good to have kids raising kids. A signature trauma for one adult woman client of Francine Shapiro (the originator of EMDR—eye movement desensitization reprogramming) was when the woman, at four years old, was dropped off at a park with her two-year-old sister whom she was supposed to take care of. It was a signature trauma because she knew that at four she couldn't do an adequate job and something horrible might happen, and the sense of anxious inadequacy continued to haunt her through her development.

• Authoritative is a parent in charge, but fair and kind. An authoritative parent has a moral compass, is attuned to self and child, and enforces rules respectfully, insisting that rules be reasonable and open to dialogue in the family. An authoritative parent will encourage kids to have opinions and even take charge when the kids are coming from mature and caring places. An authoritative parent wants everyone in the family to have power, but takes on the responsibility to maintain fairness and support with what's best for both kids and adults.[156]

There's a great book by Lynn McTaggart called *The Bond*, where she gathered studies of human cultures and social preferences. McTaggart is a genius at integrating vast amounts of scientific data into accessible and absorbing stories. The consensus of these studies was that when people are given an environment where they can exist comfortably with each other and there's enough food, security, and personal autonomy, they tend to prefer societies that are fair, where they care for each other, and where they share resources. Authoritative parenting tends to produce families, each one a little culture or society, biased to care, be fair, and share.

EXERCISE:
WHAT FLAVORS OF PARENT AM I?

In your journal write down incidences of your mother and father being authoritarian, permissive, uninvolved, and authoritative when you were a child.

- *Write how you felt about yourself and how you felt about your parent in each instance.*
- *Write how who you are today might have been influenced by any of these instances or modes of parenting.*

In your journal write down incidences of you being authoritarian, permissive, uninvolved, and authoritative—especially with your children.

- *Write how you felt about yourself and how you felt about your child in each instance.*
- *What one aspect of your parenting are you most proud of? Write about it in your journal.*
- *What one aspect of your parenting are you most ashamed of, embarrassed about, or frustrated with? Write about this in your journal, and what you would have to do—starting today—to improve in this area.*
- *Share everything with someone you trust—preferably the person or persons you co-parent with, and especially with your spouse.*

CRITICISM

Authoritarian and emotionally dismissing parents tend to be more critical than authoritative and emotionally coaching parents, and this makes a big difference to children.

Susan Heitler in her book *From Conflict to Resolution*, reports how criticism is the single most significant factor in a child's perception of the parental relationship.[157]

That's right!

CRITICISM is the single most significant factor in a child's perception of the parental relationship!

So, let's mostly be approving of our children and disapprove only when necessary, like with destructive behaviors such as violence, or distorted beliefs such as bigotry, self-loathing, or perfectionism.

Another study by neuroscientist Eveline Crone in the Netherlands found that areas associated with cognition (thought) and learning were activated in nine-year-olds' brains by positive feedback, but not by criticism. Adolescents' and adults' brains were different, with cognition/learning areas activated by both positive and negative feedback. The take-home message—children before puberty learn best by showing them new things, staying generally positive, and avoiding criticism whenever possible.

IT HELPS TO UNDERSTAND THAT GOOD PARENTS HELP TRAIN THEIR CHILDREN'S *NERVOUS SYSTEMS* RESPECTFULLY

We tend to project conscious choice onto our children. I've had parents of babies four months old accuse their children of *deliberately* crying or waking, "Just to manipulate me."

I respond to such pronouncement vehemently, "No! Your infant (two-year-old, eight-year-old, fourteen-year-old) is not consciously messing with you. They have habits of feeling, thinking, and acting. We need to help them keep their good habits like sharing, saying 'Please,' and 'Thank you,' washing their hands before they eat and after they go to the bathroom, etc. We need to help them change bad habits like tantrums, violence, disrespect, self-harm, and shutting down. Most often we are training our children's Shadow, their adaptive unconscious—their nervous systems—while their conscious selves are often clueless bystanders."

The caveat in this is that training your kid's nervous system *must* be done respectfully (and I rarely use the word "must"). An infant can feel a parent's contempt and will react negatively to contemptuous expressions and tones with no understanding of the words being spoken. All children have their own sense of personal dignity where they are exquisitely aware of what's fair and respectful and what is not.

So, if you're training your child to sleep in his own bed at six, you are training his Shadow—his nervous system—to resist the impulse to go into your bed when he has the impulse, and to stay in his own bed at night. You can do this disrespectfully by using dismissing or hostile tones when he comes into your bed, or respectfully by gently but firmly escorting him to his bed and reminding him that, "The rule is that you sleep in your bed, not ours." You may have to do this *dozens of times* before his Shadow has shifted and he calls from his room at night instead of going into your room, or doesn't go to your room when he randomly wakes up. You might have to use physical props like a privacy lock on your bedroom door, or a nightlight for his room, or get help from a family therapist.

Whatever you do, you are working with him to train his Shadow self, his adaptive unconscious, and he will tend to trust you if he hears respect in your voice, and tend to resent or rebel if he hears anger, contempt, or fear.

So, when helping our children learn and deal with difficult habits, it helps to know we are training their nervous systems—we are not negotiating with functional adults—and that we need to always be respectful of their inherent dignity as human beings.

QUALITY OF THE MARITAL RELATIONSHIP IS HUGE IN PARENTING

Authoritative parenting is certainly the best parenting style, but it's not the bottom line. In general, the bottom line *in parenting* is the quality of the *marital relationship.*

Berkeley psychologists Phillip and Marilyn Cohen randomly assigned couples to two groups and gave one group parenting training and the other group input on improving their marital relationship. Both groups improved parenting, but only in the working-on-the-marital-relationship group did the marriage also improve, and this group also improved *more* on parenting, even though they were working exclusively on their marital relationship.

Similarly, researchers from the John Gottman group in Washington State investigated emotionally coaching couples compared to emotionally dismissing couples (or couples with mixed styles). Emotionally coaching couples who both had an, "Emotions are important and we should respect and listen to them in each other and our kids," attitude reported higher intimacy and satisfaction with each other and their kids did better socially and in school.

Not surprising to me after over forty-plus years of working with couples and families, the couples who work on improving their marital relationship have better outcomes with their kids. Apparently being happier with your spouse improves your parenting better than studying superior parenting while neglecting your marital relationship.[158]

PARENTAL SHADOW IS ENDLESS

If you skim back over this chapter, read your journal entries, and examine your genogram and goodness-of-fit charts, you'll see there is an ongoing fractal interface between your constructive and destructive Shadow and your conscious awareness in all your family relationships. Shadow flows constantly through our habits and states of consciousness with our children—a flow which has to be managed for better or worse for our entire lifetime.

So let's end this chapter with a series of practices to identify constructive and destructive parental Shadow.

Please honor your constructive parental Shadow! Your adaptive unconscious holds incredible wisdom about helping each of your children thrive.

Similarly, please honor your destructive parental Shadow! When it intrudes and causes you or your family pain, seek positive influence (from your spouse, friends, therapists, books, audios and videos—there is a wealth of knowledge a click away in the twenty-first century) and cultivate growth mindsets on gradually turning these vulnerabilities and weaknesses into virtues and strengths.

The following are some indicators to help identify constructive and destructive parental Shadow.

EXERCISES:

Discover your constructive and destructive parental Shadow through answering the following questions. Write your responses in your journal and share them with people you trust and parent with:

- *Attune to yourself and your kid (be aware with acceptance and caring intent what you and your child are sensing, feeling, thinking, judging, and wanting). Easy to attune? Constructive Shadow. Trouble attuning? Destructive Shadow.*
- *Do you notice when your kid has problems and respond with warmth and compassion? Constructive Shadow. Don't notice or get easily distressed or frustrated? Destructive Shadow.*
- *Do you ignore your child's issues, or overreact and make your kid's problems about you? Destructive Shadow.*
- *Do you have high intimacy and satisfaction in your primary relationship? Does your partner? If so, constructive Shadow. If not, and you're currently addressing the problems, constructive Shadow. If you're unhappy and you're avoiding problems, destructive Shadow.*
- *Does your child feel safe discussing emotionally painful topics and events with you? If so, constructive Shadow. If not, destructive Shadow.*
- *Do you feel comfortable discussing emotionally painful topics and events with your child? If so, constructive Shadow. If not, destructive Shadow.*
- *Do you receive influence on helping your child thrive? If so, constructive Shadow. If not, destructive Shadow.*

The attunement practices we did in Chapter 1 can help you develop the self-reflective tools to enable you to expand your awareness of constructive and destructive parental Shadow. You can attune to yourself and others anytime, and I encourage you to attune as much as possible. Especially, attuned awareness with acceptance and caring intent of you and your child's inner states and processes sets the stage for thriving children and a happy family.

11
Dreams, The Royal Road to Shadow

What a dream I had
Pressed in organdy
Clothed in crinoline
Of smoky burgundy
Softer than the rain
I wandered empty streets
Down past the shop displays
I heard cathedral bells
Tripping down the alley ways
as I walked on

FROM: *FOR EMILY, WHENEVER I MIGHT FIND HER,*
—BY PAUL SIMON

THE UNIVERSE DREAM

At the moment the Big Bang occurred, the Universe Dream came into existence. The Universe Dream is the story of creation from before time until the end of time, constantly unfolding in reality and fantasy. With every level of complexity that appeared in the expanding universe, a step was taken towards sentience and self-awareness. With life came emotions, instincts, and drives, ancestral voices speaking powerfully but non-consciously. With mammals came dreams, all mammals dream and all dreams seek to influence, to wake the individual up to better possibilities of surviving and thriving. With humans came a self who could observe the dream, and now the Universe Dream began waking up to itself. With the evolution of conscious self-awareness, humans can, *in one lifetime,* personally evolve to keep waking up to the ancestral voices speaking through Shadow, accessing deeper levels of wisdom and love.

Night dreams and daydreams are stories, impulses, images, and experiences that Shadow keeps presenting us with, daring our conscious selves to attend, integrate, and grow, challenging us to wake up to new understanding and deeper consciousness. Each night dream, each day-dream—no matter how mundane or colorful—has it's evolutionary roots in the Big Bang and every new complexity programmed into matter since.

The Universe Dream kept waking up to itself through successive evolutionary waves, each one closer to self-aware consciousness. In the last fifty thousand years—a blink of an eye in cosmic time—the Universe woke up to human self-awareness.

Humans can imagine the Universe Dream from the beginning to the end of time waking up through you and me and all of us together, and then feeding back into personal and collective Shadow—potentially influencing the Universe Dream itself (Herself? Himself? Ourselves?) through morphic fields of subtle energies.

If we decide to keep waking up, we have incredible Shadow resources. We can discern healthy and unhealthy Shadow, surrender to healthy dream influences, transmute unhealthy dream influences, and live this moment in harmony with the dreams of all who have been and will come, circling back to archetypal morphic depths—to the Universe Dream.

Practices of integrating the Universe Dream began with self-awareness and progressed through Shamanic ceremony and altered states to the enlightenment and science exploding. To integrate the Universe Dream we can practice different yogas (practices that connect subtle energies and physical actions) to harness our conscious self, default mode, night dreams, working memory, and executive attention networks. We can learn to sense, observe, and shape past, present, and future dreams as they arise through us from the Universe Dream waking up to itself.

The daydreaming networks, the default mode of the brain, spontaneously generate images, impulses, thoughts, and feelings, all embedded in stories, generated by the same brain regions as night dreaming.[159]

When we focus on anything or anyone, our working memory provides us with facts, impulses, thoughts, and feelings to deal with the current situation, all embedded in stories—generated like dreams from Shadow—about ourselves and who or what we are engaged with.

Conscious awareness follows and regulates Shadow material constantly flooding up out of our adaptive unconscious, always embedded in *stories*.

Self-aware consciousness manages all the stories from night dreaming, daydreaming, working memory, and Shadow, correcting, indulging, avoiding, attacking, or integrating, depending upon levels of development on our self line, morals line, integration-of-defenses line, psychosexual line, interpersonal line, and values line of development.

Observing and working with dream states is a portal to progressing on all developmental lines. The stories of how we dream, how dreams have been held and accessed throughout history, and how psychology took the lead in unlocking the secrets of dreams is what this chapter is about.

We all know dreams connect us to Shadow, both constructive and destructive, but what are dreams? Practically speaking, what are the best ways to use our dreams to grow our Shadow?

IN THIS CHAPTER WE WILL:

- Anchor ourselves in scary and yummy dream images.
- Check out what science, psychology, and the wisdom traditions have taught us about dreams and dreamwork, and apply this to personal dream images.

- Explore fractal interfaces between conscious and unconscious, waking self and dreaming self, that help us grow Shadow.
- See how dreams can expand creativity, enhance intimacy, lead you to the Other World, and contribute to the evolutionary impulse.
- We'll return to our Unified Field Theory of Shadow and fractal interfaces we can attune and harmonize.
- We join with the Universe Dream—sweet and potent dream yoga.

NIGHTMARES—LET'S START AT THE BOTTOM

What are the scariest dream images or sequence you've ever had? Mine have been witches as a child and vampires as a grown up. The first Witch dream I remember happened when I was four or five. *I am running panic-stricken down our Street in Granada Hills, CA, finally making it to the Front Door of our House. Door opens leaving me in a Cooking Pot being held by Leering Witch.*

Notice how I describe the dream in the present tense, as if it is happening now. I also give the proper names of *"Leering Witch, Street, House, Cooking Pot, and Front Door"* to the dream images. I'll keep doing this throughout this chapter. Proper names help us relate *personally,* now in the present tense, to characters and images as individuals. Awarding qualities, landscapes, feelings, colors, sounds, and proper names helps us enliven dreams—we want present moment immediacy. In general when we work with dreams, the more vividly we feel them happening right now, the more useful they become.

> ▶ **Trauma sidebar:** *The exceptions to maximizing affective immediacy are trauma memories which can be unbearably emotionally charged, and post-traumatic stress disorder (PTSD) where sufferers are routinely flooded with horrific sensations and images, often in terrifying nightmares. Therapy for these involves reducing the emotional charges into affectively tolerable doses.*

Write your nightmare dream images down in your journal with as much sensory detail as possible. Include what you and other characters see, feel, think, and do in whatever dreamscapes they arise from. Do it in the present tense as if it is happening now. Give proper names to each aspect and character of your dream.

Nightmares inevitably involve conflict, usually between a *"Me"* who might or might not be my current body/self and a frightening *"Other."* Such conflicts often represent or involve actual conflicts we are experiencing, have experienced, or might experience in waking life, either between us and others, and/or between our conscious ego and any of our countless inner selves/voices/attitudes in the past/present/future.

Nightmare caveat: *Some nightmares are rooted in trauma, or are inherently so upsetting that they are literally too scary or too shameful to even consider. If any of your nightmare images are too uncomfortable for you to deal with alone, it's probably best for you to work on them collaboratively with a therapist.*

LOVELY DREAMS

What are the loveliest, most fun dream images or sequences you've ever had? One of mine is: *I'm soaring like Superman over Beautiful Sea dotted with Lovely Islands. I'm on my way East to something/someplace good—maybe Hawaii.* Write your delightful images down in as much sensory detail as possible.

We'll return to these later.

KEITH'S DREAM JOURNAL:

July 13, 2005: *I have a Job with a Tree Trimming Company and get a Married Couple hired. I'm surprised there is such a Big Office Contingent and only one Crew. Riddick character (Vin Diesel) is then included, followed by an Evil Guy from a Vampire Movie trying to assassinate him. Riddick cuts him in half with a Sword.*

August 10, 2014: *Making Chicken Sandwiches with Someone.*

August 11, 2014: *Becky, Barack Obama, and I are going to a Lecture I'm giving on Evolutionary Relationships. Becky wants to go on a Snowmobile and I get mad and say, "No! There isn't enough room to store the Three Books I need to take." Barack was nervous about going to see an Indie Band. I try to tease him, can't quite connect, but feel warm and protective.*

March 3, 2015: *In a Garden with Jade [a Shaman friend]. There is a Rattlesnake that shows its Fangs and goes into a Hole. Jade is unconcerned and keeps Digging in the Garden. I look for a Tool to kill the Snake, but can't seem to deliver an Effective Strike.*

What?

I will never fully understand dreams—non-linear, non-rational, multiple meanings, multiple functions. Nightly fountains of Shadow material in representative and symbolic forms relentlessly pouring out of our adaptive unconscious every 90 minutes while we sleep. Messages from our past/present/future, neuroregulators of emotional stability, and good brain health, sources of wisdom, insight, confusion, intimidation, and demands—could dreams have any more complexity and potential significance?

Not that dreams haven't been studied forever. Mystics, scientists, psychics, Shamen, psychotherapists, and visionaries have been transfixed and transformed by dreams since humans woke up to self-awareness.

I've been working with my own dreams since 1965 and with my clients' dreams since 1973. Freud called dreams the "Royal road to the unconscious." I've found dreams to be the royal road to Shadow.

EXERCISE:
BEGIN A DREAM JOURNAL

- *Either in your regular journal or in a separate journal just for dreams, begin writing your dreams every morning. Write in the first person present tense (I am...), and capitalize the names of the figures (Earth,*

Wings, Bush, Tall Man, etc). Dream images fade fast after waking, so as soon as you wake up write what you remember from the night, in as much sensory detail as possible. If you have no memory of dreams, write what you're feeling and thinking as you wake.

- Notice the emotions associated with your dreams and dream images and record them also.
- Throughout the day, allow your mind to wander to your dreams and just stay connected, feeling the feelings and noticing the insights and associations. Record what comes to you in your journal.

The goal of this exercise is more to hang out with dream themes and images rather than interpret or analyze them too much. Interpretation is fine if it doesn't take you away from the lived experience of the dream. For instance, two nights ago I dreamed about surfing, and, uncharacteristically for me, I was catching waves rather than encountering obstacles to getting in the water. A possible interpretation of this dream is that I'm currently actively engaged in meaningful activity rather than feeling blocked—for instance, this book is coming together and feeling much more coherent than it did six months ago. That being said, the image and feeling of pushing myself and my board down onto the face of a left-breaking wave has a certain alive feel that takes me back to the joy of catching waves (an injury has kept me out of the surf for a long time). The possible symbolism involved is interesting and potentially useful (if I have a chance to go for it in any way, I'm more inclined right now to take the risk), but I especially want to keep going back to that stoked moment paddling into the wave. Staying in relationship with the felt experience of the dream is a central principle of all modern forms of dream work.

MESSAGES FROM SHADOW

When I was seventeen in 1966, I had the following dream.

I'm Eating at a Long Table with many Young People on either side. Suddenly, a Young Man from across the Table attacks me and Young Man and I are wrestling and fighting on the Table. Young Man then turns into Young Woman and we're Making Love. I wake frightened and ashamed.

Later I related the dream to Joe Ericson, my psychotherapist at the time. The dream shook me, leaving me alarmed and confused. In homophobic 1966, the sexual elements were alarming and humiliating. The out-of-control qualities of the attacking and fighting were drearily reminiscent of the hostilities and tensions that seemed to permeate relationships and culture at the time.

Joe (whose approach to dreams was mainly interpretive) said, "That's a beautiful dream Keith! Dream images are all part of you. Young Man with whom you're fighting is a conflicted side of you. As you fought, he became your feminine side. Carl Jung said that we all have to integrate our masculine and feminine on the road to individuation or adulthood. What better way than making love?"

I was shocked at how true this sounded and how relieved I was. I had already decided to be a psychotherapist, and could feel the power of the elements Joe had pointed out interpreting my dream—masculine, feminine, conflict, integration of interior forces, shame/rage/anxiety/ relief, healing insight, embodied interpretation, individuation and development. Somehow the dream brought them all together in a theme that reflected my fears, my shames, my fierce dedication to psychological/ spiritual growth, and my avocation as a psychotherapist.

The message of the dream suddenly seemed clear—take on the challenges that the world presents and resolve conflicts into love. Accept the different sides of myself, both masculine and feminine. The shame and fear vanished (at least temporarily), leaving me more focused and empowered.

During that time I began writing my dreams down, working on them and studying them, and have continued to this day.

Throughout the subsequent decades I've come to understand how dreams exist on multiple levels simultaneously, all woven together by the adaptive unconscious, and presented to each of us every 90 minutes while we sleep, as well as throughout the day in daydreams and random associations.

I've found dreams to be meaningful, meaningless, predictive, chaotic, ecstatic, frightening, powerful, mundane, and reassuring. Practically, attending to dreams in most ways has always proven beneficial to me and my clients.

WHAT ARE DREAMS?

Some scientific reductionists like J. Allan Hobson have suggested that dreams are neurological events where our brains construct images and themes that involve current emotional immediacy. Hobson believes dreams have relevance to the real world, but not deep symbolic meaning.[160]

Here's what science tells us. A pulse comes up from the pons in the brain stem every 90 minutes to activate the geniculate nuclei of the thalamus (which creates the stories of our lives), which sends waves to the occipital cortex in the back of our brain associated with sight, seeing, and images. The hypothesis is that the brain—without benefit of perception and movement—creates meaning using it's reflexive metaphor-seeking, story-making faculties in service of whatever is currently most emotionally charged. The resultant dreams are fanciful conglomerates of memories, fantasies, characters, stories, and associations that are quickly deconstructed upon awakening, and not remembered due to the dearth of amines in the brain during sleep, and the flood of serotonin that accompanies waking.[161]

Neural firing in the brain generates synchronized electrical pulses that are measured in cycles per second (hertz or hz)—brainwaves. They fall into five categories, with Theta being most associated with dreaming:

- Delta: .5 to 3 hz—associated with deep dreamless sleep, many profound meditations, empathy, healing, and regeneration.
- Theta: 3 to 8 hz—associated with dreaming, the unconscious, learning, memory, and deep meditation. From birth to six years old, children spend *most of their waking hours* in Theta. Dreaming is also associated with rapid eye movements (REM), but we also

have non-REM dream states as we are going to sleep, or even while waking. Premature infants spend 70 to 80 percent of sleep in REM, babies and children 50 percent, adults 25 percent, and older adults 15 percent.

- Alpha: 8 to 12 Hz—associated with flow states, calmness, alertness, and mind/body integration.
- Beta: 12 to 38 Hz—associated with thought, waking life with an external focus, problem solving, and excitement. Low beta is 12 to 15 Hz and is fast idle or musing. Beta 2 is 15 to 22Hz and usually accompanies high engagement and active problem solving. High beta is complex thought integrating new experiences, excitement, or anxiety.
- Gamma: 38 to 42 hz (and beyond up to 60 or more hz)—is associated with simultaneous processing from different brain areas. Gamma is highly active in transcendent states of unity, love, healing, or psychic activity.[162]

THE STORYTELLING SPECIES

Two-hundred-thousand years ago when the two mutations on the 714 sites of the FOXP2 gene gave humans the capacity for I, you, we, in past/present/future and metaphor, language abilities exploded. Memory, metaphor, sophisticated language, and fantasy gave humans superpowers beyond the pale of previous evolutionary shifts. Perhaps our most powerful superpowers are our ongoing drives to create stories.

Human brains *constantly create stories* based in experiences, memories, anticipations, and metaphors. *The ocean sparkled like diamonds today and the pelicans looked like old men standing on the wave-drenched rocks—the rocks solid in the surf like troll guardians of the cliffs, waiting for someone or something to arrive.* The brain has been called an "Anticipation and association machine,"[163] and humans, "The storytelling animal,"[164]—waking, sleeping, alone, or in communion with others, always generating stories. This drive to create stories permeates our waking life (we naturally and effortlessly daydream stories and images 15–20 percent of our waking hours[165]) and our sleeping life through night dreams.

But dreams have more functions that storytelling.

In the last several decades, Hobson and other neuroscientists have found dreaming to be intimately connected with consolidating memories. Once we've dreamed something it becomes much more permanently and readily available to memory.[166]

We also know the "seeking systems" of our brain based in our nucleus accumbens (near the brain stem) and driven by the excitement neurotransmitter dopamine control the vividness of our dreams.[167]

Dreams are somehow connected to keeping us sane. Sleep researchers have established that depriving people of dreams—but not sleep—leads to disorientation and even psychotic symptoms. Somehow dreams help us be psychologically balanced, though the mechanisms involved have yet to be fully explored.

Sixty percent of night dreams are problem-solving dreams with interpersonal themes, activating many of the same neural circuits as daydreaming. Daydreams come in three categories, positive constructive, guilty dysphoric, and chaotic/poor-attention-control.[168] Most night dreams fit into these categories in the forms of wish-fulfillment/problem-solving night dreams, nightmares, and chaotic night dreams.

Problem-solving with interpersonal themes makes evolutionary sense. It seems obvious that an adaptive function of night dreaming and daydreaming is to imaginally rehearse and prepare for real life events—we can make mistakes without physical cost, and solve problems often before they actually physically or relationally arise. These powers give profound evolutionary advantages.

Hobson acknowledges that dreams draw emotionally charged material from our experiences and fit different components into currently relevant narratives or stories, but he believes his research repudiates the ideas that dreams have deeply symbolic, archetypal, or even psychic components. He and various psychoanalysts have had lively debates over the years about these issues.

Of course, Hobson is right in observing that our brains choose what is emotionally charged and imminent to create dream stories, but this begs the questions—*who* chooses and why *these* choices? Whatever the brain regions or neurochemistry, *Shadow*—the adaptive unconscious, implicit self, deepest identity, or soul—chooses settings, objects, characters, themes, and actions that are relevant to *this* individual at *this* moment of existence. To believe that these choices are not heavily influenced by deep conditioning, powerful genetic drives, and personal archetypes is naive at best, and clueless scientism at worst.

Even further, there are levels of influence in dreams from our most primitive selves to our most mature selves. When we encounter both a selfish demon and a wise guide in our dreams, both represent *living* parts of us—both weighing in on dream narratives. The wise guide can embody discernment of destructive from constructive Shadow, while the demon can be the selfish immature embodiment of angry, animalistic destructive Shadow.

EXERCISE:
DREAMS AS AWKWARD CONGLOMERATES

Look at one of your scary images and list as many components of the scene as possible. Include settings, objects, characters, feelings, themes, thoughts, and actions (all with capitalized proper names). Where do these components appear in your current or past life, or potentially in the future? How are they interacting with each other? How does this reflect your current understanding of who you are and what you are about? Write about all this in your journal.

Look at one of your yummy/fun images and list as many components of the scene as possible. Include settings, objects, characters, feelings, themes, thoughts, and actions (all with capitalized proper names). Where do these components appear in your current, past, or potential future life? How are they interacting? How does this reflect your current understanding of who you are and what you are about? Write about all this in your journal.

FREUD

Sigmund Freud believed that dreams released repressed sexual, violent, fearful, and wish-fulfillment material from the Id—the dark libidinous cauldron of the unconscious which Ego (our conscious self) and Superego (our moral self) both struggle to regulate and contain. He found that by having his clients associate on dream images and feelings he and his patients could co-construct interpretations that provided healing insights in psychoanalysis. Freud thought that his was a scientific approach because he believed dreams arose from individual brains, not the supernatural, and that dreams had psychological significance and utility.[169]

Unfortunately, Freud was too insecure to test his theories scientifically, causing his students to splinter off into creating different systems rather than uniting in a growing body of understanding of Shadow, the unconscious, psychotherapy, dreams, and human functioning.

Freud also came of age in a time when the concept of the unconscious was bewildering or ridiculous to many educated people, and yet interpreting dreams as messages about our past/present/future and inner psychological architecture felt intuitively right to many thought leaders and was a fascinating and avant-garde process that captured the imaginations of several generations of therapists and patients. The very concept of a "Talking Cure" for psychological problems was a radical departure from the scientific materialism that so captured the imaginations of academics and practitioners in the nineteenth and early twentieth centuries.

Freud's approach to dreams emphasized association and interpretation. He would have his patients *associate* on dream images, saying what came to mind as they considered each image or theme. Freud would then weave the associations into an interpretation, essentially a story about the client's life, relationships, problems, or development. In a way, Freudian interpretation of associations involved creating stories from stories, seeking always to clarify understanding and create more coherent life narratives.

Freud changed modernity with his ideas of the unconscious, dreams as symbolic representations of self, and the Talking Cure. When it comes to dreams, he opened the way for future generations of dreamworkers to journey more deeply into Shadow.

EXERCISE:
DREAM ASSOCIATIONS:

- *Find a comfortable spot, and review what you've written about your scary and yummy dreams.*
- *One by one take each person, scene, thought, family relationship, emotion, perception, context, and memory, and associate on it. Write whatever comes into your head about what you're considering. For instance, my Witch associations are Woman, Mother, Anger, Dark, Terror, Hunger, Family Home, Courage, Flight, Granada Hills, and Lemon Grove (we lived down the street from a lemon grove). In my flying dream my associations are Light, Power, Joy, Surf, Ease, Blue, White, Ocean, Peace, Islands, and Healing.*
- *Look over your nightmare associations and look for relationships between dream figures or between your associations and dream figures, and write them down. Write whatever relationships that occur to you. My Witch dream involves relationships with Outside World—I'm running from something scary—as well as relationships with Unsafe Woman and Angry Mother where I'm looking for comfort and finding terror. There are also relationships with Granada Hills House—paradoxically a source of security and terror, and relationships with my two Brothers and Father who are conspicuously absent from the scene. Finally there is relationship with my Young Body—I'm running because I'm too small and weak to defend myself.*
- *Look over your lovely associations and look for relationships between dream figures or between your associations and dream figures, and write them down. My flying dream involves relationships with*

Ocean—magic and vast; with Spirit—I am given transcendent powers; with Joy—freedom of flight and discovery; with Purpose—I know I'm doing something good and meaningful as I fly; and with Blue—my favorite color and the signature color of Krishna, a personal avatar.

- *Now read everything you wrote and look for themes, messages, warnings, and insights—essentially your personal interpretations. Pay special attention to any image, idea, or association that has a little burst of reaction in you—an emotional charge, a numbing, or any other reaction. Helpful interpretations almost always involve a shift of emotional charge, a heightening, or a numbing. Write everything down in detail.*

- *Share all that you've written with someone you trust, and talk about what you've discovered and how this is a window into Shadow. Notice how the meanings you've found often morph and shift as you discuss them with another. Notice further how objects and themes often repeat and develop in subsequent dreams you record in your journal. As always, be alert for any new ideas or insights, and then write them down.*

JUNG

Carl Jung, easily Freud's most famous student, had a much more hopeful view of the unconscious than Freud (who apparently was often quite a depressed guy), as well as Shadow in general and dreams in particular. Jung thought dreams reflected personal and collective Shadow understanding—power and wisdom that connected us with all peoples in all times. He encouraged clients to extend *association* of dream images into *amplification* where they looked for larger, mythic themes.[170] Stick picked up off a dreamscape becomes the Sword Excalibur, or Paddle Father used to punish. Angry Woman next door becomes Avenging Fury from Greek Myth, or Raging Mother from childhood.

Jung in many ways is my favorite dream theorist and worker, because of his radical willingness to reconceptualize any framework in response to the needs of an individual client. He said "[We] should in every case be ready to construct an entire new theory of dreaming."¹⁷¹ and in later life expressed dislike for "Jungians," who reified his work and tried to compress clients into theory rather than expand theory in response to clients.

The goal of Jungian psychotherapy is individuation, where increasing harmony of multiple personal and archetypal forces leads to deeper wisdom, compassion, and improved relationships. This is not the homogenization of all our selves and symbols, but their organization into coherent wholes. In this, Jung anticipated subsequent research on adult development where we've discovered that our "Self" can change through adulthood, usually growing wiser and deeper, but sometimes contracting and becoming more rigid and crazy. In other words, constructive and destructive Shadow affects us as we affect it throughout life.

EXERCISE:
DREAM AMPLIFICATIONS:

* *Find a comfortable spot, and review what you've written about your scary and lovely dreams.*
* *Choose one image or aspect of your nightmare that has the most emotional intensity. What are the qualities of this intensity? What do you feel in your body as you allow yourself to be absorbed in this image?*
* *Think of a story, myth, fairy tale, movie, book image, or character that epitomizes these qualities. For instance, my Witch can be the Wicked Stepmother Sorceress in Snow White or Kali the Goddess of destruction. You can also intensify the image into your own archetypal form. My Witch could become a Thunderstorm with dark tentacles reaching out to grab and hurling lightning bolts to burn. However you amplify, reach for this image or character to feel like a larger, more universal form of your dream aspect.*

- *Draw, sculpt, or write poetically about this amplified image. Give it as much intensity and juice as possible. Give it a proper name (like Kali, or Sorceress), and find a spot in your house that feels spiritually charged to place what you've created where you can see it daily.*
- *Choose one image or aspect of your pleasurable dream which has the most emotional intensity. What are the qualities of this intensity? What do you feel in your body as you allow yourself to be absorbed in this image? Think of a story, myth, fairy tale, movie, or book image or character that epitomizes these qualities. Reach for an image or character that feels like a larger, more universal form of your dream aspect. For instance, Ocean in my joyful dream is a character which appears frequently in my dreams and can exemplify the vast unknown of Shadow—with wonders and monsters concealed in its depths.*
- *Draw, sculpt, or write poetically about this amplified image. Give it as much intensity and juice as possible. Give it a proper name (like "Ocean"), and find a spot in your house that feels spiritually charged to place it where you can see it daily. This can be the same spot as your nightmare image or a different spot.*
- *Every day for a week, sit for as long as you like in front of your two images/figures/writings while attuning to yourself and attending to whatever thoughts, feelings, images, and memories which arise. Write everything down.*
- *After a week, read everything you wrote and look for themes, messages, warnings, and insights. Pay special attention to any image, idea, or association that has a little burst of reaction in you—an emotional charge, a numbing, or any reaction. Write everything down in detail.*
- *As you record your dreams, look for these characters returning in the same or different forms. As we relate to dream images and characters, they often change and grow, just as we change and grow over time.*
- *Share all that you've written with someone you trust, and talk about what you've discovered and how this is a window into Shadow.*

▶ **Ceremony sidebar:** *We humans are naturally drawn to ceremony, which elevates a moment to spiritual significance either alone or with others. I believe we benefit from ceremonies we create in service of love, growth, and healing. Spiritual seeker and writer Evalyn Underhill suggests that the stages of ceremony for groups include:*

1. *Awakening/initiation—people become aware of the desire to transform, and are drawn to a teaching/spiritually-connecting experience.*

2. *Purification/pacification—the environment is set, the intent is set, the group is called together and unified by the leader.*

3. *Illumination—the message/talk is delivered with the Dharma lesson for today.*

4. *Dark night—where participants encounter the shadows of doubt, fear, anger, shame, or struggle.*

5. *Unification—where unity is experienced through transcending struggle into transformation.*

6. *Benefit is dedicated to all beings.*[173]

These stages can be organized for you alone, by you for others, or by others for you. Ceremony strengthens the emotional/spiritual significance of experience and insight. You can organize your own individual and group ceremonies to involve these six stages, and you might want to do it with the last exercise of sitting daily in front of your dream representations.

EMBODIMENT

Inspired by Jung's work, practitioners like James Hillman, Marion Woodman, Jill Mellick, and Steve Aizenstat elevate dreams to almost independent status of fellow travelers with self-aware consciousness. They discourage facile interpretation (or often practically any interpretation at all), and encourage an embodied relationship that should be tended and cultivated, looking to uncover dialectics and allow ongoing communion between parts. These approaches advocate elaborate processes and ceremonies to remember, record, process, and relate to dreams and dream images.[172]

Steve Aizenstat, author of *Dream Tending*, advocates two questions to organize all subsequent dream work: Who is visiting now? What's happening here? He goes on to expand dreamwork into every aspect of living and relating, postulating a "World Dream" that encompasses and guides us all. Jill Mellick, author of *The Art of Dreaming*, emphasizes cultural relativism and radical inclusion of all approaches. James Hillman, author of many books on dreams and Shadow including *The Dream and the Underworld*, views dreams as reflections from the "Underworld," which underpins all human experience and culture. He says, "Mythology is the psychology of antiquity. Psychology is the mythology of modernity."[174]

Jung and the depth psychology movement he inspired were among the first psychotherapists to harness the power of dreams, imagination, and storytelling for psychological growth, healing, and understanding. This work anticipated the humanistic psychology movement of the sixties and seventies, which has since morphed into the Positive Psychology and Transpersonal Psychology of today, where enhancing health and supporting development have become more central to psychotherapy than diagnosing and curing psychopathology.

Fritz Perls, the founder of Gestalt Therapy in the 1960s, believed every part of a dream represented a part of the Self. Trained in psychoanalysis, he was impatient with the slow pace of psychoanalytic work. The classical psychoanalyst cultivates a neutral relationship with the patient until the patient projects old figures (father, mother, teacher, abuser, savior) onto the therapist (called positive and negative transference), thus making the underlying conflicts available to be worked on in the therapeutic relationship. Fritz found he could accelerate projection using dreams and other life events in conjunction with imaginative processes. He pioneered the now famous empty chair technique of alternately talking to dream fragments, then embodying them to respond. These dialogues often progress from initial resistance, to conflict, to reconciliation and integration.[175] For instance, you dream of a locked door in a house. Your therapist asks you to have a dialogue with Door, switching identities from you to Door:

You: "Let me in Door!"

Therapist: "Now be Door responding."

You: "I don't want to be Door!" People often initially resist Gestalt dialogues—sometimes because it feels awkward, and sometimes because it can be scary to personalize and relate with dream images and characters.

Therapist: "Try it," and you agree, imagining yourself to be Door talking to you.

Door says, "I'm closed and locked! Stay away! Don't try to come in!"

Therapist: "Be you and respond to Door. Include how you feel."

You: "Let me in, Door! I can handle whatever is in the room. This is frustrating!"

Door replies: "I'm just trying to protect you. I'm afraid you'll be hurt."

You say: "I like it that you want to protect me, but I want to go in."

Door says, "I trust you more now. I'm opening."

In your imagination you cross the threshold into the room and discover what's inside, with Door as your ally.

EXERCISE:
DREAM ANIMATIONS

- *Find a comfortable spot and review what you've written about the images we've been working with, including the associations and amplifications we did in previous exercises.*

- *Have a Gestalt dialogue with a scary amplified image/character. You can use two empty chairs and move from one to the other, you can write the dialogue in your dream journal, or you can move back and forth from you to the image/character as you sit in the same place. Make sure each time you speak you express how you feel (what emotion or sensation you're having) as you or the image/character you're embodying. If the dialogue feels unsafe, bring in a third character whom you trust—a wise dream figure, Buddha, Christ, or your imagined perfect therapist. Give them a voice and let them weigh in.*

- *Do this each day for at least three days. Write about your experiences in your dream journal. Especially attend to how you and the figure change and how your relationship changes over the series of dialogues. If this feels useful, continue it until the figure eventually becomes an ally, perhaps a personal ambassador to destructive Shadow.*

- *Have a Gestalt dialogue with a lovely amplified image/character. You can use two empty chairs and move from one to the other. You can also write the dialogue in your dream journal or you can imagine being yourself and the image/character alternately as you sit in the same place. Make sure each time you express how you feel (what emotion or sensation you're having) as you or the image/character you are embodying. Do this each day for at least three days. Write about your experiences in your dream journal. Especially attend to how you and the figure change and how your relationship with the figure changes over the series of dialogues.*

- *Now read everything you wrote and look for themes, messages, warnings, and insights. Pay special attention to any image, idea, or association that has a little burst of reaction in you—an emotional charge, a numbing, or any reaction. Write everything down in detail.*

- *Share all that you've written with someone you trust, and talk about what you've discovered and how this might be a window into Shadow.*

▶ **Gestalt sidebar:** *Back in 1974, I was in the first meeting of a Gestalt Therapy class run by then famous Gestalt therapist, Dr. George Brown. He and his wife Judith were professors as UCSB, students of Perls, and internationally-known Gestalt teachers and theoreticians. Twenty of us sat in a circle and introduced ourselves, and then George looked around the class and pronounced, "Everyone seems fairly healthy, but as I listen I hear a hint of neuroticism coming from you," pointing towards me. I was a bit of a rebel in those days and responded, "I think that's bullshit!" He asked me if I wanted to work in front of the class and I said "Yes!" He had me put Dr. Brown in the empty chair and address him, and I did, expressing my outrage. Then he had me be Dr. Brown responding. As Dr. Brown, I was smiling and telling Keith, "What's the big deal? I just had an intuition and expressed it. Why so upset?" Almost immediately I realized that I had been especially angry because I was projecting power and authority onto George, the teacher and expert. I would have been significantly less distressed if a fellow classmate had given me the feedback. It was huge moment, realizing how much relative power I gave to everyone depending on my conditioning, associations, and projections.*

George and I got to be friends during the class, and I participated in his wife Judith's Gestalt group for nine months after the class. Later I taught Gestalt myself to aspiring therapists.

DREAMS AND CREATIVITY

History is rife with problems solved during dreams. Elias Howe, stymied on his design of the sewing machine, dreamt of tribesmen threatening him with spears with holes in the spearheads, leading him to create the needle with a hole in the head for the first sewing machine. Friedrich Kirkule dreamed of a snake swallowing its tail and woke to a vision of the benzene ring which revolutionized organic chemistry. Descartes, after a series of vivid dreams, abandoned his profession of mercenary soldier and dedicated himself to developing analytic geometry, along his many other scientific achievements. Most of us have gone to bed pondering a problem and woken the next morning with a solution.

Problem-solving dreams make up 60 percent of dreams, and dream themes become more coherent over the night, with the last dream before waking often being the most elaborate and well-organized. It's no surprise that Shadow engages in information processing of whatever is most important to us and delivers us solutions, suggestions, and insights through our dream journeys. These messages can be clean constructive Shadow (a happy scene with your son, indicating your yearning to play more with him, or approval from your Shadow of your commitment to play with your son), or more difficult destructive Shadow (you're striking your son in your dream, feeling horrible shame—perhaps, upon compassionate reflection, suggesting both conflicts with him and with your immature violent self who struggles with him).

I remember a dream where a cosmic voice told me, "Keith, the secret of everything is ____" I woke and began to write feverishly, but by the time I got to "is" I had forgotten the punch line! I still feel a tingle of frustration when I remember this dream. I take this as a dream joke on me, though for the life of me I can't imagine what my Shadow jokester was intending! Maybe my adaptive unconscious was suggesting to me that the secret of everything can never be expressed in words.

When I was writing my first book on Integrally Informed Psychotherapy, *Waking Up: Psychotherapy as Art, Spirituality, and Science,*

I dreamt about the material each night for many months. Every morning I woke and wrote down whatever insight or story had occurred in the dream, and then incorporated the material into the manuscript.

EXERCISE:
HARNESSING DREAMS TO SOLVE PROBLEMS

- *During the day be alert for any problems you might have left unsolved, or questions you might have unanswered. Write them down when you think of them.*
- *Shortly before sleep read what you've written and cultivate any sense of curiosity or hunger for a solution you have associated with these questions and problems.*
- *Upon waking write down whatever dream fragments, feelings, or insights that you remember or that occur to you. These don't have to be directly related to your question or problem, just whatever you remember, imagine, or think. Let this material play in your consciousness throughout the day, and look for how it might relate to your questions.*
- *Do this daily for a week, and then review everything you've written.*
- *Share any experiences, insights, creative flashes, or solutions you might have experienced with someone you trust. Be aware of how the conversation goes and write about it in your journal.*

DREAMS AND PSYCHIC EXPERIENCES: PASSAGES TO THE OTHER WORLD

Ask any experienced therapist about the psychic experiences they and their clients have had, especially with dreams, and you'll get surprising answers. Many of us shrinks have had synchronicities, non-rational connections, and unexplainable-by-modern-science events, and have talked to lots of clients who've had similar experiences.

In 1978, my wife's father was killed by a bus in LAX in the early morning. At the moment he was hit, Becky bolted up in bed in Santa Barbara, anxious and activated for no apparent reason. We didn't find out until later that day about the accident.

Larry Dossey, an M.D. internist and famous science/spirituality writer, was once on a radio show promoting one of his books on precognition. He related a precognitive dream he'd had where he anticipated a colleague's four-year-old son tantruming his way out of an EEG brain imaging session. He went on to tell listeners he was interested in hearing their stories of precognitive dreams, and was flooded with mail in subsequent days.[176]

Researchers such as Dean Radin, progressive science writers such as Lynne MacTaggart and Larry Dossey, and many others have chronicled countess stories of people anticipating events, having the same dream on the same night, or being connected in mysterious ways to the world or to people they love through dreams. Having had numerous psychic experiences myself, I'm convinced that dreams can be passageways to what I call the Other World—the mysterious energetic Spirit realms that envelop all of us, but which none of us can fully grasp.

> **Psychic sidebar:** *A phenomenon I've noticed again and again when relating psychic experiences is selective amnesia in the listener. For instance, I'll tell someone that over my career I've repeatedly had the experience of thinking of a past client, and then within 24 to 48 hours getting a call from that person asking for a session, even though I might not have heard from him or her in years. The listener will say something like, "Wow! That's strange!" and the conversation stops and is never brought up again. My hypothesis is that many of us have no framework to store memories that seem to fly in the face of the physical laws of the universe as we understand them, and so such stories often are just not encoded into memory.*

KEEP THE DREAM ALIVE

Shadow often speaks to us from the emotionally dominant right hemisphere, and dreams always have emotional undercurrents, like the music in movies. As we consider dreams, our emotional engagement with them either strengthens or weakens—we can feel it in our bodies. Generally, we want to keep feeling engaged, looking for the physical and emotional spikes and blank spots associated with dream experiences. When we talk about, analyze, or conceptualize about dreams, they can begin to lose their emotional immediacy—one of the main reasons many modern dream workers discourage analysis and interpretation.

Even though I find analysis and interpretation frequently valuable when working with dreams, I agree with keeping a primary focus on emotional aliveness. For me, sending attention into the spikes and blank spots while staying open to shifts, insights, and new experiences is dream yoga in its purest form and often requires great skill and continuing efforts.

To plum our dreams, to remember, retrieve, hold, and relate simultaneously means *feeling* the pleasures and pains of dream images and scenes. We often resist acknowledging destructive Shadow—selfish, violent, addictive, self-indulgent, venial, or shameful parts of ourselves—in general, and our tendency can be to do the same in dreams. There are dangers of interpreting away from our weaknesses or vulnerabilities, engaging in spiritual bypass where we look for existential glory in neurotic craziness, or egocentric wish fulfillment. This is why discerning emotional engagement is so important—it helps keep us honest and in our bodies as we deal with dream material. This being said, the vast rewards from dream channels into Shadow are worth the risks.

Shadow often speaks to us in sensation, emotion, intuition, attraction, and repulsion. Attuning to ourselves while attuning to others and the world helps us receive and benefit from these messages. That's why in all our dream exercises I've encouraged you to attend to your sensations thoughts, feelings, and images at every stage of the work.

RELATIONSHIP ENHANCERS

In 1934, Kilton Stewart visited the mountains of Malaysia and studied several of the many tribes of indigenous people who lived in that area, collectively called the Senoi. Every morning dreams were discussed by families and tribe. From earliest ages, people were encouraged to challenge threatening images in dreams, to receive dream gifts, to pursue pleasures in dreams, and to make artistic renderings of dream figures and images. There seemed to be remarkably little violence and psychopathology in the Senoi, and Stewart and others concluded that the emphasis on dream guidance was a crucial variable.[177]

Couples and families are little tribes. It's been my experience that when dreams are honored and shared in relationships they can enhance intimacy if certain guidelines are followed—specifically sharing in an atmosphere of radical acceptance and refusing to offer interpretations unless they're asked for.

Sharing dreams with your spouse in an atmosphere of non-critical radical acceptance, and refusal to offer interpretations sounds easy enough, but is actually quite difficult. Observe the following two hypothetical dialogues between Gary and Ginger (married nineteen years), about the same dream and you'll see what I mean:

Conversation #1: Gary wakes up, yawns, turns to Ginger and says: "Last night I dreamt I was at a party, and this young woman kept smiling at me. I offered to get her a drink and she started dancing with the host's son and I got irritated. Then a cow stuck her head in the back door and everyone freaked out."

Ginger: "So! I suppose I'm the cow ruining your good time with the young babe! Thanks a lot!"

Gary: "I didn't say that! If anything, you're the hostess and the girl is my anima."

Ginger: "Anima shamanina!"

Conversation #2: Gary wakes up, yawns, turns to Ginger and says: "Last night I dreamt I was at a party, and this young woman kept smiling at me. I offered to get her a drink and she started dancing with the host's son and I got irritated. Then a cow stuck her head in the back door and everyone freaked out."

Ginger: "How do you feel?"

Gary: "Kind of sad. The cow reminds me of the farm in Oregon we used to vacation at when I was little. I miss the innocence of those days. The girl and the host's son makes me think of the New Year's party we went to last week. I imagine myself there and feel a little out of place being the middle-aged couple at the party. I feel a little guilty about the girl."

Ginger, laughs: "As long as she's only in your dreams!" and Gary laughs with her. She rolls over and kisses him. "I'll bet she didn't kiss you like that!"

Gary, kissing Ginger back with enthusiasm: "She didn't kiss me at all, though I did like her. She seemed friendly and interested."

In conversation #2 Gary and Ginger are hanging out together with his dream, creating an intimate moment. They are not jumping to over-interpret or overly personalize. You can imagine this version of Gary and Ginger having many matter-of-fact, interested conversations about their dreams over the years, creating shared interest, enhanced intimacy, and increasing understanding of their own and the other's Shadow.

DREAMS AND MORALITY

Humankind's most sophisticated capacities come straight from our *implicit self*—adaptive unconscious/Shadow—organized from the right hemisphere and the source of dreams.

Here's a description of my implicit self—my adaptive unconscious or my Shadow self—as a dream with the dream figures capitalized (you might try doing the same with your Shadow self):

My Implicit Self is the Seat of Intuition, Empathy, Self-reflection, Integrated Map of my Body, Morality, Metaphor, Emotionally Charged Memories and Impulses, "Keith," and the Autobiographical Narratives of Keith's Life. *Values* are here, *Creativity* roils in these Depths, Moral Reasoning occurs and is communicated to my Conscious Self with Impulses and Stories colored by Satisfaction, Pride, Joy, Sexual Arousal, Anger, Fear, Anxiety, Dread, Guilt, Disgust, Curiosity, or Shame.

Any of the above capitalized figures could be associated on, amplified, and animated. I could have Gestalt dialogues with any of them, and the dialogue would lead me deeper into Shadow.

Implicit self is Shadow that grows if we support it and receive caring influence from wise others. If we can't observe and clean up destructive Shadow—source of our most dangerous thoughts and impulses—we compromise our abilities to surrender to constructive Shadow.

Intuition, empathy, self-reflection, an integrated map of the body, morality, metaphor, emotionally-charged memories and impulses, our spoken name, and autobiographical memory all deepen and grow out of our awareness. They show up in dreams, not only with emotional overtones, but with *moral* overtones.

We can feel guilty or ashamed in dreams or blissfully engage in forbidden activity while sleeping, and wake to shame and alarm as I did at seventeen with my dream of fighting an opponent who transforms into my lover.

As we mature, we can get better at noticing personal evolution—reflected by wiser choices—in moral discernments, coherent autobiographical memories, complex metaphors, affect regulation, intuition, resilience, an integrated body awareness, and lucid dream experiences. As we age our dreams tend to be less conflicted, and we have fewer nightmares and less aggression, especially if we practice any of the dream yogas I've mentioned so far. This is how dreamwork supports moral development.

LUCID DREAMS

Dream journal, 2006: *I'm walking across a Wilderness Landscape with Brilliant Stars overhead and a Cold Wind blowing. A Night Spirit offers me a piece of Horn, a Rock, and a Flower, and the dream becomes lucid. Knowing I'm dreaming, I walk consciously West through the Plain. A Field of Earth rises up and becomes Black Woman, beautiful and sensual. We make Love and She dissolves into Mud. I turn to fly to Jade in Arizona, and rise up in the Air, Speeding East. Happy and Stoked, I Wake.*

Lucid dreams are dreams where we know we're dreaming and can direct ourselves and others in the dream. Long-term meditators as well as dedicated dreamworkers increase lucid dreams (which can also increase from high stress or sleep deprivation). Lucid dreams feel special and significant. I didn't have to review my journals to tell you this one. I *remember*.

In general, when you find yourself awake—lucid—in a dream, it's good to follow your heart and inclinations. Say "Yes" to pleasure, joy, and intimacy. Rise to the occasion! My decision to fly to Jade arose naturally from the Shamanic characters and landscapes of the dream—Mud Woman, Horn/Rock/Flower, and Wilderness.

IF LIFE IS A DREAM, LET'S LIVE EACH MOMENT AS IF WE ARE IN A LUCID DREAM

"Life is a dream," messages are misunderstood, I think. The Hindu God Mara is the deity of illusions, and the embodiment of the concept of Samsara, that all the world is a dream, an illusory mist overlaying true nature. In references to Mara, I often find subtle contempt for taking concrete reality too seriously, and undercurrents of embracing the manifest world as an illusion being a superior perspective.

I agree that non-attachment is a beneficial quality that helps us not take life too seriously, and considering physical reality to be a form imposed over a more profound reality helps expand our consciousness. After all, everything is fields and we are only aware of our tiny band of existence—our "Assembly point," as anthropologist and author Carlos Casteneda Carlos Casteneda called it[178]— between subatomic cosmic strings and the entire manifest universe.

Being fully present, nonattached to objects or outcomes is a great way to roll. The less attached we are to success/failure, approval/disapproval, life/death, our car or our phone, the more liberated we are from anxiety and obsessions.

The answer to attachment—being *overly* invested in ideas, actions, objects, outcomes, or anything—is not to dismiss life because it's a dream, but rather to live life as a dream with *us as the dreamer.*

Look around you at this moment. How do you relate to your immediate setting, the people nearby, the tasks you've done today and will do later, and who you *feel yourself to be at this moment?* All this is colored and understood by *you.* You—the sum total of your conscious self and Shadow—determine the meaning, the emotional valence, of everything you think, remember and encounter.

We *decide* on what world we walk in. We *determine* the universe that we enact and interact with. More or less compassion, wisdom, generosity, or violence *right now* is our choice.

Arguably, every state of consciousness creates a different universe—a different assembly point for our brain to *dream* our current story.

What if we *could* live life like a lucid dream, guiding ourselves in the most soulful directions? What liberation to feel the endless possibilities and potentialities!

We can! We can live each moment as a lucid dream, aware of infinite possibilities and abilities *right now* to choose direction and emotional valence.

What power we have! Yes, life *is* a dream! Yes, almost anything can happen! Yes, we can create incredible experiences and artifacts! Yes, we are the dreamers! Let's direct our dreams towards health, love, service, meaning, and supporting the Evolutionary Impulse!

UNIFIED FIELD THEORY OF SHADOW

Remember our Unified Field Theory of Shadow from Chapter 1, the fractal interfaces occurring at boundaries which both connect and separate differentiated parts? The universe is fields arising out of nothingness, self-organizing up ascending levels of include-and-transcend hierarchies to form atoms, molecules, life, and us.

Our conscious self can create emotionally alive fractal boundaries between our conscious self and our dreams—assembly points where unique moments are enacted. Consciously maintaining boundaries with acceptance and caring intent grows Shadow and wakes us up.

Our brains automatically strive to self-organize towards greater complexity. The more we link differentiated parts of our selves together with acceptance and caring intent, the more we support our personal (ontological) evolution. Ontological evolution is not merely, or even primarily, *me*—self-aware, conscious *I*, the thinker, the dreamer—progressively learning new material. We can learn endless new facts and never really mature or *evolve*. To evolve we need to move into novelty, into new, better, deeper understanding and being, always in relationships with ourselves, others, and the world.

PERSONAL EVOLUTION INVOLVES LINKING DIFFERENTIATED PARTS WITH ACCEPTANCE AND CARING INTENT

Personal evolution arises when we attune to ourselves, others, and the world, and keep linking differentiated parts—sending awareness, acceptance, and caring intent to fractal interfaces.

For instance I dream, *"I'm floating through a Clean Stone Basement in a Tower that Rises into the Sky."* I wake, write the dream down, and stay in relationship with Tower and Rising—maintaining the fractal interface. I can feel it now, warm and interesting—*Clean Stonework in the Basement rising towards Solid Bulwarks reaching into Sky. Sky illuminated with Rainbow Fields.*

Is the tower a Freudian phallic symbol? Maybe.

Is the tower the various levels of awareness I have from my root chakra through my crown chakra? Maybe.

If I hang out with the images and feelings, supporting the fractal interface of conscious Keith and dream experience, *something new* will arise, maybe including the above interpretations or maybe not. My job is just to keep the dream alive.

Attending to dreams in the ways we've discussed in this chapter enhances personal evolution—which moves us towards deeper consciousness and greater compassion, and thus more love.

How cool is that?

12
VIOLENCE SHADOW

Violence is never far away. It is possible to identify the seeds
of violence in our everyday thoughts, speech, and actions.
We can find these seeds in our own minds, in our attitudes,
and in our fears and anxieties about ourselves and others.
Thinking itself can be violent, and violent thoughts can lead
us to speak and act violently. In this way, the violence
in our minds manifests in the world...

When we recognize the violence that has taken root within
us, in the everyday way we think, speak, and act, we can
wake up and live in a new way. We can make a strong
determination to live mindfully, to live in peace. Shining the
light of awareness on the roots of violence within our own
hearts and thoughts, we can stop the war where it begins in
our minds. Stopping the war in our minds and in our hearts,
we will surely know how to stop the war outside.

—THICH NHAT HANH, CREATING TRUE PEACE (PARALLAX)[179]

Violence is *the* problem. Violence always harnesses destructive Shadow.
Even violence in service of protection and justice—necessary violence—injures everyone involved.

We have instinctual drives to care, share, and be fair—necessary for satisfying life.[180] We have drives to do violence to others and ourselves—dangerous, but also necessary for healthy existence.[181] One measure of individual development is how well we integrate and harmonize all instinctual drives—intertwined as they are with constructive and destructive Shadow.

To deal effectively with violence, I believe we need to understand it in ourselves and others, beginning with accepting how necessary violence is to the human experience and how, one way or another, we all must face the violence in ourselves and others.

IN THIS CHAPTER WE WILL:

- Define violence.
- See how violence is inevitable and necessary.
- Explore the evolutionary purposes of violence.
- Find how development involves violence.
- Discover and personalize our own Shadow violence and learn to use it for good.
- Revisit defense mechanisms and how they always involve violent impulses and/or acts to self and/or others.
- More deeply understand objectification and trauma.
- Wake up to the interplay between attribution theory and trauma, and see how to deal with Victim and Bully.
- Understand lying as violence.
- Look at evil and what we need to do about it.
- Understand psychopaths and how we're not them.
- Get how we grow best when we can face our own violence and evil and turn it into compassion and growth.

WHAT IS VIOLENCE?

The World Heath Organization defines violence as "The intentional use of physical force or power, threatened or actual, against oneself, another person, or against a group or community, which either results in or has a high likelihood of resulting in injury, death, psychological harm, maldevelopment, or deprivation."[182]

I expand this definition in several ways. I think violence can also be unintentional, occurring either accidentally like a car accident or from destructive Shadow like a vicious comment thrown out in a heated exchange—this last demonstrating how violence can also be the intentional (or unintentional) use of "emotional force." There is thoughtless violence we do to ourselves—"Keith, you jerk! You forgot to make the call!"—or the random violence that moving through the world delivers one way or another—earthquakes, bike accidents, stock market crashes, forest fires, face-plants, tsunamis, etc.

Practically, violence constitutes a necessary dimension in living and growing, and development requires us to understand and manage it in all its forms.

My friend Patricia Albere, Spiritual Teacher and founder of the Evolutionary Collective, says that violence by nature is divisive. I agree with this. Emotional and physical violence separates people spiritually, perhaps leaving them engaged, but not more authentically connected—for instance a nasty argument has lots of words and gestures but very little authentic contact. Interiorly, violence can cause us to dissociate from parts of ourselves, resisting memories, associations, and the parts of us that either committed violent acts or who were the victims of violent acts. In this sense the opposite of violence isn't nonviolence, it's authentic connection—intimacy—which supports health and growth. Activities that support authentic connection create more love and less violence, while furthering the evolutionary impulses we all share to self-transcend and care for each other.

VIOLENCE IS INEVITABLE

Violence is inevitable because genes mandate violence, cultures demand violence, development needs violence, and progressively coming to grips with our own and other's violence forms a series of milestones which help determine who we are and how we move through the world.

> ▶ **Patricia Albere sidebar:** *In the same conversation, Patricia said that some of the worst violence she's experienced has come from insecure men. "You should write a book about that!" she told me. This actually mirrors my own sense of where masculine violence most frequently arises. A man truly secure in his power or vulnerability tends to be open to influence and connection—he can be powerful, even righteous, but projects respect and protection rather than threat. A secure man can be authentic, even about his occasional lapses into inauthenticity, making him more trustable to both women and other men.*

Fear and anger are proximate emotions for most violent impulses and acts. *Perceived* threat—meaning our nervous system determines we're being threatened—leads to fear, leads to anger, leads to violent impulses, leads to our reactions to violent impulses (indulge them, suppress them, integrate them, etc.), leads to how we deal with the world, how the world deals with us, and our sense of self.

Evolution demands violence: As we've discussed in previous chapters, the three core evolutionary drivers are natural selection, sexual selection, and kin selection. On every level these require violence. How?

- Natural selection—survival of the fittest—requires personal defense through violent push-back if we are threatened, not to mention violence to other beings in service of food, shelter, and comfort. Further, dominance hierarchies—maintaining secure positions in groups—are often enforced by the willingness to do violence to maintain social positions. Violence emerges young. In all forms of mammalian play, violence occurs when the boundaries have been pushed into injury and violent response communicates a demand for de-escalation. We can see this in pups playing with each other or with mother—the boundaries are established through nips and growls. Most children's arguments (eight out of nine in one study), if uninterrupted by adults, are mostly resolved violently, with one child dominating or retreating.[183]

- Sexual selection—survival of the sexiest—requires outcompeting others for a mate. It's no coincidence that testosterone is associated with aggression, and that high testosterone men have more libido, more sexual partners, more frequent divorces, and generally more problems with violence.[184] We are also programmed to react violently when our mating bond is threatened. When we are in love with another person—or even have a primary attachment with a spouse in a sexless marriage—we are moved to violent mate protection if another seems to be honing in on "our" mate.[185]

- Kin selection—survival of the blood-kinship tribe—involves protecting the tribe from external threats. Walruses circle around females and young to violently repel polar bears, who are equally driven to kill and eat walruses. The rational for Hitler invading Poland was lebensraum—living space—he wanted his German tribes to violently take land from the Poles. Chimpanzee tribes have been observed to make war on neighboring tribes to expand territory. Humans kin selection violence shows up in countless ways. A cross cultural example is competitive sports where we identify with *our* school/community/national team and want them to physically dominate *your* community's team.

Ritualized cultural violence: Every culture has ritualized violence in conformity, entertainment, protection, initiation, and development. Sioux warriors endured torture and ritual scarring from fellow tribesmen as initiation rites. We Americans love our football, boxing, and Ultimate Fighting Championships. Iran has engaged in state-sponsored terrorism. Federal and state criminal laws are rife with measures that seek to inflict proportionate violence—punishment—on criminals who have injured innocents. These are all forms of ritualized cultural violence.

Developmental violence: Toddlers engaging in violent acting out are subject to parental disapproval and constraint, causing painful but necessary shame reactions which we need for healthy socialization.[186] In one study in the 1990s, 70 percent of parents spanked their toddlers, believing it was right to titrate and inflict violence on their children for appropriate discipline (multiple studies have shown that it is *absolutely* not in your or your kids' best interests to inflict violence on them).

Toddlers grow into progressively self-aware children who must feel and process their violent impulses to harmonize with social milieus. Ideally, this means tolerating impulses to strike and strike back without indulging them, and developing abilities to set boundaries while not developing sadism or angry attacks for emotional release.

All these tendencies to strike out *at others* are mirrored in our human tendencies to strike out *at ourselves* when we've violated personal standards or seek release/relief through self-attack. Directing ourselves to be good without punitively attacking ourselves for not being perfect constitutes a lifelong practice necessary for moral and social growth.

Adult development *requires* waking up to ourselves and the world with acceptance and caring intent, leading us to grow up developmentally.[187] We are all of us the Universe Dream waking up to itself. Waking up includes experiencing and integrating our violent selves, victimized selves, and despised selves—our despised selves whom we routinely have impulses to do emotional or physical violence to.

WHAT TO DO?

Facing and harmonizing our violent selves is harder and slipperier than it sounds—involving lifelong relationships at fractal boundaries between our conscious self and violent thoughts, impulses, and behaviors arising from Shadow.

Of all the Shadow work we do, the work with violence is the most dangerous and important. Most injuries we do to ourselves and others arise from destructive Shadow violence.

WE NEED TO BE AT PEACE WITH OUR VIOLENT SELVES

All this being said, it is a disaster to deny, ignore, or dissociate from violence. Our sense of personal power necessitates relationships with our violent selves. Men and women disconnected from, or conflicted with, Shadow violence feel weaker and more shallow to themselves and others than people with robust and pro-social relationships with their violent selves. Violence Shadow is important because our power as humans and our coherence as conscious beings needs us to tap the wellsprings of power that our violence provides.

EXERCISE:
FINDING YOUR VIOLENT SHADOW

- *Remember the last time you were angry at another person—really ticked off—with as much detail as possible. Now, answer the following questions in your journal:*
- *What did this person do to piss me off?*
- *At the time, what was my most primitive impulse? As I recall my mind and body while angry, what impulses arise? Perhaps I wanted to attack physically? Attack emotionally? Turn and walk away? Did I want to angrily surrender to the aggressor, as in, "Screw you! Have it your own way!"*
- *How do I feel at this moment remembering these impulses? Entertained? Ashamed? Guilty? Righteous indignation?*
- *What did I do at the time? Attack? Walk away? Lie? Surrender? Engage in cooperative dialogue? And how did the event eventually resolve?*
- *How do I feel right now about how I handled the situation? Good? Bad? Satisfied? Ashamed?*

- *Now consider this "me" who got angry and had the primitive impulses as a character—a person whom you can give a name to, like Angry Self, Violent Self, or Chester. What does your Chester look like? Sound like? Feel like? Create a picture, sculpture, or collage that represents this figure. What does this character want from you at this moment as you do this exercise?*
- *Have an empty chair dialogue with this figure like we did with the dream images in the last chapter. Write what you and your Chester say, and how each one of you feels each time you talk. Continue the dialogue until you feel at least an increased shared understanding between the two of you.*
- *Continue the dialogue daily for five days. On the sixth day review everything you've written and look for what has been revealed, what has changed, and what has stayed the same. Write about these observations.*
- *Share everything you've written with someone you trust and write about the conversation.*

DEFENSE MECHANISMS—VIOLENCE TO OURSELVES AND OTHERS

If you did the above exercise, you probably encountered reflections of you that don't seem very nice or attractive. As we've explored in previous chapters, we don't like seeing our ugly sides, and as children learn to instinctively deal with our ugly sides with defense mechanisms—states of consciousness that manage unpleasant material to try to reduce the discomfort. A healthy defense addresses the pain directly to encourage growth (for instance, I might acknowledge my violent impulse towards you and look for a mutually healthy resolution). An unhealthy defense keeps us clueless and unaware of what we need to change—more susceptible to violent Shadow impulses.

A primary healthy defense is seeking and receiving influence from wise others. Sometimes children seek understanding, forgiveness, and guidance from caregivers in response to distress and anger, and attuned caregivers respond with wisdom and compassion, teaching children how to eventually do the same with themselves. This is superior parenting.

Unhealthy defenses avoid awareness, responsibility, and healing action, and we all have unhealthy defenses to some extent. Inevitably, children will occasionally dissociate, project, deny, suppress, or act out to seek relief from distress, and these responses become habits carried into adulthood, strengthened through repetition and rationalization. This is what immature nervous systems naturally do—develop defensive patterns to regulate painful feelings—and defense states are normal and important components of growth, *if they are eventually faced and dialysized into more mature habits.*

Almost all defensive states are characterized by amplified or numbed emotions, distorted perspectives, destructive impulses (to do violence), and diminished capacities for empathy and self-reflection.[188] Learning how to consistently recognize these states when we enter them marks a colossal developmental achievement, opening us to accelerated emotional and relational growth. Indulging defensive states by denying, avoiding, or blaming others keeps us stuck in primitive responses to stress.

What are the most common defenses to violence Shadow? We encounter shameful or alarming impulses/behaviors/thoughts/feelings and deny them, "I did not call you a bitch!" or rationalize them, "What do you expect when you're so rude to me?" We also can repress our violence, "I don't get mad," or suppress our violence, "I feel contempt for your apparent disapproval, but try desperately not to reveal it to you."

One defense, projective identification, is particularly nasty.

PROJECTIVE IDENTIFICATION

One of the most dangerous defense mechanisms is projective identification. Someone unconsciously projects his or her meanest, most sadistic side onto you, and then is driven to keep attacking you, feeling that if you hurt enough he or she will feel better. This is essentially sadistic attack—relentless violence for personal relief and gratification—and is a signature characteristic of Borderline Personality Disorder—characterized by both rage states and extreme self-loathing (violence towards others and self).[189]

Most of us have to be particularly outraged and jacked up to engage in projective identification (sadistic attack), and relatively quickly feel regret, guilt, shame, disgust, or embarrassment and regulate to more empathic and self-reflective states. How long can *you* tolerate being *really mean* to another? Five seconds? Twenty seconds? One minute? Ten minutes? Usually we become self-conscious and ashamed pretty quickly, and have to stop being mean.

People with Borderline Personality Disorder, Intermittent Explosive Disorder, pathological narcissism, bipolar disorder, and sociopathy are easily cued to violent rage states. They often have enormous difficulty perceiving sadistic attacks, acknowledging the damage, or regulating into respectful dialogue. They can keep attacking *for days*. They can maintain violent hatred *for years*.

OBJECTIFICATION

To do violence to another, we usually need to suspend our empathic connection with that person—the multilevel attunement that naturally happens with human contact. If someone blocks empathy for your feelings, needs, and rights, they're turning you from a person into an object, and that usually feels bad. It is a subtle form of violence.

Sometimes, as with extreme narcissists or sociopaths, someone can pretend to care for you, but actually use you as an object to gratify their personal needs for power, money, sex, dominance, or recognition. Narcissists feel entitled to constant special attention, have difficulty with deep intimacy, and easily justify exploiting others.

Extreme narcissism becomes sociopathy where criminal attack and exploitation is normalized, with no concern for the suffering of others. It becomes psychopathy when extreme harm to others is a *necessary* and *valued* part of the exploitation—think Ted Bundy, Hannibal Lector, or

Charles Manson. Only 1 percent of the U.S. population are psychopaths, but they cause a disproportionate amount of damage; 25 percent of maximum security inmates are psychopaths. As psychopath researcher Kent Kiehl maintains, "Prisons are filled with failed psychopaths," which means the successful ones are out in the world doing harm, though, to be fair, he estimates that 77 percent of American psychopaths are currently behind bars.[190] We'll talk more about psychopaths later in this chapter.

We all objectify others to some extent, or we couldn't read a newspaper without being devastated. We have to have some emotional distance between us and war, famine, assault, tragedy, or catastrophe to be able to function, but most of us care about others and don't want to injure them. Narcissists and sociopaths are largely indifferent to those who cease providing praise or resources, and easily desert or injure people who wound their inflated sense of self, with little guilt or self-censure for the violence they inflict. This is pathological objectification, it is violent, and it causes much suffering.

EVERYDAY DEFENSES AND THE INTEGRATION-OF-DEFENSES LINE OF DEVELOPMENT

As Thich Nhat Han said, " When we recognize the violence that has taken root within us, in the everyday way we think, speak, and act, we can wake up and live in a new way."

Since defenses are so predictably characterized by amplified or numbed emotions, distorted perspectives, destructive impulses, and diminished capacities for empathy and self-reflection, you'd think they'd be easy to spot in ourselves. Not so!

A central function of defensive states is to hide—to keep themselves in Shadow to preserve their power—so progressively learning how to recognize and regulate them is a lifelong process. I call this process the Integration-of-defenses Line of development, and it figures heavily in our personal, emotional, moral, sexual, and relational lives.

We can accelerate progress on the Integration-of-defenses Line. How?

- Practice compassionate self-observation through mindful attunement.
- Observe defensive states—especially in *me*.
- Handle defensive states in other people. Invite them into intimacy or manage them into less crazy.
- Surrender to appropriate emotions, compassionate perspectives, and healthy impulses, always with robust empathy and self-reflection.

VIOLENCE IS A TWO-EDGED SWORD, NECESSARY AND DANGEROUS

Power hierarchies matter to each of us whether we're conscious of them or not. We all seek position on personally important social hierarchies, and we'll react with anger if that position is threatened. An area in our left hemisphere monitors social environments, determines where we fit in, and reacts with anger and distress if we are not treated accordingly.

Anger is the one painful emotion that drives us *towards the source of distress*. Fear wants us back off, shame makes us look down and away, disgust repels us, sadness and grief lead to debilitation and collapse, but anger mobilizes us to attack—anger seeks violence to protect self and right wrongs.

Neuroception of danger: When our nervous system reads threat—whether a stampeding elephant or the nasty neighbor next door—our brainstem instantly mobilizes us for fight or flight.[191] Fight involves direct violent thoughts, feelings, and actions towards another. We instantly suspend empathy, become less self-reflective, and organize to defeat or punish. Flight is often indirect attack—leaving a distressed intimate to his or her own devices is often felt by them as a violent desertion.

The fight/flight response is necessary for survival. When we successfully fight (defeat the threat), or successfully flee (get away effectively), we tend to feel pretty good.

▶ **Trauma sidebar: Trauma as a failure of the fight/flight reflex**

Many trauma reactions like recurrent nightmares, obsessive angry or frightened ruminations, high anxiety, depressed collapse—violence turned inward—actually involve the failure of the fight/flight response. If flight/fight fails, the nervous system goes to "freeze" and reprograms autonomic stress responses—sometimes in an instant. The car accident, the rape, the beating, the sudden explosion, or the daily bullying is not effectively dealt with right now, and so the brain dissociates—runs away from its own memories and experience, while simultaneously locking us into painful defensive states of numbness, alarm, irritability, depression, or self-loathing that can influence us for a lifetime—a lifetime of feeling in danger, in pain, or powerless much of the time.

A blocked or ineffective fight/fight response to pain, trauma, or threat can cue immobilized despair (totally collapsed, even passed out) or anxiety/depressive disorders where we stay hyper-jacked-up all the time, vigilant for imagined threats and frightened of anything new. This is epitomized in post-traumatic stress disorder (PTSD) where the sufferer keeps hopelessly re-experiencing traumatic images, sensations, and emotions, always trying to control them and never succeeding satisfactorily.

Violence turned inward keeps stress hormones like cortisol and adrenaline pumping when we are actually in safe environments, and makes us fear new situations and new people. It diminishes our health and drains joy from our lives.

Violence turned inward is perhaps the most common violence that therapists deal with. I see it every day of my practice and know firsthand the suffering it causes. A sound principle in dealing with violence in general and violence to self in particular is that it's always best to be kind—especially to yourself.

Attribution theory—take one shot, give two back: Basic attribution theory arose from research findings that when we feel injured by another—say you slap me across the face—we want to come back harder—I want to break your jaw. As Ariel Sharon said after he invaded Lebanon in 1982, "And if anyone even raises his hand against us we'll take away half his land and burn the other half, including the oil. We might use nuclear arms."[192] This "You step on my foot and I'll cut off your leg," philosophy characterized Sharon's entire life, and is emblematic of the genetically-driven tendency to respond to your violence towards me with *much more* violence to you.

Strangely, in life circumstances of dominator hierarchies with egocentric power-God types in charge, attribution theory works pretty well to maintain the social fabric (though admittedly, it's a miserable social fabric—these countries routinely show up in U.N. surveys as among the unhappiest on the planet). Bullies do back down from bigger, more violent bullies. Dominator hierarchy cultures foster authoritarian personalities types who position themselves socially to bully those beneath them and allow bullying from those above—think North Korea, Iraq under Saddam, and East Germany before unification.

Punishment as social justice: We also want to hurt those we fear and resent. In 2009, Avanti Mehta Sood of U.C. Berkeley School of Law did a survey of 246 American adults. She asked them whether torture was warranted as an interrogation technique in a series of hypothetical scenarios. She found:

The majority said torture of suspected terrorists is justified if they *might* know of future attacks.

People were more likely to endorse torture if they believe the subject "deserves" it.

Participants consistently recommended more aggressive interrogation of a person they regarded as "morally corrupt," compared to "morally neutral." This was true whether there was a 5 percent, 60 percent, or 95 percent chance of getting useful info.

A majority recommended aggressive interrogation even when there was *no chance at all* of useful knowledge.[193]

The "Interrogation" part of the question was clearly contaminated with profound impulses to punish those who *might* be threats. Apparently the Bill of Rights is not programmed into the human genome when it comes to threats and violence. There is an instinct to punish those we deem "morally corrupt" by our personal standards—we're programmed to want violence/punishment to satisfy an inherent eye-for-an-eye (but really two-eyes-and-a-couple-of-legs-for-an-eye) sense of justice.

This explains the enduring popularity of action movies. Invariably some morally-compromised villain inflicts unjust and despicable violence to the hero or his loved ones. The hero comes back tenfold with incredible ferocity—which we enjoy and applaud. The villain (and multiple associates) deserved it! If I were Dirty Harry, or Indiana Jones, or Aragorn, I'd do it too!

Children's dominance hierarchies: We can see social tendencies for violence in our children. As I mentioned earlier, if two kids argue and are left to their own devices, eight out of nine times one will either bully the other into submission, or one will flee the scene. Many of my clients have been victims of bullying in schools or in families by older siblings in unsupervised violent encounters, parents not present, and often in denial at the emotional (and often physical) violence routinely happening.

Contrary to popular beliefs, bullies have high self-esteem—they like dominating other kids—but low empathy.[194] For various reasons, bullies are numbed to empathically feeling bad about the suffering they inflict on others and are programmed to seek pleasure and relief through emotional/physical cruelty to weaker children, whom they recruit through monitoring who will tolerate abuse (bullies avoid kids who fight back effectively or arrange to not be available for abuse). Children who are physically abused at home are more likely to be victims of bullies (a common bully myth is that domestic violence predisposes kids to be bullies—often not so—more frequently it predisposes them to be victimized outside the home). Bullies seek out such victims and target them in schools and other kid cultures.

Since aggression is an especially enduring habit, the younger we identify bullies and help them, the better for everyone. School cultures that make bystanders responsible to challenge bullying seem to best support general security, and the strategies of walking away and social assertion are much preferable to ineffectual resistance, which is what bullies like the most. Many bullies stop abusive behavior by high school, but a significant number grow to abuse their own families, sexually harass coworkers, and generally be assholes.[195]

Interestingly, rough and tumble play, play that looks like fighting/wrestling/struggling, is good for children if it doesn't progress to injury or victimization. Kids who have strong dominant parents who roughhouse with them but decelerate the play before anyone gets upset or hurt, grow to have better concentration and non-violent peer relationships than kids who don't engage in such play, or who have weak dominant parents who let roughhousing accelerate until someone is hurt or upset (children of weak dominant parents tend to be *more violent* with peers when they get older).[196]

Similarly, children's social hierarchies, if not primarily maintained by aggression and attack, are necessary social constructs. Kids want to know who's the leader, the follower, the jester, the wing-man, or the cautious one in groups—especially who *I* am in this group. We like to be known and accepted for who we are at every social level, whether we are leaders or followers, risk-takers or risk avoiders, serious or irreverent by nature.

Non-violent communication and mediation, resolving conflicts through cooperative resolution, are developmental achievements, and we have to master our innate tendencies to be victims or bullies to learn and practice peacefully resolving conflicts. Increasingly I'm seeing this taught from pre-school through college, and I believe such standards create a more mature and civil society.

VICTIM AND BULLY, TWO BAD CHOICES

Victim vs. bully. Defensive programming gives us two bad power choices. Better choice, universe creator.

Some friends and I once started a community mental health center back in 1976. Even though I was the vice president of our non-profit corporation, I was never a particularly good administrator. I much preferred teaching and doing therapy than attending meetings, dealing with funding agencies, or managing employees.

We called it the Family Education and Counseling Center (we didn't realize until after we had our stationary printed that the acronym was FECC—try saying it out loud and I bet you ask yourself, "What were they thinking?!"). We converted an old house in an avocado grove into a counseling center offering psychotherapy and continuing education to the local community.

The director kept two chickens in a coop near the house, but he routinely let run free, and they would frequently scratch and cackle outside the rooms where I was doing therapy, and I found the noise profoundly distracting and irritating. I asked him many times to keep them in their coop, but he kept letting them out, and I got progressively more enraged. I felt victimized by him and his noisy chickens. Unfortunately, rather than patiently seek mediation, I shifted from victim to bully.

Finally I told him, "If you don't keep those two chickens in the coop, I'm going to kill them." It felt great to threaten him—the bully in me felt empowered and self-righteous. He looked a little shocked, but took my words for hyperbole, said he would be sure to keep them locked up, but they kept running free.

Infuriated, the next week I hired my friend Noel to shoot the two chickens for $20 each. Essentially, I took contracts out on two chickens.

Late Sunday afternoon, Noel came to the center with his .22-caliber pistol and, sure enough, the chickens were running free. Noel got a clean shot at one and killed it on the spot, but only winged the other (I find that a funny reference, which shows how some parts of us never mature). The staff showed up Monday morning to find one chicken gone and the other dead outside the coop.

Everyone at the counseling center was horrified—with good reason. It was crazy of me to shift into bullying and violence when I should have been insisting on communication and non-violent resolution. As a kind of karmic consequence for my acts, I've since had two clients who were profoundly traumatized by angry men killing pet chickens.

Suffice to say that other violent emotional dynamics were seething both below and above the surface of our organization, and not long after the incident I went into private practice.

This story reflects the primitive false dichotomy between victim and bully—that the answer to being a victim is to effectively attack your victimizer. Freud and Josef Breuer, in an 1894 paper, actually suggested that "effective revenge" might alleviate trauma.[197]

I've certainly heard story after story over the years of physically and/ or emotionally abused children at fifteen or sixteen effectively striking back—standing up to the bully parent or sibling, willing to return violence with violence, and backing the abuser down. Was it good for them to back down their abusers? Of course! Standing up to injustice strengthens us and guides us towards doing right.

Did violently standing up to their abusers heal their trauma wounds? Of course not! We always pay a price for violence. Family violence usually leaves lasting scars transmitted to subsequent generations, one way or another. Often these traumas echo through life, compromising self-worth and poisoning relationships. Effective psychotherapy sometimes needs to return to these memories, bring compassionate understanding and assertive action to bear, and reconsolidate them into better life stories, more coherent autobiographical narratives.

WHAT WAS THAT ABOUT "UNIVERSE CREATOR?"

The universe we live in is largely a function of *us*. How we relate to ourselves, others, and the world determines what our universe feels like and how we hold reality. We can *choose* how to relate to ourselves, others, and the world, and thus construct better or worse universes for ourselves.

There are always better choices than victim or bully, and those revolve around our capacities to self-observe even when stressed, and organize our thinking and acting to reflect compassion and wisdom. This is insisting on creating universes where we get progressively better at choosing compassionate alternatives to violent thoughts and impulses. In the above example I should have advocated for mediation to resolve the chicken problem. It would have taken time, but would have had much better outcomes for everyone, including me.

We co-create universes all the time, blending what's happening and what we are experiencing into *a personal story of now*, where I can be a victim, a bully, a Warrior, a Man of Wisdom, or clueless, depending on my capacities and choices.

Creating present moment universes reaching for compassion and depth of consciousness guides us to use our instincts to violence for good. We can observe the threat, the anger, and the destructive impulses arising from Shadow, and dialyze them with conscious compassion until we discover the way through that supports health and love *for everyone*. Even if we have to set a boundary, give our child a time-out, confront our boss or employee, repel a mugger in alleyway, or criticize our husband or wife, the actions are less violent and more in service of love.

EXERCISE:
VIOLENT SELF AS ALLY

Go back to the angry figure from our previous exercise—you know, "Violent Self, Angry Self, or Chester."

- *Think of a conflict you're currently having with anyone, and have a dialogue with your Chester about the situation. Keep going back and forth until you feel you have a just and respectful course of action. Write about this in your journal.*
- *Try this exercise around any conflict or irritating situation over the next week—talk about it with your Chester. Write about your experiences in your journal.*

- *Share everything you've written with someone you trust, and ask them what they see as the optimal integration of you and your Chester. Write about the conversation in your journal.*

LYING AS VIOLENCE

People lie all the time. Check out these stats from Susan Barash's *Little White Lies—The Truth About Why Women Lie:*

- 12 percent of adults admit telling lies.
- 80 percent of women admit occasionally telling harmless half-truths.
- 31 percent of people admit to lying on their resumes.
- Men tell an average of six lies a day to their partner, boss, or colleagues.
- 60 percent of people lie at least once during a 10-minute conversation.
- 40 percent of patients lie about following a doctor's treatment plan.[198]

Most of these lies are of course relatively harmless, but there is a particular dark side of lying. M. Scot Peck, the famous author of *The Road Less Traveled,* also wrote *The People of the Lie,* where he maintained that evil (yes, "evil") resided in lies. He made a strong case for the evolution of absolute truth in service of goodness as an optimal direction for human kind.[199]

All this being said, my opinion is that lies are often forms of violence. For instance:

"No! I didn't cheat on you! How can you ask that?" As you say to yourself, "There's no way she's going to find out about the hooker in Atlanta."

"I'm not mad. I'm disappointed!" When you're so angry you're shaking.

"I'd love to lend you the money, but I just don't have it." Thinking, *"He never paid me back the money I lent him for his truck, so screw him!"*

"I figure it would be better for everyone if I was dead!" You're completely blanking out on all the suffering it would cause everyone you know if you killed yourself, not to mention the harm you're doing to whoever you're talking to.

All these lies separate people, and separations from people tend to create problems, just as honest, loving connections create goodness and health. Even worse, when you normalize lying to others, you tend to normalize lying to yourself, and we all know the dangers of that!

Lying also lowers self-esteem, because we observe ourselves doing emotional violence. This compromises our sense of integrity, that warm internal confidence of, "I live my principles."

Of course the truths in the examples I used are also potentially dangerous, but in a different way. Speaking some of those truths can potentially put relationships on the line, evoke corresponding condemnation or desertion, and cost you time, money, and trust—even your marriage. Though 70 percent of people who discover their partner cheating decide to work on their marriage, 30 percent leave.[200] In the suicide example, we see how pain makes us egocentric and entitled to crazy beliefs and actions—emotional/physical/spiritual pain can inflame violent impulses—and truly facing these distortions initiates a long and arduous epic journey through darkness seeking a life that feels worth living.

Once you consciously prefer lies to truths, you're on a slippery slope to being an instrument of violence in the world, and—as I maintained at the beginning of this chapter—violence of thought, behavior, neglect, and action is *the* human problem.

Most people hungry for the deepest truths about themselves and others are open to new input and loving influence. Seeking understandings validated by science, self-reflection, shared intimacy, or social research tends to provide the clearest views, the best relationships, and optimal life directions.

Such clarity requires dedication to truth as we know it. Yes, there can be exceptions that protect people's feelings and self-esteem, but they're rarer than most of us think.

EXERCISE:
TWO DAYS OF RADICAL HONESTY

Decide to be fully resolved for 48 hours to completely live your principles, and tell no lies. Tell other people you're doing it—don't keep it a secret. Each day, write in your journal what you are feeling, wanting, thinking, judging, and then share it with someone you trust.

EVIL: VIOLENCE TO SELF OR OTHERS FOR PLEASURE, PROFIT, OR RELEASE

Unquestionably, evil exists. Pick up any newspaper, or watch any police procedural TV show and you'll see human beings hurting themselves or others for pleasure, profit, or release. This is my personal definition of evil—violence to self or others for pleasure, profit, or release. Some otherwise socially appropriate people hurt themselves or others for pleasure, profit, or release when extremely stressed, addicted, intoxicated, or generally lost in some extra-crazy defensive states. Other people, psychopaths, *have* to exploit and hurt others—it is their nature.

PSYCHOPATHS

As I mentioned earlier, psychopaths are neurologically and psychologically wired to exploit and hurt others. One in 150 Americans is a psychopath, and 15 to 35 percent of prison inmates are psychopaths; 77 percent of psychopaths in this country are incarcerated—they are the failed psychopaths. The successful psychopaths are out in the world, from the slums to the boardrooms, hurting and exploiting others. These people, *from childhood onwards,* lie, cheat, steal, hurt, and exploit others, with practically no remorse or sense of personal responsibility. Every human culture, from hunter-gatherers to modern democracies, generates some psychopathy.[201]

Psychopaths tend to be smart and superficially charming. Kent Kiehl, author of *The Psychopath Whisperer,* occasionally has his grad students interview a psychopath prison inmate and report on the conversation. Their responses are often some version of, "What an interesting man! He's the kind of guy I'd like to have a beer with." Dr. Kiehl then reveals the inmate's record of murder, rape, violence, robbery, manipulation, and recidivism, often leaving the poor student frightened and astounded, asking, "How could I not see that?"

The answer is that people who normalize violence, dishonesty, and exploitation are some of the best liars around. A psychopath's charm reflects abilities to attune to others and manipulate them, but with practically no empathy or real caring. They can understand other people's minds for the purpose of using them, but not care at all emotionally. For instance, "Callous and uncaring," are the core designations of the most dangerous and violent juvenile delinquents, and predict later psychopathy.

How does this happen? We don't really know. The paralimbic systems of psychopaths' brains (anterior and posterior cingulate, prefrontal cortex, and temporal lobes) are deficient in predictable ways, as Kiehl has demonstrated with EEG and fMRI studies of hundreds of psychopath inmates. Temporal lobe injuries can increase psychopathic behavior, but psychopaths don't have particularly more early brain damage than normal people.

Certainly many of these men (male psychopaths outnumber female psychopaths ten to one) have histories of being abused and exploited themselves—sometimes horribly—but only a small percentage of physically, sexually, or emotionally abused boys become psychopaths. The bottom line is that some humans are hardwired for evil—to hurt and exploit others for pleasure, profit, or release—if born with the right biological vulnerabilities into the right environments for them to grow and potentiate their destructive Shadow.

Worried you might be a psychopath? Good sign! Psychopaths never take responsibility for the harm they inflict and hardly ever self-reflect or worry about consequences of their violent acts.

You're much more likely to find yourself in relationship with a psychopath than to be a psychopath yourself. Someone who is superficially charming, arrogant, a chronic liar, manipulative, parasitic, exploitative, never acknowledging responsibility, never learning from mistakes, and easily moved to impulsive destructive acts for which he feels no remorse is bad news for anyone he encounters. When you find yourself in relationship with someone like this, it's a good idea to gracefully separate as quickly and smoothly as possible!

Such evil requires boundaries, both physical and spiritual.

- Physical boundaries for psychopaths begin in childhood as family and community members limit and punish (punishment has little effect on psychopaths), and then progress to incarceration for significant crimes they commit in young adulthood.
- Spiritual boundaries involve bringing compassionate understanding into the physical boundaries. This is necessary to protect the police/probation officers/social workers/family members from being damaged from dealing with the psychopath. Allowing each person, even a psychopath, the dignity of representation in court, no unnecessary cruelty or constraint in prison, and an emphasis on social protection rather than punishment protects the boundary-setters from being corrupted by having to engage in the physical and emotional violence involved in dealing with and constraining psychopaths.

BUT WHAT ABOUT THE REST OF US?

But what about you and me? What about our occasional impulses to hurt and exploit? We're certainly not psychopaths, we're rarely if ever callous and uncaring, but we still have destructive Shadow regularly flooding up to confuse and distress us. Since our very genes dictate at least occasional impulses to injure ourselves or others for pleasure, profit, or release, we all have to deal with our own evil tendencies—destructive Shadow in its most dangerous forms.

Luckily we are also genetically wired to care, share, and be fair, and are mostly socialized to be good—to be ashamed of evil impulses and feel even worse acting on these impulses and actually harming anyone.

What a powerful dialectic! Impulses to lash out and exploit colliding with deep desires to care and support. This is where much of our shame arises to torment us, both helping us do right, but injuring us with self-loathing and self-attacks. How to deal with this paradox?

SOCIAL STANDARDS

All societies, from two people living together, to countries with hundreds of millions of citizens, create community standards for right and wrong—stay within the standards and you're good, stray and risk negative consequences of exclusion, reprisal, or social constraint.

We absorb these standards from birth onwards, and by two we can observe ourselves and feel guilt, shame, disgust, or embarrassment when we screw up. These capacities for self-observation and self-censure mostly *keep getting stronger* throughout development. In other words, we *absorb and amplify* social standards into our Shadow, which observes us and can generate both shame emotions when we err or sin, and defensive states to protect us from the shame emotions. Growth on the integration-of-defenses line of development manifests as increasing capacities to self-observe defensive states and use them to refine values and become less clueless and more dialed-in.

Social norms change as worldviews change. Tribe to village, village to city, city to empire, empire to nation states—each progressive step creates new human capacities and demands new social norms, usually some combination of spirit-based standards and power-based standards.

Spirit-based standards arise from what our spiritual orientation feels is caring and just. The Bill of Rights, based on the spiritual standard of every person deserving respect and justice, is a great example. Ideally, cultural spiritual standards harmonize with our interior relationship with the Divine, leaving us identifying ourselves as virtuous (we feel the Divine in us supporting freedom of speech, assembly, etc. and stand up for those principles).

Power-based standards are anchored in fear—they demand compliance or suffer punishment, and are characteristic of dictatorships, oligarchies where only a few hold the bulk of power through wealth and/ or institutional corruption, and authoritarian families. A power-based standard is, if you offend me, aren't behaving as I'd like, or possess something I desire, I feel the right to punish you, demand obedience, or exploit you.

Concrete operational thinking, characteristic of seven- to eleven-year-olds and preliterate societies, is either/or, black/white, and avoids contextual ambiguities. Concrete operational thinking leans heavily to punishment solutions for breaking rules. Punishment solutions are common in more primitive social forms, as we can see in ancient (and some current) societies. Steal and lose a hand. Cheat on your husband and be stoned to death. To this day, if you ask third graders what should happen to a fellow student who hits, cheats, lies, or steals, you'll often get lively discussions of creative punishments much more than nuanced opinions about how the offender might have a problem that requires help.

Formal operational thought arises as children grow into early adolescence and their brains develop to the point they can think more relativistically, in shades of gray, and can better self-observe. Formal operational thought is more the norm in literate societies, which naturally move towards democracy (people elect leaders) and then social democracy (the collective takes progressively better care of all citizens).

As teens develop formal operational thought, self-reflective insight can help them see more parts of themselves. Apparently the capacities for empathy and self-reflection are among the most complex social skills, are heavily dependent on the development of the frontal lobes (especially the right hemisphere), and are not fully mature and online in the brain until the age of twenty-six.

More self-reflection means being able to see our own violence, our own instincts to evil, more clearly. Encountering our violent, often socially unacceptable sides creates crises—we feel shame or we generate defensive states to avoid shame. Adding to this complexity is the fact that no one's personal morality exactly mirrors cultural standards. This incongruity is often ignored by concrete operational thinkers, who tend to turn a blind eye to damage caused by violence to individuals, groups, or ecosystems from rigid beliefs—a good example is American gun laws, where ideological resistance to regulation ignores data suggesting universal background checks and registration of firearms would dramatically reduce murder and suicide in the US. Opponents of these policies want less murder and suicide, but can't consider solutions that threaten rigid cherished beliefs about having no constraints on gun ownership.

People tend to resolve such crises by either initiating self-developmental processes that dialysize destructive Shadow to create more compassion and healthy power, or by doubling down on defenses and strengthening destructive Shadow. Examples of people initiating self-developmental processes that dialysize destructive Shadow and create more compassion and healthy power are all of us who decide to grow—almost certainly including *you* since you're reading this page right now. Initiating self-developmental processes was a main focus of my last book, *Integral Mindfulness: from Clueless to Dialed-in.*[202] In it, I suggested that we deal with destructive Shadow from four different positions:

- *Clueless* is indulging destructive Shadow repetitively and resisting influence—like the alcoholic who keeps drinking even though people he loves confront him and desert him as his life falls apart.
- *Mindless* is not knowing you're behaving destructively, but changing when someone points it out or you happen to notice your mistakes—you're willing to receive positive influence to be less

violent. Your wife tells you she can't stand your drinking problem and you receive her influence to help get you into recovery.

- *Mindful* is being aware of your states with acceptance and caring intent, and especially noticing defensive states and states of healthy response to the present moment. You notice when you're unkind and trust your thoughts, feelings, and impulses *less,* while also noticing when you are attuned and compassionate and trusting your thoughts, feelings, and impulses *more.*

- *Dialed-in* is observing yourself screw up, either catching it or being confronted by another, and adjusting to superior perspectives and actions based on a broad understanding of self, others, and the world. For instance, Father Shane finds five-year-old Daughter Betsy pouring flour on the floor, and begins berating her with withering scorn. Wife Bobbie interrupts, "Betsy's only five and you're furious and hurting her. You need to be more gentle!' Shane catches himself, looks Betsy in the eye, and says, "I'm sorry I'm yelling. I got super-upset seeing the big mess. Let's clean it up together, and, please, it's against the rules to pour stuff on the floor!" Bobbi now looks approvingly at Shane as he and Betsy clean the floor together.

Doubling down on defenses is being particularly clueless. Examples of doubling down on defenses and strengthening destructive Shadow are chronic self-criticism, refusal to receive caring influence, becoming a solitary depressed/violent loner, being a bully or a victim, chronically blaming others, never taking responsibility, or joining kid or adult cultures which support destructive impulses to abuse drugs and alcohol, commit crimes, oppress others, or indulge cynical or hostile belief systems—essentially cultures that normalize violence to others and/or self. For instance, adolescent boys are much more likely to engage in destructive or oppositional behaviors in groups than alone—they're vulnerable to co-creating cultures which can indulge violence for relief or pleasure. In the above example, doubling down on defenses might be

Shane responding to Bobbi's confrontation with, "Shut up! You clean up the mess and to Hell with both of you!"

Resisting self-awareness and doubling down on defenses creates much modern suffering. I see it every day in my therapy practice. Strangely, it is often the people with the most robust moral sense, the highest standards, who struggle the most with their inherent violence. Someone will come into a session with some version of, "It's intolerable to me that I am envious of my neighbor's wealth, that I want sex with the babysitter, that I regularly have selfish impulses, that I'm mean to my husband or children when I'm tired, that I'm guilty about hurtful things I did and said in the past, or that I feel like screaming at my supervisor when he unfairly criticizes me."

Part of my job with such morally-demanding clients is to remind them that being harsh and violent with yourself is as immoral as being harsh and violent with others.

Self-awareness of destructive Shadow often requires we take the hit of shame emotions (regret, guilt, embarrassment, self-doubt, disgust, mortification, or humiliation) when we acknowledge the destructive thought, impulse, or act, before we can feel the relief of resolving to do right in the present moment, and to behave better in the future.

Part of doing right is recognizing that an impulse or fantasy is not an act, that the past can't be changed, and that I always have a choice to listen to my wiser, more loving self right now, and act on what wise self tells me.

Exercise:
Take the Hit and Adjust to Compassion

Remember the last time you were mean or unkind—emotionally or physically violent—to another person. Write about this in detail in your journal. Include:

- *Details of what happened.*
- *How you felt about yourself and the other at the time.*
- *How you feel about yourself and the other right now.*

Remember the last time you were mean or unkind—emotionally or physically violent—to yourself. Write in your journal.

- *Details of what happened.*
- *How you felt about yourself at the time.*
- *How you feel about yourself right now, remembering the episode.*

Now go back to each example and write your most compassionate under-standing of you and the others in the scenes. Include:

- *Contexts—what might have motivated the behaviors.*
- *Defensive states that you and the other might have been in.*
- *What positives you forgot about others and yourself—things like, "She always does her best to not hurt people," or "I was trying to solve the problem and got sidetracked by frustration."*
- *Write how understanding this situation can help you think, feel, and act better in the future.*
- *As you do this, how do you feel about yourself? Do you feel like a kinder and better person? Do you feel wiser and more mature? Less ashamed? Write about this.*
- *Share everything you've written with someone you trust.*

THE FLAVORS OF VIOLENCE

As we've explored, violence injures for relief or pleasure, or through coercion, duty, habit, or chance. Violence takes many forms—phys-ical violence, material violence in damaging or stealing another's property, or emotional violence such as insulting, discounting, or verbally attacking.

"Duty" justifies violence when one person feels a moral respon-sibility to hurt self or other—often in extreme situations with no apparent non-violent options, like war, self-defense, police actions, or vicious self-castigation after a mistake. Interestingly, violence in service of duty is less likely to amplify defensive states and cause lasting emotional damage.

"Coercion" means control through fear of punishment.

Chance violence—like car accidents and meteor strikes—can activate many of the same brain circuits as other violence and put our health and development at risk, but chance violence independent of human intent tends to injure us less psychologically than other forms. The same is true for consensual violence associated with athletics, martial arts, and extreme sports. I loved tennis tournaments, wrestling matches, and karate sparring contests. The rough-and-tumble play circuits in my brain were activated, not primarily rage/dominance circuits. I would get angry, even vindictive, but it was also fun! It was play! My opponent and I shared respect for rules and were cooperating in creating an exciting competition. There was not an explicit agenda of doing violence to hurt or diminish. I've always found deliberate violence to hurt or diminish repulsive and debilitating. Facing a bully in the high school food court was worlds different from facing the most formidable opponent on the practice floor.

Human spirits are injured when doing deliberate violence to hurt others, for whatever reasons. We're less injured when we feel violence is morally justified and proportionate to the situation, and more injured when we feel that we have violated social norms. The "proportionate" part of this is slippery because of attribution theory ("Step on my foot, I cut off your leg.").

All forms of violence radically affect both constructive and destructive Shadow. Whether we're the perpetrator or the victim, implicit Shadow material arises demanding our attention.

FINAL EXERCISE:

Review all your responses to the exercises in this chapter, and ask yourself, "What have I learned about my Shadow violence?" Write your answer in as much detail as possible in your journal.

Now ask yourself, "What have I learned about Shadow violence in general?" and then write your answer in as much detail as possible in your journal.

Finally, ask yourself, "What am I likely to notice in the future that I didn't notice previously?" and then, "How am I likely to be different in the future than I have been previously?" Write your answers in as much detail as possible.

Share everything with someone you trust, and write about your conversation. Notice if this talk leads you to deeper intimacy or more separation from this person, and, if possible, share this with him or her.

13

CREATIVITY—SHADOW DEMANDING EXPRESSION

"Logic will get you from A to B.
Imagination will take you everywhere."

—ALBERT EINSTEIN

Y ou are a creator! You are an artist the likes of which the universe has never seen until the incredible miracle of self-aware consciousness somehow emerged—after thirteen and three-quarter-billion years—from pure plasma exploding out from the Big Bang.

Your thoughts, dreams, daily activities, hobbies, and conversations are creative miracles. The dinner you prepare, the outfit you choose, the comfort you offer your child, the warmth you offer your husband, the flowers you buy for your wife, the point you construct on the tennis court, the email you compose to your friend—even the ridiculous angry hyperbole you come up with in arguments—are all creative acts, impossible for other species.

Habituation numbs us to the flood of creativity that constantly emerges through us from constructive and destructive Shadow. Waking up to our inherent phenomenal creativity is one of the pleasures of development.

Creation needs perception. Perceiving new things helps us create new things, and we can *create* new perceptual systems. Am I fulfilled in my relationship? Is my partner? Am I in a defensive state or state of healthy response? Am I speaking or thinking primarily from my deepest, most authentic self? Am I speaking or thinking from pride? Ego? Instinct gratification? Altruism? Interdependence or codependence? Am I being true to my deepest purpose, or betraying my deepest purpose? Learning how to consistently answer these questions grows us new perceptual systems. As we develop them our capacities to generate love, wisdom, and art amplify and expand, because these new perceptions push the fractal boundaries between what we know and don't know into greater complexity. This is especially true if we can harness our default mode networks, executive attention networks, salience networks, and mindwandering networks with focused intent and action, in service of principle, and driven by resolve—always in relationships with others and the many parts of ourselves.

All this book's exercises encourage self-awareness and new sense organs—creative new perceptual capacities. All the exercises encourage new insights and opportunities for growth and love. One reason you're probably reading this book is that, as we grow, we increasingly seek out like minded others to share our manifestations and service, because like attracts like, creativity attracts creativity, and love attracts love.

CREATIVITY EXERCISE:

In your journal, write about the last time you felt the pleasure of making something. A poem, meal, garment, picture, party, date, collage, song, dance—anything you did/made/composed/thought/imagined/said that gave you pleasure.

- *What motivated you to create? Was it momentary discomfort? For example, "I'm hungry. I need to create a meal," or, "I'm bored. I need to create entertainment." Was it an emotional surge that required expression—like a poem, song, painting, or conversation? Was it a direction from (or obligation to) another person—like homework, a request, a work assignment, or an inspirational idea? Write in detail about how the motivation felt, and how your feelings changed as you became engaged in the creative process.*

- *Did you experience flow states during your task—some kind of effortless, timeless pleasure feeling in sync with forces seemingly larger than yourself?*
- *If you did have periods of flow, write about how they felt and how you transitioned into them and out of them. Did focused intent and action lead you into flow? Did minor interruptions jerk you out of flow?*
- *How did you feel right after you accomplished your goal? Satisfaction? Dissatisfaction? Loss? Pleasure? Narcissistic delight? Remember that healthy narcissism is feeling appropriately great about yourself, while unhealthy narcissism dismisses or demeans others. Some studies suggest that experiential thinkers who value perception, intuition, and emotional surges in their creative work have more anxiety and self doubt after finishing a project than rational thinkers who prefer logical analysis of problems.[203] Write about how you felt in your body and what thoughts accompanied the feelings right after you accomplished your goal.*
- *Now look at your daily routine with new eyes—alert for every moment that requires your creative manifestation. What is your reaction to this view of yourself as constant creator? How does it feel and what do you think? Write about this in your journal, recognizing that your journal entries are all creative acts.*

THE UNIVERSE CREATES

The universe creates. Cosmic strings, quarks, atoms, molecules, compounds, stars, planets, gravity, electromagnetism, the laws of physics, morphogenetic fields, my daughter's pet rat Cherry; name it, and it is, has been, or will be created. The Big Bang was certainly the most significant—easily the loudest—creation of all time, leading billions of years later to the evolutionary miracle of you reading these words.

Life creates. Seeds grow into trees, single cell organisms divide and replicate, ants work constantly, birds build nests, chimps make primitive tools, and human consciousness creates art, literature, philosophy, music, multiple social systems, skyscrapers, space shuttles, and spinach soufflés.

English biologist Rupert Sheldrake believes that each species is influenced—physically and behaviorally—by subtle energies he calls morphic fields. These fields combine with DNA to teach life how to grow, and they change as members of a species change. His hypothesis is that when enough members of a species learn a new skill or demonstrate a new

---

▶ **100th Monkey sidebar:** *Morphic fields have often been explained by the 100th Monkey Phenomenon, which happens to be mostly urban legend. The story is that a troop of monkeys on Koshima Island near Japan started washing their sweet potatoes, and the practice spread throughout the troop. Eventually a monkey troop on another island started washing their sweet potatoes, apparently supporting the idea of a morphic field effect. In reality, the Koshima troop acquired sweet potato washing skills through normal social learning channels as the practice was spread through friends and families, and there was no evidence of monkey troops on other islands spontaneously knowing how to wash sweet potatoes.*

On the other hand, there have been rat studies showing how members of an inbred strain learn a maze quicker when a large number of the same strain successfully learned the maze. My conclusion is that some version of morphic fields exist and influence species and family members via subtle energies we have yet to accurately observe or measure.

behavior, a tipping point is reached and the morphic field of that species is changed. He believes morphic fields extend out and help guide the evolution of the universe. This means that every creative act we engage in potentially influences everyone—to some extent potentially affecting cosmic habits, which can deepen into laws of nature—constant creation in constant motion.[204]

This chapter is about Shadow and creativity in people. Humans continually create and co-create (and procreate!). From first waking in the morning to our last thoughts before sleep we co-create with the people and objects surrounding us. As we sleep our brains create dream worlds, populations of characters, new identities, and endless stories.

IN THIS CHAPTER WE WILL:

- Explore the miracle of human creativity.
- Harness our capacities for mindful manifestation.
- Hear the story of Vatsyayana manifesting the Kama Sutra.
- Look at creativity and the brain, and how to harness the default mode network and the executive attention network to maximize creativity.
- Learn about E. Paul Torrance and the Beyonder Checklist.
- Define downloads and how to encourage them.
- Elaborate what researchers have discovered to boost creative output.
- Discover our different worldviews and how creativity shows up in each of them.

HUMAN CREATIVITY IS SPECIAL

Human creativity can utilize consciousness in service of beauty, goodness, and truth. A bonsai tree—guided by genes, nature, and subtle energetic fields—grows from a seed into a tiny lovely tree. Only human consciousness can take that tree and delicately prune and shape it into art. Hungry dogs do not share willingly with others. Hungry humans can generously give food to others while creatively preparing and presenting it. Chimpanzees can remember a bitter berry and not eat it again, but only humans yearn to know the chemical makeup of the berry, sometimes just for the pleasure of discovering new truths, and sometimes to literally change the berry—create a new species—to make it sweet and nutritious.

Ken Wilber suggests that any universe needs matter, principles, and an evolutionary flow—telos, logos, and eros.[205]

- "Telos" is stuff like atoms, molecules, stars, forces, and planets.
- "Logos" is organizing principles like Newtonian physics, relativity, quantum theory, and complexity theory.
- "Eros" is evolutionary drive and direction—constant creation. Eros is the flow of the universe toward greater complexity and deeper self-awareness—a flow of atoms to suns to planets to life to consciousness to art to unity.

Conscious creation is the crest of the evolutionary wave. Sure, the second law of thermodynamics says that energy dissipates and all systems degrade into entropy, but complexity theory tells us that complex systems of linked, differentiated parts (like a human brain, or a social group), that are open, hierarchical, energized, and capable of chaotic activity tend to move toward *greater complexity* and *more energy efficiency.* They essentially reverse the second law of thermodynamics. This creative flow happens at the fractal boundaries (which both divide and connect) permeating the universe and omnipresent in each of our lives. As we have seen again and again in previous chapters, we can bring our attention to such fractal boundaries and amplify their creative outputs—Godlike power if you think about it. That's why conscious creativity is the current summit of evolutionary expression in the known universe.

YEARN, DISCERN, AND ACT

Throughout history, the main blocks to human creativity have come from other humans. Lack of education, opportunity, or interpersonal support, religious intolerance, abject poverty, social injustice, authoritarian families, and political corruption all inhibit creative spirit. An historical shift in the last century involving the combination of (relative) political stability, education, technological prowess, mass communication, separation of church and state, significant numbers of people with rational and pluralistic worldviews, and a generally accessible middle class for hundreds of millions has resulted in an explosion of creative output. One estimate is that between the years 2011 and 2014 the amount of knowledge in the world *doubled*. In other words, all the accumulated knowledge and art of ten thousand years of recorded history was doubled *in four years*.

There are many systems that have been developed to support creativity—all effective. Mostly they simply teach us to yearn, discern, and act. "Yearn" is attending to what draws us. "Discern" is evaluating and clarifying what goals, perspectives, and actions serve our deepest purpose and values. "Act" is where the rubber hits the road and we *do* something in service of our goals.

MINDFUL MANIFESTATION AND CREATIVITY

It's six PM and you're hungry. You yearn for food. You discern that you have some chicken and lettuce in the refrigerator. You make a Chinese Chicken Salad. You have manifested dinner. What most proponents of mindful manifestation maintain is that the main difference between manifesting dinner and manifesting a million dollars (or a painting of a sunset, or tap dancing) is that we are certain we can make dinner and are willing to keep at it until dinner is ready, while we tend to be uncertain about whether we can manifest the million, paint the sunset, or learn to tap, and tend to be discouraged when we encounter problems along the way.

COMMON ELEMENTS OF MINDFUL MANIFESTATION

We all unconsciously create all day long, but we also *consciously* create, where we deliberately choose a goal and move towards it—*mindful manifestation.* There are almost as many mindful manifestation systems as there are teachers. Even though they sometimes don't use the terms "Creativity," or "Manifestation," people from every walk of life, discipline, and profession have methods for setting goals and realizing them. The systems I've encountered tend to have five elements in common:

1. Self-reflective centering while establishing goals.
2. Visualization and embodiment of goals into images and language, often using present tense ("I am…") affirmations while cultivating gratitude for the goal *already realized* (I can imagine the joy of generating a pill that cures Alzheimer's, a book that changes a culture, or a movie that captures a zeitgeist).
3. Ceremonies of daily activities often involving regular productivity, contemplative practice, networking, generating teams, resting and recuperating, and welcoming input from many sources.
4. Inevitable problems that are best met as interesting challenges and growth opportunities rather than as humiliating rationales for avoidance and desertion of project and self.
5. Personal transformations, unexpected life consequences, and subjective experiences of being in harmony with vast spiritual/energetic beings or forces.

EXERCISE:
WRITE A PERSONAL MANIFESTATION STORY

* *Remember a time that you wanted something and then created it or otherwise made it happen.*
* *Write a story of how it happened, with you as the central character, in as much detail as possible.*
* *Go back over the story and underline or highlight all the parts related to yearning with one color of marker, all the parts related to discerning with another color, and all the parts related to acting with a third color.*

- *When you're done, put the pages on the floor in front of you in sequence, and observe what you feel, think, and imagine as you see your personal manifestation story spread out and highlighted before you.*

EXERCISE:
MINDFUL MANIFESTATION

What is a current goal of yours? A new car? More fun with your children, husband, or wife? Lose ten pounds? Make a movie about dog training? A trip to Bali? Learning how to make pasta? Write down your goal in as much detail as possible.

- *Find a comfortable spot, and attune to yourself, breathing deeply in your belly and attending to what you sense, feel, think, judge, and want with acceptance and caring intent. As you feel stable in your attunement, send your attention to your goal.*
- *Visualize your goal already accomplished, and describe it in your journal in present tense terms—"I am driving my new car to the beach," "I see the delight in my son's eyes as we walk into Disneyland together," "I feel intense love and desire for my husband as I kiss him and relax into his embrace."*
- *Make a list of specific actions you could do daily for the next month to move towards your goal, with as much specific detail (what, where, when, and how many) as possible. Include asking others for help, and networking to support your project.*
- *Anticipate at least four problems that will arise and what you'll need to do specifically to resolve them towards accomplishing your goal. Write the problems and solutions in your journal*
- *Resolve to follow your plan for a month, and be open to insights and personal transformations along the way.*
- *Enact your plan and record daily experiences and progress.*
- *After a month, review everything and write about how you feel differently or the same about yourself or your goal than when you started.*
- *Share everything you've done with someone you trust.*

VATSYAYANA AND THE KAMA SUTRA

One of my favorite manifestation stories is how Vatsyayana created the Kama Sutra.[206]

India in the fourth century was at the height of the Gupta period where political stability, relative wealth, education, and a twelve-hundred-year-old culture allowed science, art, and commerce to bloom. Vatsyayana, an enthusiastic sensualist, felt called upon to integrate the sacred and secular texts of the day—some of which dated back to the Upanishads from eight hundred B.C.—in a compilation entitled *The Kama Sutra.* "Kama" means "erotic practice," and "Sutra" means "coded text."

In a classic yearn/discern/act fashion, Vatsyayana felt a deep calling to integrate the erotic classics of his day with his own considerable experience in a work that was designed to instruct children, teens, and adults of the privileged classes in the principles and practices of intimacy and erotic bliss, which he believed were sourced in deep spirituality. He didn't want each generation to have to rediscover sex. Rather he wanted each generation to build on hundreds of years of cumulative cultural wisdom in creating intimate sensual/emotional bonding—providing opportunities to grow through levels toward supreme love and sexual transcendence. This was a sacred activity for Vatsyayana, who remained celibate during the writing, and apparently experienced the process as channeling divine wisdom into the world.

The Kama Sutra is five books that provide instruction in amorous advances, acquiring a wife, duties and privileges of the wife, other men's wives, courtesans, and occult practices. It deals explicitly and practically with most forms of erotic activity including homosexuality, multiple partners, and creating erotic environments and moods. For instance, in advice to a man seducing a woman, Vatsyayana suggests the man engage in innocent play with children in her presence, thus cultivating her trust and affection.

Reading the Kama Sutra, it's easy to like Vatsyayana. He suggests that the husband of a virgin refrain from intercourse for three days after marriage and each day talk intimately to her about her life, her friends, and her family. He prescribes playful cuddling and the lightest kisses each day, gradually including more intimate caress and erotic touch. He advises women and men to create a room in their house filled with sweet smells, comfortable beds, beautiful art, and delicate fabrics to magnetize the eye, relax the body, and delight the senses. He promotes eroticism as a yoga (twenty-seven modes of copulation with infinite variations), a spiritual practice, and a duty to marriage.

I love Vatsyanayana's utter pragmatism. Rather than refuse to deal with topics that he finds generally immoral such as infidelity and prostitution, he acknowledges their presence in society and gives advice on how to create minimum damage and enjoy maximum pleasures. He promotes monogamy, saying, "Happy is the possessor of a single lover. He whose heart goes after other loves kills his family, destroys virtue, loses his fortune, and drifts away from happiness." On the other hand, he gives detailed instructions on how to optimally pursue other men's wives, how women can free themselves from marital constraints, and how to relate to courtesans. This eerily parallels the harm reduction models of sex and drug/alcohol education/treatment that have been tested in Europe and with Australian adolescents and indigents. These studies demonstrate significantly less cumulative damage to groups participating in harm reduction programs as compared to abstinence-based programs. Similarly, harm-reduction approaches to alcohol abuse by American college students are significantly superior to abstinence-based programs.[207] It's a testament to the miracle of human consciousness when a fourth century visionary predicts controversial twenty-first century social research.

IF IT'S SO EASY, WHY AREN'T WE CREATING EVERYTHING WE WANT ALL THE TIME?

Yes, we can manifest amazing things by consciously yearning, discerning, and acting. Yes, we constantly manifest and can't *stop* manifesting (we'd be manifesting stopping manifesting!). So, why aren't we always making our dreams come true?

What stops us from yearning, discerning, and acting spontaneously, naturally, and consistently in every important area of our lives are bad habits, poor information, defensive states, limiting belief systems, and fixed mindsets (where we can't risk failure so we won't pursue success)— destructive Shadow involved in every one. All these blocks are present to some extent in each of us due to the nature of human development—we learn good habits and bad habits as we grow. Luckily, these difficulties can all be addressed and gradually resolved with *attention* and *intention* directed into yearning, discerning, and acting—essentially using our human superpowers of focused intent and action, in service of principle, and driven by resolve.

What propels us forward are instinctual drives for food, shelter, security, affiliation, sex, artistic expression, recognition, love, social position, authentic harmony with our deepest masculine or feminine essences, and the need to create meaning. What enables us to stay on task and transcend obstacles are depth of consciousness, growth mind-sets, mindful awareness, knowledge, guidance and support from others, deep purpose, love, and self-discipline, *all of which can be learned and cultivated, and all of which involve constructive Shadow.*

CREATIVITY AND THE BRAIN

Since we create constantly, our brains are organized to *manage* the creative outflow, with capacities to either enhance or inhibit the flow. Even further, our nervous systems *enjoy* creativity! When we enter flow states of creative absorption, we're having a good time and respond with irritation when interrupted, even when someone compliments our work![208]

Since we're constantly creating consciously and unconsciously in every way imaginable, there is no part of the brain *not* involved in creativity. Rather than engage in mind-numbing categorizations of what brain areas are associated with what forms of creativity, let's look for a practical understanding of our brains and creativity.

▶ **Flow sidebar:** *This irritation at having flow states interrupted ends up causing all kinds of problems with couples. People living together often interrupt each other's flow states. He's playing video games and she walks in on him (or he's watching sports, or doing puzzles, or researching a project), and he gets irritated. She doing a crossword, focusing on a recipe, finishing the report for her boss, or reading her new Susan Elizabeth Phillips romance, and he wants a hug, or to tell her that Stephen Curry just scored thirty-six points in one quarter—she couldn't care less about the NBA and thinks to herself, "Can't he see I'm busy?!"*

These flashes of irritation can turn into defensive relationship patterns of dismissal, attack, contempt, or denial unless each partner can accept the feelings and resolve the little injuries into warmth and appreciation. As I write this, Becky might knock on my study door to tell or ask me something—it's happened countless times—and I'll tell her to come in while feeling a little surge of irritation at having my writing flow state interrupted. She usually waits patiently the two or three seconds it takes me to adjust to being glad to see her, and then we deal with the issue—with her leaving my study to mutual smiles. This doesn't look like a big deal, but it's taken us decades to consistently resolve such flow-state-interruption-irritations back to love.

Wow! Becky just knocked and we're doing it right now! "Hi Becky! What's up?"

DEFAULT MODE NETWORK, EXECUTIVE ATTENTION NETWORK, AND THE SALIENCE NETWORK

We discussed the default mode network in Chapter 3 when we talked about the neurobiology of consciousness, and in Chapter 11 when we talked about daydreams. 15 percent to 20 percent of our time is spent in daydreams or reveries about problems to be solved, relationship issues, future possibilities or past mistakes or triumphs. All this material is spontaneous creation flowing right out of Shadow into conscious or semi-conscious awareness—it happens naturally without conscious intent.[209]

The default mode network *doesn't*:

- Reason about mechanical objects.
- Retrieve factual information from long term memory.
- *Consciously* label a facial expression.
- Infer the knowledge state of another person.
- Emotionally react to another's skillful performance or physical injury (*I find this last one fascinating—our brains naturally mobilize focused attention, our executive attention network, on another's skillful performance or physical injury, moments when others really need and want our full attention*).

The default mode network *is associated with*:

- Mindwandering (which combines the default mode network with the executive attention network).
- Daydreaming.
- Creative improvisation and evaluation.
- Imagining the future.
- Self-awareness.
- Retrieval of deeply personal memories.
- Reflective consideration of the meaning of events and experiences.

- Simulating the perspective of another person (*I love how we do this automatically—we are wired through prosocial mirror neurons and interpersonal resonance to try to understand each other*).
- Evaluating the implication of self and other's emotional reactions.
- Moral reasoning.
- Reflective compassion.

Remember how daydreams come in three general categories?

- *Positive constructive* where we are happily solving problems or lost in fantasy.
- *Guilty dysphoric* where we generate memories, images, or fantasies involving shame, anger, sadness, fear, confusion, disgust, or anxiety.
- *Poor-attention-control/disjointed* where we can't focus and are easily distracted.

Those positive constructive daydreams are the heart and soul of human creativity and constructive Shadow. They pull us into what's *personally* important, yummy, beautiful, and good, giving us flashes of emotions, insights, impulses, stories, and images that can be harnessed into creative acts. Positive constructive daydreams generate creative fantasy, problem solving, and happy reverie—all gifts of self-aware consciousness and central to understanding, processing, and moving through the world. Positive constructive daydreams serve creativity in multiple ways, and are generally constructive Shadow happily informing our moment to moment life.

DAYDREAM EXERCISE:

Pay attention to what kinds of daydreams you have today and tomorrow and write about them in your journal.

- *If they are positive constructive, relax into them with interest.*

- *If they are guilty dysphoric, ask yourself, "What positive constructive thoughts can I have about this topic?" and pay attention to what feelings, thoughts, images, or ideas emerge—especially about you.*
- *If your daydreams are poor attention control/distracted, kindly direct yourself back to the task at hand.*
- *Consider an ongoing practice of cultivating positive constructive daydreams and recording insights/ideas/images etc. that emerge.*

THE EXECUTIVE ATTENTION NETWORK, MINDWANDERING, AND THE SALIENCE NETWORK

The default mode network, our daydreaming system, happens automatically on the edges of conscious awareness. The executive attention network involves us deliberately bringing our minds to bear on a problem, task, or process. The executive attention network does what the default mode doesn't—it retrieves factual information from long term memory, reasons about mechanical objects, infers the knowledge state of another person, etc.—and much more. When we consciously focus on anything, the executive attention network is activated.

Mindwandering harnesses both the default mode and the executive attention mode to generate creative options and evaluate ideas—somewhat unusual since typically the default mode network and executive attention network inhibit each other. Not so in mindwandering, which fosters creativity.

Highly creative people are able to switch modes when generating and evaluating ideas. They can go from an inward focus (often associated with the default mode network and intuition) to an outward focus (often associated with the executive attention network and rational analysis) more or less at will. The circuits that enable this switching are collectively called **the salience network,** and the salience network is particularly robust in highly creative people.

The neuroscience I've studied on consciousness, memory and creativity seems to indicate that the neurological bottom line in creativity is that brains have evolved to be relational creative organs (as we discussed in Chapter 1, "Everything is relationships"). Whether in relationship with ourselves, others, or the world, brains create. In all my studies, I can't find any brain areas *not* associated with relationship and creativity in one way or another.

> ▶ **Writing sidebar:** *Often the way I write a chapter is to let myself wander through books, articles, and lectures on the topic, paying attention to what attracts, repels, and excites my interest. I'll connect new information and insights with other disciplines, talk with my family, friends, colleagues, and students about what I'm discovering, and be ready to record insights and new data on 3" by 5" inch cards. I'll move back and forth from the material I'm studying to my feelings and insights until forms begin to emerge and a rough draft begins to form. All the time there is a subjective sense of going outward into new areas while going inward looking for experiences, memories, impulses and connections. Like many writers, I'm utilizing my salience network to shift back and forth between my default mode network and my executive attention network. This is fun, seeker-system-do-pamine-bursts-of-pleasure both alone and when I'm cocreating with others—flow states of absorption and meaningful action.*

CONVERGENT AND DIVERGENT THINKING

How people think, create, and solve problems has fascinated psychologists over the last hundred years. Of special interest has been logically deducing solutions to problems, often called *convergent thinking*, contrasted with generating different alternatives and applications of ideas, often called *divergent thinking.*[210]

Convergent thinking is bringing ideas together into solving a problem with rational analysis and working memory—working memory being the facts and ideas your constructive Shadow generates and holds in awareness when you're thinking about anything. In the 1940s and 1950s Lewis Terman and others thought that rational analysis plus working memory equaled intelligence, and they designed IQ tests like the Stanford Binet to determine how children and adults compared on g—a term for general intelligence.

Other theorists—led by E. Paul Torrance—disagreed with Terman that intelligence was mostly rational analysis and working memory. Torrance believed that divergent thinking—being able to generate new ideas, perspectives, and applications—was as important or more important to creativity, productivity, innovation, and general intelligence.

As you might imagine, research over the years has validated both schools of thought. Both convergent and divergent thinking contribute to creativity and intelligence. We just explored how the salience network switches and harmonizes the default mode network and the executive attention network to combine convergent and divergent thinking to maximize creative output.

That being said, divergent thinking has been a more slippery research area, given that the line between creative and crazy can be pretty thin. As far as divergent thinking in creativity goes, E. Paul Torrance was a giant in establishing that creativity involves *way* more than just IQ.

ELLIS PAUL TORRANCE AND THE BEYONDER CHECKLIST

Ellis P. Torrance knew something about creativity—at least if one measure is *volume*. His work includes 1,871 publications: 88 books; 256 parts of books or cooperative volumes; 408 journal articles; 538 reports, manuals, tests, etc.; 162 articles in popular journals or magazines; 355 conference papers; and 64 forewords or prefaces—what a prolific guy! He also was a good guy. By most accounts Torrance was a warm friendly companion, colleague, and husband. He lived from 1917 to 2003 and was obsessed with creativity in all its forms. His test of creativity—the Torrance Test—is a foundation instrument in the field.

Torrance was the one who predicted that creativity and IQ would be correlated at low but not at high scores, known as the threshold hypothesis, and this was born out by subsequent research. He found other variables associated with the highest levels of creative output, the sum total of which he called "The Beyonder Checklist." These qualities are all learnable and include:

- Love of work.
- Sense of mission.
- Deep thinking.
- Tolerance for mistakes.
- Well-roundedness.
- Feeling comfortable as a minority of one.

He measured these qualities in a number of teens and young adults and followed them for fifty years (*think about doing an experiment for fifty years! You have to have a lot of patience and passion to keep one study going for five decades!*). Sure enough, the subjects high on the Beyonder Checklist had the most creative output in their lives.

The *big variable*—the one measure with the most predictive power—was falling in love with your dream, with your image of the future.[211]

This last was also validated by Catherine Cox who studied the creative output of people from 1450 to 1850 and found that passion plus persistence predicted creative output more than simple genius.

EXERCISE:
FIND YOUR PASSION AND PERSISTENCE

In your journal write down each of the following sentence stems at least three times, and as you repeat them to yourself generate different answers that you write down.

- *The most important work of my life is ...*
- *One situation where I have the most willpower is ...*
- *The creative activity that gives me the most pleasure is ...*
- *Someone whose work and mission I admire is ...*
- *I yearn for ...*
- *I'm jealous of ...*
- *I desire ...*
- *I envy ...*
- *I despise ...*
- *I would be satisfied if ...*
- *I would be happy if ...*
- *I love ...*
- *Read your answers every day for a week, and then write what you've discovered about your passion and persistence in your journal. Clarify these goals as specifically as possible by writing, drawing, or gathering images or literature reflecting them already accomplished. Put key messages and images that support your missions on your mirrors, your refrigerator, or your dashboard where you can see them daily, and cultivate gratitude for them already accomplished.*
- *Share everything with someone you trust.*

So we create constantly, but how do we boost creativity? How can we harness our Shadow flow to further our happiness, intimacy, success, and development? What does creativity *feel* like?

DOWNLOADS

I experience creative insights as downloads from my adaptive unconscious—constructive Shadow—informed by other, larger forces. Not surprisingly, this is consistent with what neuroscientists (such as Bogen and Bogen[212]) have observed as common to creative processes which often seem to progress through stages and involve flow states:

- You find or generate a question you want answered or a goal you want accomplished.
- You gather information and experience about your question/goal, hungry for wider knowledge and deeper understanding.
- You become frustrated and feel like giving up at some point.
- You have a rush of insight, a transformative image or idea, or a vision of a complete work you *experience* as image or sound—in other words, a *download*.
- You turn your vision into steps you can take in real time and commit to taking those steps—translating your new understanding into the common tongue, painting the picture, building the house, etc.

Downloads can come unexpectedly, during a time you set aside for creative reflection, in conversations with others, or when your left hemisphere rational self is impaired by fatigue, sleepiness (you just got up), intoxication, or distraction. As I mentioned in Chapter 2, Mozart would have whole concertos come to him in "Round volumes of sound" which he would then transcribe. Einstein's most important insights came to him in images of people and objects in motion and in relationships with each other.

Most people who pursue creativity simultaneously research their areas while keeping track of little insights and major downloads. I keep 3" by 5" inch cards in my pockets for big and little downloads and—like many artists, writers, seekers, and enthusiasts—have more cards than I can count loosely organized throughout my house. I find all downloads extremely pleasurable.

Artists, energy healers, mystics, and contemplatives often have the sense that the download is coming from *someplace else through them.* Experiential thinkers (as opposed to more linear rational thinkers) routinely report this—it's a common aspect of flow states—and it's often felt like that to me. One study by Barnaby Nelson and David Rawlings involved a hundred artists who routinely reported that, during creative activity, they felt a loss of self awareness and a sense of contact with a force beyond their individual selves.[213]

Is this force beyond individual self an objective reality, or just a subjective experience that we have in flow states and creative activities? I think the answer is "Yes!" In flow states we often subjectively feel connected to larger forces, but there is also a huge body of psychic research supporting the idea that there are collective field effects that influence individuals, groups, and living organisms. Check out the books of Dean Radin, Joseph Chilton Pearce, Lynne MacTaggart, Larry Dossey, and Gregg Braden for some incredible data supporting the existence of subtle energetic fields generating experiences and knowledge that can influence, guide, and connect us. Some of my favorite research involves algae and plant studies where thinking nasty thoughts and loving thoughts *towards algae and plants* had significant effects on how well they grew.

WHAT ARE SOME OTHER METHODS TO MAXIMIZE CREATIVITY?

We've established that humans create constantly, do it both consciously and unconsciously, and that we can cultivate downloads, but what are some other ways to boost creative capacities and maximize what we've already got? Science and the wisdom traditions have yielded some obvious and not-so-obvious answers to these questions. Let's visit some of them.

- Set aside a regular time and spot for creative activities, and then relax into whatever comes during that time. Early morning is usually good since we often are solving problems in our dreams. Between four and five pm is also good because our conscious mind—centered in our left hemisphere—is fatigued and thus our non-conscious, Shadow driven right hemisphere has less obstructions to sending us creative insights. In general, be curious and open when the left hemisphere is fatigued or cut off (as in intoxication, taking a shower, or absorbed in a non-demanding task).

- Engage in creative activities regularly! Nothing supports creative output more than the activity of creation. You're more likely to paint a masterpiece if you do a hundred paintings than if you do three paintings.
- Embrace influence from wise others! Share your work with people you trust and admire and ask for direction in making it better. In this sense, dialectics with others where we are authentically reaching for new perspectives are priceless intersubjective fountains of creative thoughts, ideas, and actions.
- Write or record dreams, insights, images down as they arise. Think about them, look at them later during your dedicated creative times, share them with others, and look for patterns to arise.
- Rub different knowledge areas or disciplines against each other, creating fractal boundaries where novelty can arise. My friend Ken Wilber—author of numerous books and the main originator of Integral theory—once told me he'd read to a Ph.D. level in twenty-three different disciplines (the guy reads a lot!). It's no wonder he came up with Integral meta-theory (a theory about theories) that unifies the empirical with the phenomenological, and adds valuable new perspectives to any approach put through the Integral lens.

Speaking of Ken Wilber and Integral theory, a central feature of Integral psychology is how worldview affects the universe we live in. Let's look at worldviews and creativity.

YOUR MANY CREATIVE SELVES

One bedrock of Integral psychology is the understanding that we grow through different worldviews:

- Toddlers and little children live in magical worlds where the sun comes up because Mommy wakes up, or presents are delivered Christmas morning by Santa Claus. Cultures such as hunter-gatherers maintain magical thinking as a central mode of moving through a world filled with mysteries, spirits, and living myths. In the magic world, creativity is for the tribe, for beauty, for gratification, for the nature spirits, and for our ancestors.

- As an egocentric four-year-old, your worldview is often very much about *me* and what *I* want. I can be in charge of you, or even dominate you, or you can be in charge of me or even dominate me. Fascist cultures like North Korea maintain this social organization at every level, and it creates general unhappiness. Creation must not alienate the Leader, and must be ultimately in service of the Leader, and only secretly in service of our own passions.

- As a more traditional conformist six-to-eleven-year-old you likely want to fit in with the rules and roles of your family, school, team, church, or organization   you want to be the roles and follow the rules to *belong*. Traditionalist societies insist that to belong to our group, your creations must be with and for God (as the priests and leaders define Him), in keeping with the sacred text, and committed to protecting *us*—the followers of the Book—from unbeliever enemies of True Faith. The Taliban insisting on Sharia law is an example of this. During much of the middle ages, *all art* in many parts of Europe was required to have religious themes.

- As a rational fifteen-year-old you might yearn to be recognized and accepted as a unique individual and be successful in school, sports, and social life. It's virtuous to win, succeed, self-gratify, and compete successfully on fact based and merit based hierarchies. Objective measures like SAT scores and batting averages determine perceptions, self-identity, and conclusions about others. If profit is your measure, profit will determine success/failure, winning/losing. Credit and recognition is competed for. Leadership is rising in the hierarchy. Creativity needs to involve profit or success to be legitimate. Capitalist democracies like the United States are examples of (mostly) rational worldviews (*though, I must say, sometimes observing American politics I wonder how rational the U.S. really is*).

- As a pluralistic young adult you might be distressed by social injustice and want to help bring care and rights to the world—to care for all. Creative expression is valued, but critical evaluation is frowned upon. Credit is shared, hierarchy is resisted. Egocentricism is present, but kept in Shadow to emerge passive aggressively through disapproval of other worldviews. Seeking victory, primacy, or individual eminence is frowned upon. The social democracies of northern Europe tend to be pluralistic.

- As a mature adult who has felt appreciation for all points of view, you might grow to find that all forms of creation have healthy and unhealthy forms, and your bias is towards the healthy forms. This is often called Integral consciousness. Whatever the motivation, the background sense is that each person's creativity serves the evolutionary impulse uniquely. A few companies like Zappos, Google, and Apple seem to be organized in this fashion.

- As a Man or Woman of Wisdom, you desire to join with like minded others to serve the world, with an understanding that there is a beauty and spiritual connectedness with all we feel, share, and create. Billionaires joining in commitments to leave at least half of their wealth to charity are example of this impulse made manifest.

These worldviews don't disappear as we grow, they progressively include and transcend each other, with any one of them likely to show up under the right circumstances or life conditions. I might want what's in the highest good for mankind (pluralistic), but I also want to have a good time at the Super Bowl party (egocentric), be accepted by my friends, clients, colleagues, and family (conformist), and succeed in my work and play (rational). I'd love this book to be fun to write (egocentric), be a best seller (rational), be celebrated and accepted by psychologists, lay people, and spiritual teachers everywhere (conformist), and generate lots of opportunities to teach, and help further the evolutionary impulse (pluralistic). In other words, my egocentric self likes to create for gratification, my more conformist, wanting-to-belong-and-be-accepted self likes to create for approval and acceptance, my more rational self likes to create for success and recognition, my more pluralistic self likes to create to serve the world, and my Integral self appreciates the healthy forms of all these motivational forces.

In the last century, Claire Graves noticed how individuals, groups, and cultures tended to lean towards these different worldviews, and his work has informed such developmental luminaries as Ken Wilber, Don Beck, Chris Cowan, Robert Kegan, Terri O'Fallon, and Susanne Cook-Greuter. Everybody agrees that individuals and couples grow through these stages in an include-and-transcend manner, and often are more informed by one motivational system than another.

What are *your* relationships with your different selves and their creative outputs?

EXERCISE:
MEET SOME OF YOUR DIFFERENT SELVES

Get a big sheet of paper and list in a column down the left side egocentric, conformist, rational, pluralistic, and Integral. Now let's get to know these parts of you better!

- *Think about your egocentric self, the part of you concerned with your pleasure, safety, personal power, and comfort. Pick an image, character, or dream person that most personifies this part of you, and write about him, her, it in detail opposite "Egocentric" on your sheet. Give him or her a name if you'd like. I imagine Keith happily catching a wave on a sunny day, or lying on my couch with a glass of wine watching my favorite Ultimate Fighter in a championship fight. When you are done, imagine that character/image/dream figure sitting opposite you and look into his or her eyes and say what you're feeling and wanting. Especially ask that figure what he or she wants you to create for him/her/it. Then change places and be that character looking you in the eyes and answering. Go back and forth like this at least several times, and write in your journal what you say, think, feel, judge, want, and imagine as you do this.*

- *Think about your conformist self, the part of you concerned with fitting in and being accepted by people with your beliefs. Pick an image, character, or dream person that most personifies this part of you, and write about him/her/it in detail opposite "Conformist" on your sheet. Give him or her a name if you'd like. I imagine Keith out to dinner with my favorite interpersonal neurobiologists and colleagues (as well as my wife and two kids) and we're enjoying each other's stories and ideas—feeling comfortably part of the same belief systems. When you are done, imagine that character/image/dream figure sitting opposite you and look into his or her eyes and say what you're feeling and wanting. Especially ask that figure what it wants you to create for him/her/it. Then change places and be that character looking you in the eyes and answering. Go back and forth like this at least several times, and write in your journal what you say, think, feel, judge, want, and imagine as you do this.*

- *Think about your rational self, the part of you concerned with success, recognition, and being consistent with the way the world really works. Pick an image, character, or dream person that most personifies this part of you, and write about him, her, it in detail opposite "Rational" on your sheet. Give him or her a name if you'd like. I imagine Keith in a $2000 suit presenting to rollicking laughter and thundering applause at UCLA's yearly Lifespan Learning conference, while Shadowlight is hitting the bestseller lists. When you are done, imagine that character/image/dream figure sitting opposite you and look into his or her eyes and say what you're feeling and wanting. Especially ask that figure what it wants you to create for him/her/it. Then change places and be that character looking you in the eyes and answering. Go back and* *forth like this at least several times, and write in your journal what you say, think, feel, judge, want, and imagine as you do this.*

- *Think about your pluralistic self, the part of you that feels that everyone's opinions and feelings count, and that everyone should be treated equally well. Pick an image, character, or dream person that most personifies this part of you, and write about him, her, or it in detail opposite "Pluralistic" on your sheet. Give him or her a name if you'd like. I imagine me making a case before congress for universal healthcare and massive material and social support for mothers, fathers, and children from conception through high school. When you are done, imagine that character/image/dream figure sitting opposite you and look into his or her eyes and say what you're feeling and wanting. Especially ask that figure what it wants you to create for him/her/it. Then change places and be that character looking you in the eyes and answering. Go back and forth like this at least several times, and write in your journal what you say, think, feel, judge, want, and imagine as you do this.*

- *Think about your Integral self, the part of you that appreciates and accepts all the above characters and motivation systems, and can mostly discern the healthy and unhealthy aspects of each. Pick an image, character, or dream person that most personifies this part of you, and write about him, her, it in detail opposite "Integral" on your sheet. Give him or her a name if you'd like. I imagine me in a Shrink and Pundit dialogue with my good friend Jeff Salzman, trying to help everyone live, love, and work more joyfully and successfully, while knowing that everyone enacts a different universe requiring different insights and missions, and that every worldview has destructive and constructive Shadow influences. When you are done, imagine that character/image/dream figure sitting opposite you and look into his or her eyes and say what you're feeling and wanting. Especially ask that figure what it wants you to create for him/her/it. Then change places and be that character looking you in the eyes and answering. Go back and forth like this at least several times, and write in your journal what you say, think, feel, judge, want, and imagine as you do this.*

- *Talk with each of these (going back and forth looking into each other's eyes at least two or three times) every day for the next month. As the days pass, notice how you become more marginally aware of all of them at different times. You are developing new sense organs to monitor these parts of you, as well as new powers to listen, respond, and self-regulate. You are also learning how to discern the healthy and unhealthy manifestations of each worldview's constructive and destructive Shadow.*
- *Cultivate relationships with these five of your most central selves, all of whom want you to create, but who all have different emphases of motivations. As these relationships become a background hum to your life, you are amplifying the fractal interfaces between your conscious self and adaptive unconscious. From these interfaces will arise insights, images, desires, feelings, and stories.*
- *The more you have a felt appreciation for the strengths and weaknesses of all these selves, the more your Integral self becomes the central voice, with a felt appreciation for the strengths and weaknesses of all points of view and dramatically less fear of the world, including of your own death.*

Multiple points of view interacting, cross-validating, and mutually enriching, have been associated with amplified creativity in all disciplines, and *you contain all these voices*—they all send Shadow messages to you each day. These worldview are *always informing you* one way or another.

Do these exercises and you accelerate and clarify new material arising from constructive and destructive Shadow into your conscious awareness—you expand your boundaries of understanding and amplify your creative output.

CREATIVITY SHADOW EVERYWHERE

If you go back to each chapter in this book, you'll see how the information, stories, and exercises all involve cultivating the creative flow of constructive Shadow into your life, as well as transmuting destructive Shadow into constructive Shadow.

In Chapter 1 we practiced an attunement exercise to enhance our abilities to be aware with acceptance and caring intent of our own and others' sensations, feelings, thoughts, judgments, and desires. This was to create new perceptual capacities to compassionately observe self and others.

In Chapter 2 we looked at relationships everywhere and how to send our attention to them to maximize their creative outputs.

In Chapter 3 we learned how to use shame as a spiritual guide, and how to optimize our neurobiology to support constructive Shadow.

In Chapter 4 we explored the neurobiology of Shadow work and how to integrate our consciousness with our neurobiology.

In Chapter 5 we dived into the Hero's Journey, how to guide yourself through the dangers and distractions, and what new gifts to expect and cherish from your personal trials, ordeals, and transformations.

In Chapter 6 we identified the Warrior and Man of Wisdom and how to harness our superpowers of focused intent and action, in service of principle, and driven by resolve to support our missions in life.

In Chapter 7 we communed with the ingénue, the Divine Mother, and the Woman of Wisdom, seeing how feminine power is becoming a driving force in this century and how to honor that feminine in ourselves and others.

In Chapter 8 we delved into sexual Shadow and how to focus on creating fulfilling sexuality as a vehicle for love, growth, and bliss.

In Chapter 9 we explored how to turn marital entropy into marital transcendent bliss by identifying constructive marital Shadow and surrendering to it, and transmuting destructive marital Shadow—especially evident in defensive states.

In Chapter 10 we drew genograms to discover new family strengths, weaknesses, and opportunities for love.

In Chapter 11 we plunged into the Universe Dream and discovered how we can tap into its wild creative beauty and power.

In Chapter 12 we explored our own and others' violence—it's dangers and gifts—and how integrate our violent selves into our identities as prosocial loving people.

In Chapter 13 we are finding creativity everywhere in our lives, and learning how to amplify and enhance it in services of love, joy, health, and service.

In Chapter 14, Spiritual Shadow, we'll bring it all together in the light and dark of our individual spirituality—discovering that ultimately we are all part of one continuing creative and mystical explosion through time.

14

SPIRITUAL SHADOW

THE CREATION OF MAN BY PROMETHEUS (BY J.M. HUNT)[214]

Prometheus and Epimetheus were spared imprisonment in Tartarus because they had not fought with their fellow Titans during the war with the Olympians. They were given the task of creating man. Prometheus shaped man out of mud, and Athena breathed life into his clay figure...

Prometheus had assigned Epimetheus the task of giving the creatures of the earth their various qualities, such as swiftness, cunning, strength, fur, and wings. Unfortunately, by the time he got to man Epimetheus had given all the good qualities out and there were none left for man. So Prometheus decided to make man stand upright as the gods did and to give him fire...

Prometheus loved man more than the Olympians, who had banished most of his family to Tartarus. Prometheus lit a torch from the sun and brought it back to man. Zeus was enraged that man had fire. He decided to inflict a terrible punishment on both man and Prometheus...

To punish man, Zeus had Hephaestus create a mortal of stunning beauty. The gods gave the mortal many gifts of wealth. He then had Hermes give the mortal a deceptive heart and a lying tongue. This creation was Pandora, the first woman. A final gift was a jar which Pandora was forbidden to open.

Thus completed, Zeus sent Pandora down to Epimetheus, who was staying amongst the men...

Prometheus had warned Epimetheus not to accept gifts from Zeus, but Pandora's beauty was too great and he allowed her to stay. Eventually, Pandora's curiosity about the jar she was forbidden to open became intolerable. She opened the jar and out flew all manner of evils, sorrows, plagues, and misfortunes. However, the bottom of the jar held one good thing—hope...

Zeus, furious with Prometheus, had his servants, Force and Violence, seize Prometheus, take him to the Caucasus Mountains, and chain him to a rock with unbreakable adamanite chains. Here he was tormented day and night by a giant eagle tearing at his liver. Eventually, Chiron the Centaur agreed to die for Prometheus and Heracles killed the eagle and unbound him.

In this myth Prometheus gives humankind the gift of fire. Zeus is appalled that such power has been given to humans—justifiably, since deepening consciousness led the Greeks away from pantheism and towards rationalism. In punishment Prometheus is chained and tormented until he's delivered from suffering by Chiron the Centaur, Shamanic teacher of the Heroes, and Heracles the half human warrior/hero with God-like powers. The Heroes like Heracles, Perseus, and Theseus were half God/half human hybrids who formed a bridge between the Spirit Realm and the Material Realm. People have always searched for some explanation for the divine that they intuitively feel inherent in *us,* humanity—and the half God, half human heroes metaphorically fit the bill for the ancient Greeks, just as the saints would for future Christians.

Humans are punished by "...all manner of evils, sorrows, plagues, and misfortunes," released from Pandora's jar.

I believe our gift of fire is self-aware consciousness, and the Prometheus myth illuminates human consciousness coming with a price. Self-aware consciousness can suffer infinitely. As Ken Wilber maintains, with each ascending level of development, new pathologies and problems arise.[215]

IN THIS CHAPTER WE WILL:

- Revisit stories, relationships, and bring in Ego and Soul.
- Offer definitions of spiritual Shadow.
- Connect Shadow spirituality with waking up.
- Explore how levels of shame both block and guide spiritual development.
- Practically define enlightenment and the hazards we face pursuing it.
- Look at cultural spiritual Shadow.
- Define spiritual bypass and how it shows up in different forms.
- Learn how spirituality can involve taboos like sexuality taboos, and how spirituality is central to psychotherapy.
- Explore how Integral Mindfulness can help us move from clueless to dialed-in.
- Discover Buddhism's great blind spot.
- Learn a 9 Chakra meditation for cultivating 28 transcendent states.

STORIES, RELATIONSHIPS, EGO, AND SOUL

So far in this book I've claimed that everything is relationships between our conscious self, the world, and our many interior aspects and selves across time. I've also claimed that everything is stories. Dreams, daydreams, working memories, beliefs, myths, etc, are all stories which inform our decisions consciously and non-consciously, which in turn become our actions which we integrate into ongoing autobiographical narratives—the stories of our lives. Humans are relational, story-generating species. Stories are matrices of relationships. Everything is relationships. Everything is stories.[216]

Do we examine and cross-validate our stories through science, experience, inner wisdom, and social networks? Sometimes.

Do we receive influence from the world? From others? From ourselves reflected through others? Sometimes.

A person refusing influence resists validation by science, experience, or social networks, thus locking stories down in rigid forms which inevitably cannot adequately reflect a changing world. This amplifies destructive Shadow and leaves a lot of people believing delusions like evolution is a false construct, that global warming is not caused by human pollution, or that it's a great idea to eat three doughnuts, ten strips of bacon, and three cups of coffee for breakfast.

Stories constantly arise from deep genetic drives, from our brain's mandate to constantly create stories, from morphegenic fields, from our lived experience, from our intersubjectivity with others, and from who knows what else? Where ever and whatever is involved, life *is* stories!

SOUL AND EGO

Soul is our closest connection to Spirit, hovering at the edge of—the intersection between—the vast unknown collective and our individual self. Soul feels and loves everyone and everything, which makes Soul the purest story teller.

Ego is our conscious self. The "I" that you experience reading these words. Ego is our personal interior ally, opponent, lover, friend, mother, father, sister, brother, stranger, son, daughter, guide, self, and interpreter. One way or another, Ego is always directing the show, and the show must go on!

Ego can self-observe and clarify—including and transcending—until Ego identifies primarily with Soul. Meditation, contemplative work, and tantric engagement with others can accelerate ego development. This opens up stable channels into the other world and clarifies the flow of stories cocreated with Shadow and conscious self, connecting us to the Universe Dream and our special place in it.

Integral theory maintains that all physical bodies have energy bodies. Soul is a so-subtle energy body, but does the Soul energy body cease to exist when the physical body turns to dust? If energy body Soul endures past death, where is the physical body to sustain it? Does our living body provide the physical body of our soul across time? Do we have a self-aware consciousness after our death through transtemporal forces anchoring Soul to a physical body that will always exist (and has always existed) somehow outside of time?

The destructive Shadow of Spirituality—turning away from problems, challenges, and disturbing feelings with spiritual language and practices—deflects us from considering such questions. Turning towards the big questions, open to influence and change, amplifies constructive Spiritual Shadow and helps us wake up.

WAKING UP

A basic tenant of *Shadow Light* is that the more senses we develop the more Shadow is revealed to us. The more Shadow we can perceive, the deeper we can become, and the faster we can grow our adaptive unconscious, our implicit self, our Shadow selves. This speeds up understanding of everything—it *wakes us up*.

This is why I titled my first book on Integrally Informed Psychotherapy *Waking Up*. When we learn something *interestingly* new, our brains give us a little boost of the seeker/pleasure neurotransmitter dopamine. These dopamine driven pleasures we feel when we encounter flashes of insight and new understandings are the evolutionary impulse rewarding us, shaping us to keep seeking and growing both alone and with each other.

Seeking and growing leads to more love—at-one-ness—with our many different selves, others, and the world. Contemplatives consistently report that thousands of hours of practice translate into increasing feelings of unity of consciousness, form, time, and space. Is this merely subjective, or also objective where there are non-local, transtemporal dimensions encompassing us all? Perhaps all moments are one moment, outside of time, encompassing time, everything all at once. Thinking this makes me achingly grateful for the present moment, connected as it is to all moments.

BIG REVEAL: EVOLUTION WAKES UP

Until life appeared in the universe, evolution worked chemically. Energized systems with linked differentiated parts self-organized into more complex forms—atoms to molecules, to suns, to solar systems. Fractal boundaries, biased towards greater complexity, kept bringing novelty into existence.

When life arose, evolution accelerated with natural selection (survival of the fittest), sexual selection (survival of the sexiest), and kin selection (survival of the blood kinship group). These forces in combination with random mutations created millions of new species, almost all of which evolved to eventually fail and be supplanted by new life.

Up until humans, evolution worked relatively randomly. Species would adapt as well as they could to slowly changing ecosystems (or sometimes quickly changing ecosystems as with cataclysmic meteor strikes). At the edges, genetic mutations and variants would appear, mostly not giving particular advantage for natural selection, sexual selection, or kin selection. Occasionally a variant provided an advantage that could be passed down genetically or behaviorally with social learning (like whales teaching babies how to breathe, or wolves teaching youngsters how to hunt). This genetic upgrade, or social milestone, would work its way into the group, eventually changing entire species.

With humans, evolution literally began to wake up to self-awareness, and *sped up*. Humans began *consciously* changing genomes and environments. They bred for characteristics in animals like dogs and horses, in plants, and in other humans. The advent of cities accelerated human physical evolution a hundred times—*ten thousand percent.*

Humans deliberately and dramatically altered the balance of entire ecosystems. For instance, the Aborigines of Australia, in the first hundred years after arriving on the Australian continent, completely eliminated fifty species of large land animal—presaging the current sixth great die off in the history of life on this planet, this one caused by human activity. The sixth great die off is an ecological catastrophe, but it is the first great die off with a conscience. How this will eventually play out is still up for grabs.

With Darwin's *On the Origin of Species*, and the subsequent discoveries of genes, chromosomes, cloning, epigenetics, and genetic engineering, humans took over the evolutionary process *on the genetic level*, deliberately engineering genetic changes in plants and animals.

We, you and I, are evolution in action. We are the evolutionary impulse waking up to itself, and guiding our personal evolution as well as human evolution.

The direction of personal and relational evolution is fascinating and revealing. We grow on the cognitive line towards more complex and inclusive thinking. We grow on the moral line to more relativistic and caring morality. We grow on the interpersonal line to greater compassion and care for all. We grow on the psychosexual line towards tantric relationships which help us feel more intimacy and love. We grow on the spirituality line towards more felt unity.[217]

It's pretty obvious that the evolutionary impulse is driving matter towards identifying itself as self-aware Spirit.

We—you and I—are evolution waking up and discovering itself as Spirit, transformed into matter, growing towards felt unity with Spirit.

The universe is composed of holarchies—fields embedded in atoms, embedded in molecules, embedded in living creatures, embedded in more complex living creatures. Holarchies include and transcend, drawing from the energy and resources of previous levels.[218]

In terms of sustenance, each level literally feeds off of previous levels, from life needing water and oxygen, to humans consuming animals and plants, to perhaps spirit arising and being nourished by human consciousness.

I suspect that, if this is the case, that a loop exists comprised of spirit nourished by our depth and compassion, informing us from our intuitive core (our constructive Shadow), to grow towards felt unity with Spirit—a virtuous circuit which strengthens everyone. This is a positive feedback loop in the best sense—a loop that potentially takes any one of us or all of us all the way to stable identifications with pure Spirit.

Meditations, contemplative practices of all sorts, strengthen frontal lobe brain regions associated with morality, affect regulation, intuition, self-awareness, empathy, response flexibility, and general self-observation. The more we bring compassion to bear on our experiences, the more we can access these networks to clarify the stories saturating our existence and surrender to our optimal roles in the Universe Dream.

It sounds so simple and obvious to identify with Spirit, to bring compassion to bear, to faithfully engage in contemplative practices, so why aren't we all happily connected to and informed by Spirit all the time? What makes it so hard and painful to be human? What are we not seeing?

What is the Shadow of Spirituality?

DEPRESSION, SHAME, ANXIETY, AND THE HUMAN CONDITION

Even though we are Spirit waking up to itself, practically speaking, life and development are messy processes which need constant attention on every level. Constructive Shadow guides us towards enhanced development, which is great, but destructive Shadow keeps arising and demanding attention. This is the dance of life.

Recently I was talking to my good friend David who was depressed. He was frightened he would sink into the kind of lingering despair he had once struggled through decades ago, requiring the help of a therapist and antidepressant medications.

David asked me, "Why does this happen? Is it karmic? Past lives? Childhood trauma? When I went through depression before, I didn't think that it had to do with shame, but, looking back, shame was everywhere. I know you wrote about this in your book, *The Gift of Shame*. Is there an explanation?"

LEVELS OF SHAME

Often people have asked me, "Why do I have this pall of depression enveloping me or threatening me all the time?" "Why am I so anxious? Why am I afraid I won't be able to cope with my life, or that something bad is going to happen?" "Why do I feel like a failure often, even though I've had many successes?" "Why do I feel so alone when there are people in my life who love me and value me?" "Why is it so easy for me to be ashamed of who I am, or who I've been—so easy to doubt my worth or lovability?" "Why does suffering happen? Is it karmic? Past lives? Childhood trauma?"

My book, *The Gift of Shame,* was written to help people make sense of these questions, and my understanding has expanded since. The bottom line? It's hard being human because shame/fear hit us developmentally in multiple waves. Each encounter has spiritual significance, because it deals with how we feel existentially in a world where everything is connected, but often doesn't *feel* connected.

FIRST LEVEL OF SHAME: SECURITY OF ATTACHMENT

As we explored in previous chapters, 55 percent of American babies become securely attached to a caregiver. A securely attached infant has confidence that the world will give her the attention, space, and love she needs. This baby will play and communicate with interest. She'll explore her immediate environment, come back for contact and comfort, and then explore some more. When distressed, this baby is confident of a trusted comforter either being there or arriving soon, and easily receives comfort when it shows up. All babies are programmed to create secure attachment if they have a primary caregiver (almost always a woman—usually Mom) with a secure, autonomous, autobiographical narrative—meaning her life story makes positive sense to her and she can stay present and attuned to herself and her baby.

An insecurely attached infant is emotionally shut down, or chronically anxious or irritable, and has been either neglected or raised by an insecure mother. Insecure mothers generally lean towards being either emotionally dismissive, preoccupied with past trauma, or disorganized, and they can't consistently be present, congruent/contingent, and attuned, so their babies don't feel securely known, accepted, and protected. Their babies develop insecure attachment styles where they are mostly either emotionally cut off, pervasively anxious or irritated, or disorganized and disoriented.

Secure or insecure attachment styles are in place by ten-months-old and *remain relatively stable throughout life.* Trauma (such as physical, sexual, or emotional abuse) can shift attachment style from secure to insecure. An intimate relationship with a secure other (like teacher, therapist, family member, minister, or even friend) can help someone shift from insecure attachment to secure (called "Earned secure attachment" in the literature).

A secure caregiver can attune to herself and her baby, and can create a low arousal, warm, predictable, manipulable, safe environment consistently with her baby. 70 percent of the time mother and infant pairs are emotionally miscoordinated, and secure mothers notice this and repair these tiny attachment ruptures back to mutual attunement with holding, caressing, vocalizing, eye-gazing, and care giving.

Securely attached children still develop psychological defenses— all humans do—but they generally have underlying feelings of basic safety and connection. Their lives make positive sense to them most of the time—gradually developing secure, autonomous autobiographical narratives as they grow into adulthood.

You can see how secure attachment sets the stage for spiritual development. Feeling consistently known, loved, and attended to makes it easier to have the realization that I am basically good and connected to others, the world, Soul, and Spirit.

As I just mentioned, secure or insecure attachment styles are in place by ten-months-old and *remain relatively stable throughout life.* Think about what this means to our sense of self. If we are in the 45 percent of kids with an insecure attachment style (or sometimes if we're secure but have suffered trauma or neglect), as we develop more cognitive capacities from preoperational, to concrete operational, to formal operational, to post-formal operational, we increasingly wake up to the fact that something is *profoundly wrong* with us. (This can also happen with securely attached children through the normal defenses they develop, but they are generally more available to change as they mature.)

To many of us, the world, relationships, or life, *never* feel completely safe or secure. We look at others and imagine them happy and secure, and feel shame. "What's wrong with me that I can't feel that person's simple pleasures of a happy life?" Insecure attachment programs are unsolved problems that cause destructive Shadow to send regular messages of, "It's not safe. You are not adequately loved. You are not adequately lovable."

SECOND LEVEL OF SHAME: SHAME PROGRAMMING DURING THE PRACTICING PERIOD OF DEVELOPMENT

When we are between 10 and 20 months old our parents are constantly either approving (we sense positive connections with parent and feel good) or disapproving (we sense emotional separation and dismissal from parent and feel shame). Our nervous systems read minor exclusions from the social fabric with each small disapproval, and major exclusions with each major disapproval. Toddlers' nervous systems react to all disapprovals with shame responses—blushing, immobilization, loss of energy, and weakening of the chest and neck as they look down.

Nervous systems do not like shame and try to get away from it with a variety of strategies such as seeking comfort, distraction, looking away, stimulus seeking, or collapse. Our neurological reactions to the shame, fear, and distress of these experiences are hardwired as synaptic substrates for defenses like projection, scapegoating, obsession, rumination, denial, suppression, etc.

Major disapprovals are interpreted by nervous systems as potential death threats because our genes know we need our tribe around us to survive. Thus fear of death is associated with shame material and psychological defenses, and becomes programmed into destructive Shadow.

THIRD LEVEL OF SHAME: NEED FOR EXTERNAL AFFECT REGULATION LEADING TO FEAR OF MADNESS

Until we're teenagers, we can't regulate distressing emotions very well alone (and most teens have problems with it too), and we often need external regulation from parents, friends, teachers, and others. Without it, we have both the fear of negative emotion run out of control, and shame at *being* out of control.

Whenever we exceed our window of tolerance for a negative emotion our nervous systems tend to go into shame-humiliation-rage cycles. In other words, without others' help in managing our affects, our Shadow knows that we might go mad. Knowing this, when we feel disapproved of, excluded, or unable to receive help regulating painful emotions, we can suffer both fear of madness and shame at imagined madness. This pain isolates us and cuts us off from feeling connected to Spirit.

FOURTH LEVEL OF SHAME: WE CAN ALWAYS SEE FATHER THAN WE CAN BE

As we develop our human superpowers of fantasy and mental time travel to the past and future, we can remember past mistakes and anticipate future humiliations and feel shame.

We can also *always* imagine ourselves wiser, more successful, and more beautiful, happily related, and secure than we are now—a setup to feel critical judgments (and accompanying shame emotions) about our current levels of wisdom, success, relationship, attractiveness, and security.

This is especially devastating if we have programmed an internal value/ motivational system driving us forward by telling us that we'll only feel OK if we meet our ideal standards. This is a common response of children in demanding American culture, where active parents want success and achievement in every arena. Our adaptive unconscious—Shadow—knows it's impossible to ever completely meet our ideal standards, and so the inherent anxiety and shame in never being good enough becomes a constant companion. These critical judgments of ourselves can generate devastating shame and hopelessness, leaving us always striving and rarely feeling like we're enough. The despair that accompanies such distress isolates us and cuts us off from any sense of Spirit in the first person (me as an embodiment of the divine), Spirit in the second person (Spirit as a God or Goddess I can talk to), or Spirit in the third person (Spirit as infusing all objects and processes, big and small).

FIFTH LEVEL OF SHAME: SHAME AT NOT SURRENDERING TO SPIRIT

At some point many of us realize either consciously or unconsciously that self-aware consciousness is the most unobstructed expression of pure Spirit in the known universe. We can feel Spirit's voice deep inside us at the Soul level, but the voice is shrouded and muted by our drives, habits, defenses, ego, and judgments.

We know we should completely surrender to Spirit's voice, but very few people develop a stable enough channel into the other world (or soul, or atman, or even the adaptive unconscious) to rely on as a daily guide. Even those who do can lose felt connection with Spirit when distressed, caught up in destructive habits or cravings, or in pain. Even the primary Christian exemplar of Spirit on earth, Jesus, while suffering horribly on the cross, cried out, "O lord! Why have you forsaken me?"

Our disconnections from Spirit can be felt as empty holes in our souls, compensated for by our personalities trying to fill them up with success, ambitions, material goods, relationships, sexual gratification, obsessions, addictions, etc—but the holes are never filled and we are distracted from the real problem of disconnection from Spirit.[219] Our Shadow generates shame at our failed attempts to fill the holes, leaving us ontologically devastated and separated from Spirit.

GROWING UP, WAKING UP AND INTEGRATION ARE THE ANSWERS

Until we grow up and wake up enough to consistently integrate all the systems with our developing Ego, purpose, death, relationships, past/present/future, culture, and a larger sense of Unity, we can feel overwhelmed, confused, ashamed, and lost in the weeds of life.

Integration requires enough ego development to *be able* to understand and observe all five levels of shame, enough knowledge about them to *know what's going on*, and enough interior tools to regulate and harmonize everything *on a moment to moment basis* in an ever-changing and stressful world.

All five levels operate constantly in relationship with different parts of ourselves (including our bodies, feelings, memories, fantasies, and dreams), everyone we encounter or know, and the manifest universe. Until we feel in harmony consistently, we periodically are vulnerable to becoming lost, depressed, anxious, or ashamed—challenging our affect regulation skills, spiritual faith, relationships, and cultures to right our ship and bring us back to harmony.

Nervous systems resist shame by building hard wired shifts to different states (defensive states), still painful, but feeling more self-protective than shame. This begins in infancy and accelerates until we can finally take charge of the process and turn defenses into growth.

What do these defensive avoidance states look like? Let's visit four-year-old Karen and her Mom, Kate. As I enumerate a few of little Karen's possible defenses, imaging how they might play out in adulthood if she *never* learns how to perceive and transform.

Momma Kate leaves Karen alone in the living room with new crayons—big mistake, Kate! When she notices five minutes of suspicious silence, she gets an uneasy feeling and walks in to see Karen happily drawing on the walls, eliciting an angry, "Oh no! Stop that right now!" from Kate. Let's look at a few paths their nervous systems might take to deal with the anger and shame:

- **Healthy reactions:** Karen looks down in shame, "I'm sorry Mommy." She begins to cry, getting that she screwed up and feeling bad about it. Kate takes a deep breath, resists her impulse to keep yelling and blaming, and says with the kindest tone she can muster, "You know you're not supposed to draw on the walls?" Karen says, "Yes Mommy, I won't do it anymore." Kate hugs her and says briskly, "Alright, let's clean everything up!"
- **Reaction formation**. Karen looks down in shame, and then recoils to energizing rage. She throws down her crayons and starts a full-on temper tantrum. This leads to a power struggle and an unsatisfying time-out while pissed off Kate cleans the wall alone.
- **Projection**. Karen says, "Tommy (her younger brother) did it!"
- **Denial**. "I didn't do anything."
- **Rationalization**. "Look at the pretty colors I put on the wall."
- **Scapegoating**. Karen turns to her long-suffering puppy, and screams, "Go away!" as it cowers down.
- **Retroflection**. Karen says, "I'm sorry Mommy. I'm a bad girl and you should spank me." Jumping on the "I'm bad, punish me," bandwagon is a strategy many diligent children develop to try to control the pain of shame.

We all have programming like this, ready to pop out if we feel shame, anxiety, or distress. Most such defenses are distortions which block us from sensing and feeling Soul.

DEFENSE EXERCISE:

When you were little, or a grade schooler, or in high school, what were your go-to defenses to deal with disapproval? Did you project and blame others for doing what you were caught doing? Did you deny? Did you rationalize destructive behavior with elaborate excuses and explanations? Did you attack the person disapproving? Did you attack yourself? Write about this in your journal with special attention on:

- *How connected or alone you felt when in a defensive state.*
- *How willing you were to give up the state when confronted (or soothed) by yourself or another.*
- *How much you still practice these particular maneuvers, with which people, and how it feels when you do it.*
- *What the impact these defensive habits have had on your life.*
- *How close or disconnected to Spirit you have felt when in the grips of such states.*

When you're done share everything you've written with someone you trust.

Self aware consciousness comes with a price. This is the deeper meaning of the Prometheus myth, where the cost of fire was eternal suffering, but the light and creative powers were worth it.

WE CAN'T KNOW EVERYTHING, BUT WE CAN KNOW OF EVERYTHING

Enlightenment has been discussed by most Eastern teachers, but what is it, and how does it figure into spiritual Shadow? Ken Wilber has defined enlightenment as being at one with all the states and stages existing in our personal universe.[220] But what does this mean? When we're in an enlightened moment, do we know everything?

Of course not! Nobody knows everything, but in an enlightened moment we know *of* everything. There are no surprises because everything is feelable, acceptable, and think-aboutable. Contemplative practices over time tend to deliver more and more of such moments, and these enlightened moments are central to a felt sense of Spiritual connectedness.

A Shadow hazard of seeking such moments is to dismiss other states as inferior or less than—states like talking about the basketball game with a friend, or laughing at the cat tangled up in yarn. Even worse is feeling continuing dissatisfaction with self because "I'm never as enlightened as I can imagine myself to be."

The dialectics between ambitions of all sorts—and especially spiritual ambitions—and the inhibiting effects of attachment to success, failure, security, appearances, etc. are necessary fractal interfaces in authentic spiritual development. As long as we are embodied with genetic drives we will encounter these dialectics. Managing them—not denying or eliminating them—is necessary spiritual Shadow work. Avoiding this work is spiritual Shadow.

An example of this is the following excerpt from a session I had with Alice.

Alice is a thirty-nine-year-old woman who scheduled an appointment with me because she was distressed during her spiritual retreats by how difficult it was for her to participate in and feel the power of the guided imagery exercises that are staples of such groups.

Alice: "I just don't get the exercises. The leader tells me to take the elevator down and open the door to a guide on the other side, and I don't see anything."

Keith: "You can just make up an elevator door opening, and make up a person on the other side."

Alice: "That's what the leaders say. But it doesn't feel like it's…"

Keith: "Real?"

Alice: Looking a little embarrassed. "Yes. It doesn't feel real, like it means anything or has any kind of effect. It feels like we're all just kidding ourselves."

Keith: I can sense how her genuine yearning for spiritual growth is being frustrated by her integrity at not wanting to believe something that is not "true." She is struggling with the shame of, "I am not good at guided imagery." Alice's undergraduate and graduate studies trained her to understand and trust empirical data, so I ask her, "Are you familiar with Lynne McTaggart's book, *The Intention Experiment,* or Greg Braden's *The Divine Matrix?*"

Alice: "Yes, I've read both of them. I don't see how they can help me do visualizations better."

Keith: "The research they present establishes that there is a quantum field that we all are part of and can influence with our thoughts and actions." Alice nods her head. "If you'll recall the studies, the question isn't whether we have an impact through our conscious intent, but how much impact we have. If you focus positive intent on me right now, do you believe it has a positive effect on me, *to some extent?*" She nods again. "Similarly, if you focus positive intent on *you, your husband, or your children* right now in the past, present, or future, do you believe it has positive effects, *to some extent?*"

Alice: "Of course. I feel it and I believe that science supports my experience."

Keith: "What I've found personally is that if I become invested in *how much* effect I'm having with positive intent, my Ego-attached-to-success-and-failure is driving the process. Ego-attached-to-success-and-failure wants to prove something, have something, or control something. If I put out attention and intention with the understanding that it has benefits, but without needing the benefits to be a certain way, then I'm optimizing the intention process and minimizing egoic involvement."

Alice: Her face relaxes and lights up with a look of awakening that is one of the most beautiful things to see in psychotherapy. "I get it. I do believe the studies. I do know that visualizations harness some aspects of my desires to grow and help people. I've been feeling one down because I've thought that my efforts were less than other people's."

Keith: Laughing. "Sounds like Ego-attached-to-success-and-failure to me."

Alice: Also laughing. At this moment seeing, disidentifying with, and being amused by her instincts to compete with other seekers—a tiny enlightened moment where she's identifying with a deep, caring witness in herself. "It doesn't matter how much or how little I'm into the exercises. Just doing them has an impact."

Keith: "Yes. The more you relax into this understanding, the more coherent your emotion will be. Coherent emotion amplifies psychic effects."[221]

Alice: "I'm remembering those studies now. It feels different to me when I let go of that Ego."

Most spiritual suffering involves dialectics like Alice's. Facing and working with the dialectics between shame and spiritual hunger can move us forward and resolve destructive spiritual Shadow conflicts.

CULTURAL SPIRITUAL SHADOW

A huge shift in spiritual orientation has taken place over the last three decades. Since ancient times, spiritual authority has resided primarily in the sacred text, the guru, or the priest. In conformist cultures like traditional churches and ashrams, the sacred texts as interpreted by the leader have almost always superseded and trumped individual beliefs or discernments.

Most current spiritual teachers I encounter these days see every human being as a unique expression of the divine, and that the teacher's mission is to use the traditions, offerings, ceremonies, and everything else to clarify and strengthen each person's individual expression of Spirit on earth, and to help them contribute as they are called to.

In a way, this shift is away from spiritual seekers deferring to authorities, towards seekers becoming spiritual consumers—in charge of their spiritual paths and purchasing the "products" of teachings and guidance.

Even though this orientation dominates current approaches, I haven't heard it widely acknowledged or discussed explicitly—it seems to be cultural spiritual Shadow transforming the zeitgeist of millions before our very eyes, but strangely unobserved.

This shift towards individual authority and liberation is consistent with the Integral view that, when you consistently have felt appreciation for all points of view, diminished fear of death, and are able to more clearly see the worldviews you've grown through, you have shifted qualitatively into Integral consciousness which is naturally flexible about authority. Sometimes one perspective or person best organizes the moment, sometimes another perspective or person—constituting what we call flex/flow thinking and relating.

In groups operating from Integral consciousness, natural authority is generally recognized as residing in different individuals depending upon different situations and capacities. At the Integral level, it becomes increasingly obvious who should be the leader and what the superior perspective is *right now.*

This orientation changes how we experience the world in countless ways. One effect is being alert for wisdom where ever it arises, whether from your three-year-old son or your Aunt Dorothy. Another effect is that it becomes easier to have compassionate understanding of the present moment and to share it skillfully. For these reasons and others, individuals stable at Integral consciousness have been referred to as "Universal donors."[222]

SPIRITUAL BYPASS

Buddhist psychotherapist John Welwood created the concept of spiritual bypass over thirty years ago. He defined it in a 2011 Tricyle Magazine interview with Tina Fosella as: "[Spiritual bypassing is] a widespread tendency to use spiritual ideas and practices to sidestep or avoid facing unresolved emotional issues, psychological wounds, and unfinished developmental tasks."[223]

For me, spiritual bypass is any time our deepest, most loving wisdom—our soul—is not calling the shots. If my soul, my personal interface between me and universal Spirit, is OK with a thought, action, or story, I'm in pretty good shape. If my violence, distress, or selfishness is making the call in spite of Soul's protest (however faint), I'm generating a rationalization—a story—to support why this is a good thing, and I'm in the midst of a spiritual bypass.

My friend Mark Forman, author of *A Guide to Integral Psychotherapy,* sees four levels of spiritual bypass, each with progressively more potential problems. He described the four levels in a 2015 blog briefly summarized below:[224]

- **Expectable bypass** is the normal dialectic at each stage to objectively confront reality and the tendency to add subjective elements of fantasy to it—to project or imagine what we would like life to be like. This is normal, inevitable, a necessary part of growth.
- **States-driven bypass** is a powerful spiritual opening or obsessive state that can cause us to neglect or ignore reality's needs and demands like self care, or maintaining relationships. Such an opening can activate a drive that, like romantic infatuation in a love affair, often runs its course over months or years.
- **Problematic Bypass** involves someone clearly using spirituality to avoid very pressing needs or aspects of self when they could likely do otherwise. This is contrasted with helpful retreats used as authentic healing processes where the reintegration into daily life finds you deeper and wiser (you come back from the eight days of silence, yoga workshop, or the meditation class at Esalen more ready to take on the challenges of work, family, and body). The normal crazy person experiencing problematic bypass receives influence and adjusts towards health, while extra crazy doubles down, resists influence, and defends the bypass.
- **Narcissistic Bypass** is melding of destructive Shadow material with spiritual practices or principles within someone with narcissistic traits or personality disorder. This destructive melding stays stable (in pathology) through level changes on other developmental lines—essentially giving a dangerous person more power to do harm. One probable cause of narcissistic bypass is early developmental arrest, with spirituality becoming a vehicle for narcissistic tendencies. This is a *big* problem. Someone caught up in narcissistic bypass has potentials to normalize emotional and/or physical violence, habituate to objectifying others for personal gratification, and to generally engage in extra crazy excesses. In its worst form, narcissistic bypass is sociopathy, involving tendencies to seriously damage others for selfish purposes.

▶ **Rivers sidebar:** *We each are a river of consciousness—implicit and explicit, Shadow and conscious awareness—composed of all the aspects/ selves/memories/habits/programming we are. All share the river of human consciousness which is the self-aware evolutionary edge of everything arising.*

Our ultimate work seems to be to help every consciousness integrate/ harmonize to unity.

Borrowing from interpersonal neurobiology and attachment theory, we optimize this development by being present, congruent, and marked with others and ourselves, so that all facets of self can be known, accepted, and protected.

Words can't capture this fluid dynamic process. Songs like 100 Years by Five For Fighting, poems like The Waking by Theodore Roethke, books like Transformations of Consciousness by David Hawkins, and The Inner Journey Home by A. H. Almass, evoke flavors of soul and universe, but can't fully mirror the huge, fluid vastness that includes and transcends time and space.

All words become rigid structures as they are spoken and written. All created objects are reifications that subtly resist the morph and flow of the undulating and unfolding Kosmos. Words are reifications, metaphors, rhythms, and evocations. They can guide our intent toward progressive awakenings. They can help us discover we ourselves as rivers of consciousness. We are—have always been—the Kosmos.

The first stanza of the Tao Te Ching says the Tao is unqualifyable and cannot be described, but only spoken about and occasionally pointed to. The next 80 verses all point towards the Tao.

Moments of identification and illumination are sensory signposts that lead us to deeper intimacy with ourselves, our beloved, our friends and families, until we finally identify with all and become all—one movement, one breath, one taste.

Robert McKee in his brilliant *Story: Substance, Structure, Style, and the Principles of Screenwriting* makes the point that there is a continuum from evil to good, a path that often characterizes the Hero's Journey as he struggles from darkness to illumination. The continuum progresses from the evil masquerading as good (the worst), through in-your-face-evil, to ignorance, to courageous self-knowledge and transformation in service to the higher good.[225]

Unfortunately, narcissistic bypass is evil masquerading as good—extra crazy, extra dangerous.

We see examples of this with charismatic leaders caught sexually, emotionally, or financially exploiting others, rationalizing the abuse with spiritual language or constructs. The Catholic priest pedophilia scandals mushrooming through the last fifteen years, chillingly depicted in the movie *Spotlight,* often involved priests giving spiritual rationales for abusive behaviors—evil masquerading as good—extra crazy, extra dangerous.

SPIRITUALITY LIKE SEXUALITY

A particular form of spiritual Shadow seems to be a curious reluctance to discuss personal spiritually charged experiences. My general impression is that acknowledging and discussing personal spirituality often has similar taboos to acknowledging and discussing personal sexuality. Certainly the Tibetan tradition was to keep quiet about huge insights or peak experiences to avoid spiritual pride.

I think personal spirituality, like personal sexuality, benefits from frank and accepting talk. I often ask my friends, family, and clients what they experience when they pray or do contemplative practice. Interestingly, people seem most comfortable talking about God in the first person ("I" in unity with all) and third person (God in nature and every object and experience), but reluctant and halting in discussing God in the second person (God as "You" whom I address and relate with).

Meditation students seem most comfortable talking about their experiences phenomenologically. "I have *this* subjective experience when

I do Loving Kindness Meditation." "I have *this* subjective experience when I do mindfulness attunement."

Perhaps we are reluctant to make claims of connection with another world, or feel our delicate identifications with Spirit will be injured by too much scrutiny.

Whatever the cause, it leaves Spirituality as an often unspoken subtext in many conversations and practices—in Shadow. A great example is modern psychotherapy.

MODERN PSYCHOTHERAPY REQUIRES A SPIRITUAL ORIENTATION

Every therapist and change worker is a spiritual teacher. Progressive graduate schools are beginning to teach this, but integrating spirituality into psychotherapy remains controversial.

Luckily, there is a magnificent bridge between psychological and social science and spirituality, and that bridge is mindfulness practices plus the willingness of therapists to legitimatize and work with spirituality and spiritual practices in psychotherapy.

My earlier session with Alice is an example of the psychotherapy/spirituality link. Everyone has values that feel like moral imperatives based in something larger than self—the Golden Rule, protecting children, speaking compassionate truth, helping the disadvantaged, protecting the innocent from injustice, and seeking unity with God or Goddess are all examples.

These spiritually charged core values need to be honored, admired, and resourced in effective therapy. I tell my clients that the purpose of therapy is less about change and more about being more purely yourself, honoring your core values, and being more at one with your Soul (or Higher Self, or Moral Self depending on the language and worldviews of my clients). This commitment to personal values broadens our current worldview and eventually leads to developing new, more caring and understanding worldviews.

Many psychology teachers and professors in the late 60s and 70s discouraged such talk, but the field has grown since then, and almost any therapist who actively works with clients would agree with encouraging and sourcing each client's spirituality in psychotherapy.

INTEGRAL MINDFULNESS, FROM CLUELESS TO DIALED-IN

My book, *Integral Mindfulness, from clueless to dialed-in,* was written with all of the above in mind (as were my books on Integrally Informed Psychotherapy, *Waking Up,* and *Sessions*). Integral mindfulness begins with learning basic mindfulness practices such as cultivating awareness with acceptance and caring intent of sensation, feeling, thought, judgment, and desire in self and others. From that foundation we can examine all dimensions of life—very much as we have in this book—looking for clueless moments (destructive thoughts/behaviors that resist change), mindless moments (destructive behaviors that change when pointed out), mindful moments (self-observing with acceptance and caring intent), and dialed-in moments (mindfulness informed by both wide and deep understanding of self and the world).

One of the pleasures of observing these clueless, mindless, mindful, and dialed in moments is that we become interested in what we haven't previous seen and how it connects to what we know. With dialed-in spirituality we become more interested in spiritual Shadow.

For example, take Buddhism's great blind spot.

BUDDHISM'S GREAT BLIND SPOT—THE ULTIMATE CONSTRUCTIVE SHADOW FORCE OF CREATION

A while ago I was listening to David Loy talking with my friend Terry Patten about his excellent book, *Money, Sex, War, Karma* on Terry's podcast, *Beyond Enlightenment,* and their conversation illustrated to me Buddhism's great blind spot—the myth of nonattachment in an embodied evolving universe.

David was explaining the three poisons of Buddhism—ignorance, attachment, and aversion—which have been widely understood in the modern world as narcissism, desire, and anger. He suggested that these have been culturally institutionalized in drives to be rich, famous, powerful, and erotically fulfilled. Like many who are appalled at the excesses of the modern world—climate change, environmental degradation, income disparity, overpopulation, bigotry, objectification of other people, institutional corruption and political polarization—David implied that these problems could only be solved by recognizing the inherent sickness of the three poisons and embracing the nonattachment so popular in Buddhist teachings.

From an evolutionary standpoint, this approach is somewhat misguided at best, and completely antithetical to the spiritual imperatives of our evolutionary roots at worst. Yes, it is healthy and possible to be progressively less attached to the outcomes of our purpose driven goals and activities, but the universe requires us to be *more surrendered to, more attached to,* the mandate to evolve and create. Even further, embodied humans always must experience and manage drives for safety, affiliation, sexual expression, social position, pleasure, safety, recognition, success, etc. Denying the legitimacy and importance of genetically mandated drives is not nonattachment, it is dissociation.

Especially, at its core, the evolutionary impulse demands that we *create.* Creation always arises from dialectics—self/other, thesis/antithesis, possible/impossible, emptiness/form, etc. From the differentiations of the Big Bang, to life, to male and female, to conservative and progressive, novelty emerges from the fractal interfaces between dialectically opposing forces—always biased towards greater complexity. In those fractal boundaries that connect and separate, creation arises.

Self-aware you and me are driven to *create*—we must create. Often the primary drive to create is experienced as a drive to *acquire, build, dominate, possess, transform, affiliate, heal, sexually bond, become secure,* or *help*—all genetically based. All these drives are generally secondary to the primary drive to *create,* and in that sense they are second-order drives.

Second order drives tend to be expressed in more primitive or less primitive ways. Lust can be rape or a charming overture. Hunger can be killing a rabbit with a stick and immediately consuming it raw, or spending six hours creating a gourmet meal. Art can be finger painting or building the Taj Mahal.

As any drive evolves, it generates greater complexity that is usually characterized by deeper understanding and more compassion. Our drive to create absolutely amplifies hungers for—even obsessions with—wealth, fame, erotic fulfillment, and power over others, the world, and ourselves, but the answer to the excesses of those expressions isn't pure *nonattachment*, but rather *more surrender* to the evolutionary impulse to create beautiful, good, and true artifacts and experiences from these hungers.

As long as we're embodied, we'll either feel the satisfaction of serving the evolutionary impulse, or the suffering of frustrating it. Creative output has been linked to passion and persistence—to falling in love with an area, becoming intensely *attached* to goals and the process of pursuing them.[226] Ask any accomplished person, and they will tell you that no achievement, skill, or material success satisfies forever. Eventually the drive to create seeks new purpose, new meaning, and we either surrender or suffer. An embodied being *cannot* be completely nonattached from this organizing principle, and a self-aware being especially is driven to be in harmony with the evolutionary impulse to create.

In other words, our drive to create—to evolve—can't be *denied,* or we cultivate pathological dissociation. It can be *refined,* where increasingly we are more attached to being in harmony with the creative evolutionary mandate in the present moment, and progressively *less attached* to *outcome*—but never completely *nonattached.*

"Less attached" can never be "nonattached," because our nervous systems will always prefer success over failure, satisfaction over dissatisfaction, and approval over disapproval.

In the wisdom traditions, this is beautifully illustrated by Karma Yoga, detailed in the *Bhagavad-Gita,* in which the God Krishna instructs the Warrior Arjuna to make every act an expression of God, while accepting all outcomes.[227]

The question isn't how to eliminate the three poisons of narcissism, desire, and anger, but how to transmute them into elixirs of love and life. This involves discovering the constructive and destructive Shadow inherent in each, and surrendering to constructive and transmuting destructive until the elixirs support healing and growth on every level, from raising babies to solving global warming and harmonizing the ecosphere and noosphere.

ONE OF MY CORE PRACTICES—9 CHAKRA MEDITATION

Raising the Kundalini energy is a central tantric practice found in many Eastern yogas. Cultivating centered, peaceful, or transcendent states defines most contemplative traditions. One of my foundation practices is raising Kundalini energy while practicing twenty-eight different transcendent states.

Each time you enter a state of consciousness, the neural networks associated with it become more mylinated and hard wired. Particularly in my work I wanted my constructive Shadow to have ready access to a wide variety of transcendent states to show up when needed while I'm teaching, writing, or doing psychotherapy. I also want it to become easier and more habitual to discern and surrender to constructive Shadow in all its forms. I developed this meditation to practice transcendent states the way a pianist practices scales.

This particular practice is informed by the Wilber/Combs Lattice (from Allan Combs and Ken Wilber[228])—a charting of the ascending chakras as they manifest in gross (concrete materialistic), subtle (imaginative and energetic), causal (pure emptiness), and nondual (everything at once). Lighting up each chakra, starting with the root chakra and moving up nine chakras is one of my favorite daily routines.

This practice combines the Integral state concepts of gross, subtle, causal, and nondual with the process of raising the Kundalini. Through nine chakras this yields 28 distinct states, since causal—pure emptiness—is the same for each chakra. Doing this meditation strengthens each state as well as abilities to shift states, and I've found it enormously useful as well as personally transformative. I'll define some terms and then show you how it's done. Feel free to take any or all of these steps in combinations that feel right to you, and to include them in your personal spiritual activities.

GROSS, SUBTLE, CAUSAL, NONDUAL:

- **Gross** is "real world" concrete manifestation. It is the first level of concrete experience.
- **Subtle** is all the variations of this level, including imaginative, subtle energies and spiritual variations, in this universe and beyond.
- **Causal** is pure formlessness—emptiness, no-thingness—which is the same in all chakras.
- **Nondual** is the all-at-onceness of self/world/everything-as-that-chakra as one taste or experience.

THE PRACTICE:

Sitting meditation: This practice can be done sitting in stillness, with eyes open or shut.

Moving meditation: This practice can be done exercising, walking, or any other safe activity (your attention gets divided so you need to use relatively safe, easy, repetitive activities). I do it sitting, laying in bed, swimming, and walking in nature.

Choose which states to practice: It's not necessary to do all 9 chakras, or even all four states in any chakra. Feel what's most comfortable and transformative for you and practice those states. Each one of them is a particular flavor of bliss. I will describe my experiences, but yours will be your own flavors.

Choose how long you inhabit any given state: You can hold any one of the states for seconds, minutes, or longer. Teaching yourself to shift from one to the other strengthens your salience network, divergent thinking, and access to the other world.

1ST CHAKRA: THE ROOT CHAKRA/PHYSICAL EMBODIED REALITY—ASSOCIATED WITH THE BASE OF THE SPINE

- **Gross:** I feel my physical being connected with everything in gross reality such as gravity, electromagnetism, atoms, and molecules, etc, all the way up to the universe expanding at a constantly accelerating rate (physicists are still puzzling about what causes *that*). I relax into expanding universe.
- **Subtle:** I am aware of all the forms—from cosmic strings, to tiny drops of water, to galaxies—as unique expressions of holarchies, connected and separate. I usually feel a sense of devotional awe for the mysteries of subatomic to transgalactic manifestation.
- **Causal:** Anchored in admiration and adoration for all forms, I feel for pure emptiness from which everything is constantly arising. This is often a fade-into-black dissolution experience that is pleasurable, but requires some practice if you're moving around. I've occasionally walked into cars or collided with another swimmer if I don't make sure I stay oriented to the physical world.
- **Nondual:** From pure emptiness, I sense the miracle of the universe continuous arising—flowing from emptiness into fullness, into one taste of all physical reality.

2ND CHAKRA: LIFE IN ALL ITS FORMS—ASSOCIATED WITH THE PELVIC/ABDOMINAL AREA

- **Gross:** I feel fields of all life, including mine, connecting in the fields of life that encompass earth and beyond. Inherent in me and everything are the sensual drives to survive, thrive, be intimate, procreate, and create. I feel the sweet pleasures of life with a little thrill up and down energy channels from above my forehead through my root chakra and legs into the earth.

- **Subtle:** I see each blade of grass, tree, microorganism, animal, person, as a miracle of life with genetic roots back to our first single celled ancestors. This usually involves floods of love for each plant, bird, animal, insect, and microorganism I consider.
- **Causal:** Anchored in admiration and adoration for all life, I relax into pure emptiness from which everything is constantly arising.
- **Nondual:** From pure emptiness, I feel the unity of all life, past/present/future, as one joyful song/motion/taste/sensation. I'm intensely aware of my sensual interfaces with everything, even as I experience all life as joyful suchness.

3RD CHAKRA: THE POWER CENTER—ASSOCIATED WITH THE SOLAR PLEXUS

- **Gross:** I feel myself connected to all the powers of the universe, from supernovas to a single virus, to a sub-atomic particle that might become another Big Bang, to any human capacity for choice, action, thought, and influence. The sense is relaxing into dancing with unimaginably powerful forces, adding my infinitesimal powers to the constantly moving/evolving energies of the universe and beyond.
- **Subtle:** I feel profound respect and admiration for all the powers, and sense the increasing consciousness and choice as power ascends the evolutionary scales into individual capacities for violence and compassion, unwise influence and wise influence. I feel all my own powers existing in this energetic matrix.
- **Causal:** Anchored in respect and resolute acceptance of all powers everywhere, I feel for pure emptiness from which everything is constantly arising.

- **Nondual:** From pure emptiness I feel one with the power of the universe, channeled through me as Warrior, willing to die for principle, one with both the void and infinite torrents and shapes of energy.

4TH CHAKRA: THE HEART CHAKRA OF ALL LOVE—ASSOCIATED WITH THE HEART AREA

- **Gross:** I feel my love contributing outward to all the fields of love that encompass everything in loving embrace.
- **Subtle:** I am aware of how all holarchies are expressions of love, of matter reaching to affiliate with matter in coherence and increasing harmony with the whole, dramatically amplifying love up the evolutionary ladder to the fields of love that each person, couple, family, and tribe have for one another, into Universal Love. A line from a Jim Steinman song, *Heaven Can Wait,* sometimes comes me at this point, *"And all the Gods come down here just to sing for me."*
- **Causal:** Anchored in love for all the fields everywhere, I feel for pure emptiness from which all love is constantly arising.
- **Nondual:** The universe is all love all the time and I am that love, serve that love, and surrender to that love. Big Heart. Divine Love.

5TH CHAKRA: EXPRESSION AND COMMUNICATION—ASSOCIATED WITH THE THROAT

- **Gross:** I feel my voice/being/transmissions as part of the universe as language in the broadest sense. Subatomic particles communicating with other subatomic particles, to all the conversations, books/videos//verbal/non-verbal expressions of matter and life. Terrence McKenna once said that the universe is language. I feel immersed in endless communication.
- **Subtle:** I feel each expression as a miracle, from atoms informing atoms, to sap flowing through the oak tree, to all human

exchanges, both trivial and profound. I am part of a cornucopia of communication, all self-organizing and fluid.

- **Causal:** Riding the torrents of all the communications—the universe as language—I feel for pure emptiness from which communication is constantly arising.
- **Nondual:** From emptiness I feel the Kosmic "Om" from before the Big Bang to after the end of the universe, with all my communications, contributions, and transmissions being multiple channels where I give and receive simultaneously, constantly transforming others as others transform me—*all at once.* I get senses of fields projecting endlessly in all directions from my throat chakra.

6TH CHAKRA: THOUGHT—CENTERED BEHIND THE THIRD EYE

- **Gross:** I feel my thought fields interpenetrating with all the thought fields, all the beliefs and thoughts that coexist in the universe—especially dense around life, and superdense around self-aware humans.
- **Subtle:** I feel how thoughts influence and ultimately harmonize/alter/cross-validate each other with infinite variations. These thoughts are fields connecting and mutually influencing, and I relax into their interpenetrating clouds, feeling peaceful and intensely *aware.*
- **Causal:** Anchored in connection to thought fields everywhere, I feel for pure emptiness from which consciousness is constantly arising.
- **Nondual:** Pure presence flows from emptiness in the sixth chakra. I rest in pure presence, and often think about Eckhart Tolle saying how he loves sitting in presence.

7TH CHAKRA: ALL CREATION—ASSOCIATED WITH THE CROWN AROUND THE TOP OF THE HEAD

- **Gross:** I feel myself relaxing into the evolutionary force for greater complexity that permeates every particle and field in the universe.

Pure creation is the field from which evolution arises. To me it's a subtle bubbly energy that permeates everything and sparkles with all colors.

- **Subtle:** Evolutionary forms are manifest in matter, life, and rising into humanity waking to the Universe Dream. I feel awe at eight billion humans, each generating a unique cosmos, all connected and spilling over into each other, iterating back into the collective as novelty expands into the unknown and unformed. Behind is the past, constantly reevaluated and reunderstood as we surf the crest of the evolutionary wave towards countless imagined futures.
- **Causal:** Surrendered to the interpenetrating evolutionary fields of consciousness, I feel for pure emptiness from which creation is constantly arising.
- **Nondual:** I am Big Mind, created and creator, timeless and timefull. I feel mature, *big*, centered and intimately entwined with creation.

8TH CHAKRA: FIELDS OF CONSCIOUSNESS—THE UNIVERSE AS FIELDS UNDULATING INTO DENSER AND LESS DENSE LEVELS OF ORGANIZATION—FROM QUARKS TO YOU

- **Gross:** I am aware of everything as fields, popping in and out of existence, self-organizing to greater coherence at every level.
- **Subtle:** I feel how all the fields are constantly relating and feel myself as multileveled coherent fields. The Keith consciousness (a blob of fields) blends with people and nature fields, and with time and space fields. This is enormously peaceful, because my sense of self shifts to a subtle conglomeration of fields imbedded in fields—pure witness consciousness of my fields of awareness interfacing with all other fields.
- **Causal:** Surrendered to the self-organizing fields that comprise everything, I feel for pure emptiness from which they constantly arise.

- **Nondual:** Everything is simply lively awareness, and I remember Daniel P. Brown talking in awe of feeling everything as lively awareness in a lecture he gave on Mahamudra Buddhism in Terry Patten's Beyond Awakening webseries.

9TH CHAKRA: NONLOCAL, TRANSTEMPORAL—I EXPERIENCE NO SPECIFIC PLACE FOR THIS CHAKRA, BUT THE AREAS ABOVE MY HEAD FEEL VERY ALIVE

- **Gross:** I click into no-time, no-space, all-at-onceness, and everything seems like one taste, touch, note, event.
- **Subtle:** Every moment of every object that's ever existed and will exist, all at once, each object having an epic story from the Big Bang to the end of the universe, connected to everything else all the time. Indescribable sense all-at-onceness.
- **Causal:** From the overwhelming sense of all-at-onceness, it is relaxing to drop into pure emptiness.
- **Nondual:** Avatars start inhabiting my body, usually beginning with Krishna as a man or youth. Avalokiteśvara in her female form and other archetypal figures occasionally show up. I feel their delight in my precious human body and their desire to manifest and serve through me.

  As I suggested earlier, this practice like any other used to expand understanding and compassion supports liberation and the integration of conscious self into constructive Shadow.

> **Be careful sidebar:** *One cautionary note is that these states are blissful and intoxicating. If we use these (or any other) practices to avoid necessary pains, they become a form of spiritual bypass.*

How do we know the difference between healthy use and spiritual bypass? Stay open, curious, available to caring influence, and willing to change perspectives, opinions, and practices as you find better alternatives. Find guides, teachers, and friends you resonate with, and receive influence from them.

When you're curious about (often entertained by) destructive spiritual Shadow, your own and other's spiritual bypasses, and grateful for constructive spiritual Shadow you are probably doing just fine.

Struggling with all these issues is the Shadow of Spirituality.

15

EPILOGUE: ILLUMINATIONS AT THE EDGE OF DARKNESS

I hope you've enjoyed our journey through Shadow.

We humans are so amazing, powerful, dangerous, and beautiful! Daily I'm delighted and horrified by all we do, have done, and can do.

Each one of our personal relationships with Shadow reflects who we feel ourselves to be and the nature of our personal universe—how we hold and experience our bodies, relationships, missions, stories, and yearnings.

I'm convinced that continuing to expand understanding and acceptance of constructive and destructive Shadow supports personal evolution and is good not just for each of us, but for our families, friends, clients, and everybody.

As you reflect on what you remember from *Shadow Light,* I encourage you to witness all your reactions with acceptance and caring intent, open to see what you haven't seen before, to know what was previously unknown, and to care more than you ever thought you could care.

Much love to you and yours on this magnificent life journey we've all been blessed with. Strangely and wonderfully, Shadow might be our most powerful ally, guiding us on our Way.

ENDNOTES

1. Lyubomirsky, Sonya (2007). Helliway, John. Layard, Richard. Sachs, Jeffrey, (editors), (2016).

2. Kahneman, (2011).

3. Chess, Stella Thomas, Alexander, Birch, Herbert, (1965).

4. Duhigg, Charles (2012).

5. Porges S.W. (2011).

6. Siegel, Daniel J. (1999).

7. Schore, Alan (2014). Wilber, Ken. (2000).

8. Siegel, Dan (1999).

9. Marks-Tarlow, Terry (2008).

10. Davidson, Richard (2012).

11. Schore, Allan (1994).

12. Wilber, Ken (2016).

13. Siegel, Dan (1999).

14. Wilber, Ken (2006).

15. Wilber, Ken (2000).

16. Duhigg, Charles (2012).

17. Fisher, Helen (2004).

18. Pearce, Joseph Chilton (2002).

19. Wilber, Ken (2015).

20 Pearce, Joseph Chilton (2002). MacTaggart, Lynne (2007). Radin, Dean (2006). Braden, Gregg (2008).

21 Whitehead, Alfred, North (1929).

22 Siegel, Daniel J. (2007).

23 Thomson, Paula (2008).

24 Schore, Allan (2003).

25 van der Kolk, Bessel (2014).

26 MacTaggart, Lynne (2012).

27 Masterson, James F. (1981), Twinge, Jean, M. and Campbell, W. Keith (2009).

28 Dunbar, Robin (2010).

29 Witt. Keith (2006), (2015).

30 Siegel, Daniel J. (2007).

31 Pearce, Joseph Chilton (2002).

32 Mekel-Bobrov (2005).

33 Schore, Alan (1994).

34 —————. (2014).

35 Witt. Keith (2006).

36 Wilber, Ken (2006).

37 Baumeister, R. F. (2011), Siegel, Daniel J. (2007).

38 Kaufman, Scott, Barry (2013).

39 Siegel, Daniel (1999).

40 Poitras, Laura (2014).

41 Witt, Keith (2007).

42 LeDoux, Joseph (2015).

43 Panksepp, Jaak (2007), (2015).

44 Ibid.

45 Witt, Keith (2007).

46 Ecker, Bruce (2012).

47 Wilber, Ken (2016).

48   Witt, Keith (207).

49   Schore, Allan (2003), (2014).

50   Shapiro, Francine (2014). Schore, Alan (2014).

51   Cloniger, Robert C. (2004).

52   Porges SW (2011). (2006).

53   Wilber, Ken (2000).

54   Twinge, Jean, M. and Campbell, W. Keith (2009).

55   Wilber , Ken (2016).

56   Porges SW (2011).

57   Kotier, Steven (2009).

58   Siegel, Daniel J. (2005). (2007).

59   Gottshall, Jonathon (2012).

60   Ibid.

61   Schore, Allan (2003), (2004). Siegel, Daniel (1999), (2007).

62   Campbell, Joseph. (1949), Gottshall, Jonathon. (2012).

63   Campbell, Joseph (194).

64   O'Hanlon, Bill (2007).

65   Deida, David (1997), (2006).

66   Zelazny, Roger (1967).

67   Keller, Greg (2015).

68   Goodman, Leslee (2015).

69   Baumeister, R. F. and Leary M. R. (1995).

70   Deida, David (2006).

71   Cherlin, Andrew (2009).

72   Fisher, Helen (2004).

73   Ibid.

74   Fisher, Helen (2003).

75   Dunbar, Robin (2010).

76   Sapolsky, Robert (1994).

77   Pearce, Joseph Chilton (2002).

78   Mekel-Bobrov (2005).

79   Liedloff, Jean (1975).

80   MacTaggart, Lynne (2012).

81   Prabhavananda, swami, and Isherwood, Christopher (1944).

82   Mushashi, Miyamoto (1974).

83   Witt, Keith (2005).

84   Cherlin, Andrew (2009).

85   Wilber, Ken (2000).

86   Gilligan, Carol (1993). Eliot, Lise (2009). Fisher, Helen (2003), (2004).

87   Jung, Carl (1959).

88   Wilber, Ken (2006). Gilligan, Carol. (1993).

89   Rampton, Martha (2008).

90   Taylor, Shelley E. (2002).

91   Armstrong, Alison (2007).

92   Witt, Keith (2007).

93   Murdock, Maureen (1990).

94   Gottman, John (2005).

95   Davin, Anne (2015).

96   Freud, Sigmund (1949), (1961).

97   Wilber, Ken (2000).

98   Levine, Judith (2002).

99   Buss, D. M. (1997), (2003).

100   Fisher, Helen (2004).

101   Hutson, Matthew (2006).

102   Trivers, Robert (2015).

103   Fisher, Helen (2004).

104   Ibid.

105   Witt, Keith (2015).

106   Clark, Russel & Hatfield, Elaine (1989).

107   Conley, Terri D. (2011).

108   Fisher, Helen (2004).

109   Ibid.

110   Deida, David (2006).

111   Fisher, Helen (2004).

112   Northrup, Chrisanna; Schwartz, Pepper; Whitte, James (2013).

113   ABC News Prime live Poll (2004).

114   Witt, Keith (2007).

115   Fisher, Helen (2003).

116   Symons, Don (1979).

117   Gottman, John (2015).

118   Buss, D. M., and Shmitt, D. P. (1993).

119   ABC News Prime live Poll (2004).

120   Carnes, Patric (2002).

121   Cunningham JA. (1999).

122   Levine, Judith (2002).

123   Orstein, Peggy (2016).

124   Finkelhor, David (2008).

125   Maltz, Wendy (2009).

126   Fisher, Helen (2003), (2004).

127   O'Hanlon, Bill (2007).

128   Schore, Allan (2015).

129   Witt, Keith (2007).

130   Fisher, Helen (2003), (2004).

131   Cherlin, Andrew (2009).

132   Masterson, James F. (1981).

133   Fowler, J. H.; Christakis, N.A. (2008).

134   Gottman, John (2015).

135   Witt, Keith (2015).

136   Schore, Alan (2014), (2015).

137   Friston, Karl (2002).

138   Marks-Tarlow, Terry (2008).

139   Schore, Allan (1994), (2003). Siegel, Daniel (1999).

140   Chess, Stella; Thomas, Alexander; Birch, Herbert (1965).

141 Baumrind, D. (1966).

142 Gottman (2007).

143 Nichols, Michael (2007).

144 Witt, Keith (2006).

145 Tronic, Ed (2008).

146 Ware, Bronnie (2011-2012).

147 McGoldrick, Monica, and Gerson, Randy (2008).

148 Dweck, Carol (2006).

149 Schore, Allan (2003). Bateman, Anthony, and Fonagy, Peter (2004).

150 Cloniger, Robert C. (2004).

151 Chess, Stella; Thomas, Alexander; Birch, Herbert (1965).

152 Fisher, Helen (2004).

153 Young, Larry, J. and Wang, Zuoxin (2004). Shetty, Priya (2008).

154 Westermarck, Edward (1891).

155 Cameron, Elissa, and Dalerum, Fredrik (2009). Rickard, Ian (2008).

156 Baumrind, D. (1966).

157 Heitler, Susan (1990).

158 Gottman, John (2005).

159 Kaufman, Scott, Barry (2013).

160 Hobson, J. Allan (2002).

161 Ibid.

162 Brainworks.

163 Siegel, Daniel (1999).

164 Gottshall, Jonathon (2012).

165 Kaufman, Scott, Barry, (2013), Singer, Jerome (1976).

166 Siegel, Daniel (1999).

167 Panksepp, Jaak (2007).

168 Singer, Jerome (1976).

169 Freud, Sigmund (2010).

170 Jung, Carl G. (1961).

171 Jung, Carl G. (1959).

172 Aizenstat, Steve (2009), Hillman, James (1979), Mellick, Jill (1996).

173 Wilber, Ken (2000).

174 Hillman, James (1979).

175 Perls, Fritz (1969).

176 Dossey, Larry (2013).

177 Domhoff, G. W. (2003).

178 Almaas, A. H. (2004).

179 Hanh, Thich, Nhat (2016).

180 MacTaggart, Lynne (2012).

181 Buss, D. M. (1999).

182 Krug et al. (2002).

183 Marano, Hara Estroff (2014).

184 Fisher, Helen (2004), (2003).

185 Marano, Hara Estroff (2009).

186 Witt. Keith (2006).

187 Wilber, Ken (2016).

188 Witt, Keith (2006), (2007).

189 Bateman, Anthony, and Fonagy, Peter (2004).

190 Kiehl, Kent (2014).

191 Porges SW (2011).

192 Sharon, Ariel (1989).

193 Sood, Avani, Mehta (2009).

194 Marano, Hara Estroff (2014).

195 Ibid.

196 Gottman, John (2015).

197 van der Kolk, Bessel (2005), (2014).

198 Barash, Susan (2008).

199 Peck, M. Scott (1985).

200 Cherlin, Andrew (2009).

201 Kiehl, Kent (2014).

202 Witt, Keith (2015).

203 Kaufman, Scott, Barry (2013).

204 Sheldrake, Rupert (2009).

205 Wilber, Ken (2000).

206 Danielou, Alain (1994).

207 Resnick, Michael D. et al., (1997).

208 Csikszentmihalyi, Mihaly (1990).

209 Kaufman, Scott, Barry (2013).

210 Ibid.

211 Ibid.

212 Bogen, Joseph E.; Bogen, Glenda M. (1988).

213 Kaufman, Scott, Barry (2013).

214 Hunt, J.M. (1978).

215 Wilber, Ken (2000), (2006).

216 Siegel, Daniel J. (1999), Gottshall, Jonathon (2012), McKee, Robert (1997).

217 Wilber, Ken (2000).

218 Ibid.

219 Almaas, A. H. (2002).

220 Wilber, Ken (2006).

221 Braden, Gregg (2008).

222 Wilber, Ken (2000), (2006).

223 Fossella, Tina (2011).

224 Forman, Mark (2015).

225 McKee, Robert (1997).

226 Kaufman, Scott, Barry (2013).

227 Prabhavananda, swami, and Isherwood, Christopher (1944).

228 Wilber, Ken (2006).

BIBLIOGRAPHY

ABC News Prime live Poll: (2004). The American Sex Survey. Released Oct. 21, 2004). http://abcnews.go.com/images/Politics/959a1AmericanSex Survey.pdf.

Aizenstat, Steve. (2009). *Dream Tending.* New Orleans, Spring Journal Inc.

Almaas, A. H. (1987). Diamond Heart: Book One: Elements of the Real in Man. Boston: Shambhala Publications.

————. (2002). Facets of Unity. Boston: Shambhala Publications.

————. (2004). The Inner Journey Home: Soul's Realization of the Unity of Reality. Boston: Shambhala.

Anand, Margot. (1989). *The Art of Sexual Ecstasy.* New York Tarcher/Putnam.

Armstrong, Alison. (2007). *Making Sense of Men.* 417 W. Foothill Blvd. Glendale, CA. UnderstandMen.com.

Barash, David. P. and Lipton, Judith Ever. (2009). *Strange Bedfellows: The surprising connection between sex, evolution and Monogamy.* New York: Bellevue Literary Press.

Barash, Susan. (2008). *Little White Lies, Deep Dark Secrets: The Truth About Why Women Lie.* St. Martin's Press: NY, NY.

Barratt, Barnaby. (2005). *Sexual Health and Erotic Freedom.* Philadelphia: Xlibris.

Bateman, Anthony, and Fonagy, Peter. (2004). *Psychotherapy for Borderline Personality Disorder: mentalization-based treatment.* Oxford: Oxford University Press.

Baumeister, R. F. and Leary M. R. (1995). *Desire For Interpersonal Attachments as a fundamental human motivation.* Psychological Bulletin, 11. 7. 497-529.

Baumeister, R. F. (2011). *Willpower: Rediscovering the Greatest Human Strength.* New York: Penguin.

Baumrind, D. (1966). Effects of Authoritative Parental Control on Child Behavior, *Child Development, 37(4)*, 887-907.

Beck, Don Edward, and Cowan, Christopher C. (1996). *Spiral Dynamics; mastering values, leadership, and change.* Malden, MA: Blackwell Publishing.

Bergner, Daniel. (2009). What Do Women Want? *The New York Times Magazine,* Jan 25, 2009.

Bodkin, J.A. (1995). Buprenorphine treatment of refractory depression. *Journal of Clinical Psychopharmacology.* 1995 Feb: 15(1):49-57.

Bogen, Joseph E.; Bogen, Glenda M. (1988). Creativity and the corpus callosum. Psychiatric Clinics of North America, Vol 11(3), Sep 1988, 293-301.

Boon, Suzette, Steele, Cathy. (2011). *Coping with Trauma Related Dissociation.* W.W. Norton and Co: New York, NY.

Bowen, M. (1961). *Family Psychotherapy.* American Journal of Orthopsychiatry. 31: 40-60.

Bowlby, J. (1988). *A secure base: Parent-child attachment and healthy human development.* New York: Basic Books.

Braden, Gregg (2008). *The Divine Matrix.* New York: Hay House.

Brainworks: "What are brainwaves." http://www.brainworksneurotherapy.com/what-are-brainwaves.

Brizendine, Louann. (2006). *The Female Brain.* New York: Morgan Road Books.

Buss, D. M. (2003). *The evolution of desire: Strategies of human mating* (Second Edition). New York : Basic Books.

Buss, D. M., & Shackelford, T. K. (1997). Susceptibility to infidelity in the first year of marriage. *Journal of Research in Personality, 31,* 193-221.

Buss, D. M. (1999). *Evolutionary Psychology: The New Science of Mind.* Boston, MA: Allyn and Bacon.

Buss, D. M., & Shmitt, D. P. (1993). Sexual strategies theory: A contextual evolutionary analysis of human mating. "Psychological Review": 100, 204-232.

Cage, Arlan. (2008). *Modern Physics and the Science of Qi.* drcage@southbay-totalhealth.com, www.southbaytotalhealth.com.

Cameron, Elissa, and Dalerum, Fredrik. (2009). A Trivers-Willard Effect in Contemporay Humans: Male-Biased Sex Ratios among Billionaires. PLoS ONE. 2009; 4(1): E4195.

Campbell, Joseph. (1949). *The Hero With a Thousand Faces.* Princeton: Princeton University Press.

Carnes, Patric. (2002). *Out of the Shadows, Understanding Sexual Addiction.* Hazelden, Minn.

Cassidy, J., & Shaver, P. (Eds.). (1999), *Handbook of attachment: Theory, research, and clinical applications.* New York: Guilford Press.

Chen, Ingfei. (2009). The Social Brain. *Smithsonian,* June, 2009.

Cherlin, Andrew. (2009). *The Marriage-Go-Round.* New York: Vintage.

Chess, Stella, Thomas, Alexander, Birch, Herbert. (1965). *Your Child is a Person: A Psychological Approach to Childhood without Guilt.* The Viking Press, New York.

Christensen, Beth, Maslin, Mark. (2008). Rocking the Cradle of Humanity: new thoughts on climate, tectonics and human evolution. *Geotimes,* Jan. 2008.

Clark, Russel & Hatfield, Elaine. (1989). Gender differences in receptivity to sexual offers. Journal of psychology and human sexuality. V2(1) 1989. The Haworth Press.

Cloniger, Robert C. (2004). *Feeling Good, the Science of Well-Being.* Oxford University Press.

Cowan, P. A., & Cowan, C. P. (2002). Interventions as tests of family systems theories: Marital and family relationships in children's development, and psychopathology. Development and Psychopathology. Special issue on Interventions as tests of theories. 14, 731-760.

Combs, Allan. Krippner, Stanly. (2003). Process, Structure, and form: An Evolutionary Transpersonal Psychology of Consciousness. *The International Journal of Transpersonal Studies,* 2003, V. 22.

Conley, Terri D. (2011). Perceived proposer personality characteristics and gender differences in acceptance of casual sex offers. Journal of Personality and social Psychology, V100 (2), Feb 2011.

Coyle, Daniel. (2009). *The Talent Code.* New York. Bantam.

Cozolino, Louis J. (2002). *The Neuroscience of Psychotherapy.* New York: W.W. Norton & Co.

Csikszentmihalyi, Mihaly. (1990). *Flow: the Psychology of Optimal Experience.* New York: Harper & Row.

Cunningham JA. (1999). Resolving alcohol-related problems with and without treatment: the effects of different problem criteria. J Stud Alcohol. 1999;60:463–6.

Czaplica, M. A. (1914) *Aboriginal Siberia, a study in social anthropology.* Oxford: Clarendon Press, p 243.

Danielou, Alain. (1994). *The Complete Kama Sutra.* Rochester, Vermont: Park Street Press.

Darwin, Charles. (1872). *The Expression of Emotions in Man and Animals.* London: John Murray.

Davidson, Richard. (2012). *The Emotional Life of your Brain.* New York: Penguin.

Davin, Anne (2015). The Heroine's Journey: an emerging mythology on how to live, love, and lead. Web course: http://annedavin.com/offerings/intensives/#the-heroines-journey.

De Becker, Gavin. (1997). *The Gift of Fear, and other survival signals that protect us from violence.* New York: Dell Publishing.

Debroski, T. M., MacDougal J. M., (1985). *Components of Type A, hostility, and anger-in: relationship to angiographic findings.* Psychosomatic Medicine. Volume 47, Issue 3.

de Chardin, Pierre Teilhard. (1955). *Le Phenomene Humain (The Phenomenon of Man).* Bernard Wall translation. New York: Harper and Row.

Deida, David. (2004). *Enlightened Sex.* Boulder, Colorado: Sounds True (audio recording)

————. (1995). *Intimate Communion.* Deerfield Beach: Health Communications, Inc.

————. (1997). *The Way of the Superior Man.* Austin: Plexus.

————. (2006). *David Deida, live, volumes 1, 2, 3.*

Dement, William C. and Vaughan, Christopher. (1999). *The Promise of Sleep.* New York: Dell.

Diagnostic and Statistical Manual of Mental Disorders 4th edition: Washington D.C. American Psychiatric Association.

Dixit, Jay. (2010). Heartbreak and home runs: the power of first experiences. *Psychology Today:* Jan/Feb 2010.

Domhoff, G. W. (2002). *The Scientific Study of Dreams.* APA Press.

Domhoff, G. W. (2003). *Senoi Dream Theory: Myth, Scientific Method, and the Dreamwork Movement.* Retrieved from the World Wide Web: http://dreamresearch.net/Library/senoi.html

Donbek, Kristin. (2015). Supply and Demand. The New York Times Book Review, Sept. 13, 2015.

Dossey, Larry. (2013). *One Mind.* Hay House Inc: New York, NY.

————. (2009). *The Power of Premonitions.* Hay House Inc: New York, NY.

Dubberley, Emily. (2013). *Garden of Desires: The evolution of women's sexual fantasies.* Black Lace.

Duhigg, Charles. (2012). *The Power of Habit.* New York: Random House.

Dunbar, Robin. (2010). *How Many Friends does one Person Need?* Harvard University Press: Cambridge, Massachusetts.

Dweck, Carol. (2006). *Mindset.* New York: Ballantine.

Ecker, Bruce. (2012). *Unlocking the Emotional Brain.* New York: Routledge.

Eliot, Lise (2009). *Pink Brain, Blue Brain.* New York: Houghton Miflin Harcourt Publishing Company.

Elton, Catherine. (2010). Learning to Lust. *Psychology Today:* May/June, 2010.

Finkelhor, David. (2008). *Childhood Victimization: Violence Crime and Abuse in the Lives of Young People.* Oxford University Press, 2008.

Fisher, Helen. (2004). *Why We Love: the Nature and Chemistry of Romantic Love.* New York: Henry Holt.

————. (2009). *Why Him? Why Her? Finding real love by understanding your personality type.* New York: Henry Holt.

————. (2003). The Anatomy of Love. Presented at *Anatomy of Intimacy Conference,* Life Span Learning Institute. Available through www.lifespanlearn.org.

Forman, Mark. (2015). A new way to approach spiritual bypass. Blog entry, Jan 2, 2015: http://citintegral.com/2015/01/02/a-new-way-to-approach-spiritual-bypass/

Fossella, Tina. (2011). Human Nature, Buddha Nature: On Spiritual Bypassing, Relationship, and the Dharma. Tricycle Magazine, 2011.

Fosha, Diana. (2008). *Transformance: Recognition of Self by Self, and effective action.* In K. J. Schnieder (ed.), *Existential-Integrative Psychotherapy: Guideposts to the core of Practice.* New York: Routledge.

Fowler, J. H. Christakis, N.A. (2008). Dynamic spread of happiness in a large social network: longitudinal analysis over 20 years in the Framingham Heart Study. BMJ. 2008 Dec 4.

Fox, Matthew. (2014). *Meister Eckhart: a Mystic-Warrior for Our Times.* New World Library. Novato, CA.

Frankl, Viktor. (2004). *Man's Search for Meaning. An Introduction to Logotherapy.* Boston: Beacon and Random House , first published 1946.

Fredrickson, Barbara. (2014). *Love 2.0.* New York: Penguin.

Freud, Sigmund. (1961) *Civilization and its Discontents.* New York: Notion.

Freud, Sigmund. (1949). *An Outline of Psycho-Analysis.* New York: W.W. Norton and Company.

Freud, Sigmund. (2010). The Interpretation of Dreams the Illustrated Edition. New York: Sterling Press.

Friday, Nancy. (1987). *My Secret Garden.* New York: Pocket Books.

Friston, Karl. (2002). Functional integration and inference in the brain. Progress in Neurobiology, V68, Issue 2.

Gardner, Howard. (1983). *Frames of Mind.* New York: Basic Books.

Gawande, Atul. (2009). *Hellhole: The United States holds tens of thousands of inmates in long-term solitary confinement. Is this torture?* New Yorker Magazine. March 30.

Gigy, L. & Kelly, J. B. (1993). Reasons for Divorce:—Perspectives of Divorcing Men and Women. *Journal of divorce & Remarriage, 18(1).*

Gilligan, Carol. (1993). *In a Different Voice: Psychological Theory and Women's Development*. Cambridge, Mass.: Harvard University Press.

Glausiusz, Josie. (2009). *Devoted to Distraction*. Psychology Today, March/April, 2009.

Goodman, Leslee. (2015). The Mystic and the Warrior: Radical Priest Matthew Fox On Loving And Defending Our World. The Sun, July 2015.

Gottman, John, M., Silver, Nan. (1999). *The Seven Principles for Making Marriage Work*. New York: Three Rivers Press.

Gottman, John. (2005). Presented at a conference, *The Anatomy of Intimacy*. Foundation for the Contemporary Family, UC Irvine, November 5 and 6.

—————. (2007). Meta-Communication, *Presented at the conference, "The Healing Power of Emotion."* By the Lifespan Learning Institute, www.lifespanlearn.org.

—————. (2001). *The Relationship Cure, a 5 Step Guide for Building Better Connections with Family, Friends, and Lovers*. New York: Crown Publishing.

—————. (2015). *Principia Amores: the new science of love*. New York: Routledge.

Gottshall, Jonathon. (2012). *The Storytelling Animal*. Houghton, Mifflan, Harcourt: New York, NY.

Hanes, Stephanie. (2010). In an Affair's Wake. *Christian Science Monitor,* February 14.

Hanes, Stephanie. (2012). Time for Play. *Christian Science Monitor,* January 23, 2012.

Hanh, Thich, Nhat. (2016). *Creating Peace*. Parallax, from Shambhala Sun. Jan 2016

Hawkins, Jeff. (2000). *On Intelligence*. New York: Henry Holt and Company.

Hebb, Donald. (1949). *The organization of behavior: A neuropsychological theory*. New York: Wiley.

Heitler, Susan. (1990). *From Conflict to Resolution*. New York: Norton.

Helliway, John. Layard, Richard. Sachs, Jeffrey (editors). (2016). World Happiness Report: V1: http://worldhappiness.report/wp-content/uploads/sites/2/2016/03/HR-V1_web.pdf

Hesketh, Theresa. Min Min, Jiang. (2012). The effects of artificial gender imbalance. Science and Society Series on Sex and Science. EMBO Rep.

2012 Jun; 13(6): 487–492. Published online 2012 May 15. doi: 10.1038/embor.2012.62.

Hill, Catey. (2013)....Spouses Won't Tell You. *The Wall Street Journal,* August 25, 2013.

Hillman, James. (1979). *The Dream and the Underworld.* Harper: New York.

Hobson, J. Allan. (2002). *Dreaming: an introduction to the science of sleep.* New York: Oxford University Press.

Hunt, J.M. (1978). The Creation of Man by Prometheus. The Hellenic Society Prometheus: Washington D.C. http://www.prometheas.org/index.html

Hutson, Matthew. (2006). *The heat of the moment: what will you do when in the mood?* Psychology Today, September 1, 2006.

—————. (2016). Triver's Pursuit. Jan 7, 2016 issue of Psychology Today.

Isaacson, Walter. (2007). *Einstein: His Life and Universe.* New York: Simon and Schuster.

Jaffe, Eric. (2012). What do men really want? Psychology Today, March and April of 2015.

Jaynes, Julian. (1976). *The Origin of Consciousness in the Breakdown of the Bicameral Brain.* Houghton Miflin Company. New York.

Johnson, Robert A. (1971). *Owning Your Own Shadow.* HarperSanFrancisco.

—————. (1986) *Inner Work: Using Dreams and Active Imagination for Personal Growth.* HarperSanFrancisco.

Johnson, Susan. (2005). Presented at a conference, *The Anatomy of Intimacy.* Foundation for the Contemporary Family, UC Irvine, November 5 and 6.

Jones, Andrew, Zimmerman (2015). What is the Higgs Field? About Education, http://physics.about.com/od/quantumphysics/f/HiggsField.htm

Jung, Carl G. (1961). *Memories, Dreams, and Reflections.* New York: Random House.

—————. (1959). *The Archetypes and the Collective Unconscious.* Princeton: Princeton University Press.

—————. (1959). *The Basic Writings of C. G. Jung,* ed. Violet Staub De Laszlo, New York: The Modern Library.

—————. (1957). *C. G. Jung: The Collected Works.* Princeton University Press.

Kanazawa, Satoshi. (2009). A chip off the best block. *Psychology Today,* September/October, 2009.

Kahneman, Daniel. (1999). *Well-Being: Foundations of Hedonic Psychology.* Portland, Oregon: Book News, Inc.

—————. (2011). *Thinking Fast and Slow,* Penguin Books.

Kaplan, Karen. (2008). Your whole world smiles with you. LA Times: 12-5-08.

Kaufman, Scott, Barry, (2013). *Ungifted: Intelligence Redefined.* Philadelphia, Basic Books.

Kegan, Robert. (1982). *The Evolving Self: Problems and Process in Human Development.* Cambridge, Mass: Harvard University Press.

Keller, Greg. (2015). France: Americans subdue gunman on train. Associated Press. Santa Barbara News-Press, August 22, 2015.

Kernberg, Otto. (1975). *Borderline Conditions and Pathological Narcissism.* Northvale, New Jersey: Jason Aronson Inc.

Kettlewell, Julianna. (2004). "Fidelity gene" found in voles. *BBC Online News,* June 16.

Kiehl, Kent, (2014). *The Psychopath Whisperer: the science of those without conscience.* New York, NY: Random House.

Kinsey, Alfred Charles. (1948). *Sexual Behavior in the Human Male.* Indiana University Press.

—————. (1953). *Sexual Behavior in the Human Female.* Indiana University Press.

Kohn, Alfie. (1993). *Punished by Rewards: The Trouble with Gold Stars, Incentive Plans, A's, Praise, and Other Bribes.* New York: Houghton Mifflin Company.

Kolbert, Elizabeth, (2011). Sleeping with the Enemy. *The New Yorker,* August 15 & 22, 2011.

Kotier, Steven. (2009). Escape. *Psychology Today,* Sept. 10, 2009.

Krug et al. (2002). "World report on violence and health," World Health Organization, 2002.

Lakoff, George, Johnsen, Mark. (2003). *Metaphors we Live by.* London: The University of Chicago Press.

Langer, Ellen J. (1997). *The Power of Mindful Learning.* Cambridge, MA: Da Capo Press.

LeDoux, Joseph (2015), *Anxious.* New York: Viking.

Lehmiller, J. J. (2009). Secret romantic relationships: Consequences for personal and relational well-being. *Personality and Social Psychology Bulletin,* 35, 1452-1466.

Lemonick, Michael D. (2004). *The Chemistry of Desire.* New York: Time Magazine, Jan. 19, 2004.

Levine, Judith. (2002). *Harmful to Minors.* Minneapolis: University of Minneapolis Press.

Liedloff, Jean. (1975). *The Continuum Concept.* Reading Mass: Addison-Wesley Publishing Company, Inc.

Lipton, Bruce. *The Biology of Belief.* (2005). www.hayhouse.com: Hay House.

Loy, David. (2008), *Money, Sex, War, Karma.* Somerville, MA: Wisdom Publications.

Lyubomirsky, Sonya. (2007). *The How of Happiness.* New York: Penguin.

MacTaggart, Lynne. (2007) *The Intention Experiment: Using Your Thoughts to Change Your Life and the World.* New York: Free Press.

MacTaggart, Lynne. (2012). *The Bond.* New York: Free Press.

Maltz, Wendy. (2009). *Private Thoughts.* New York: Magna Publishing.

Mareno, Hara Estroff. (2010). The Expectation Trap. *Psychology Today:* March/April 2010.

Marks-Tarlow, Terry. (2008). *Psyche's Veil: Psychotherapy, Fractals, and Complexity.* New York: Routledge.

Masterson, James F. (1981). *The Narcissistic and Borderline Disorders, an integrated developmental approach.* New York: Brunner/Mazel.

Marano, Hara Estroff. (2014). *Bully Pulpit.* Psychology Today: May/June, 2014.

———. (2009). *Love's Destroyer.* Psychology Today: July/August, 2009.

McGoldrick, Monica, & Gerson, Randy. (2008). *Genograms, Assessment and Intervention, 3rd Edition.* W.W. Norton and Co. New York, NY.

McGonigal, Kelly. (2012). *The Willpower Instinct.* New York: Penguin Books.

McKee, Robert. (1997). *Story.* New York: HarperCollins.

Mekel-Bobrov (2005). *Ongoing adaptive evolution of ASPM, a brain size determinant in Homo sapiens.* Science: Sep 9;309(5741): 1720-2.

Mellick, Jill. (1996). *The Art of Dreaming: Tools for Creative Dreamwork.* Canari Press Books.

Monto, M. A., & Carey, A. G. (2014). A new standard of sexual behavior? Are claims associated with the "hookup culture" supported by General Social Survey data? *Journal of Sex Research*, online publication ahead of print.

Murdock, Maureen (1990). *The Heroine's Journey.* Boston, Mass. Shambhala Publications Inc.

Mushashi, Miyamoto. (1974). *A Book of Five Rings.* Woodstock, New York: The Overlook Press.

Nichols, Michael. (2007). *The Essentials of Family Therapy.* New York: Pearson.

Northrup, Chrisanna, Schwartz, Pepper, & Whitte, James. (2013). *The Normal Bar: The surprising secrets of happy couples and what they reveal about creating a new normal in your relationship.* New York: Harmony.

O'Hanlon, Bill. (2007). *Positive Psychology.* J&K Seminares. www.JKSeminars.com.

O'Neil, George and Nena, (1972). *Open Marriage.* New York: M. Evans and company, Inc.

Orstein, Peggy. (2016). Dutch Masters of Sex ed. L.A. Times, April 10, 2016.

Oz, Amos. (1984). *In the Land of Israel.* translated by Maurie Goldberg-Bartura. Vintage Books: New York.

Panksepp, Jaak. (2007). The Emotional MindBrain: The Foundational Role of Core Affects in Consciousness and Psychotherapy. Lifespan Learning Institute conference, *The Healing Power of Emotion.* Lifespan Learning Institute.

—————. (2015). *The Archeology of Mind:* New York: Norton.

—————.(1998). *Affective Neuroscience.* New York: Oxford University Press.

Paris, Wendy. (2010). Still doing it. *Psychology Today:* May/June 2010.

Pearce, Joseph Chilton. (2002). *The Biology of Transcendence: A Blueprint of the Human Spirit.* Rochester, Vermont: Park Street Press.

Peck, M. Scott. (1985). *People of the Lie.* New York: Touchstone.

Perel, Esther. (2006). *Mating in Captivity.* New York: Harpers.

Perino, Kaja, (2014). A Perfect Devil. *Psychology Today:* May/June 2014.

Perls, Fritz. (1969). *Gestalt Therapy Verbatim.* The Gestalt Journal Press: Gouldsboro, ME.

Pink, Daniel. (2007). How to make your own luck. *Fast Company,* December, 2007.

Poitras, Laura. (2014). *Citizenfour.* Documentary movie, directed by Laura Poitras.

Porges, S. W. (2006). Presented at a conference, *The Embodied Mind: Integration of the Body, Brain, and Mind in Clinical Practice.* UCLA, March 4 and 5.

Porges SW (2011). *The Polyvagal Theory: Neurophysiological Foundations of Emotions, Attachment, Communication, and Self-regulation.* New York: WW Norton.

Porter, Bruce. (1998). Is Solitary Confinement Driving Charley Chase Crazy? *New York Times Magazine,* November 8.

Prabhavananda, swami, and Isherwood, Christopher. (1944). *The Song of God: Bhagavad-Gita.* New York: The New American Library.

Radin, Dean. (2006). Entangled Minds: Extrasensory Experiences in a Quantum Reality. New York: Paraview Pocket Books.

————. *(2007).* Theater of the Mind Interview with Dean Radin. *Podcast by Kelley Howell.*

Rampton, Martha. (2008). The Three Waves of Feminism: Pacific Magazine, 2008 Fall issue.

Resnick, Michael D. et al. (1997). Protecting Adolescents From Harm: Findings From the National Longitudinal Study on Adolescent Health. *Journal of the American Medical Association,* 1997; 278 (10): 823-832.

Rickard, Ian. (2008). Kanazawa's Generalized Trivers-Willard Hypothesis' and the Heritability of Offspring Sex-Ratio. J. of Evolutionary Psychology, 6(2008)4.

Rodgers, Joann, Ellison. (2014). Go Forth in Anger: *Psychology Today:* March/April, 2014.

Salmon, C. and Symons, D. (2003) *Warrior Lovers.* Yale University Press.

Sapolsky, Robert. (1994). *Why Zebras don't get Ulcers.* New York: Henry Holt.

Sheldrake, Rupert. (2009). *Morphic Resonance: the nature of formative causation,* Rochester, Vermont: Park Street Press.

Peters, S., Braams, B.R., Raijmakers, M.E., Koolschijn, P.C.M.P.*, Crone, E.A* (2014). The neural coding of feedback learning across child and adolescent development. Journal of Cognitive Neuroscience, 26 (8): 1705-1720. *shared last authorship.

Schnarch, David. (1997). *Passionate Marriage, Keeping Love and Intimacy Alive in Committed Relationships.* New York: Henry Holt and Company.

Schiller, Daniela. (2009). Preventing the return of fear in humans using reconsolidation update mechanisms. *Nature, 12-9-09.*

Schore, Allan. (2006). Presented at a conference, *The Embodied Mind: Integration of the Body, Brain, and Mind in Clinical Practice.* UCLA, March 5.

Schore, Allan. (2003). *Affect Regulation and the Repair of the Self.* New York: W.W. Norton and Company.

——————. (1994). *Affect Regulation and the Origin of the Self.* Lawrence Erlbaum Associates. New York.

——————. (2014). Affect Regulation and Healing of the Self. Affect Regulation and Healing of the Self (full audio program) 2014 Annual Interpersonal Neurobiology Conference full conference. Available through Lifespan Learning.

——————. (2015). Lecture in Lifespan Learning Institute conference, *Current Approaches to the Treatment of Trauma.* Lifespan Learning Institute. Available from Lifespan Learning Institute.

Schulz, M. S., Cowan, C. P., & Cowan, P. A. (2006). Promoting Healthy Beginnings: A Randomized Controlled Trial of a Preventive Intervention to Preserve Marital Quality During the Transition to Parenthood. Journal of Consulting and Clinical Psychology, 74, 20-31. See more at: http://psychology.berkeley.edu/people/philip-cowan#sthash.4JhlAFIN.dpuf.

Shapiro, Francine. (2014). *Getting Past your Past.* New York: Rodale.

——————. (2014). Lecture in Lifespan Learning Institute conference, *Current Approaches to the Treatment of Trauma.* Lifespan Learning Institute.

Sharon, Ariel. (1989). *Warrior.* New York: Touchstone.

Sharot, Tali, (2012). The Optimism Bias. *Time Magazine,* March 26, 2012.

Shetty, Priya. (2008). Monogamy gene found in people. Daily news, September 1, 2008.

Siegel, Daniel J. (1999). *The Developing Mind*. New York: The Guilford Press.

Siegel, Daniel J. and Hartzell, Mary. (2003). *Parenting from the Inside Out*. New York: Penguin

Siegel, Daniel J. (2005). *The Mindsight Lectures: cultivating insight and empathy in our internal and interpersonal lives*. Mind Your Brain, Inc.

Siegel, Daniel J. (2007). *The Mindful Brain*. New York: W.W. Norton and Co.

Singer, Jerome. (1976). *Daydreaming and Fantasy*. New York: Routledge.

Slater, Lauren. (2006). *Love*. National Geographic, February.

Smiler, Andrew. (2013). Challenging Casanova. Psychology Today, March/April 2013.

Sood, Avani, Mehta. (2014). Revenge may be a factor in torture. LA Times, 12-24-14.

Sood, Avani, Mehta. (2009). The Fine Line Between Interrogation and Retribution. *Journal of Experimental Social Psychology*. 191 (with Kevin Carlsmith).

Symons, D. (1979). *The Evolution of Human Sexuality*. New York: Oxford University Press.

Talbott, Shawn. (2007). *The Cortisol Connection*. Berkeley, CA: HunterHouse.

Tart, Charles. (1990). *Altered States of Consciousness*.

Taylor, Shelley E. (2002). *The Tending Instinct: How Nurturing is Essential to Who We Are and How We Live*. New York: Henry Holt and Co.

Teilhard de Chardin (1959). *The Phenomenon of Man,* Wm. Collins and Sons, Harper and Row, New York.

Thomas, Alexander, Chess, Stella, and Birch, Herbert. (1970). The Origin of Personality. *Scientific American, pp 102-109, 1970*.

Thomson, Paula. (2008). Mommy and Me: Shared Trauma During Prenatal Development. Conference, Adult Attachment in Clinical Context. Available through Lifespan Learning.

Tolle, Eckhart. (1999). *The Power of Now*. Novato, Vancouver: New World Library.

Trivers, Robert. (2005). *Natural Selection and Social Theory*. New York: Oxford.

Tronic, Ed. (2008). Recorded panel discussion at UCLA conference: Towards a new psychology of interpersonal relationships. Lifespan Learning Institute.

Twinge, Jean, M. and Campbell, W. Keith. (2009). *The Narcissism Epidemic: Living in the Age of Entitlement.* New York: Free Press.

Ucia, Anca. (2014). Spare the Rod. Psychology Today, April, 2014.

van der Kolk, Bessel. (2005). Presented at a conference, *The Anatomy of Intimacy.* Foundation for the Contemporary Family. UC Irvine, Nov. 5 and 6.

van der Kolk, Bessel. (2006). *Clinical Implications of Neuroscience Research in PTSD.* Annals of N.Y Acad. Sci. 1071: 277-293Boston University School of Medicine, The Trauma Center, Brookline, Mass. 02446.

—————. (2014). *The Body Keeps the Score.* New York: Penguin.

Vanity Fair Interview, Jan 2012, *Lady Gaga Opens Up About Bad Romance and Marriage Proposals.*

Wade, Nicholas. (2010). New adventures in recent evolution. *New York Times News Service.* July 25, 2010.

Wahoo, Jade. (2005). Personal communication, at a men's retreat on the green river in Arizona.

Wai, Jonathon. (2014). *7 Strategies for Innovation: how to boost your creativity:* Psychology Today: May/June, 2014.

Ware, Bronnie. (2011-2012). *The Top Five Regrets of the Dying.* Balboa Press.

Wedekind, C. et al. (1995). "MHC-dependent preferences in humans." *Proceedings of the Royal Society of London* 260: 245-49.

Welwood, John. (2011).Human Nature, Buddha Nature: On Spiritual Bypassing, Relationship, and the Dharma: An interview with John Welwood by Tina Fossella: Tricyle Magazine, Spring 2011.

Westermarck, Edward. (1891). *The History of Human Marriage.* MacMillan & Co, New York, NY.

Whitehead, Alfred, North (1929). *Process and Reality.* The Free Press, Simon and Shuster, New York, NY.

Whitman, Walt, (1892). *Song of Myself,* from *Leaves of Grass.* The Walt Whitman Archive.

Wilber, Ken. (2000). Sex, Ecology, Spirituality, the spirit of evolution. (revised from 1995). Boston: Shambhala Publications.

—————. (2000). *Integral Psychology*. Boston and London: Shambhala.

—————. (2000). *A Brief History of Everything*. Boston: Shambhala.

—————. (2003). *Kosmic Consciousness*. Boulder: Sounds True (audio recording).

—————. (2006). *Integral Spirituality*. Boston: Shambhala.

—————. (2004). *The Simple Feeling of Being*. Boston: Shambhala.

—————. (2013). *Address in The Integral Living Room*. Boulder, Nov. 1, 2013.

—————. (2015). Personal communication.

—————. (2016). *Full Spectrum Mindfulness*. Integral Life.

Willsher, Kim. (2015). A train ride, a shot, then: 'Let's go!' Los Angeles Times, August 23, 2015.

Winter, Angela (2014). The One You're With: Interview with Barbara Fredrickson. *The Sun* magazine, July, 2014.

Wiseman, Richard. (2003). *The Luck Factor: Changing Your Luck, Changing Your Life: The Four Essential Principles*. Miramax.

Witt, Keith. (2006). *The Attuned Family: How to be a Great Parent to Your Kids and a Great Lover to Your Spouse*. Santa Barbara Graduate Institute Publishing/iUniverse.

Witt. Keith. (2006). *The Gift of Shame: Why we need shame and how to use it to love and grow*. Santa Barbara Graduate Institute Publishing/iUniverse.

Witt, Keith (2015). *Integral Mindfulness: from clueless to dialed-in*. Integral Publishers.

Witt, Keith. (2006). *Sessions, All Therapy is About Relationships integrating toward unity*. Santa Barbara Graduate Institute Publishing/iUniverse.

Witt, Keith. (2005). *Waking Up: Psychotherapy as Art, Spirituality, and Science*. Santa Barbara Graduate Institute Publishing/iUniverse.

Witt, Keith. (2015). Loving Completely. Audio class available through IntegralLife.com.

Wormser, Gary. (2010). Voice indicator of male strength. *Santa Barbara News press,* July 25, 2010.

Wright, S. C., & Aron, A. (2009). The Extended Contact Effect. In J. M. Levine & M. A. Hogg (eds.), Encyclopedia of group processes and inter-group relations, Thousand Oaks, CA: Sage Publications.

Young, Larry, J. and Wang, Zuoxin. (2004). The neurobiology of pair bonding. Nature neuroscience 7. Published online: 26 September 2004.Zelazny, Roger. (1967). *Lord of Light.* New York: Doubleday.

Zimmerman, Eilene, (2012). Modern Romance. *Christian Science Monitor, February 13, 2112.*

Zuk, Marlene. (2010). Is the man you call Dad really your father? *L.A. Times, June 30, 2010.*

CPSIA information can be obtained
at www.ICGtesting.com
Printed in the USA
BVOW08s1435110517
483863BV00009B/176/P

Also by Nicci Cloke
Under pseudonym Phoebe Locke

The July Girls
The Tall Man

HER MANY FACES

Her
Many
Faces

A Novel

NICCI CLOKE

wm

WILLIAM MORROW

An Imprint of HarperCollins*Publishers*

HER MANY FACES. Copyright © 2025 by Nicci Cloke. All rights reserved. Printed in the United States of America. No part of this book may be used or reproduced in any manner whatsoever without written permission except in the case of brief quotations embodied in critical articles and reviews. For information, address HarperCollins Publishers, 195 Broadway, New York, NY 10007. In Europe, HarperCollins Publishers, Macken House, 39/40 Mayor Street Upper, Dublin 1, D01 C9W8, Ireland.

HarperCollins books may be purchased for educational, business, or sales promotional use. For information, please email the Special Markets Department at SPsales@harpercollins.com.

hc.com

FIRST EDITION

Designed by Bonni Leon-Berman

Library of Congress Cataloging-in-Publication Data has been applied for.

ISBN 978-0-06-339504-6

25 26 27 28 29 LBC 5 4 3 2 1

For Chris, for everything

1

Katie

COCKTAIL HOUR. MARCH HOUSE COMES alive with the slosh of martini, the stench of aftershave; business is over for the day.

I weave through them all, take the elevator down to the calm and quiet of the lobby. Step into the corridor, where the only eyes on me are oil-painted and safely trapped in their frames.

I take a breath. Tray steady, the palm of my hand perfectly flat. Cocktails balanced precisely. Door opened with my other hand, quick swoop of the tray through the gap, and I'm into the private dining room again, listening to the four of them laugh.

"So I told her, 'Listen, sweetheart, I could buy this plane, your entire fleet of them, right now,'" one of them says. I dig my nails into my palm.

Lucian catches my eye. Fatherly smile. Grandfatherly, I guess. Anyway: he's not a lech. I get a lot of *those* smiles, slimy and hard-eyed, a snake's tongue flickering over my skin. But Lucian looks only at my face, wants to know how I am, are they working me too hard, have I brought any of my sketches to show him?

Smile. Set the drinks down and murmur politely back. Short and sweet. I'm supposed to be invisible tonight.

"You should have told her, 'Sweetheart, I could buy *you*.'"

Hyenas laughing. They don't care I'm here. The things I've heard in this room, in all of the rooms in March House. Sharp, the feeling of it, like walking over broken glass. Each prick a shock.

I retreat. Wondering how to get through the night.

It's simple, really.

Step back outside into the quiet of the corridor. Leave them to it;

listen to the tick of the clock, the night slipping slowly by. The wine with it. Their faces flushing, their voices getting louder.

Wait on their every need; appear before they even know they want me. Decant and pour, serve and clear.

My moment will come.

Wait.

2

Tarun

"Katherine"

YOU WERE A CHALLENGE. I should be honest about that.

I'd just sat down at my desk in chambers when my phone rang. When I looked down and saw Ursula's name on the screen, my first instinct was to ignore it. I answered only out of a sense of duty to someone who had been a good friend to me when I really needed it, and I regretted it almost as soon as I heard her brisk voice.

"Welcome back," she said, and then she told me about you.

You were twenty-two, a waitress at March House—a private members' club in the heart of Mayfair whose patrons were some of the wealthiest and most powerful people in London. You were accused of murdering four of them.

I imagined the scene. The private dining room with its antique oak table; at the head, Lucian Wrightman, the owner of the club, with the poisoned bottle of brandy in front of him. Two of his guests, the property magnate Harris Lowe and the Chief Secretary to the Treasury, Dominic Ainsworth MP, had died in their seats, while the third, oil baron Aleksandr Popov, had been found on the floor several feet away. An attempt to raise the alarm that he had been unable to complete before being overcome.

A lethal dose of hydrogen cyanide prevents the body's cells from using oxygen, resulting in confusion, dizziness, seizures, and rapid cardiovascular collapse before a victim's inevitable loss of consciousness and death.

It was a cruel way to kill someone. I had, unfortunately, seen worse.

You'd abandoned your post and been captured on CCTV leaving the club shortly after midnight, and had subsequently been arrested attempting to flee London via an early-morning train at Paddington. You told the arresting officers, "They deserved it."

So yes, you were a challenge.

You refused to speak during your interviews in custody. Ignored the duty solicitor and were equally unwilling to communicate, at least initially, when your father hired Ursula as her replacement. And while she seemed confident in your case now, it was clear to me that you would need a highly competent barrister to represent you in court if you were to have any chance of walking free.

I should have been flattered, then, that Ursula had chosen to instruct me. Instead, as I read through her notes again, I felt only dread.

3

John

"Kit-Kat"

YOU WERE A GIFT. UNEXPECTED but not unwanted, a daughter making her late entrance after two sons. Your mum turned thirty-eight three days before you were born; no age at all, really, but we'd thought, after Bobby, that she couldn't carry another baby. We'd been lucky enough to have the boys and had made our peace with it, been content with our little family.

And then there you were. The sweetest girl, seven pound nothing and happy to be held by anyone who'd have you. Born smiling, we used to say, though Bobby, who was having trouble adjusting, would always tell anyone else in earshot, "It's just wind!" He had a habit of eavesdropping on adult conversation, snatching up phrases like a magpie. You may remember a time when you were small and he liked to tell people you were an "axe-dent."

It was Stephen, eleven years your elder, who took his role as your protector seriously, right from the start. When you were a toddler, he used to hold your hand to cross even the quietest street, and as you grew, he was always there to swoop in when you—adventurous, mischievous, ever the explorer—decided to climb a tree or a fence, or to try and ride your little blue trike backward or to crawl into the chimney looking for Father Christmas. You loved the stories he invented for you, a bear called Howard and a brave girl named—at your insistence—Pancake, adventuring through faraway lands and magical worlds with the dubious guidance of the WotsitPotsit Bird. Nothing made you laugh more than that badly behaved bird, and whenever we were out in the garden or on the beach, I'd catch you craning your face to the sky, hoping to catch a glimpse of him.

Your mother and I worried about you as you got older, more so than we did the boys. Perhaps that's normal. It's frightening, sending a daughter out into the world. And you were so headstrong, so fearless, that I would lie awake some nights, wondering what the world would make of you. Wondering what you would make of it. It seemed to baffle you, sometimes—at four, five, six, you were a ball of questions: *Why is that man sleeping on the pavement? Why is that lady sad? Why do I have to go to school? Why do we live in a house and not on the beach? Can I learn to fly a plane? Can I have cake for breakfast? When is it Christmas again?*

So often I felt I was disappointing you with my answers, realized the inadequacy of saying *Well, sometimes people are sad* or *That's just the way we have to do things.*

You were angry one weekend, aged six, when I wouldn't let you camp alone in the field behind our house. Your mother had been trying to get you into the stories she'd loved and so you'd been listening to audiobooks of the Secret Seven and Nancy Drew and had fallen in love. You wanted to look out for robbers and smugglers, making notes in one of your schoolbooks by torchlight. I told you it wasn't safe. "But why, Dad?" you asked, so impatient with me. And I found I couldn't tell you that smugglers are not one of the things people fear, out in the dark of night. Stephen, humoring you, offered to camp in the garden with you, and Bobby, always afraid of missing out, suddenly became enthusiastic too.

Stephen and I set up the tent together, you bouncing in before we'd even finished pegging the guy ropes to the ground.

"Perfect," you said, flopping onto your front, a notebook already open in front of you, an old pair of binoculars your uncle had bought the boys looped around your neck. "Get in, get in!"

I left you to it, and later, I watched through our bedroom window as night fell, the glow of your torches flickering through the canvas of the tent. It was colder than forecast and when I came out to check on you, I half expected you to want to come back inside.

But you were already tucked in a sleeping bag fast asleep, your brothers reading their books peacefully on either side of you. Stephen, aged seventeen and probably wishing he was out with his friends, smiled at me and took the extra blankets I'd brought. Bobby, ten and usually far too cool to be seen with any of us, pointed at the notebook. "No smugglers or robbers," he said, "but we heard one owl and one car alarm."

You came in the next morning, not long after dawn, your hair a scarecrow's nest and your pajamas damp with dew from the grass. You had your toy cat, Pudding, under one arm and your notebook under the other, and you were the happiest I'd ever seen you.

4

Max

"Killer Kate"

YOU WERE THE STORY I'D been waiting for.

Everyone had heard about March House. A place where you needed more money than sense and an invitation to join. Where rock stars snorted coke in the toilets with world leaders, and Hollywood heart-throbs hobnobbed with royals, and where some of the biggest business mergers and policy decisions of the past century were said to have been made.

A murder there would always have been a peach of a headline, but the identity of the victims made it particularly fucking juicy. The owner, Lucian Wrightman, wasn't exactly a household name, but he was richer than God and tipped for an OBE in the coming honors list. Dominic Ainsworth, a political cartoonist's wet dream with his neat little side parting and eager pink face, had had a disastrous outing on breakfast telly two years earlier as a junior minister, and had somehow since been promoted to a role at the Exchequer, despite giving the impression he'd struggle to manage a weekly shopping budget, let alone the country's finances.

Then you had Popov, a billionaire tycoon with fingers in lots of pies, not least as the new owner of a Championship football club—spawning a slew of Mumsnet threads about how hot he was. Harris Lowe looked practically pedestrian in comparison; he was heir to the Lowe's Diamonds fortunes and head of Lowe Estates, which happened to own half the property in Mayfair—including the very building you murdered him in.

They had a clutch of marriages and affairs and a shocking—sickening—amount of personal wealth between them. Very naughty boys. We were all just waiting to hear exactly what they'd done to become targets.

Then came news of your arrest: a waitress at the club, aged twenty-two, barely five feet two and a mousy little face, looking like you wouldn't say boo to a goose.

The whole thing went from nought to feeding frenzy in record time, headline after headline for days, click rates to die for on every article we posted. And once you were charged, I set about finding out everything there was to know about you.

5

John

"Kit-Kat"

YOU BROUGHT ME FLOWERS ONE Father's Day. You'd been for a walk with Stephen while the rest of us were out, had broken off stems from people's front gardens while he wasn't looking. You presented them to me with your hands still streaked with soil, a gap in your smile where you'd lost a bottom tooth and a smear of green pen still staining your cheek where you'd drawn yourself "a tattoo" days earlier.

"Sorry," Stephen said. "I did tell her not to."

"Boys don't like flowers, stupid," Bobby told you, and you looked genuinely puzzled.

"Everyone likes flowers," you said, and you turned to me for confirmation.

"I love flowers," I told you.

"So did the people who planted them," your mum said. "Bobby, get your things. Kit, are you ready?"

You looked at me and shook your head. "I want to stay here today," you said.

You'd always loved going to the gym when Bobby was training. As a toddler, you'd treated the place like a giant soft play, often needing to be fished from the landing pits beside the parallel beams and the vault table, where you liked to bury yourself beneath the foam blocks. Now that you were older, Julia, who adored you, would sometimes take time out to help you practice your handstands or to plait your hair in various complicated ways, while Peter ran through Bobby's routines with him.

"You can't," your mum said. "Come on, get a move on."

"Please," you said, turning to me.

"I have to drive Stephen back," I said. "You don't want to be stuck in the car the whole day."

"Yes I do," you said, case closed, and you ran to get your shoes and your Nintendo DS.

Your mum shrugged and smiled at me. "At least you won't get lonely on the way home."

"Can't you come and watch me?" Bobby asked, his small frame dwarfed by the kit bag slung across his body.

I tried to make it to as many of his practices and meets as possible. We had hired a new vet at the surgery, making my workload a little more manageable, and your mother and I divided things equally between us where we could—drop-offs and pickups and birthday parties and your swimming lessons and playdates. But Peter was your mum's friend, now Julia too, and so gradually it became her thing, the other commitments mine.

"Next weekend, I promise," I told him. I kissed them both and herded you and Stephen into the car.

I hadn't wanted Stephen to go to Sandhurst. It hadn't really occurred to me, when marrying your mum, that the military line in her family might be expected to continue with any children of our own. When the three of you were younger, I'd tuned out your uncle's and your granddad's comments, had thought that Stephen—endlessly patient and kind to a fault—would be a good teacher or a nurse, perhaps a writer. You still talked about Howard and Pancake and the Wotsit-Potsit Bird.

But Stephen had been set on it, and even I could see it had been the making of him. Glancing at him in the passenger seat, confident and calm, his hair shorn, I almost did a double take, unable to reconcile him with the skinny, sweet little boy I remembered.

As we joined the motorway, we passed the time talking about some of Stephen's fellow officer cadets and his instructors and the exercises he would be taking part in during his final term. You played your game, ignoring us. At first, you'd shown some interest in the survival skills he'd learned, were particularly excited about building your own

camouflaged shelter behind your mum's rose beds, but you'd been upset when, in his second year, Stephen had been on an exchange to
West Point in the States and you hadn't seen him for three months,
and since then you ignored all talk of his training as if that might make
it go away.

"Will you be home in time to go to the farm?" you asked when we'd
fallen quiet.

"Not this year." Stephen turned in his seat to talk to you. "But when
I get back, I'll take you to London, okay? Top deck of the bus, all the
sights. Like I promised."

"Fine," you said, rolling your eyes and turning the volume up on your
game.

But when we dropped him off, you, suddenly solemn, hugged him so
tightly he let out a surprised puff of air. I met his eye, and he smiled at me.

"Be good, okay?" he said to you, ruffling your hair, and you pulled
back and told him that you would.

Aged seven, you liked to draw, working your way painstakingly through a
book you'd found at the library, though it was too advanced for you, your
tongue poking out of the corner of your mouth as you tried again and
again to follow the steps to draw a dog. You loved to learn about the world,
liked copying pictures of things you thought Stephen might like—Angkor
Wat and the Great Wall of China, the "Great 8" animals of the Great
Barrier Reef, and a cockscomb plant whose flowers looked like brains that
you found in an old gardening manual of your mum's.

You were helpful, always appearing at my side in the kitchen or garden, asking if I had a job for you. "Your little shadow," your mum said
once, though you were just as likely to curl up next to her on the sofa
while she was marking homework. You liked company, liked to talk. You
always had something to say, always a question to ask.

The four of us traveled up for Stephen's passing-out parade, you and
Bobby dressed smartly with your hair combed neat. I felt so incredibly
proud of you all as I moaned at you to pose nicely for the photos. And
as we walked back to the car afterward, you and your mum were ahead,
you tugging at the waistband of the tights that were too big for you, a

grass stain on the hem of your dress. Your mum put her arm round you and squeezed you, and you looked up at her and beamed.

I think of that moment often, perfectly framed in my mind, a postcard from another time. I want to step inside it, race to catch up with you both, to fold you into my arms and never let go.

You turned eight the following summer. Your birthday was on a Monday, an injustice you were deeply unhappy about, only compounding your upset that Stephen was still two months away from returning from his first deployment to Helmand Province. But you'd been cheered up by your presents—the beautiful set of encyclopedias that your mum had found for you, the games and clothes and hair braiding set you'd chosen for yourself—and had gone off to school happily enough.

That morning we went shopping for the birthday dinner you'd requested: burgers, hot dogs, and your mum's macaroni cheese. We drew the line at the champagne you'd asked for.

"Where has she even heard the word *canapé*?" your mum asked, frowning at the list you'd carefully written out for us.

I pushed the trolley on, adding mince for the burgers. "I blame *Ratatouille*."

"Maybe *we* have the champagne," she said, consulting the list again. "That seems fair, don't you think?"

It was unusual for us both to have a day off together—your mum's school was closed for emergency water pipe repairs, and I'd taken one of my many accrued annual leave days after repeated badgering from the practice manager. Back at the house, I made us sandwiches, and we took them into the garden, the day warm and bright. We sat and listened to the birds singing in the oak tree above us.

"She was such a lovely baby," your mum said. "Remember the cheeks?"

"The wrist rolls."

Your mother pressed a hand to her chest. "Perfection."

There was a single, sharp ring of the doorbell. "It's probably the cake," your mum said as I got up. "The woman said between one and two."

But when I opened the front door, there was a man of about my own age, sweating in his suit. Everything about him precise, calm. Only the slightest tremble in his voice gave him away as he came into the living room, sat us both down, and delivered the news.

Stephen, killed by a car bomb on a patrol base in Nad Ali.

Your mum, sitting beside me on the sofa, let out a single, indecipherable sound and curled over onto her knees, her hands covering her face.

You liked our casualty visiting officer, a young man from the same regiment as Stephen who had sisters of his own and often took the time to sit and talk with you. I heard you once, on the afternoon he'd come to assist us with funeral plans, telling him about the letters Stephen had sent you, proudly showing him the little blue sheets of paper with their jokes and doodles, Stephen's descriptions of the camp and the things he missed most from home. I noticed the way you spoke in the present tense about him—*he says it's really hot and the food's okay and that Cheryl Cole is visiting soon for Pride of Britain and he'll say hello from me*—and the gentle way the CVO used the past tense in response: *It sounds like he was a lovely brother. I bet he missed you a lot.*

When your mum found the letters on the kitchen table, she gathered them up and hid them on a high shelf in a cupboard. "It's upsetting her," she said, though I worry, now, that the opposite was true.

Stephen was buried in a military cemetery in West London, and your uncle Neil traveled down from Scotland to be a pallbearer. He'd served in the Gulf War before returning to run your mum's family's farm when your grandfather had become too ill to do so, and when I came down that morning, feeling sick to my stomach, he was dressed in uniform in the kitchen, making breakfast while you and Bobby sat quietly at the table. For a second, I thought it was Stephen standing there, and it was only in that moment, as Neil turned round and I saw it was him, that it truly hit me that I wouldn't see Stephen again.

Afterward, you kept a photo of Stephen in his uniform—one of the ones I had taken at his passing-out parade, you grinning beside him—on your bedside table. I noticed, over the months that followed, how it moved position every few days. Sometimes facing your pillow, at other times looking out at the room, once or twice on your windowsill or dresser.

And I felt *glad* that you were touching it, holding it, while I was walking round the house with my eyes fixed on the floor, too scared to look at any of the family photos we'd hung so carelessly, so obliviously, as if they were from a never-ending supply. You were remembering Stephen. As if you were the only one brave enough to do so.

6

Tarun

"Katherine"

I STAYED LATE AT CHAMBERS that night, rereading Ursula's email. I was grateful that she had contacted me directly rather than my clerk. I'd felt that the time was right for my return to work, but now, looking at the details of your case, I was no longer sure.

I focused on the specific points of law a jury would need to be convinced of to convict you of the murders. In doing so, I set about applying pressure to each piece of the prosecution's case in turn. Searching for the gaps, the weak spots. The things that said *there is doubt here*.

There was no doubt you were in an undesirable position. You had served the group all night, in a dining room on a floor separate from the rest of the club and its patrons, and the only fingerprints found on the poisoned bottle of brandy belonged to you and Lucian Wrightman himself. You had fled your shift early without telling anyone you were doing so and, when apprehended by police, had declared that the victims deserved it.

But that didn't mean I couldn't see those weak spots in the case against you. I could begin, reading those notes, to imagine myself standing up in court, the lines of cross-examination I might pursue against the witnesses who would be called by the prosecution. I stepped unexpectedly back into a self I had once known so well, and it felt good.

Just as quickly, a familiar feeling crept over me: the sensation of walking along a cliff edge, not knowing when the ground might crumble beneath me. I read what Ursula had written about you again, and then, knowing it was a terrible idea, I read some of the news coverage of your arrest.

There is a principle in my profession known as the cab rank rule: a barrister may not discriminate between clients and must take on any case, provided that it is within their competence and that they are available and will be appropriately remunerated. Justice must be freely accessible to all, meaning that one cannot turn down a client simply because a case may be contentious, unpopular, or difficult to defend. I had never strayed from this code of conduct. Had always represented every client to the very best of my ability.

But I was not the same person anymore. And I was no longer sure that this case—or any—was within my competence.

I called Ursula as I walked home.

"I'm not sure," I said, when she answered. "I'm not the right person for this."

"Of course you are," she said.

"I'm not ready—"

"You are ready," she cut in, in a tone that brooked no argument. "And you can help her."

I was silent, the entrance to the Underground station looming ahead of me.

"She isn't Marla, Tarun," Ursula said.

I hesitated for a second, winded.

"Come on," she said. "I need you. And you need this."

7

John

"Kit-Kat"

IN THE MONTHS AFTER STEPHEN'S funeral, when the house felt too quiet, too still, you were always there with your questions, your stories about your day, your funny little ways. You insisted on coming with me to walk the dog each night, waiting by the door in your pajamas with your coat zipped over the top. You and me and Wilbur, who endured your hugs and teasing and your games of hide-and-seek, walking the same loop across the meadow and the dunes and down to the beach. You told me it was the best bit of your day, but once, a couple of months in, I overheard you telling your mum that you didn't want me to be lonely.

As time went on and we settled into a new kind of normal, you were always trying to make us laugh. You could make your mum and me cry with your impressions of celebrities and neighbors and my customers at the surgery; I still remember how uncanny your old Mrs. Pollock was, the way you'd stand with one hand on your hip, berating the imaginary receptionist: *I've told you a thousand times, this waiting room is too* cold *for Bitsy!*

Though you weren't particularly academic, you liked school. You loved art and anything creative, especially when your teacher brought in a sewing machine for you to try. You came home so excited about it that your mum went up to the loft and brought hers down, and the two of you spent the rest of that summer going to charity shops, buying baggy old T-shirts and dresses that you cut with painstaking concentration, trying out stitches and techniques from another library book.

She wore a top you made when she went out for dinner with Julia one evening, and I thought you might actually burst with pride.

All the while, the collection of medals and trophies displayed proudly in Bobby's room grew larger, his confidence with it. I stood watching him on the parallel bars one afternoon in early 2010, not long after he'd turned fourteen, and was completely blindsided by how strong he looked, how elegantly he moved.

"I think he might be one of the most naturally talented gymnasts we've ever worked with," Peter said, coming up beside me. "You must be very proud."

"I am."

"Big things," he said, clapping me on the back. "The boy's going to do big things."

The after-school and weekend training sessions and meets intensified after that. I tried to be around as much as I could, so that you could stay at home instead of waiting for hours on end on the balcony of the gym, reading or drawing in your notebook. You told me repeatedly that you hated it, that everyone was annoying, that gymnastics was the stupidest sport.

But your mum said that you often asked if you could have a turn, could sometimes be found in whichever corner of the gym was quietest, trying out the balance beam or the horse in your school uniform and socks. You came home upset one evening because Peter had told you off for climbing on some old equipment you'd found in a storeroom.

"It was dangerous," your mum said. "Don't sulk about it."

"It wasn't dangerous," you told me later. "Peter was horrible to me. He said I had to stop sneaking around and trying to be the center of attention all the time." Your eyes filled with tears again as you said, "I don't even know what that *means*!"

Bobby was invited to a selection event for an official Team GB development program. It meant staying in London for three days, time off school. Peter would attend as his coach, and I managed to book leave so I could go with them.

"I want to come," you said, a week or so before. "I want to see Diagon Alley."

"It's not real, idiot," Bobby said, at the same time as your mum told you, "You've got school."

"It's not fair," you said, your voice growing plaintive. "Bobby gets to go everywhere."

"You'll get plenty of trips when I'm in the Olympics," Bobby said, grinning, and you rolled your eyes.

"*Not* going to happen," you said, but Bobby, on cloud nine, took no notice of you.

Your night terrors began around that time. Waking soaked in sweat, or sleepwalking into our room, babbling about bad men, death, fire. It had been two years since Stephen died and your mum banned you from taking out scary books from the library, grounded Bobby for showing you horror movie trailers on YouTube. When I suggested, six months on, that we actually needed to find some kind of counseling for you, she dismissed the idea. "She'll grow out of it," she said. "I was the same, at her age."

"This is different," I said. "She's gone through something traumatic, we all have. She needs to talk about it."

"You're making connections that don't exist." She was irritated now. "It's just a normal thing, and she'll grow out of it."

"But why *should* she, when we can get her some help?" I was tired by then of the belief, handed down to her by your granddad and his father before him, that things should be borne or suffered silently through, that airing our problems only gave them oxygen to burn brighter.

"I'm not having this conversation again," she said, going into the en suite and closing the door on me, and I walked over to the bed and screamed into a pillow.

But to you, we always presented a united front, and when you had a run of good nights, sleeping soundly through, I let the idea of counseling drop.

One afternoon, Bobby came storming into the kitchen, complaining that he couldn't find his grips.

"Those are new. Please tell me you haven't lost them," your mum said.

"I *haven't*," Bobby said hotly. "They were in my room, and now they're gone." He thundered back up the stairs and went into your room.

"Hey!" I heard you shout. "You have to knock—"

There was a crash, and your mum and I both hurried up to see what was going on. Bobby had pushed your books and pens and pencils from your desk, and now began ransacking the drawers.

"*Bobby*," your mum said, shocked, as you leapt from your bed, the wool you'd been attempting to knit with tumbling to the floor.

"Stop touching my things," you shouted, your mum just catching you before you could get to him.

"Enough." I pulled Bobby away by the shoulder. But as he removed his hand from the back of the bottom drawer, he brought out the brand-new grips. We all stared at them.

"I was just borrowing them," you said in a small voice.

There were several similar incidents over the following weeks. A track-suit top went missing, never to be found again, and Bobby's kit bag was left unzipped on the front step in the rain. A leotard had a tear down the back when I came to remove it from the washing machine.

Your mum sat you down after your bath one night, you wrapped in your dressing gown with your hair still wet.

"It's normal to feel jealous," she said, combing your hair. You winced. "But I want this behavior to stop," she continued. "You should be happy for your brother. You should be supporting him."

You opened your mouth, ready to argue, but then you closed it again. "Okay," you said.

That weekend, I took you and Wilbur up the coast for a walk through the forest, a place you'd loved to come to when you were little and liked to help Stephen and Bobby make dens between the trees. I could picture you in your tiny wellies, arms loaded with twigs and sticks and your face scratched and beaming, so pleased with yourself. Now you were quiet, walking along with your hands stuffed into your pockets, your shoulders slumped. You barely looked up as we followed the trail, ignored the ball Wilbur kept dropping at your feet.

"Let's go and get cake," I suggested. "Maybe a hot chocolate?"

You smiled and nodded, but you still seemed a million miles away.

When we were sitting in the café, our drinks steaming in front of us, I asked you if everything was all right.

You bit your lip. "I need to tell you something."

"Okay." I folded my hands in my lap.

"I don't think you're going to like it," you said.

"You can tell me anything."

You swallowed. "When I was at the gym with Mum the other day, I saw Peter taking pictures," you said.

Your cheeks were burning; that's the thing I remember most. You were never shy, rarely blushed, and yet now you could hardly meet my eye.

"What do you mean? Pictures of the session?"

"No." You shook your head. "Pictures afterward. In the changing room. In the . . ." You blinked at me. "In the showers," you said, your voice almost a whisper now. "He was standing at the door and nobody had seen him and he was taking pictures."

8

Max

"Killer Kate"

MY WIFE, ANYA, HAD HER own opinions of you. "She looks so sweet," she said, scrolling through her phone at breakfast. "It's sad, really, isn't it?"

"Sad for the men who were murdered, sure."

She got up from the table, started clearing the mess of crumbs and juice our hurricane of a six-year-old had left in his wake. "Imagine how her parents must be feeling. What do you think happened?"

I shook my head. "I'd like to find out."

I found the picture of you she'd seen on the BBC, an old one ripped from social media: you in a park, smiling like sunshine personified with an ice cream in your hand. She was right: you did look sweet. I imagined that same conversation happening over coffee and cereal in kitchens across the country. What had happened in that club? Why had you done it?

Good questions. I wanted to be the one to answer them.

That day, I started trying to track down people who knew and would be willing to talk about you. Your parents had been easy enough to find—your mum's picture all over the school's website, and the one for the veterinary surgery where your dad worked listing a phone number and email address for me to try. I'm guessing I wasn't the first or last journalist to contact them, and I didn't hold out much hope of my calls being returned.

Your brother was on Instagram. Not much personal information given away, just artsy-fartsy shots of London—blurry buildings through rainy bus windows and nighttime streets streaked with headlights—and pretentious flat lays of books he was reading: a classic Agatha Christie with a coffee and croissant, a P. D. James beside a boiled egg and soldiers and a chintzy teapot. None of his own face and none of yours. But in his bio, the place to find him: *Owner of @wilburscoffee.*

Wilbur's was already busy, the tables out on the pavement full and a queue for the counter inside that never really seemed to subside. I joined the end of it, pretending to admire the display of cakes. The place was full of yummy mummies and hipsters with their matcha lattes and cold brews, buggies and expensive bikes parked between tables. It was a prime spot, right off Newington Green, and I bet the rent was astronomical.

There were two girls behind the counter, no sign of Bobby. Maybe keeping a low profile while your mug shot was still fresh in people's minds. I toyed with the idea of using a cover story to ask for him, possibly pretending to be a concerned friend, which had worked for me in making reluctant sources materialize in the past. But no need—just as I reached the front of the queue, he appeared, a phone wedged between his shoulder and ear. I ordered a black coffee from one of the girls, watching him as he stood at the other end of the counter, searching through a stack of documents. In person, there was some family resemblance, same mousy hair and freckled skin, but he was more striking than you, strong jaw and bright blue eyes, and looked like he took better care of himself.

He found whatever he was looking for just as the girl handed me my coffee. I tapped my card on the reader without really paying attention, instead noticing the way your brother kept his head down as he weaved his way out through the tables and onto the pavement. He looked bruised somehow, scared, like he was afraid of being noticed or spoken to. I took my coffee and hurried after him.

He was walking fast, already a little way down the street when I called his name. He turned, and when he saw me, a stranger, his face hardened. But he stopped walking.

"Max Todd," I said, jogging to catch up with him. The paper cup was thin, and I hadn't taken a sleeve for it, the heat of the coffee already burning my hand. "I work for the *Herald*. I'd really love to talk to you about your sister."

He flinched, already turning away. "No comment."

"It must be a terrible shock, all of this," I said, because a little kindness right off the bat usually goes a long way. You'd be surprised how far a bit of empathy gets you with some people.

To my surprise, he laughed. A bitter, hurt kind of laugh that told me he'd talk. Eventually.

"Nothing Kit does shocks me anymore," he said. "Please, leave us alone."

But he took my card when I offered it. I watched him walk away, turning that line over in my head. *Nothing Kit does shocks me anymore.*

Now I really was interested.

9

John

"Kit-Kat"

THE DAYS THAT FOLLOWED WERE rough; I find it difficult to remember them now. That night your mum asked you, over and over, *Are you sure?* while you sat at the kitchen table and cried. Bobby flew at you when he heard what you'd said, his face scarlet as he spat, *Liar.* I grabbed him, his wiry frame now knotted with hard muscle, my heart pounding against his back as I locked my arms round him and held him.

Your mum tried to stop me at the door when I said I had to report it. Over her shoulder I saw you standing there, looking small and scared. I pushed past her and found my phone.

When a member of staff rang to let us know the gym was closing temporarily, Bobby punched a wall so hard that his knuckles split open with the plaster. I cleaned and bandaged his hand, and when I was done, I kept hold of it. "I know this is awful," I said. "But I'm here for you."

"She's lying," he said. "And you believe her and not me." He pulled his hand away.

You refused to leave your room all week. That night I came up to see you with two plates of food on a tray. You were curled at the end of your bed, reading a book, and I noticed you were wearing an old sweatshirt of Stephen's.

"Hi," you said.

"Hi." I put the tray down on the bed beside you and then took a seat. You watched me, cross-legged on your kitten-print duvet, trying to eat lasagna, and then picked up your own knife and fork and started eating too.

"Everyone's going to hate me," you said. "They're all talking about it at school."

"It's a small town," I said. "Everyone talks about everything and then they forget."

"Okay," you said, though you didn't sound sure.

"You did the right thing," I told you, and I saw your shoulders drop, just a little, as if a weight had been lifted from you.

We ate in companionable silence after that. I took the plates down to the quiet kitchen and washed them while Bobby and your mum watched a film in the living room.

10

Tarun

"Katherine"

MY FIRST MEETING WITH YOU made me nervous; I won't pretend otherwise.

I'd told Ursula I wished to see you alone, and if she thought that unusual—or the fact I had asked to do so at this early juncture—she said nothing. Perhaps she thought I was still finding my feet again, overcautious about ensuring I had everything I needed to proceed with the brief.

The truth, however, was that I wondered if you were guilty, and hoped I might be a better judge than she was.

You were sullen, staring at me as I took my seat opposite you in the private room the prison had assigned for us. You were sitting on your hands, the sweatshirt you were wearing swamping you, and your hair was unwashed and uncombed.

"Hello, Katherine," I said. "My name is Tarun Rao, and I'm the barrister that Ursula has instructed on your behalf."

You eyed me warily and then looked away. "She says you're the best," you said.

My last murder client had said something similar to me, and this did not reassure me.

"There is significant evidence in the case against you," I said. "I'd like to hear your version of events."

You began picking at a loose thread on the cuff of your sweatshirt. "She didn't tell you?"

"I'd like to hear it from you."

You chewed your lip. Nerves, perhaps, or the pause of someone trying to ensure they had their story straight.

"I went to work as normal," you said. You still didn't meet my eye. "It was a private dinner, one of Lucian's, and I did what I always did. I served the food, served the wine, served the brandy. I didn't kill them."

"The Crown Prosecution Service are proposing that you brought the poisoned bottle of brandy into the club."

"I didn't. It was already in the room when I arrived."

You looked at me as you said it, your clear green eyes locked on mine, and I understood for the first time why Ursula believed you.

"You ran away before your shift was over," I prodded.

"I hated it there. I'd had enough."

"So you just walked out, there and then, without telling anyone?"

You nodded, your expression hardening. You didn't like being questioned, which did not bode well.

"You told the police the men deserved it."

Again, you hesitated. "I didn't mean that. I didn't know what I was saying."

I sat back in my chair and let a silence unfold between us.

"What's going to happen to me?" you asked.

"If you're found guilty, this offense meets the criteria for a whole life order, meaning a life sentence with no possibility for parole."

You looked as though I had slapped you. "*Will* I be found guilty?"

I knew that I should respond reassuringly, pragmatically. But instead the only answer that came to mind was *Should you be?*

11

John

"Kit-Kat"

IN THE SUMMER OF 2014, we headed for Scotland. It had been three years since Peter and Julia had moved away, two and half since we'd heard the investigation had been dropped. You'd cried when I told you the news.

Peter had been popular locally, and I can't pretend I didn't notice the way people avoided me after he left, the slight frostiness with which a lot of my patients spoke to me.

But you'd turned eleven, then twelve, then thirteen, seemed to be doing well at senior school. You still spent hours carefully sketching or sewing, sometimes doing your maths homework at the dining table so one of us could help you. When I look back now, it seems obvious how little you talked about friends. How few names you mentioned when recounting your days at school. We were too distracted to notice.

Bobby had failed his exams and refused to retake them, had begun smoking cannabis so regularly that I'd stopped noticing the smell on his clothes, stopped being shocked by his red eyes, his long disappearing acts to friends' houses. He sat in the backseat of the car now with his headphones in, ignoring all of us. As we drove up the rutted track to the farmhouse, I looked in the rearview mirror and saw he'd fallen asleep, his head bouncing gently against the window.

As children, you'd all loved Neil, who had taken over the family farm when your granddad retired. We'd always spent our summer holidays there, Neil telling you ghost stories out in the dark barn or letting you sit too close to the firepit he'd built so you could toast marshmallows.

But when we arrived this time, he wasn't going to play the fun uncle.

"You've grown, kitten," he told you, barely glancing at you before switching his attention to Bobby. "And what's the problem with you, then, eh?"

"Good to see you too," Bobby said, but the sarcasm fell flat, and I could tell he was nervous.

"Go and put some trainers on," Neil said. "We're going for a run in ten minutes."

"Can I come?" you asked, and Neil shook his head. "Me and Bobby have got some talking to do."

That night I walked in to find Bobby at the kitchen table with a laptop, applying for jobs, and realized that your mum had been right. Neil had known how to get through to him.

I went to our bedroom to tell her and found her at the window, watching you in the garden with Wilbur. You were getting him to chase you, one of his favorite games, your hair flying behind you and your cheeks flushed. You looked the happiest I'd seen you in a long time.

"I'm glad we came," I said, and your mum startled, lost in thought.

"She's so like my mother," she said, still watching you. "I hadn't noticed."

I hesitated. She rarely spoke about your grandma, who'd died when you were still a toddler, but when she did, it often sent her mood spiraling to a dark place.

I put my arm round her. "I think she's just our Kit," I said.

12

Max

"Killer Kate"

AFTER I MET YOUR BROTHER, I realized this was going to be a big deal for me. I mean, obviously you were clickworthy. You were young, reasonably attractive; the four victims were high-profile enough that there was plenty of mileage to be had in that alone. That was my job: finding the headlines that people couldn't resist opening, making sure we were always first in line with those stories. It was never going to win me a Pulitzer but I think old József P. himself would've understood: the sensational stuff was what got the traffic, and that paid the bills. I was good at it.

But there was more to this. There was more to you.

And that was the *point* of it all. The reason I went down this path in the first place, the way I'd felt when I read *In Cold Blood* for the first time, aged fifteen. Writers like me were supposed to shed light on the darkest parts of our society, to truly show the reality of the world we live in. To explain why people do bad things, to find closure—justice—for everyone involved.

Your story? It felt like a chance to really do that.

Especially when I realized Hasan was working your case. That, I guess, was my first real stroke of luck.

We'd met five years earlier, when I'd been working on my first book, a deep dive into the cocaine trade in the UK, formed entirely of conversations with five anonymized real people connected to it: a dealer, a middle-class dinner-party user, the mother of an addict, a kid caught up in county lines, and a detective from one of the Met's crackdown operations.

The Met officer was Hasan, and we'd been friends ever since. The book, meanwhile, had generated a brief flurry of moderate excitement from the industry and then been conspicuously absent from the shelves or the review pages, and nowadays it was something that Hasan and I didn't speak about. C'est la vie. Genius hits a target that no one else can see, as Schopenhauer said.

We met at a pub just off Broadway Market, and I bought the drinks as usual. Fair enough; I remembered what it was like to be young and hemorrhaging most of my salary on rent, working too many hours to actually spend any time in the shoebox flat it was all going toward. Hasan's girlfriend was drifting along like a typical Gen Z, but he reminded me of myself: a workaholic, hungry for it. That day, his hair was still wet from the shower, the bags and circles under his eyes telling a tale of naps grabbed between night shifts, his stomach growling as he glanced at the menu.

"Sounds like this March House thing's going to keep you busy," I said.

"Understatement." He rolled and then unrolled his sleeves, his foot tapping against the tiled floor. He was a ball of energy and caffeine, just like I'd been at his age, and that was usually when it was easiest to catch him off guard.

"I've been doing some digging into Kate Cole. It's hard to see how she ended up doing something like this."

He raised an eyebrow at me, a kind of *you don't know the half of it.*

"I shouldn't be telling you this," he said, taking a sip of his beer, enjoying it, "but check out a site called the Rabbit Hole."

13

Gabriel

"K. C."

YOU WERE THE PRETTIEST GIRL I'd ever seen.

I was fifteen and had wet dreams about Jennifer Lawrence, my maths teacher, and you. Back then, I blushed pretty much as soon as you walked past me, but that didn't matter. I was invisible to everyone then, even you, and that suited me just fine.

Before everything, I grew up sick. That's how it feels, when I think of being a kid. Chicken pox, a thousand puking bugs, one long Christmas spent picking impetigo scabs. Chest infections, allergic reactions, every cold and flu that came to town. And then, when I was fourteen, a virus that hit me hard, for no reason anyone could ever figure out, and left me stuck in bed while they tried to decide what the hell was wrong with me.

When I told you that once, those exact words, you laughed. "Any day now," you said.

The summer of the sickness was also the summer my mum finally saw sense and broke up with her boyfriend, Dave of the bad breath and polo necks, and decided it would be best for both of us if we moved somewhere new, ideally somewhere with fresh sea air, like I was a Victorian kid with rickets.

She settled on Devon and then on Combe Little—close enough to see the sea but from a flat we could just about afford the rent on—and we packed up our stuff into a grand total of twenty-three boxes and loaded up a hire van with my auntie Shelley in the driving seat. Shelley bought us a pizza while we unpacked, and the three of us sat out in the flat's little courtyard, listening to the seagulls and the silence while Shelley drank three Cinzanos—the box of booze being the only one she'd helped unpack—and Mum hummed happily to herself.

A week later I started school, painfully and obviously the weird new kid, and I did my best to shrink into the shadows at every opportunity, scuttling around like a wood louse running from rock to rock and wondering how long I could get away with nobody noticing me. Choosing the quietest corner of the canteen to eat my sandwiches, trying not to make eye contact with anyone or in any way draw attention to myself.

You sat at the table in front of mine about ten minutes before the end of lunch with a half-eaten slice of pizza and a can of cream soda. You had your back to me, and I watched you carving your initials into the bench as you ate. *K. C.* I liked the sound of them in my head, the way they made a name of their own.

Mum got a job at a guesthouse near the beach, cleaning the rooms and washing the sheets, which meant she got up at five each morning, and I got myself breakfast and went off to school without saying a word to another human until my form teacher called my name in registration. In the evenings, Mum worked in an old people's home on the outskirts of town, helping with the dinner trolley and washing more sheets and playing cribbage with an old man who thought she was his daughter, and I got myself dinner and made sure there was always enough for her and that the flat was tidy and warm when she got home. She was happy, and that made me happy.

I finally worked up the courage to join Warhammer Club, which was a great decision because I made a friend, Bart, who was kind and funny and, most important, could help me navigate my way round the school. Once we were walking to biology and you were hurrying in the opposite direction, your head down. "Who's that?" I asked, feeling uncharacteristically brave.

He looked at you and then raised an eyebrow at me. Bart's eyebrows did a lot of the talking for him a lot of the time, sometimes disappearing up under his fringe or crawling right down into one long line when he was really thinking about something. "Katie Cole?" he asked. "Why?"

I shrugged, already embarrassed. "Just wondering."

"She's trouble," he said. "Everyone will tell you that."

But I didn't have everyone to ask, just him, and it didn't stop me looking for you each time my mind started wandering at school.

My mum turned forty that winter, and I decided I was going to make her a cake. I'm not usually ambitious, but I'd watched a lot of *Bake Off* that year, and I guess might have developed unrealistic ideas about what was achievable with a bit of time and a positive attitude, so I chose a Black Forest treble-tier number with chocolate-dipped cherries on top. I waited till her first night shift at the old people's home that week and headed straight off on my bike to buy all the stuff for it, riding down the hill toward town and picking up speed.

I didn't see the car reversing off the drive in front of me. Probably I was miles away, imagining myself winning *Bake Off* or running through the *Call of Duty* mission I was meant to be playing that night with Bart, with no bandwidth left available to see the souped-up Vauxhall crossing the pavement in front of me. I smashed into the side of it, and the next thing I knew, I was on the ground as the bike hit the pavement in front of me, its back wheel spinning.

The wind must've got knocked out of me or something, because I remember just lying there and hearing a car door open, the clump of boots on the pavement.

The next thing, I'm being lifted up by my T-shirt or my neck, and my ears are still ringing, and there's this red-faced guy launching spit all over my face while he's telling me I'm a fucking moron and a little shit and that he's going to rip my fucking head off.

"Hey," you said, from the pavement on the other side of the car. "Want to say that again so I can be sure I got it?"

We both turned to look at you, and you waved and pointed at your phone held up in front of you.

"I didn't quite catch you reversing into my friend," you said, with the sweetest smile. "But I definitely have you threatening to kill him, which really seems like a strange way to apologize for a situation that was one hundred percent your fault."

I'd never, ever, in my whole life been happier to see someone.

The guy let go of me. Or at least my feet touched the ground again.

"He's dented my car," he said.

"Then you should look where you're going," you said, the phone still held up, you still giving him that sweet smile.

The guy looked at you and then at me.

"Fuck this," he said, or something like it, and before I could even draw a full breath, he was storming back round to the driver's side, the car reversing the rest of the way into the road with a squeal.

When he was gone, there was just you and me and a valley of pavement between us, and I finally got round to feeling the full force of the humiliation of the whole thing.

"Thank you," I said.

"Are you okay?"

I looked down at myself. "I . . . think so?"

"Are you sure?"

I was worried my legs were shaking so much I'd have to sit down on the curb before I fell over. Or that I might cry, which in front of you might actually have been even worse than getting beaten up.

"I'm fine," I said. "Honestly."

You smiled at me, like you were waiting to see what I'd say next, and I realized I was gawping at you like some bug-eyed fish, like you were some mythical being who'd swooped down on a lightning bolt or Pegasus or something.

"Thanks," I said again, like a total idiot. I swear, with every second that passed, a little bit more of me curled up and died inside.

You stepped forward and lifted my bike up from the ground. "Look where you're going this time, okay?"

I took the handlebars from you and watched as you walked away in the orange glow of the streetlights.

"Hey," you said, turning back round. "What's your name, anyway?"

14

John

"Kit-Kat"

YOU GREW QUIETER AS YOU turned fifteen and started studying for your GCSEs. You frustrated easily—emptying the wastepaper bin in your room, I often found scratched-out notes and crumpled attempts at essays or art assignments. You still made clothes, your room filled with stacks of fashion magazines and scraps of fabric, the sewing machine often juddering through the floorboards late into the night. You also liked to listen to music while you were alone, sometimes lying on your bed with your eyes closed, your speaker turned up as loud as it would go.

Your mum was not shy about strolling in and turning it off. But I liked some of the artists you liked, had taken you to see Joanna Newsom and Sufjan Stevens before. You tried to teach me about the others when you were in a chatty mood, playing me Wolf Alice and Kendrick Lamar, Alabama Shakes, Jenny Hval and Beach Slang.

I came into your room one afternoon with a stack of books and magazines you'd left scattered around the house, and found you at your desk, frowning at your laptop. I told you that dinner was almost ready, and you nodded, distracted.

"Can I show you something?" you asked.

You played me a video of the footage from 9/11: the planes colliding with the twin towers, one after the other, the footage slowed right down as someone in the corner of the screen speculated about inconsistencies in the way the buildings had collapsed.

"Isn't this crazy?" you asked. "Can you believe we haven't heard about this before?"

I put down the books on the edge of your desk. "We haven't heard about it because that person doesn't know what they're talking about. Where did you even find this?"

You ignored me. "But what if it *was* staged, Dad? And the war was all because of a lie?"

You said it so earnestly that I felt unnerved. "It wasn't, Kit-Kat. This is just a made-up conspiracy theory. There's a million of them out there, about all sorts of things."

"I don't think it is! If you look into it, there's so much evidence. We've been lied to."

"Stop," I said. "You're smarter than this."

"But—"

"Really, Kit," I said, firmly now. "If Mum heard you saying things like that . . . It's disrespectful to Stephen's memory."

Your eyes filled with tears. "I didn't . . ."

"I know you didn't mean it like that. But this stuff . . . it's delusional."

After a final look at the screen, you closed the laptop lid. "Okay. Sorry."

We went down to dinner together after that, and I thought, I suppose, that was the end of it.

15

Max

"Killer Kate"

LET'S NOT BEAT AROUND THE bush: this wasn't my first conspiracy rodeo. I'd spent a lot of time on the Rabbit Hole before, and back then it'd been far more personal. In the grim early days of 2020, I'd been put on our Covid coverage, running the liveblog in the first few months of lockdown, going to the press conferences, rounding up all those eerie images of empty public spaces around the world, and generally trying to be a voice of calm and reason in what felt like an unprecedented shitstorm.

It hadn't taken long for the conspiracy theorists to surface. Posting comments under my articles, sending threats to my work email. People calling me a traitor, a stooge, a puppet of the cabal. I was told I should be lynched, executed for war crimes. My habit of periodically googling myself started turning up results on sites like the Rabbit Hole. Users posting about whether I was being paid or blackmailed or whether I was even a real person, long discussions about how I should be punished for peddling my lies about the virus, the vaccine, the hospitalization rates.

Then someone shared my home address on one of those threads, and I stopped finding it mildly amusing and started feeling fucking unnerved. I wrote a complaint to the email address that was listed for the moderator—as if anyone were actually monitoring that place—and the post got taken down a couple of days later. It didn't make me feel much better, wondering how many weirdos had made note of it before that, and I started checking the thread obsessively. I even thought